Knowledge and Money

Knowledge and Money

Research Universities and
the Paradox of the Marketplace

Roger L. Geiger

STANFORD UNIVERSITY PRESS 2004

Stanford, California

Stanford University Press
Stanford, California
© 2004 by the Board of Trustees of the
Leland Stanford Junior University

Library of Congress Cataloging-in-Publication Data

Geiger, Roger L.
   Knowledge and money : research universities and the
paradox of the marketplace / Roger L. Geiger.
       p. cm.
   Includes bibliographical references and index.
   ISBN 0-8047-4925-6 (cloth : alk. paper)—
   ISBN 0-8047-4926-4 (pbk. : alk. paper)
       1. Research institutes—Economic aspects—United States.
2. Research—Economic aspects—United States.   3. Universi-
ties and colleges—Economic aspects—United States.   I. Title.
Q180.U5G345 2004
001.4'06073—dc21

                                    2004001622

Printed in the United States of America
Original Printing 2004
Last figure below indicates year of this printing:
13   12   11   10   09   08   07   06   05   04

Typeset at Stanford University Press in 10/13 Galliard

For Burton R. Clark

Acknowledgments

This volume brings the ever-changing story of American universities into the first years of the twenty-first century. The history of these institutions as research universities began near the close of the nineteenth century. The challenge then, as I described it in *To Advance Knowledge*, was to elevate academic scientists and scholars in the United States to the highest world standard, which was then being set in Western Europe. By 1940, with the strategic assistance of philanthropic foundations, that goal was attained. A new challenge emerged when World War II and the events following demanded that academic expertise be channeled to the needs of the nation. *Research and Relevant Knowledge* depicted how the federal government became not only the new patron of academic research, but also its principal consumer.

This relationship was modified appreciably in the years around 1980 as a concerted effort was made to relate academic research more closely to the civilian economy. The consequences of these last changes provide the focus for *Knowledge and Money*. As university knowledge became more valuable to society, universities themselves enlarged their activities and were rewarded with greater resources. For somewhat different reasons, the education they offered became more valuable as well. But these enlarged responsibilities have carried a price. Universities find that insatiable needs and increasing competition constrain their freedom of activity. At times, their involvement with markets appears to threaten the wellspring of knowledge that is the source of their value. I have called this increasing tension the paradox of the marketplace.

Since I began writing *To Advance Knowledge* some twenty years ago, the evolving fortunes of universities have been either my vocation or avocation. Still, a concentrated effort during the years 2000–2003 was needed for the analysis presented in this volume. This effort would not have been possible without assistance from many sources. A grant from the Alfred P. Sloan Foundation allowed me to explore and resolve some of the initial difficulties. This process was aided as well by the opportunity to write an overview of the U.S. system for a project of the American Academy of Arts and Sciences comparing German and American higher education. Support from the Spencer Foundation and a sabbatical leave from the Penn State College of Education permitted much of the research to be accomplished during the 2000–2001 academic year. Particularly valuable was my time as a visiting fellow at the University of California Berkeley Center for Studies in Higher Education. Special thanks are due to John Douglass for this hospitality. Material for this study was also gathered during visits to many university campuses, and I would like to thank those individuals too numerous to name who took time to help me better understand their institutions.

The Higher Education Program at Penn State aided this project in numerous ways. Program assistant Trudi Haupt provided invaluable assistance. Carlo Salerno, Dmitry Suspitsin, and Steve Cunningham acquired and sorted the data on which this analysis rests. And the study group that grew into the Research Universities Colloquium provided a stimulating forum to air and discuss many of these issues. I would like to thank all the participants. In addition, I particularly appreciate the collegial encouragement of Nancy Diamond and Hong Shen, fellow students of research universities.

This manuscript has benefited greatly from the critical eye of David Jones. I also value the comments of David Breneman and Carlo Salerno. Creso Sá and Christian Anderson helped greatly with the completion of the manuscript. Finally, in special appreciation of Burton R. Clark for placing knowledge foremost in university organization and for continued intellectual support over many years, I dedicate this volume to him.

Roger L. Geiger

State College, Pennsylvania
January, 2004

Contents

Tables and Figures

Tables

Figures

Knowledge and Money

Introduction

THE RESEARCH UNIVERSITIES of the United States entered the twenty-first century in the strongest position in their storied history.[1] Scholars and advanced students from around the world seek opportunities to share in their learning. Scientists, on balance, regard these institutions as among the best places to do research. The most able graduates of American high schools prefer these institutions for their undergraduate studies. Donors have shown their appreciation with ever-larger gifts. And universities deliberately and successfully have made themselves more useful to American society, justifying their somewhat prophetic designation as "central institutions of post-industrial societies."[2]

These undeniable markers of achievement, as one might suspect, do not tell the whole story. In what might be a classic case of "doing better and feeling worse," universities have been beset by a seeming legion of critics. University-bashing became a cultural fixture after Allan Bloom published *The Closing of the American Mind* in 1987. Legislators in Congress and the states took to heart some of the charges made against universities and proposed their own crude remedies for the alleged maladies. In addition, a minor industry developed to purvey prescriptions for improving the operations and effectiveness of the nation's institutions of higher education.

This book offers a different sort of critique, predicated on the contribution of universities to American society and, reciprocally, on how society's demands and conditions have shaped the nature of universities. It presupposes a conception of the university that transcends its specific functions of teaching, research, and service. These functions, and the university's unique role, are predicated on its privileged position in the generation and dissemination of advanced, specialized knowledge. The contemporary American university is in fact a knowledge conglomerate in its extensive activities, and this role is costly to sustain. The expenditures of the ninety-nine universities that are the focus of this inquiry, for example, account for 1 percent of the U.S. economy. Indeed, the need to garner such a magnitude of resources powerfully affects the behavior of universities.

Historically, this was much less true. European universities were traditionally accorded comfortable support by the state to cultivate and profess learning. Private patrons similarly supported American universities before World War II, if more irregularly. Both sets of institutions were more modest in scope—"elite" in the small numbers they graduated. The same kind of tacit traditions governed their human resources. Students were seldom recruited, but rather followed well-established paths from secondary schools to universities. Professors were commonly trained at their home institutions. Universities described their work in absolute, normative terms, and would have found repugnant any suggestion that they competed with other kinds of institutions or with one another.

In the United States, this situation changed in key respects after 1945. The federal government began to support a preponderant share of academic research. Universities argued that such support was justified by the intrinsic value of advancing knowledge, but government agencies provided these funds chiefly to further their own missions. These cross-purposes did not prevent an extremely fruitful relationship from developing, but the latent tension surfaced whenever policy issues were considered. Over time, support for academic research grew steadily because of its relevance to a host of external purposes. Universities necessarily accommodated the interests of patrons to win support for research, and they also competed with one another in doing so. In the area of human resources the direction of change was much the same. The vast expansion of higher education induced a more pronounced differentiation of tasks. For universities the challenge became recruiting the most able students from across the country, and indeed around the world. The same was true for faculty and researchers. The success of a university as an educational institution and as a knowledge conglomerate came to depend on its ability to compete for scarce and vital inputs.

Although these developments had deep roots, their current features were largely shaped in the last two decades of the twentieth century. Throughout much of the 1970s, higher education looked wistfully to the federal government for a resumption of the liberal support it had provided in the 1960s.

Only around 1980, for reasons that will be explored, did a fundamental re-orientation begin to take place. Universities embraced the mission of contributing to the economy, especially by forging links with private industry. They substantially revised the pricing and marketing of their principal product, undergraduate education. And they modified their labor inputs, especially the utilization of faculty. By the 1990s, these practices became the new realities for higher education, but especially for universities. In the hothouse economy of the late 1990s, these approaches yielded undreamt of prosperity for those institutions best able to exploit them. The marketplace—really a number of different markets—on balance was generous to universities to this point, but to what ultimate effect?

The impact of the marketplace on the fundamental knowledge tasks of contemporary universities is the theme of this study. Much that has been written on this broad topic has taken a piecemeal and often negative cast. Markets have conventionally been associated with revenue-generating activities, raising tuitions, or patenting faculty discoveries. In fact, some of the most important markets in which universities compete are those for human, intellectual resources. The university now depends on the marketplace for the resources essential to its core knowledge tasks; the interaction of intellectual and financial resources now lies at the heart of its existence. But what does it mean to depend on the marketplace?

"A market system," writes Charles E. Lindblom, "is a method of social coordination by mutual adjustment among participants rather than by a central coordinator." As such, it makes two important claims for enhancing the production of goods and services. First, "market systems practice a rough efficiency pricing widely and routinely," and "efficiency prices . . . permit a drastically improved degree of efficient choice." Second, "informed by efficiency prices, participants are powerfully motivated to act because they gain specific contingent benefits from doing so." Thus, pricing that reflects inherent value and the motivation for informed action underlie the voluntary acts that produce mutual adjustment in market coordination.[3]

How does this relate to higher education? The outcomes of education are a vital concern for society as a whole, and education is consequently subject to a high degree of central coordination. Pricing in higher education, it will be shown, is more arbitrary than efficient. Prices only partly guide participants seeking contingent benefits. The markets of higher education are thus quite imperfect, if not downright strange. Nevertheless, they can be better understood with reference to Lindblom's fundamental elements of social coordination, mutual adjustment, pricing, and motivation.

These elements, even in very imperfect markets, generate the market forces that have increasingly shaped universities in the current era.

Specifically, an increasing prevalence of market forces ought to produce changes in the ways higher education operates. First, central coordination should be displaced in some degree by market forms of coordination. Second, prices ought to play a growing role in influencing the choices made by participants. Finally, the motivation of individuals will be determined to a greater extent by those "contingent benefits" derived from higher education. This perspective thus generates some preliminary notions about the probable effects of the American university's deepening involvement with the marketplace. These specific concerns are revisited in the final chapter, where they guide a deeper probing of the meaning and significance of the developments that are about to be described.

The first chapter establishes a foundation for the topics that follow. The distinctive characteristics of universities are depicted as resulting from their purposes of creating, processing, and disseminating knowledge. These inherently qualitative undertakings produce two loosely related kinds of status, one for quality in undergraduate education and the other for distinction in scholarship and research. Next, the chapter describes how market forces impinge on these processes and ends by defining the current era of privatization that began around 1980.

The next four chapters comprise the substance of this study. Each begins by placing its topic in a broad context, including important developments since 1980.

Chapter 2 addresses the issue of rising university costs from the perspective of the competition for excellence and resources. Private universities have manipulated federal and institutional financial aid to establish a regime of differential charges that has escalated list tuition and optimized revenues. Public universities have only partially been able to follow this formula of high tuition and high student aid. Although most universities have increased their revenues in the current era, a large gap has opened between private and public universities. The sources of rising costs in universities are identified, as are specific university strategies for meeting financial challenges.

Undergraduate education remains the foremost task of American universities; however, the competition for status has made selectivity in admissions more salient than excellence in instruction. Stung by criticism that they neglect undergraduates and by poor selectivity-based rankings, public universities have had to improve their image and compete more vigorously for top students. "Student-centered research universities," however, established a dubious record. Heightened competition for able students has brought some improvements to undergraduate education, but it has also greatly furthered student consumerism, thus weakening university control over student learning.

Despite a litany of complaints and worries, academic research has thrived during the current era. Chapter 4 documents that it expanded far more than enrollments or faculty. Understanding these developments requires monitoring the academic core of departmental faculty as well as an autonomous research role in medical schools and organized research units. Among public universities, financial health was associated with expansion of core research, but at private universities affluence was not necessarily used to expand research. Attitudes toward research are volatile, however, and at the turn of the century universities made advancing their research missions a higher priority.

The key factor bolstering academic research has been its link to economic development. Chapter 5 synthesizes a large body of material on university relationships with industry and economic development. It details a traditional and largely noncontroversial role that university research has played in enhancing research in industry. Public policies in the current era have encouraged universities to stretch that role in order to further technology innovation and regional economic development. A different paradigm emerged in biotechnology that encouraged the direct commercialization of academic research through patenting and start-up firms. The forces driving these developments are analyzed in order to assess the threat to academic norms and possibly university integrity. Kept within acceptable limits, however, ties with economic development are a stimulus to the continuing vitality of academic research.

The final chapter attempts to explain the dynamics at work in these four areas at a deeper level of generality. Social coordination through markets has undoubtedly grown in the current era and in the process has detracted from the capacity of policy makers and university leaders to influence events. Market coordination acting on universities, as elsewhere, has brought greater inequality of wealth. It has also increased the social stratification of students at high-quality institutions. It first erected a seemingly unsustainable system of exorbitant tuition and need-based financial aid, and has now begun to undermine the same with competitive merit aid. It has in biotechnology engendered a process of commercialization that is beyond academic control. Nevertheless, the immersion of American universities in the marketplace has, on balance, brought them greater resources and better students, as well as a far larger capacity for advancing knowledge. The contrast between these benefits for universities and the unwelcome social consequences engenders the paradox of the marketplace.

CHAPTER ONE

Universities as Knowledge-Based Institutions

THE AMERICAN UNIVERSITY of the twenty-first century is a distinctive organization. Compartmentalized in structure, it performs a multitude of functions that are largely predicated on a single qualification — the possession of expert, specialized, theoretical knowledge.[1] University faculty and researchers are distinguished chiefly by their expertise over delimited areas of knowledge. Such dominions are inherently specialized and esoteric. Distinct from other specialized expertise, academic knowledge strives for generality, an ineluctable tendency toward theory. Indeed, the modern university is above all a repository of this kind of knowledge. Universities literally store knowledge in their libraries, museums, archives, and institutes. However, the most important fund of knowledge lies in the expertise of faculty and professional staff.

The overriding norm for universities is to seek what was once called *truth*, although, given the prevailing relativism in some fields, many academics would shun this term. A more neutral formulation of this norm might be to establish "valid knowledge through systematic inquiry." It falls to academic disciplines, or equivalent forms of organized consensus, to define what modes of inquiry are legitimate and what knowledge is thereby validated.

Most university activities emanate from this foundation of academic knowledge, be they educating neophyte students or fledgling experts, extending the frontiers of knowledge, applying knowledge to praxis, or disseminating knowledge within and outside of the academy. There are many loose ends in this basic scheme. Universities have long been engaged in such apparently ancillary activities as the performing arts or athletics, but these fields too invoke expertise and are subject to a relentless imperative to expand and improve the possibilities for expression or performance. A core of academic knowledge forms the basis for the bulk of university activities.

Knowledge-centered organizations generally allow a substantial degree of autonomy and discretion to professional employees. Software firms, biotech companies, and universities are largely compelled to allow knowledge workers the latitude to use their expertise in ways that only they know best. Knowledge-based organizations are consequently decentralized by nature, or bottom-heavy in organizational terms. Universities especially so. Individual faculty members work mainly alone when organizing the knowledge they will teach or when seeking to extend their own expertise. Research is a more interactive process, but decentralized nevertheless. For the purpose of structuring activities like courses and degree programs, academics are gathered into departments on the basis of recognized domains of knowledge. Departments in turn are grouped into schools or colleges in order to administer even larger knowledge domains. Authority over what is most important—knowledge—remains the basis of these organizational tiers. Each unit consequently possesses a large degree of autonomy, and integration into larger structures is inherently consensual.

The institution as a whole nevertheless requires some means of organizational control, and for the American university the most powerful lever is fiscal. If consensual authority flows upward from the bottom of the organization, fiscal control is exerted downward from the top. In most universities a provost or academic vice president, directly under the president, governs the academic units, being at once responsible for overseeing academic matters and disbursing funds. The provost's office allocates funds to the separate schools or colleges according to the policies and priorities of the university. College deans in turn determine the budgets of the departments according to the policies and priorities of the individual colleges. The departmental budget is heavily committed to the salaries of faculty and staff. Thus departments can undertake few initiatives without seeking additional funding from the dean. The same principle applies to deans, who must request additional resources from the provost. Administrative units thus retain a large measure of fiscal control over components, while at the same time permitting the operational autonomy of knowledge workers in their own spheres.

Individual universities naturally operate according to numerous permutations of this basic structure. Units or professors who generate their own income, for example, have correspondingly greater autonomy—the exceptions that prove this rule. This dual structure of authority nevertheless represents the first principles of university organization. These principles have important corollaries for universities.

Cohesion and inward focus characterize the knowledge domains that form the operating units of the university. Gathered together in an institution, such units assume a highly compartmentalized structure. Indeed, the earliest American universities have been described as thriving "on the patterned isolation of [their] component parts."[2]

The university itself provides a general framework of regulations, services, and resource disbursement, but each unit then fits the imperatives of its own operations into this loose framework. Faculty work and student learning are organized quite differently in a laboratory science such as chemistry, an applied field such as business, or a liberal art such as history. Moreover, with attention concentrated on their own affairs, members of one unit have neither understanding of nor meaningful influence over other domains. But compartmentalization extends well beyond academic units. Most universities, for example, have felt the need to create separate centers or institutes for certain kinds of research. At the University of California these have long carried the generic label of "organized research units," or ORUs, an acronym now widely used. In fact, adding largely self-contained and often self-financed units has allowed universities to perform a host of different tasks related to academic knowledge.

The multipurpose nature of universities is evident within academic units and across university units. Again, knowledge, or learning, is the common denominator—fostering student learning, facilitating faculty learning, and making the university's store of learning available to society. These different aims are felt by the individual faculty member, who must use professional judgment to balance obligations to students, research, the tasks of internal self-governance, and service to external constituencies. The balance of such activities varies greatly among the faculty according to individual proclivities and abilities, and it also varies for individuals over the course of a career.

The university also relies on special units to perform many of its associated and auxiliary tasks. In addition to academic departments and ORUs, a typical major university today operates a hotel and a dormitory system, a research park, probably with a business incubator, a hospital, a university press, a radio and perhaps a television station, a division for continuing education, and an athletics and entertainment complex. Such institutions are now billion-dollar operations. Measured in dollars, the instruction of students might represent less than half of their activities, that of undergraduates still less. Most of this welter of activities bears some relation to the university's knowledge core, but the ties are sometimes tenuous.

The knowledge-centered nature of universities, in combination with the means of fiscal control, produces another set of consequences. University units at each level of the organization seek to maximize their own sphere of activity by obtaining as much revenue as is feasible. The same principle applies to universities as a whole. Howard Bowen's famous "law" holds that "in quest of excellence, prestige, and influence . . . each institution raises all the money it can . . . [and] spends all it raises."[3] In a like manner, colleges and departments within the university generally seek to expand their allocation of funds. The motive is not greed or gluttony, however, but something more like chronic undernourishment. In most universities, most of the time, academic units believe they need additional means to accomplish the job that should be done, or better still, to achieve even higher levels of performance.

Thus academic units are consumers of resources, divorced for the most part from the business side of the organization that collects and disburses funds. Numerous approaches have been devised to alter this situation, to give the consuming units incentives to produce more with less rather than the other way around.[4] But this relationship remains fundamental—and not particularly unusual: it exists widely among nonprofit organizations.

Nonprofit Organizations and the Pursuit of Knowledge

It would be strange indeed if higher education conformed to the free-market model in which competition drives down costs and achieves market-clearing prices. Colleges and universities offer highly differentiated products. Even where products are comparable, as they are for certain skills and credentials, competition is not entirely based on stated prices. The ease and convenience of delivery strongly affect the opportunity costs of consumers. Undergraduate education for young people, particularly in its traditional residential forms, shares few free-market characteristics. Besides being differentiated, it is a heavily subsidized service, involving third-party payers, that is appropriately located in public and nonprofit institutions.

Economists have had to develop a different conceptual lens in order to analyze nonprofit organizations. By definition, these organizations are forbidden to distribute surplus revenues (profits) to their officers or directors, but instead must devote their assets to their own stated purposes. Such organizations are clearly preferable to for-profit firms in cases where trust is a paramount issue, as it is in higher education. An asymmetry of information exists between the provider and consumer, making the quantity and quality of the service difficult for the purchaser to evaluate. Because enrolling in a university is a long-term commitment with high transaction costs consumers should have confidence that the institution will not use its inherent advantage for its own profit. In addition, the nonprofit form creates appropriate objects of philanthropy in which donors can be confident that gifts will be used for their intended purposes.[5]

For these same reasons, theory holds, public universities too can be trusted not to take unfair advantage of their customers, but here another set of considerations predominates. The state has a powerful interest in assisting every citizen to attain a level of education commensurate with his or her inclinations and abilities. Just as full employment promises to maximize the production of goods and services, *full education* in this sense should contribute to maximizing the productivity and well-being of all members of society. In recent decades governments at all levels have implicitly acted on this theory, building colleges and supporting access to higher education for most who wish it. But the public provision of higher education is nevertheless circumscribed by what governments—and voters—regard as appropriate levels of expenditure. Individuals who desire different or more costly alternatives have in large measure looked to the private nonprofit sector.[6] Most private colleges and universities claim to offer education that is "distinctive" in some respect. Some of them also offer what is perceived as greater quality through ample provision of faculty, facilities, and amenities. Most of these institutions charge a high price, but much of their ostensible quality results as well from a high level of subsidization.

American higher education is subsidized in numerous ways. Public colleges and universities rely chiefly on state appropriations, but other forms of public support, including student financial aid, flow to both public and private institutions. Exemption from taxation is another implicit subsidy, predicated on a contribution to the public good. The capital costs of higher education constitute a huge sum that takes the form almost entirely of subsidy.

Throughout American history, students have rarely been asked to pay for the land and buildings in which they were educated.[7] Rather, governments and private donors have largely supplied such capital, leaving institutional budgets to reflect direct operating costs almost exclusively. Finally, American universities, like no others in the world, have reaped large subsidies from the beneficence of donors. Both current gifts and the legacy of past gifts preserved as endowment provide subsidies in magnitudes that vary enormously across institutions. All these subsidies allow higher education to be priced below costs, thus contributing to full education and the resulting benefits to society. Conversely, one could say that subsidization allows far better higher education to be offered than most people could otherwise afford. This qualitative differential, or *margin*, created by subsidization exists from community colleges to the Ivy League.

The instructional costs of any given institution can be expressed as the sum of what students pay for their education in the form of tuition and the amount of subsidy that is added. Together, the magnitudes of these revenues largely determine to what extent universities can accomplish their distinctive knowledge tasks. If higher education services were all the same, and offered at a market-clearing price, it would scarcely be possible for all of these activities to exist. Labor for instruction would be bid down to no more than minimal competence, complementary service activities could not be sustained, and no means would be available to permit the advancement of knowledge.[8] In fact, the margins that allow the proliferation of knowledge-related activities vary enormously across institutions. This margin of actual expenditures over a hypothetical market-clearing minimum makes possible the conditions that most distinguish universities—what might be called the overqualification of instructors, the generation of academic knowledge, and the synergies of multiple purposes.

The overqualification of university teachers is fundamental to universities as places of learning. It is also part of the distinctive character of faculty labor. The ticket of entry into the academic profession is the Ph.D., a prolonged, expensive, and narrowly specialized form of training for which the individual alone is responsible. Once employed in a university, faculty members are expected to devote their career to fairly well defined tasks predicated on their expertise.[9] The institution supports the further development of this expertise by supporting professional development, but chiefly by underutilizing the instructional capacity of its faculty.

In an efficient academic labor market, positions that afford the greatest opportunity for intellectual growth—the largest institutional investments—will be awarded to scholars who have the greatest promise to contribute to learning. Potential faculty members are in fact exhaustively evaluated on precisely this criterion. The eminence of the departments in which they did their graduate work, the recommendations of doctoral mentors, and initial scholarship all attest to a candidate's potential to advance knowledge in the field. Sponsorship plays a large role in fitting doctoral students for academic careers, but even those less favored can advance to more nurturing positions through the strength of their scholarship.

The process of fitting scholar and place is continuous. During the six probationary years that precede consideration for tenure, academics are expected to realize some of their promise. Universities that make the largest investment in junior faculty expect substantial and impressive accomplishments in order for tenure to be earned. Where less is invested, less is generally expected. This same process of measuring achievements against expectation, relative to the richness of the academic environment, continues throughout an academic career. The result is the development of expertise that far exceeds the minimum requirements of teaching all but the most advanced students.

Hence, tenured and also untenured faculty members know far more than is necessary to teach the largely codified knowledge that is transmitted in undergraduate classes. Universities acknowledge as much by liberally substituting less-qualified teachers—graduate teaching assistants or part-time instructors—for less-advanced courses. But overqualification in this sense allows faculty, as experts in specialized fields, to make more singular contributions in advanced instruction, in service to knowledge consumers, and in furthering knowledge in their field.

This bundle of activities is probably the most misunderstood and easily criticized feature of American universities.[10] It is also the basis of the remarkable ascendancy of the American university in the twentieth century. Rather than asking how it might be changed, one should first ask, why has it proven so effective? Faculty overqualification in fact enables the other two distinguishing university traits: the generation of knowledge and the symbiosis of multiple purposes.

The generation of knowledge in universities has an intrinsic value of its own. Universities are by no means the only place where new knowledge is discovered, but their role is distinctive nevertheless. The broad teaching mandate of universities requires the development and maintenance of a large repository of basic knowledge. Teaching sustains the nexus between the frontiers of knowledge and a more general disciplinary base. Academic expertise also reproduces itself in universities through the training of new scholars—the universities' special role. This process not only yields the next generation of experts, but also serves powerfully to stimulate creativity and discourage stagnation. To a significant extent, the value of academic knowledge attracts its own stream of resources, thereby enhancing the initial economic and intellectual base.

Considerable complementarities exist, for society and for individuals, in the multifarious activities based on this knowledge. Teaching, research, and application reinforce and fertilize one another in numerous, unpredictable ways. Research informs applications, but applications also raise questions or even findings that stimulate further research. Similarly, the organization and synthesis of knowledge for teaching provide feedback for application and research. Each of these activities, of course, is pursued by itself in other settings, and appropriately so. The rarified conditions of a university seem best fitted for pursuing systematic, theoretical knowledge. Efficiencies are gained when these activities are pursued in a complementary fashion. Individually, these three activities interpenetrate one another, often being performed simultaneously. Moreover, individuals with highly specialized knowledge can probably use their expertise more productively in a combination of different types of activities than by pursuing a single one, such as research or teaching, to the point of diminishing returns.

The deep expertise of faculty scholars, the intrinsic value of repositories of knowledge, and the complementarities of multiple knowledge tasks together constitute one ideal for the American university. However, the very nature of this ideal—its requirement of scarce resources—means that it can only be approximated by a relatively small number of institutions. The university system consequently forms an inherent hierarchy based in part on the capacity of institutions to fulfill these knowledge tasks.

A Dual Structure of Prestige

The American system of higher education is inherently hierarchical in ways that reflect much more than the national passion for rankings. Unlike continental European systems, where governments are constrained to treat all universities somewhat evenhandedly, the American system has been shaped by free student choice, uncoordinated distribution of federal and state support, and multiple sources of private support. This confusion of inputs and the resulting competition produce wide disparities among institutions of higher education, and thus a natural segmentation of tasks. Prestige, which is the subjective reflection of these hierarchical effects, is segmented as well. However, to the extent that institutions compete for resources, prestige has real consequences.

Prestige is also a slippery concept. Those who attempt to model the complex behavior of universities sometimes assume that institutions' actions are calculated to maximize prestige.[11] Taken literally, this notion is misleading. Universities seek to hire the best possible faculty, *given the salaries they can afford*; and they admit the most qualified students, *given the students that apply*. At this point universities essentially must play the cards they are dealt. The bulk of their energy is devoted to doing the job at hand, a large part of which is instructing students with the resources available.

In carrying out these tasks universities are scrupulously concerned with upholding their reputation—by maintaining academic standards and integrity in research, for example. However, there is little scope in these quotidian activities for "maximizing prestige."[12] Yet universities remain intensely concerned with reputation and prestige, and properly so. At the margin, consequential decisions about building, hiring, and fund-raising are likely to hinge on such considerations. With comparable universities behaving in identical ways, universities must continually seek improvement even to remain in the same relative position. This competition is played out in two principal arenas—one comprising the knowledge tasks described above, and the other reflecting the recruitment of undergraduate students.

University prestige based on faculty scholarship reflects the prestige structure of science itself. Recognition and rewards in science are based chiefly on how important or fundamental a contribution is to the field. As described by sociologists of science, the recognition and reward of scientists serve a crucial sorting function by ensuring that the most productive scientists will be given the most propitious places in which to work. That is, universities with the greatest resources will over time recruit and employ the best scientists. This process was monitored throughout the twentieth century. At the beginning of the century the first effort was made to identify the nation's most accomplished scientists. By noting where they worked, a ranking of universities could be had as well. Since 1960, four systematic assessments have been conducted to determine the prowess of academic departments for research and, concomitantly, graduate education (in 1966, 1970, 1982, and 1995). In these ratings, the expertise of individual faculty members is aggregated into a rank ordering of departments in each academic discipline and, by implication, for whole universities.[13]

Other indicators are employed to gauge a university's research role. Total expenditures for research, or for federally supported research, provide a volume measure for separately budgeted research (that is, virtually all research in the sciences). Data on the number of faculty publications and how often they are cited can also be used to gauge the productivity and influence of the faculty.[14] These measures, to be sure, are relevant to a limited number of institutions. The Carnegie Classification of 1994 designated 125 institutions as research universities; 120 universities expended 85 percent of the funds budgeted for academic research; and a like number had more than ten departments deemed worthy of evaluating in the 1995 ratings. But among these universities, measures of research and scholarship reflect substantial differences in relative capacity to fulfill those fundamental knowledge tasks of a university.

The largest single task of American higher education nevertheless is undergraduate education, and institutions are sharply differentiated according to their respective roles. This prestige hierarchy is based implicitly on the attractiveness of an institution for the nation's most able secondary school graduates. Attractiveness translates into selectivity, which can be and is measured. Dozens of commercially published college guides rate institutions according to the number of applications, percentage of applicants accepted, and the proportion of the latter who matriculate. The greatest importance is accorded to the collective qualifications of those matriculates—their standardized test scores, high school grades and standing, and other accomplishments. Although guidebooks have no difficulty scoring institutions by these criteria, this hierarchy too has its ambiguities.

Selectivity has different implications for public and private institutions. Private colleges and universities for the most part have far smaller first-year classes and thus can set a higher standard for admission. Selectivity is far more consequential for them as well. For private colleges and universities, selectivity is tantamount to market power. Large pools of qualified applicants translate rather directly into revenues and resources needed to support fundamental knowledge tasks. Of course, liberal arts colleges typically eschew a large portion of such tasks, most of them being too small to excel in laboratory sciences or to sustain doctoral programs. For private universities, however, prestige in undergraduate selectivity is closely associated with financial and academic strength.

For public universities as well, academic strength serves to attract high-ability students. But with large first-year classes, these institutions are inherently less exclusive. The profile of undergraduate students at a given state university varies according to its educational role in the state. The size and the quality of the applicant pool contribute to the prestige of a public university, but they have less direct financial impact. For all these reasons, state universities have more variable commitments to undergraduate selectivity even though they attract a large share of high-ability undergraduates.

The prestige hierarchies for public and private universities are somewhat asymmetrical. Nevertheless, universities in both sectors are similar in being dedicated to core knowledge tasks, in their compartmentalized structures, and in their multipurpose natures. Thus they all crave most of the same scarce resources to fulfill their missions. How these resources are distributed is a fundamental feature of the American system of universities. Moreover, imbalances in the distributive mechanisms can provide the motive force for evolutionary change.

Universities in the Marketplace

When universities and markets are mentioned together, the subject is usually university ventures into the commercial realm: patenting and licensing, developing real estate, or taking equity positions in new firms.[15] A note of disapproval often accompanies the participation of not-for-profit universities in markets predicated on profitable returns on investments. As controversial as commercial undertakings have been, they still represent a tiny portion of all university activity. Conversely, the universities' core functions involve markets that are largely internal to higher education—markets for students, faculty, and key university resources.

Markets in this sense are systems for the allocation of scarce resources. In the economic paradigm of a free market, resources are allocated through the price mechanism, subject to the discipline of supply and demand. In higher education the basic outputs of teaching, research, and service are heavily subsidized. Prices are consequently poor signaling devices. With instruction in most cases underpriced, for example, demand should in theory exceed supply, and under certain circumstances it does. In that case, rationing must be introduced into the allocation process. Institutions—the sellers—have the power to choose their customers; students—the buyers— become supplicants. In this inverted relationship prices play a different role.

In such a market, supply and demand do not set a market-clearing price, but they are by no means irrelevant. Imbalances between supply and demand generate *market forces* that have significant consequences for the allocation of resources. In higher education, prices seldom change dramatically or rapidly. Most prices are adjusted only once for an academic year. Higher education prices thus tend to be "sticky," but they are nevertheless affected over the long run by the sway of market forces.

Taken as a whole, higher education is a mixed, not a market economy. Governments supply a large portion of revenues. Income from endowments in theory gives some institutions a degree of independence from market pressures. In the language of nonprofit organizations, universities are both donative and commercial enterprises in the ways they derive their revenues. But universities need other resources too. The allocation of human resources creates markets internal to higher education. Moreover, these are virtually zero-sum situations, where institutions must compete for shares of finite resources. These areas are seldom analyzed in market terms, but market forces substantially affect them.

Doctoral education, particularly in the sciences, represents one of the most perfectly competitive markets in higher education. Each winter a limited number of students with the requisite qualifications apply to those science and engineering departments that they would most like to attend and that would be most likely to accept them. The applicants are highly informed about the training they seek, and they are highly mobile as well. Each department is a small, autonomous producer, and the departments in each subject area collectively form a national market. Except for pricing, doctoral education approaches the requirements for perfect competition.

Doctoral students are a necessary input for university science departments, serving as research and teaching assistants and sustaining doctoral programs. For that reason, almost all of them are supported while undertaking their studies, in most cases with full tuition, some benefits, and a livable stipend. Each spring this market clears as participants work out the best match between applicants and departmental offers.

The key feature of this market is that the quality of both applicants and departments varies in ways that are fully understood by both parties: applicants and departments can therefore be ranked according to desirability. Thus a dual competition takes place—departments seek to attract the most preferred students, and students seek places at the most preferred departments in their field. This situation produces a *queue and overflow* process of allocation. Top departments choose, and are chosen by, the best students; departments in the next tier do the same with the remaining students; and so on down the list. However, this market is highly competitive and the terms of competition fairly delimited. Even top departments could not attract the students they wanted if they offered too low a price; nor can top students bargain for a stipend much above the norm. Nevertheless, over time the interplay of market forces affects the terms of this competition.

Since the late 1970s the supply of qualified students seeking doctoral education in the sciences and engineering has tended to be less than the number of places potentially available for them. Market forces, in other words, have favored the applicants, with evident consequences. One effect has been a substantial increase in the number of international students. Universities have thus enlarged and improved the supply of qualified applicants by substituting highly qualified international students for lower-ranked (or nonexistent) domestic ones. The number of doctorates granted to foreign nationals tripled from the late 1970s to the early 1990s, exceeding 50 percent of graduates in engineering and 30 percent in the natural sciences. A second development has been the gradual improvement of the support packages given to doctoral students. As they competed for better students, departments lengthened the time of guaranteed support and increased the value of stipends.

The markets for professional schools—medicine, dentistry, law, and to some extent business—resemble those for doctoral studies, at least for institutions serving the national market. Regional and local markets exist as well, where location strongly affects recruitment, but in the national markets the queue and overflow process predominates. Top students are certainly prized, but professional schools are less likely to pay students to attend. Rather, the prevailing assumption is that students embarking on presumably lucrative careers should themselves pay for much of their training. Demand for places in professional schools has waxed even as interest in doctoral programs waned (the result of another set of market forces). Market forces since the 1970s have thus favored the purveyors of professional training. Their reaction, it would seem, has been to gradually increase prices. Tuition to professional schools has accordingly risen well above that charged for undergraduate or graduate studies.

The vast market for undergraduate education is less easily described. It is segmented by geography, by type of institution, by mode of attendance, and above all by the level of academic rigor. The picture can be simplified somewhat by looking only at beginning freshmen—overwhelmingly recent high school graduates—attending four-year institutions, nearly all on a full-time basis. Here is a market that clears each spring as high school graduates match themselves with colleges befitting their aspirations and accomplishments.

This market has been remarkably stable since the middle of the 1970s in terms of institutions and enrollments. More than one-third of four-year students have consistently chosen to attend private institutions, for example. But more surprising, nearly the same number of freshmen, between 1.1 and 1.2 million, has enrolled each year for a quarter-century, even though the number of high school graduates has fluctuated from 3.2 million down to

2.3 million and back to 2.8 million (1998).[16] This fact strongly suggests that freshman enrollments at these institutions are in the aggregate largely determined by the supply of places.

The supply of students for four-year colleges is not limited to recent high school graduates. An immense pool of students, nearly 4 million in 1997, attends degree programs at two-year colleges either full- or part-time. Only a small portion of these students makes the transition to baccalaureate-granting colleges, but they more than compensate for attrition among freshmen at those colleges. The number of undergraduates at four-year institutions has crept upward since the mid-1970s at a rate of 1 percent per year. The number of bachelor's degrees awarded annually—the output of American colleges—has grown at a barely higher rate. The expansion of American higher education was extremely slow from the mid-1970s to the mid-1990s, although it seems to have accelerated somewhat since then.

It is difficult to reconcile the notion of supply constraints with some readily apparent conditions. Unused capacity obviously exists among many nonselective colleges and universities, from struggling liberal arts colleges to stagnant regional state universities. But much of this supply of places may not correspond geographically, vocationally, or culturally with existing demand.

In the large middle of American higher education, most of those colleges and universities fortunate to have more applicants than places have generally chosen to increase the qualifications, rather than the number, of the students they admit. This behavior is consistent with the prestige attached to selectivity, but it usually makes sense financially as well. To extend enrollments beyond an optimal point requires extraordinary expense for additional space or personnel—a jump in marginal costs. Extra expenditures might better be devoted to improving conditions for existing students, particularly in ways that enhance prestige. One cannot generalize across hundreds of institutions, each of which carefully evaluates when, where, how, and which additional students might be accommodated, but the calculus on balance has not favored expansion.[17]

The highly selective sector of higher education resembles in a more complicated way the market for doctoral and professional education. That is, institutions compete for the most talented applicants, and applicants compete for the most coveted places. One might envision a number of queues: for liberal arts colleges, private universities, top state universities, and engineering schools. On the institutional side, colleges and universities do not choose students on the basis of a single criterion, but rather act as if they had multiple lists of desirable characteristics. Their goal is to form a class of students with strong academic skills, but also one possessing a diverse range of talents and qualifications. Needless to say, the process of queue and overflow is complex, and so are the market forces that it generates.

The number of applicants seeking places in the highly selective sector is an important market factor, but one that can only be inferred (see Chapter 3). Nevertheless, the demand for places in this sector has been indisputably robust during the current era. Moreover, since the desire of students to attend a particular institution tends to increase with its prestige, this pattern produces strong demand for the peak institutions even while colleges at the ill-defined lower boundary of this sector struggle to attract students of the caliber they would prefer. Conditions have thus been favorable for the peak institutions—the pricing leaders—to consistently raise tuition. Selective private institutions and to some extent public universities implemented a high-tuition/high-aid policy, which is explored more fully in the next chapter. Most noteworthy, this development raised the stakes in the selectivity competition, as Chapter 3 explains.

In the dual prestige structure, private institutions have far more at stake in the competition for selectivity. For liberal arts colleges, selectivity corresponds with both public reputation and financial strength. For private universities, the selectivity of the undergraduate college similarly contributes to the prestige and viability of the institution. And public universities more recently, refusing to concede superiority in this area to the private sector, have recruited top students more actively. In the 1990s, all these institutions became increasingly preoccupied with selectivity. In a case of theory following practice, the scholarly literature identified student peers as a crucial input in the educational process. Hence a college's selectivity is predicted to have a material effect on educational outcomes, upping the stakes for applicants. As the competition of colleges for students and students for colleges intensified in the 1990s, the financial consequences of selectivity appear to have grown as well. Universities reacted accordingly.

Universities adjust the emphasis they place on their multiple ongoing activities. The operating budgets may reflect incremental shifts in emphasis, but decisions to launch new programs or undertake new investments are telling indications of current priorities. During the 1990s, universities largely responded to the intensifying competition for the most desirable undergraduate students by increasing investments in this area. To some extent this included undergraduate education, but the larger stimulus and response concerned admissions and selectivity. The characteristic student-centered university of the 1990s focused primarily on the recruitment of desirable undergraduate students, which has now become the most competitive market in higher education.

The student-centered university has had ramifications for the other markets in which universities compete: those for faculty, research funds, and other sources of institutional support. Indeed, the expressions and implications of these market forces are the subject of this book. The common feature of all these markets is the compulsion they exert over university behavior. The actions of all market participants create conditions that severely restrict the range of choice and action for any individual institution—Adam Smith's invisible hand. One might demur from this view by pointing out that American higher education has always been decentralized and competitive, and that institutional behavior has also been highly mimetic. To some degree this is true. However, the new conditions reflect a significant change in the degree of competitiveness. The current era and the present marketplace had their origins in the confluence of trends and events at the start of the 1980s.

The Era of Privatization

In order to understand the reorientation of American universities that occurred around 1980, one must first appreciate the malaise of the 1970s. That decade marked the culmination of a trend of expanding governmental coordination in American higher education that extended back to the 1930s. More immediately, the preceding decade had experienced an unprecedented expansion of public investments ranging from scientific laboratories to work-study subsidies for needy students. The final touches of this system were completed early in the 1970s: state and local governments largely finished constructing a nationwide array of community colleges; and the federal government offered long-promised systemic support for higher education in the form of need-based financial aid, enacted in the 1972 Amendments to the Higher Education Act. But with these last large efforts the trend was exhausted. Relative increases in government outlays to higher education could no longer be sustained, and perhaps no longer be justified. And, as predicted by early critics, government money was followed by greater government interference.

To add to the woes, after 1975, for the first time in U.S. history, enrollments in higher education ceased to grow. Economists, scanning the diminishing size of college-age cohorts and the shrinking wage premiums of college graduates, confidently predicted that enrollments would decline in the years ahead.[18] Finally, persistent high inflation eroded university assets.

From the early 1970s to the early 1980s, real educational expenditures per student declined for higher education as a whole. Personnel were most severely affected as the salaries of faculty and administrators lost 20 percent of their value from the previous peak. As higher education lagged behind the inflation-ridden economy, it became more affordable, at least in inflation-adjusted dollars, in the public sector and throughout much of the private sector as well.[19] Universities in general probably weathered these conditions better than other institutions of higher education, but they too experienced intermittent crises. Private research universities had expanded with alacrity during the golden age of burgeoning federal research support, but then spent much of the next decade making painful adjustments. For public universities, the worst fiscal squeeze occurred around 1980. In both sectors the response was to reduce commitments and pare back costs. Retrenchment was the watchword, hiring freezes a common experience.

Even as universities struggled to balance their individual budgets, the overweening presence of government dominated their outlook. From the federal government came a stream of regulatory requirements covering matters from accounting to affirmative action. Besides having to cope with the rising prices of the goods and services they purchased, universities had to devote a larger share of shrinking revenues to administrative tasks. Among the states, "coordination" was in the ascendancy: if each institution could be restricted to its own sphere, the conventional wisdom held, "waste and duplication" might be extirpated. In sum, not only had the environment for higher education turned harsh, but government policies, to which universities were now bound, were no longer benign.

The beginning of the 1980s witnessed the kind of shift in the zeitgeist that is more readily described than explained. The size and scope of government's role continued to be vigorously contested, but the preponderance of opinion gradually tilted from government-sponsored solutions toward less government as the solution—from nationalization to privatization. Internationally this conflict was perceived as the crisis of the welfare state. In the United States concern focused on the declining competitiveness of industry, allegedly caused by too much government and too little research. The elections of Margaret Thatcher in the United Kingdom and Ronald Reagan in the United States enshrined and advanced this transformation. Both leaders were also monumentally unpopular on the campuses of their respective countries. Accordingly, a catalyst was required for privatization to take root in American universities. That role was filled by the great American inflation.

From 1978 to 1982, inflation eroded one-third of the purchasing power of the dollar. Although this development wreaked obvious hardships on universities and especially on their employees, it also affected behavior and attitudes. Hardly decisive in itself, the inflation had the subtle influence of tilting universities and their clienteles toward new, privatizing, courses of action. The most significant developments were the rapprochement between universities and private industry, the aggrandizement of university management, the renewed popularity of elite institutions, and the transformation in the financing of a college education.

In the early 1970s, relations between universities and industry reached low ebb. The radicalism that had set the tone of campus discourse in the preceding years evolved toward a self-serving concern for social justice, dedicated to criticizing rather than cooperating with capitalist firms. Links with industry nevertheless persisted in places like chemistry departments, engineering colleges, and medical schools, where ties with professional practice outweighed ideology. These ties tended to strengthen in the following years, but three developments at the decade's end transformed university attitudes.

First, the well-publicized crisis of economic competitiveness argued for a greater investment in academic research by industry and better means for transferring the fruits of academic research to the commercial sector. Second, this case was powerfully reinforced by the emergence of biotechnology. Here was an example of basic academic research that was directly relevant to the development of pharmaceutical and agricultural products. As university biologists formed or joined biotech firms, commercial links were forged that universities could scarcely prevent. Third, the increasingly apparent success of those universities that had become active in patenting or had established research parks formed another kind of compelling example. For universities, starved for revenues by the great inflation, greater cooperation with industry and even direct participation in commercial ventures seemed to promise much-needed income. Harvard president Derek Bok spoke for his counterparts when he noted that such windfalls could "stir the blood of every harried administrator struggling to balance an unruly budget."[20]

Campus opinion tended to remain skeptical, if not actually hostile, but the elements fell in place for university involvement with commercial firms and in commercial markets: the strong vested interest of faculty in the relevant fields, administrative leadership in creating new organizational units for this purpose, and soon government policies to subsidize university-industry cooperation.

An influential book in the early 1980s reported that a "managerial revolution" was taking place in American higher education. Universities belatedly recognized management as "a body of knowledge and techniques indispensable for any complex organization."[21] In the B.C. era (before computers) universities were rudimentary organizations, particularly in financial and administrative support services. This changed in the 1970s as the scope of these activities ballooned. Regulatory and reporting requirements increased administrative chores enormously. Large offices had to be maintained for "grant and contract administration," for "student financial aid," and for far more complicated budgetary operations.

The financial crisis prompted more fundamental changes in management. In order to understand and gain control over their financial predicament, universities resorted to a new dimension of managerial analysis. Consultants were brought in and computer programs deployed, but more far-reaching, strategic planning in some form became the new managerial imperative. This development occurred sooner and more thoroughly at private universities, as they were forced to deal with looming financial crises.

An additional change largely followed the managerial revolution. A new standard of economic rationality tended to pervade university decision-making. This was most visible when universities privatized inefficient operations, like bookstores. But many more university units were now expected to pay their own way. As a further ramification of these trends, significant portions of university affairs were withdrawn from faculty influence. As one manager explained his five-year plan: "naturally, we regretted not having faculty endorsement. . . . Anyway, ours by necessity is not a bottom-up planning process. It is a top-down process."[22] Going forward, the new managerialism facilitated the implementation of privatizing policies from the top down.

In the cynical climate of the 1970s a thorough liberal arts education in a residential setting was no longer held in high regard. Students were encouraged to "stop out" of college in order to learn from experience or, conversely, to graduate early by attending summer school, thus saving money. The decade also witnessed a pronounced swing of graduates toward vocational majors. Plummeting credentials among prospective students jeopardized traditional liberal arts colleges further.[23]

The prospects for the 1980s appeared even more dismal for these institu-

tions, but they were not borne out. Key factors began to change. The earnings differential between high school and college graduates began to widen,
raising economic incentive. Students, perhaps sensing the effects of inflation (or the apparent glut of college graduates), adopted more materialistic
aspirations and corresponding educational strategies. Selective colleges, for
their part, responded to their straitened circumstances by redoubling recruitment efforts with more staff, more direct mailings, and market analysis. Among prospective students, interest in the leading private colleges
clearly grew. The behavior of applicants became more aggressive too as they
began sending multiple applications to preferred colleges.[24] Perhaps most
remarkable, demand rose at the most expensive institutions despite rapidly
rising tuition.

The years of the great inflation marked a restructuring of the way Americans paid for college. The system of federal student financial aid enacted in
1972 established two types of need-based grants, one for basic support (now
called Pell grants), the other to help pay for attending more expensive institutions. A program of subsidized loans was intended to back up this core
aid for students with additional, extraordinary needs. As inflation pushed
the nominal costs of attendance higher, however, this system came under
intense political pressure to offer succor to the middle class. The Middle Income Student Assistance Act of 1978 addressed this alleged "squeeze" on
families who were neither aided nor affluent by removing the income ceiling for guaranteed, low-interest loans. Interest rates in the economy soon
shot upward, creating a situation in which both lenders and borrowers
could profit handsomely from the government's generous terms. The volume of loans increased by 60 percent in real terms in just three years. Moreover, the number of borrowers ballooned as well. When the provisions for
federal student loans were subsequently tightened, neither borrowers nor
loan volume subsided. At these new higher levels, loans overshadowed federal grants as the largest form of student aid.[25]

At virtually the same time, the leading private universities shifted their
policies slightly but significantly. Harvard and other Ivy League colleges
raised tuition aggressively to cope with their financial straits. In keeping
with their strong sense of social justice, however, they also assisted needy
students with additional financial aid, ostensibly from their own fisc. An
open window for federal loans after 1978 greatly facilitated this approach.
Thus the high-tuition/high-aid strategy was born out of a subtle adjustment
of institutional practice and reinforced over several years by relentless infla-
tionary pressure. By appreciably raising the tuition ceiling, the pricing lead-

ers provided other private colleges and universities ample headroom to boost their charges too. In the years following, the logic of this situation was steadily realized.

Thus when something like prosperity returned to American higher education in the mid-1980s, the system itself had materially altered. Conditions were ripe for raising university prices and university expenditures. The latter could be used to increase the attractiveness of institutions for preferred undergraduates. Additional spending could also be used to enhance the internal research capacity of universities, which in turn fortified the newfound goal of contributing to the economy. And if these signposts were not clear enough, university operations were now directed by a new group of managers with the skills and authority to read the signs and set the course. What this new era produced is the subject of the chapters that follow.

CHAPTER TWO

University Costs

IN 1997 the United States Congress created a National Commission on the Cost of Higher Education to undertake within six months a comprehensive review of college costs and prices. The escalation of tuition prices was the most persistent public concern about higher education from the mid-1980s through the 1990s, but this exceptional federal attention testified to both the sense of urgency and the depth of concern. The commission's charge and its 1998 *Report* were consequently focused on public definitions of this "problem": Why did colleges and universities spend so much? And how could students afford the mounting prices?[1] Largely ignored was the institutional point of view on these issues.[2]

This focus was notably different from the previous federal attempt to gauge the financial difficulties of higher education. A National Commission appointed in 1972 as part of the overhaul of federal programs supporting postsecondary education had explicitly addressed the financial distress then experienced by numerous colleges and universities.[3] It was also concerned with ensuring that all qualified individuals would have both access to higher education and a reasonable choice among institutions. Furthermore, it expected the federal government to implement programs to achieve those ends. The 1997 commission, in contrast, assumed a market environment. It focused on the rising level of producer prices, the adequacy of product information for consumers, and the effects of the subsidies, discounts, and credit arrangements that allow this market to operate.

This study is closer in spirit to the 1972 commission. It asks what factors have shaped the financing of the major U.S. universities, and explores the consequences, chiefly for institutions but also for students. It assumes that revenues are the lifeblood of these and all other universities rather than social costs that ought to be minimized. The level of resources that universities command from society greatly affects the scope and effectiveness of their activities; and who provides these resources greatly affects their behavior.[4] During the 1980s, universities generally were able to lift their resource levels above the depths of the late 1970s; in the 1990s, progress became more uneven. The university expenditures that lie at the heart of the current controversy were shaped during these two decades, the current era for higher education.

Revenues and Rising Costs

University finance underwent fundamental changes in the current era. First, as needs and expenditures rose, the additional costs of university study were substantially borne by students and their families. Second, student financial aid was transformed from the exception to the norm. Most full-time undergraduates now receive some form of financial aid, with federal loans being most common. In private universities, institutional grants, or tuition discounts, have similarly become the rule, so most students pay different amounts for the same education. These developments have strongly influenced university costs.

The *costs* of higher education are the expenditures of colleges and universities for instruction-related purposes, or what might be called production costs.[5] Costs are conceptually different from the price of higher education (the cost to students), which, because of financial aid, may vary considerably from what is now tellingly termed the "sticker price." Universities have other costs that are not directly related to instruction. The direct costs of research are separately budgeted and for the most part externally funded. These expenditures thus vary independently from other internal costs. The costs of public service are similarly met through designated funds and vary widely and randomly across institutions. Costs for operating dormitories, food service, and hospitals are lumped under auxiliary enterprises, which are expected to be self-supporting. The remaining expenditures represent the core costs of an institution of higher education: what is spent for instruction and its support, faculty learning, student needs, administration, and maintaining the campus. These costs are by no means identical to the cost of instruction alone, a concept that eludes precise specification in a multipurpose institution. Rather, the core costs reflect the resources an institution of higher education applies to its core tasks of cultivating and disseminating knowledge.

For the purposes of this study, core costs have been estimated for ninety-nine research universities—thirty-three private and sixty-six public (see Appendix A). These are major research universities engaged in both graduate and undergraduate education.[6] They perform nearly 70 percent of academic research and graduate 68 percent of earned doctorates. They also award 28 percent of bachelor's degrees and 34 percent of first professional degrees. They include the largest and in many respects the finest institutions in the vast system of American higher education. Because they are multipurpose institutions and expend their resources for multiple and complementary ends, their spending patterns are difficult to compare. For this study, the income they have to spend for these purposes—revenue—is employed as the best comparable measure of expenditures across institutions and over time. This approach is consistent with Howard Bowen's revenue theory of costs, which holds that "each institution raises all the money it can . . . [and] spends all it raises."[7] In practice, the size of each year's budget is determined by the amount of projected revenues.

Core educational revenues per student have been calculated by adding net tuition (gross tuition minus institutional student aid), spending from endowment, and, for state universities, state appropriations, and dividing that sum by the number of full-time equivalent (FTE) students. All data are adjusted for inflation to provide comparisons in 1996 dollars. The results are given in Appendix A.

This definition of core university costs yields an approximation that permits comparability across institutions and over time. It ignores certain kinds of revenues, such as gifts for current use, indirect cost reimbursements for research, and earnings from patent licenses. These revenues tend to be committed to specific purposes, most of which are tangential to instruction. On the other side of the ledger, this method also overlooks the fact that some restricted income from endowment may also be directed toward similar, noninstructional ends. This definition of costs, while hardly precise, is feasible to calculate and reasonably accurate. If anything, it underestimates expenditures.

In contrast, the alternative approach of calculating expenditures related to instruction is fraught with complications. Foremost, different categories of expenditures must be divided into instructional and noninstructional components. Institutions can and do make such calculations using internal

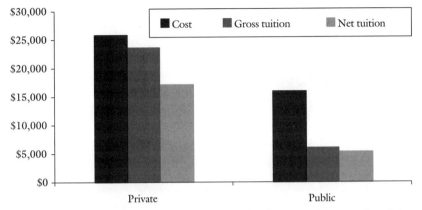

Fig. 1. Average Costs and Tuition Revenues per Student at 33 Private and 64 Public Universities, 1999–2000

accounting systems, but such results are virtually impossible to employ for purposes of comparison.[8] This definition also omits capital costs. Although the land and buildings of universities are an undoubted cost of education, there is no agreement on how to determine or depreciate such costs. Nor are they included as direct expenditures in annual operating budgets.[9] University costs as employed in this study represent the current income used to support the core, integrated educational enterprise.

A key concern of the current era has been how many of these costs are charged to students. This amount is represented by net tuition. The remainder of costs is considered a subsidy, provided by income from endowment and, in public universities, state appropriations. A critical consideration, especially for private universities (see later discussion), is the relation between the tuition sticker price and net tuition. For public and private universities in 1999–2000, these figures are shown in Figure 1. Figure 1 shows that private universities spent, on average, $25,781 for each FTE student. Tuition provided $17,095 of that total, and the institution provided the rest ($8,686). Of this latter figure, $6,474 consisted of grant aid to students who did not pay full tuition, and $2,212 was a general subsidy received by all students.[10] (See Appendix A for costs of individual universities.)

At public universities the general subsidy received by all students was $9,927, and institutional grant aid averaged just $704 per student. The implications of these figures are examined in the next two sections. First, some background on how and why these patterns evolved.

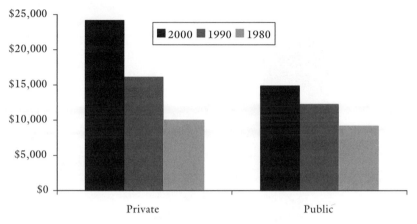

FIG. 2. University Cost per FTE Student at 33 Private and 64 Public
Universities, 1980–2000

In the 1980s and 1990s, university spending (controlled for enrollments
and inflation) grew at more than twice the rate in private universities as in
public ones (Figure 2). While the average difference between public and private universities was small in 1980, the gap widened steadily in the years
that followed.

Much of this increased spending came from students in the form of tuition, but here too the sectors differ (see Figure 3). The growth in net tuition revenues at private universities has been steep indeed, more than doubling in real terms. Public indignation has focused chiefly on the nominal
rise in the stated tuition price of the leading institutions, which ballooned
to $24,000 in 2000 from around $4,000 in 1976. Actually, average net tuition rose by 138 percent from 1980 to 2000 and university spending rose by
almost the same amount (142 percent). Students paid more, but the subsidies and the educational value they received grew proportionally. The same
has not been true in public universities. Net tuition there increased even
more rapidly (176 percent), albeit from a much lower base, but spending
grew by just 62 percent. At public universities, students paid roughly
$3,200 more in net tuition, but their subsidy, due to the sluggish growth in
state appropriations, grew by $2,500. These developments in research uni-
versities mirrored national trends. Overall, the amounts paid by students
for higher education increased enormously. How did students and their
families afford such expense?

The simple answer to this question is that they have borne only a fraction of these expenses directly. Federal loans covered a large portion of ad-

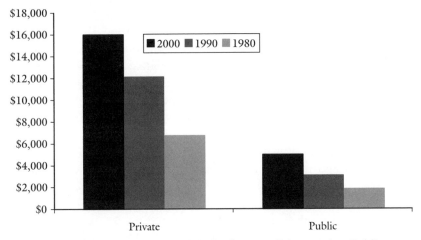

FIG. 3. Net Tuition Revenues per FTE Student at 33 Private and 64 Public Universities, 1980–2000

ditional student costs. But loans are still an expense, in fact a double one: not only must students repay them with interest, but operating these programs costs taxpayers between one-third and one-half of the amounts loaned. However, such expenditures differ from those paid from—and constrained by—current income or savings.

The costs of higher education borne by students nearly doubled in real terms from 1978 to 1996. In the same years, gross domestic product (GDP) and disposable personal income each grew slightly more than 50 percent. The cost of going to college, then, grew nearly twice as fast as the economy. Such a dramatic a rise in a national accounting category usually requires some new source of revenue to be tapped. In this case the future earnings of students (and in some cases parents) were transformed through loans into current expenditures. The distinction is an important one. This new source of purchasing power permitted students to extend their outlays to keep pace with the rising level of tuition.[11] A crude comparison suffices to make this point. From 1980 to 1996 gross revenues from tuition in American higher education increased from $24 to $55 billion (in 1996$). In the same period, federal student loans grew from $9 to $27 billion. Thus well over half of the additional purchasing power came from federal loans alone.[12] Loans of course are not grants because borrowers are obligated to repay them. Higher education is obligated as well: to federal student loans for its financial sustenance.

Since the 1980s, an ongoing debate has contested the relationship between student financial aid and the spiraling price of tuition. Critics have alleged that universities have exploited federal programs for student financial aid in order to raise tuition. In the case of Pell grants and campus-based aid, any independent effect would have to be negligible. These programs have stringent financial need requirements and are capped at levels that limit their impact on high-tuition institutions. The situation with loans is more suspicious. Those who would deny a link between loans and tuition point to the absence of a short-term correlation between increasing loan volume and tuition boosts. But given the sheer magnitude of loan volume, it scarcely seems possible that the substantial increase in the cost of attendance could have occurred without them.[13] This latter position becomes more plausible when one examines the actual process of determining and awarding student financial aid.

The financial aid process is highly standardized in higher education. It could be depicted as a balance scale, where the "estimated cost of attendance" for a given institution is first placed on one side. The various forms of payment are then added to the other side until the cost is met. First comes the "expected family contribution," which is calculated using a standard methodology from the information on savings and income entered on the financial aid application form. The next addition is "need-based aid" for which the student qualifies (if any). This group of payments includes Pell grants and the so-called campus-based federal programs (Supplemental Educational Opportunity Grants, Work-Study, and Perkins Loans). The latter are all limited in size and restricted to lower-income students. Any state aid would also be added at this point. The remaining deficit is met through "federal subsidized loans" and "institutional financial aid." Most public universities have limited amounts of aid to offer, and some of that is often awarded for merit rather than need. Hence, the entire deficit would usually be met through loans. In private colleges and universities, the deficit is filled with a combination of loans and institutional aid (or tuition discounts). This last addition to the scales is critical, for it allows the cost of attendance to be met and the transaction to be completed.

Several details of this last stage are crucial to the operation of the system. First, guaranteed student loans, which are subsidized, have annual and total caps. These limits were last extended in 1992. Most students with substantial need at high-priced institutions borrow at the annual maximums. For additional needs they might have recourse to the unsubsidized loan programs, for students or parents. Hence, despite loan limits, the system is elastic in accommodating higher prices.

Second, at private institutions, a trade-off exists between loans and tuition discounts. This allows universities room for maneuver in playing what Michael McPherson and Morton Owen Schapiro have called the "student aid game"—basically, offering more attractive terms to more desirable (or more reluctant) students.[14] Hence the availability of loans by itself can facilitate tuition increases, but the combination of loans and discounts is far more powerful.[15]

Third, despite such manipulations, the last dollar of aid comes from the institution. For that reason, in high-tuition institutions, increases in the cost of attendance, whether for tuition, room, or board, largely have to be matched by increases in aid to eligible students. This creates a multiplier effect whereby cost increases produce proportionately larger increases in tuition prices. For example, given a tuition discount rate of 25 percent, which is near average (see Figure 1), a university would need to raise tuition by four dollars in order to get three dollars of additional revenue.

Although the process of constructing an aid package allows institutions to influence student financial decisions, discretion still lies with students. Student loan volume first exploded at the start of the 1980s, when highly advantageous loan terms created a strong incentive to borrow. Loans increased only moderately thereafter until the Higher Education Amendments of 1992 expanded eligibility and raised loan limits. Loan volume shot upward by 77 percent in the next two years. The next seven years (1994–2001) saw a 50 percent rise, despite unprecedented prosperity. Much of this growth occurred in unsubsidized loan programs, which now are larger than the capped and income-restricted guaranteed loan programs. Thus much of the post-1992 growth seems to have been used for larger loans to middle-income students.[16] Such evidence suggests that the current escalation of loans is driven less by dire need and more by a culture that encourages borrowing as a first resort. Another factor bolstering the loan culture is that student borrowers must begin repayment if they leave school. They thus have strong incentives to remain in college even if that means, as it usually does, additional borrowing.

In the final analysis, the rise of the student loan culture, in combination with tuition discounts, created a situation in which the final increment required to meet the cost of attendance was always readily available. Under these conditions, student resistance to price increases in an economic sense (that is, reduced demand), especially at the more prestigious and expensive institutions, has been virtually nil.[17] Constraints on tuition increases of other kinds nevertheless persist. They include the pricing structure of the industry, the nature of the student aid system, and the potential threat of public opprobrium. However, since the 1980s, conditions have favored the growth of a *high-tuition/high-aid* policy. Accordingly, tuition revenue has been a major contributor to meeting the burgeoning costs of universities.

Costs at Private Universities

The high-tuition/high-aid policy has a long lineage. Studies in the 1960s ostensibly showed that state funding of public universities resulted in an income transfer from less wealthy Americans to the more affluent, who enrolled disproportionately at flagship campuses. This theory was a focus of the economic studies that preceded the Higher Education Amendments of 1972. Attention at that time was focused on public institutions, where students paid on average one-sixth of estimated costs. Equity would be served, most analysts seemed to agree, if those students who could afford it paid a larger share of the cost of their education, and those who could not received aid based on their financial need.

One radical interpretation of this approach proposed that well-off public university students be charged full costs and all others receive aid commensurate with need. However, the Carnegie Commission on Higher Education articulated a moderate consensus, recommending that public tuition prices be gradually raised to one-third of educational costs and that these increases be "matched by increased aid to low-income students."[18] The Carnegie Commission took pains to justify their benchmark of one-third of costs, but their reasoning largely reflected the historical circumstances of the era. One might plausibly argue that equity would be served more fully by charging wealthy students a larger fraction, full cost, or a premium. The commission's benchmark became highly respected in theory, but no economic rationale, then or now, could determine just how high high-tuition ought to be.[19]

Despite the persuasive case made by the Carnegie Commission, actual tuition prices in the 1970s lagged behind inflation in both the public and private sectors. Numerous factors weighed on the pricing power of universities, including the cessation of enrollment growth, massive new capacity, and the lowest-ever wage premium for college graduates.[20] Only at the end of the decade, in response to double-digit inflation, were tuition prices boosted, but private universities took that initiative.

Throughout the twentieth century a tacit ceiling price for college tuition existed, set by the most prestigious northeastern universities. A group of the wealthiest and most selective schools in the region have been joined since 1975 in the Consortium for Financing Higher Education (COFHE), which tracks admissions and financial data for its members. These institutions, and particularly the Ivy League trio of Harvard, Yale, and Princeton, tend to move largely in tandem since they compete most seriously among themselves. In the late 1970s, Harvard posted the highest tuition price, and it appears to have been first to raise prices aggressively. In 1978, before inflation spiked upward, Harvard boosted its tuition by 18 percent, to $5,265 from $4,450.[21] For the next ten years its tuition increases averaged $840 each year. Before these hikes, Harvard tuition had been 4 percent above the COFHE average; by 1984 it was 12 percent higher. But then the others began to close the gap.

Pricing leadership was exerted by the institutions with the strongest market position and the greatest capacity to offer their students financial aid. When their gambit succeeded, an example was set for others. Not only did COFHE institutions follow in the wake of Harvard's lead (Yale and Princeton were close behind), but so too did private colleges and universities elsewhere in the country, where tuition prices generally were lower than in the Northeast.

As private tuition escalated in the 1980s, far from alienating students, it became identified more closely with quality and prestige. Thus more and more institutions embraced the high-tuition approach, their bad social consciences always mollified by doling out increasing amounts of institutional financial aid.[22] By 2001 the tuition ceiling had risen to $27,000, with most of the private universities in this study tightly clustered above $25,000. The role of tuition in their finances remained relatively stable.[23] But this aggregate stability and the similar sticker prices belied great differences in the financial condition of individual universities.

Private universities with large endowments were already granting substantial amounts of need-based financial aid. They embraced policies of "need-blind" admissions and then met the full financial needs of the students they admitted. They supported their escalating tuition with more of the same, greatly abetted by the availability of loans.[24] The portion of gross tuition devoted to student aid—the tuition discount—changed little at Harvard and Yale during the 1980s.[25] However, the finances of universities with smaller endowments were more affected. Tuition discounts rose on average from 12 to 19 percent for the five least wealthy universities during the decade—a trend that would accelerate in the 1990s. For the decade of the 1980s, nevertheless, the high-tuition/high-aid strategy of the private universities can only be termed a resounding success.

The private universities increased their real per-student spending base by 63 percent, and this prosperity was experienced, with few exceptions, across the sector. The bottom five, for example, expanded spending by 75 percent. No single factor can explain this phenomenon. The academic leaders, in retrospect, seem to have been underpriced in terms of the intrinsic value they offered and the latent demand from highly qualified applicants. Institutions in the middle and lower reaches of this group succeeded in associating themselves more closely with the leaders, which allowed them to command the same premium tuition and, they hoped, attract more applicants. The buoyant economy of the mid-1980s played a role as well by boosting both endowments and the incomes of upper-bracket families. Spending from endowment roughly kept pace with rising tuition revenues, although actual endowments grew faster. Around 1980, when tuition prices started their rapid ascent, private universities were clearly stretched. The spending rate on endowment for this group peaked at 6.5 percent in 1983, but by the end of the decade it had dropped nearly two percentage points. Thus tuition seems to have been maintained at roughly 70 percent of core expenditures by choice, as endowment spending was adjusted down to more prudent levels.

The rising economic tide of the 1980s lifted most boats. Even the underperformers among these thirty-three universities increased real spending by at least 25 percent (see Appendix A). This situation did not persist during the first half of the 1990s, however. Glaring discrepancies soon became apparent between the wealthy and less wealthy private universities. Real spending per student increased by 17 percent from 1990 to 1996. All but two of the wealthiest ten exceeded that figure; only three from the bottom ten did that well. The middle group, as might be expected, was mixed, but the gains of the best performers did not match those in the top group. In general, a striking picture of the rich getting richer. The boom years of the late 1990s showed a similar pattern, although better for all. The bottom third increased spending by 17 percent; the middle by 28 percent, and the top third by 31 percent. Again, the rich got richer, especially Harvard, Yale, and Princeton, with gains of 50 percent. After the strong performance of the less wealthy in the 1980s it is not obvious why the situation changed in the 1990s.

Closer examination reveals that the high-tuition/high-aid policy itself was implicated. Each institution employs its own guidelines for determin-ing the relation of sticker price, student financial aid, and endowment spending. For example, assumptions and calculations might differ for un-dergraduates, doctoral students, or professional schools. However, warning lights should flash when institutional aid substantially exceeds spending from endowment. When this occurs, leaving aside other university rev-enues, an institution may have less to spend on each student than its full sticker price.[26] In 1980, eight of the thirty-three private universities were in this situation. In 1990 the number increased to twelve, and in 1996 it reached twenty before the boom years reduced it to sixteen in 2000.

The high-tuition/high-aid policy is effective only within certain parame-ters.[27] It depends on capturing significant amounts of "other people's money," either through expected family contribution, student loans, or other state and federal student financial aid. Thus it is sensitive to the ratio of aided students to full-payers and to the amount of need to be met, or put more simply, to parental income. The higher parental incomes, the more tuition revenue; the lower parental incomes, the more financial aid.[28]

This policy is also sensitive to the level of government financial aid. However, all need-based aid programs have upper limits. Boosting these caps would allow universities to capture more federal dollars, either through higher tuition or less institutional aid. But given these limits, the final increment of student cost is met through institutional aid. Perhaps for this reason the federal government has shown little inclination since 1992 to raise these caps, even though other forms of student aid have been in-creased.

For an institution to improve its yield from tuition, it must either in-crease the number of full-payers in the mix or raise expected parental con-tributions. Otherwise, each year's annual tuition hike will expand that final increment of institutional aid, as more students require aid in larger amounts. In that case, the amount of revenue realized from each additional tuition dollar will decline. In the 1990s, this is what happened to the weaker private universities, but not to the stronger ones.

The fourteen universities with the lowest spending per student were all affected. Three received about fifty cents for each additional tuition dollar; three others received even less. These six institutions (plus one other with the next lowest marginal yield) had the lowest spending levels in this group. The remainder of these fourteen received less than seventy cents for each additional tuition dollar, a figure that was lower than their overall tuition discount rate. In other words, all of these institutions were headed in the

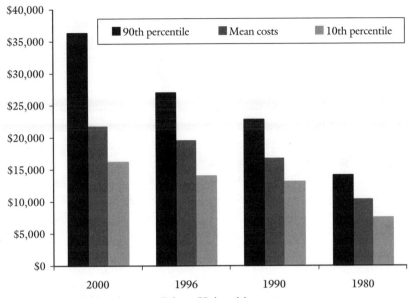

FIG. 4. Cost Dispersion at 33 Private Universities, 1980–2000

wrong direction—toward higher tuition discounts—to the detriment of their income.[29]

The growing disparity of financial means is graphically evident in Figure 4, even after the highest and lowest 10 percent are excluded as outliers. The range of costs extended from $16,000 to $36,000 in 2000. In contrast, net tuition revenue per student varied between $12,000 and $18,000, compared with sticker prices between $18,500 and $22,900 (tenth to ninetieth percentile, 1996$). The great difference in costs among these universities resulted from the enormous discrepancies in endowment income (see Figure 5). Universities with little endowment income in effect used the tuition income from wealthier students to subsidize those with financial need. Universities with large endowments can tolerate large tuition discounts (or reduced tuition revenue) and still support high costs.

The high-tuition/high-aid policy produces a peculiar price structure for private universities (see Figure 6). Tuition prices are quite similar despite large differences in expenditure levels. This pattern is not novel for American higher education, but it seems to have become exaggerated by the explosion of financial aid. In 1980, tuition levels at these schools (again, excluding the highest and lowest 10 percent) ranged from $4,500 to $6,200, a variation of 27.5 percent. In 1996, tuition prices ranged from $18,000 to

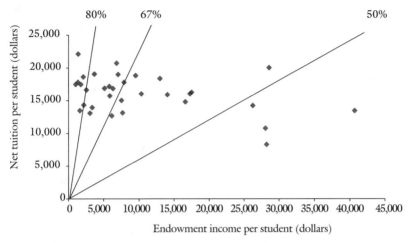

FIG. 5. Tuition Dependence at 33 Private Universities, 2000

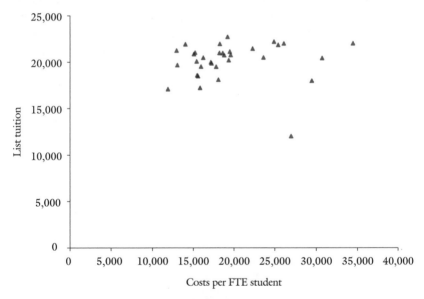

FIG. 6. List Tuition and Cost per FTE Student at 33 Private Universities

$22,000, a variation of 18 percent.[30] Thus pricing became more uniform even while differences in spending levels grew. This trend can only be regarded as an anomaly, unlikely to persist.

The prevalence of tuition discounting produces a second anomaly. Within any given university, students pay widely different prices for the same education. The situation itself is not new; assistance for needy students is as old as the American college. But now the majority of students at private universities pay different prices.

Moreover, in the 1990s private universities were using financial aid more strategically to improve the quality of their students and their capacity to pay. As these practices become more prevalent, the legitimacy of pricing disparities becomes more difficult to defend, in effect creating a third anomaly. Strategic aid reflects in principle neither academic merit nor financial need. Rather, it is predicated on the financial interests of the institution. This situation would seem to violate one of the bedrock rationales of the nonprofit sector: the crucial role of trust (see Chapter 1). Here too, financial aid practices seem to produce an inherent contradiction.[31]

These three anomalies have ominous implications. Yet during the boom years of the fin de siècle they persisted unchallenged. In many ways these years were a new golden age. Private universities were afforded the opportunity to bolster their financial and academic strength. But the basic pattern of the decade—the rich getting richer—persisted. Looking only at endowments, the ten universities with endowments under $500 million in 1995 grew by an average of 101 percent by 1999. The endowments of the thirteen universities that started with more than $1 billion increased by 128 percent. Of course, translated into dollars these percentages represent enormous differences. The $8 billion Harvard *added* to its endowment in these years roughly equals the *total* endowments of those ten universities that merely doubled their wealth. Massive and growing inequality seems to rule in the private sector in the twenty-first century.[32]

Costs at Public Universities

Public and private universities relate to the marketplace in different ways. Each private university is unique, fashioned by its distinctive history, leadership, and constituencies. Each institution also stands alone in relation to the national marketplace. But as a consequence, all must contend with the same market forces and are shaped by those forces in similar ways. The policy of high-tuition/high-aid is one example; another is the fixation on undergraduate selectivity, which is discussed in the next chapter.

Public universities, in contrast, exhibit many common features. As creatures of the state, receiving a significant portion of their core funding as legislative appropriations, they have an ineluctable obligation to the polity. In practical terms this means providing access to large numbers of the state's young people; teaching practical fields of study, whether in a land-grant institution or not; and providing certain services to taxpayers and the economy. These obligations have not precluded academic excellence, at least for a large subset of state universities, but they have engendered a latent tension between these two objectives. Beyond these common traits, though, the fact of being rooted in their particular states creates great variety among public universities. First, undergraduates are largely drawn from within the state, and each state university's composition is affected by the division of labor among state institutions. While some state institutions have (or used to have) virtually open enrollments, others have traditionally been selective. Second, governance arrangements differ widely from state to state, as does the degree of campus autonomy. Third, aspirations and possibilities for academic distinction have been markedly different and continue to fluctuate. Finally, the financial means to achieve their missions vary according to the economy, demography, and politics of each state. The public research universities examined here exhibited common themes in their evolution during the 1980s and 1990s, but there were important variations in how those themes played out.

Throughout most of the twentieth century state universities looked to their legislatures for the bulk of their operating funds. For much of this time, the amounts allotted were comparatively modest. Nevertheless, when state revenues plummeted during hard times, state appropriations most often were cut as well. When conditions improved these cuts tended to be restored, and the growth curve of increasing appropriations generally resumed. This pattern occurred at the start of the 1970s and again at the beginning of the 1980s. In 1980, states provided these public universities with seventy-eight cents for every twenty-two cents paid by students (or a tuition ratio of 22 percent; see Figure 7). This was less than they appropriated a decade before, but still more than the sixty-seven cents on the dollar that the Carnegie Commission had recommended in the early 1970s.

The funding history of state universities from that juncture is shown in Figure 7. The 1980s, despite beginning with raging inflation and a double-dip recession, was a reasonably prosperous decade for most. State appropriations grew by 32 percent in constant dollars. Tuition grew by a higher percentage, as already noted, but the original base was fairly low. States as a whole contributed more additional dollars than did the average student ($3,278 vs. $2,394), and the tuition ratio approached 28 percent. But results were actually mixed. Five universities received more revenues from students

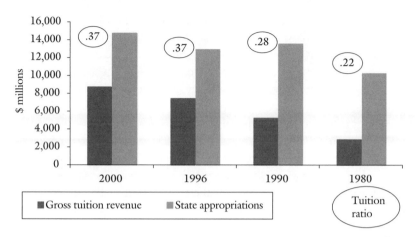

FIG. 7. Tuition Revenues and State Appropriations at 64 State Universities, 1980–2000

than from their states (the Universities of Colorado, Delaware, Michigan, and Pittsburgh, and Pennsylvania State University), but others experienced little or no erosion.

During the 1990s, the basic relationship between states and their universities shifted. State appropriations for these universities declined in real terms through 1996, so revenue growth came entirely from student tuition. The largest disaster occurred at the University of California, where reduced state revenues required that the traditional policy of low fees and ample appropriations be jettisoned. After the state appropriation was cut by 15 percent and student charges were more than doubled, the university's tuition ratio rose to near the national average. And the movement to higher tuition was nearly pervasive. The only exceptions were several sunbelt states (Florida, Georgia, New Mexico, North Carolina) that preserved tuition ratios close to the 1980 national average.[33]

To some extent these steps were forced by economic conditions. The recovery from the recession of 1990 was long and shallow. Additional years passed before tax revenues grew sufficiently for states to expand their budgets. Still, the restoration phase of the budget cycle was unusually weak in the 1990s. The most common explanation was that growth in other categories of state expenditures—particularly Medicaid and corrections—were "crowding out" the share of state budgets previously claimed by higher education.[34] But state spending reflects political choices. In these years the popularity of universities was at low ebb (see Chapter 3) and was a likely factor in constraining state appropriations or delaying their restoration.

In the boom years of the late 1990s, most states remained tentative about raising appropriations, but at least the tuition ratio remained stable. For the entire decade, real state appropriations increased by only $1.2 billion while student tuition dollars added three times that amount. A pattern became established in which good economic times brought less restoration and bad times brought greater deterioration. The latter scenario was replayed with a vengeance after the mild recession of 2001. Many states reduced university appropriations, some repeatedly; and the 2002 academic year brought the largest absolute increases in public university tuition.[35]

The prevailing mood of suspicion during the 1990s emboldened states to intervene in the internal affairs of universities to a greater extent than at any time since the postwar anticommunist hysteria. Much of this meddling was motivated by outright distrust. Hence there was widespread support for the notion that state colleges and universities must be held accountable—for the amount that students learned, for the amount that faculty taught, and for the amount of money they spent. Never mind that university leaders were already accountable, directly or indirectly, to elected officials: legislators preferred to assume that university administrators were incompetent at their principal tasks. As of 1996, fifteen states had frozen or indexed tuition; eighteen had launched inquiries into faculty workloads; and twenty-one had tied institutional funding in some degree to performance measures.[36] These and other state interventions in university management invoke fundamental governance issues that cannot be untangled here. More consequential, such steps constricted the ability of universities to deal with the difficulties imposed by shrinking state appropriations.

Distrust of state universities also may have influenced states to direct funds toward students instead of institutions. This phenomenon represented a public version of the high-tuition/high-aid policy. State officials are often of two minds about this approach. Low tuition has a strong appeal for voters who patronize state institutions of higher education, and in a number of states a powerful tradition upholds this principle. In other states the equity argument can readily be invoked to rationalize higher tuition, often coupled with greater state provision of student financial aid.

While total state appropriations for higher education shrank slightly in real terms from 1990 to 1996, support for the smaller grant programs grew by 55 percent. This development reflected a growing inclination to favor funds for students over funds for universities. During this period state programs awarded an additional $1 billion (1996$) in student aid, while student tuition payments at state schools rose by $7.25 billion. In most states these awards were available to students in both public and private institutions, reflecting the political strength of the private sector. The programs are also fairly concentrated: New York, California, Illinois, New Jersey, and Pennsylvania (with 32 percent of all students) appropriated three-fifths of all state student financial aid.

During the late 1990s the political popularity of state grants for students persisted, but programs of merit aid assumed greater prominence.[37] In 1993, Georgia began offering Hope scholarships to all state students who completed high school with a B average. In 1997, Florida instituted a similar large program that demanded higher levels of achievement. Michigan followed in 1999.[38] In 2000, California committed to a substantial expansion of its financial aid programs, employing both merit and need criteria.[39] It is noteworthy that in those four states student aid programs were not instituted at the expense of institutional appropriations. Georgia and Florida dedicated new lottery revenues for this purpose; Michigan used its windfall from tobacco litigation; and California, having largely restored the cuts of the early 1990s, was committing its budgetary surplus. Other states initiated more limited programs, usually to encourage very high achievers to remain in-state.

Student financial aid has become a popular program in state houses across the country. The rationale, in part, is to mitigate the impact of high tuition imposed during previous years, but, ironically, the market forces created by this additional aid, by expanding student purchasing power, may encourage higher public (and private) tuition in the future.

The pricing structure of public universities is quite different from that in the private sector. Tuition for resident undergraduates varies widely according to state traditions and policies. For 2001–02, in-state undergraduate tuition ranged from around $2,500 (in Arizona, Florida, and Utah) to nearly $7,500 in Pennsylvania. This variation was not too different from 1980, when the range was $500 to $1,500. Moreover, as with private universities, there is no relationship between the sticker price and institutional costs (see Figure 8).

In some states, appropriations contribute less than student charges, but in others they are as much as four times greater. These differences are unrelated to the amount of tuition charged or to the quality of the education purchased. Tuition for in-state students is often more like a copayment than a price reflecting the value of the purchased service. State appropriations provided five-eighths of total costs in 2000, and these subsidies actually varied more widely than tuition prices. Thus, despite the pervasive rise in tu-

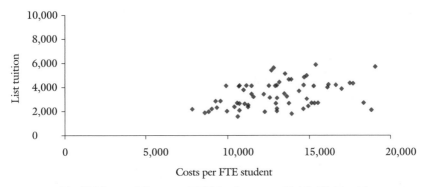

F I G . 8. List Tuition and Costs per FTE Student at 64 Public Universities, 1996

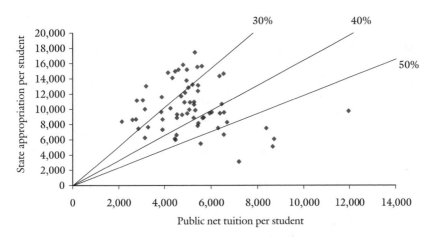

F I G . 9. Tuition Dependence at 66 Public Universities, 2000

ition, basic state appropriations are still crucial to the finance of these universities. To place state funding in perspective: the average 2000 appropriation of $250 million was roughly equivalent to an endowment of $5 billion for a private university with a 5 percent spending rule. The distribution of state appropriations versus tuition revenues is depicted in Figure 9.

Another remarkable feature of the pricing of public university education is that net tuition per student exceeds the sticker price for resident undergraduate tuition. At private universities, it was seen, net tuition revenues were 24 percent *less* than gross tuition. At public universities, average net tuition per student was 24 percent *more* than the listed resident tuition (1996). Public universities accomplished this feat in several ways. First, they inflated the tuition charged to out-of-state students. Nonresident tuition at state universities now averages about three times that for residents. Thus when 35 percent of students are nonresident—about the maximum level that any state will tolerate—the "foreigners" would contribute more than 60 percent of tuition revenue. This policy of soaking nonresident students—or charging them "full costs," as some states put it—became widespread in the 1980s. In the 1990s, however, it became a conscious strategy for revenue maximization. Many state universities now quietly direct their recruitment efforts beyond their borders, even offering scarce merit aid to attract those lucrative students. Thus, much like private universities, state universities have allowed their behavior to be shaped by the need for income from high tuition.

The practice of charging different tuition rates is also becoming more widespread in public universities. Some institutions charge upperclassmen more, and graduate students still more. Tuition for most professional schools has been raised well above undergraduate levels. In an extreme case, the trustees of the University of Virginia in 1995 withdrew all state support from the schools of law and business, making them self-supporting, largely through tuition.[40] Finally, state universities have been squeezing extra revenues from their students by imposing a variety of user fees. Altogether, public universities have found ways to maximize tuition revenues while keeping the sticker price for resident undergraduates, their most visible and politically important clientele, as low as possible. Still, many public universities have followed the path of private universities toward a high-tuition/high-aid policy. Fundamental differences nevertheless exist between the two sectors.

Private university education, on average, is overpriced, so it must often be sold at a discount. Public university education is underpriced, so a substantial minority of its clientele is willing to purchase it at a premium. Interestingly, these two separate practices converge to create a distinctive sector of the national market for undergraduate education. Nonresident tuition at most flagship universities tended to fall in the range of $11,000 to 15,000 (in 2001); tuition at a private university discounted by 40 percent would be a similar amount. Such pricing represents a mid-point between in-state public and full-price private expenses. In the 1990s this market sector became highly competitive, pitting public and private universities against one another.

If most public universities possess the pricing power to charge more, in practice they have been discouraged from doing so largely by political constraints. Many state universities do not have the authority to set their own

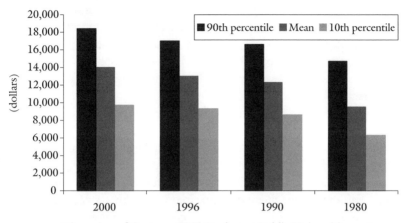

FIG. 10. Dispersion of Costs per FTE Student at Public Universities, 1980–2000

tuition. Others face legislated restrictions, and another group probably fears that raising tuition too rapidly would prompt a punitive reaction. But a few state universities now charge all that their markets will bear. In these cases further increases would harm enrollments and revenues. States have good reason to impose constraints on tuition. Public universities have an obligation to provide access to quality higher education to an appropriate portion of the state's undergraduate students rather than recruiting, as do most graduate programs, the best students available in the country or the world. And state universities clearly do not have the resources to sustain a high-tuition policy by providing tuition discounts to the bulk of their numerous students.

The range of spending levels among state universities from 1980 to 2000 shows that (as in the private sector) universities with the lowest levels made genuine progress in the 1980s, but advanced more slowly in the following decade (see Figure 10). Universities with high spending levels advanced fairly steadily throughout these decades. The halting gains from 1990 to 1996, and the more robust gains afterward, may be largely attributable to the collapse and recovery of state funding for the nine-campus University of California. Around the country, the funding of state universities showed steady progress over these two decades—roughly 2 percent per year for the mean institution. However, this tangible progress obscures two growing structural problems.

First, the dominant trend of the current era toward lower relative state support and greater reliance on tuition shows no sign of abating. Developments in the late 1990s gave some hope that fears of unrelenting privatization were exaggerated. With state coffers full or even overflowing, state support for universities generally recovered its traditional momentum. But larger appropriations often came with strings attached, and student charges, with few exceptions, did not decline (see Figure 10). The pattern of the new decade, however, promised to replicate the 1980s and 1990s — only worse.

The states themselves were among the worst victims of the economic downturn of the early 2000s, and they reacted predictably by constricting funding for higher education. State universities, perhaps wiser from experience, regarded these well-publicized cutbacks as a window of opportunity. Many imposed substantial tuition hikes and embraced greater reliance on tuition. Tuition dependence now appeared preferable to dependence on state appropriations. Forced to choose between compromising quality and compromising access, they chose the latter. In doing so they reacted to the market rather than the polity, for reasons that are partly due to their second structural problem.

The 2 percent annual spending growth of public universities pales when compared with that of private universities, where spending by the mean institution grew at more than double that rate. Comparisons of the two sectors can be distorted by the spectacular success of the wealthiest institutions. Nevertheless, in 1980 the range of costs was coextensive for public and private universities, even though the mean was higher among the privates. In 2000 the range of costs for the lower half of the private universities was roughly coextensive with the upper half of the publics. The academic competitiveness of public universities may have grown in absolute terms, yet it declined relative to that of private universities. This widening gap is ominous. Still, evaluating these differences requires asking what costs signify and why they inexorably rise.

University Costs: Finding the Problem

Many assume that the average costs of education in all colleges and universities rose with implacable regularity throughout the twentieth century. In fact, the tempo of these changes varied, as did their causes. The average cost of a year's study in a college or university (that is, what institutions spent) nearly doubled in real terms from 1939 to 1972, but the level of spending reached in 1972 was not exceeded until 1984. During the decades when costs doubled, universities became far more complex organizations offering larger and richer instructional programs. From 1984 to 1995, educational costs rose by 19 percent, but, given the previous stagnation, the same could be said for the twenty-three years since 1972. The mid-to-late 1980s were the years when higher education as a whole overcame the losses of the previous decade and advanced financially.[41] During the 1990s costs rose too, but at roughly the same rate as the gross domestic product.[42] For the research universities monitored in this study, however, spending increased far more, especially in private universities (see Figure 1).[43]

The preceding discussion has focused on the resources that made greater spending possible. The other side of the question, which has attracted far more attention, is what does such spending purchase? From an economic perspective, there are three possible explanations for rising costs: *inefficiency*, or spending more for less output; *quality enhancement*, or increasing inputs to raise the quality of outputs; and *rising factor prices*, or higher prices for identical inputs.[44] The first seems deplorable, the second laudable, and the third perhaps inescapable (unless substitutes can be found). But in fact these diagnoses are not easily made.

Inefficiency is the charge most often hurled by critics, and no doubt any dedicated Taylorite would have little trouble finding examples of waste, duplication, or dubious expenditure on a typical university campus. But critics allege that universities are inherently inefficient, and point to practices such as sabbatical leaves, tenure, and provisions for faculty research.

Such attacks ignore the knowledge-centered nature of universities, including the overqualification of teachers, described in the previous chapter. In this respect, comparisons with business corporations or even with educational institutions teaching textbook subjects are misleading.[45] To be fair, universities should be compared with institutions performing like functions. On this basis, the scale and scope of universities would appear to produce some notable efficiencies. For example, universities are usually the lowest priced performers of advanced research.[46] Overhead costs tend to be much less than those in independent or industrial laboratories. And when purchasing advanced, individualized instruction, business and government routinely pay prices that exceed those for even elite college education.[47]

These efficiencies stem above all from the multipurpose nature of universities. There are real and valuable synergies that result from the combined pursuit of instruction, research, and knowledge-based services. But these synergies also make it difficult to evaluate the efficiency of a single purpose, particularly instruction.

Nevertheless, some potential sources of inefficiency would seem to exist in the inherent structure of university work. Most fundamental is the unitary academic year and the accompanying twelve-month budget on which all universities operate. This structure requires that all planning for the next academic year take place during the current one. The budgets, plans, and course offerings thus established are exceedingly difficult to alter in midstream. Midcourse adjustments are most likely to occur only in response to crises. Worse perhaps, any significant change requires a time horizon of two years or more—to formulate an innovation, which usually entails painstaking negotiations, and to integrate it into future plans. Thus the annual clock discourages adaptive change.[48] The disadvantages of this system are exacerbated at most public universities by the practice of not allowing budget surpluses to be carried into the next fiscal year. Instead of prudently managing resources, units must spend them or lose them at the end of each year.

The annual setting of teaching assignments and advance course scheduling make it difficult to achieve optimal course enrollments. Although average course enrollment might look healthy, for any given semester it conceals a host of underenrolled and dropped courses. The problem is not unlike that of load factors for airlines, except that each course is a half-year commitment. Achieving high load factors is relatively easy for introductory and required courses, but more elusive for advanced undergraduate and graduate courses. Most universities probably have underused capacity in the latter courses, which also employ greater faculty expertise. In this respect, institutions that enroll more upper- than lowerclassmen, like the University of California, probably make more efficient use of faculty.

Few students of academic organization have confidence in the capacity of universities to make efficient decisions about staffing and resources. While metrics are employed for creating and allocating faculty positions, no solid criteria seem to exist for determining how much administration is necessary or desirable. Allegations about the proliferation of administration are common, but data are sparse. The proportion of reported expenditures devoted to administration grew moderately between 1980 and 1996 at both private (from 13 percent to 14.6 percent) and public (from 10.5 percent to 11.3 percent) research universities.[49] But there is no way of knowing how much of the additional administrative cost was justified. Both spent relatively less on administration than other types of institution in their respective sectors, which suggests that economies of scale exist in administering these large institutions.

In similar fashion, universities place a high priority on building academic community, but results from such expenditures defy cost efficiency analysis. Equity is an important component of this value, which probably results in above-market wages for faculty in purely academic subjects. Norms of equity in the treatment of faculty may also cause research time to be allocated to faculty members who are not productive scholars. More serious is the suspicion that universities devote excessive resources for the comfort of their employees, academic and administrative. Similarly, universities may have a weakness for producing, for the sake of the organization, intermediate products that do not enhance real outputs.[50] In these latter matters especially, wise and judicious leadership might prevent these pitfalls. But the nature of the university is such that different constituencies press competing claims using incommensurate arguments and invoking different missions and long-term aspirations. Because such claims cannot be readily weighed against one another, the result is what organizational theorists call "garbage can decision-making."

The countertendency to these basic inefficiencies does not assume superhuman managers, but rather stems from the chronic scarcity implied in the revenue theory of costs. Because funds are always insufficient for the level of operations to which universities aspire, they have an ever-present incentive to minimize costs that are less central to their mission and redirect resources toward more valued ends. It seems likely, for example, that a decline in the relative expenditures on physical plant resulted from such a process.[51] In fact, most universities in the current era have consistently outsourced nonessential tasks. More generally, operating under a quality deficit forces these institutions to stretch existing revenues in order to obtain savings wherever possible. That need was heightened in the early 1990s by the repeated budgetary tightening that universities experienced.[52] A number of universities institutionalized variants of this cost-reduction strategy in the hope of moving toward greater efficiency.

Given the discipline of revenue constraints, it seems unlikely that universities have become *more* inefficient in the current era. Perhaps more than most organizations, universities should be mindful of their inherent efficiency challenges, but it is doubtful that higher costs are attributable to inefficiency.

Quality in higher education is routinely assumed by economists to increase with cost, but how this takes place is something of a black box. By one interpretation, greater costs are associated with a larger and better package of services, which can be accepted as a proxy for better quality.[53] Such services would typically include the learning of the faculty, the intellectual abilities of student peers, and student amenities—all of which could be assigned market values. Educational quality is more likely to result from the chemistry of these elements than from their sum, but clearly larger and better packages are preferable to smaller and weaker ones. The data on costs indicate that universities at the ninetieth percentile spend nearly twice as much per student as those at the tenth percentile in both sectors (see Figures 4 and 11). Are the differences in quality proportional to spending? Such a conclusion seems doubtful.

Peering into the black box, one can hypothesize that the general association between spending and quality in practice is due to several interrelated factors. The most telling distinctions can be drawn between spending levels at private and public universities, but the following factors pertain to individual institutions in both sectors.

1. *Mix of programs.* Each university has a unique mix of academic and professional programs with widely varying unit costs. High-cost private universities tend to have a higher proportion of costly professional schools. Some professional schools, like schools of medicine, are tremendously expensive; others, like law and business schools, spend freely because they have abundant incomes. Doctoral programs too are inherently expensive, so universities with more doctoral students will have a higher cost basis.

2. *Cost of courses.* The cost of offering courses varies considerably by subject. Speech and sociology seem to have the lowest per-student costs at research universities; however, biology costs twice as much and engineering three times as much. Such figures are less sensitive to input prices (instructor salaries) than they are to enrollments. Hence professional subjects are more expensive when taught predominantly to upperclassmen and graduate students in small classes. Similarly, distinguished universities tend to support small academic programs in esoteric fields, in spite of the expense. The difference in costs for the same subject in different universities is about 60 percent from the twenty-fifth to the seventy-fifth percentile.[54]

3. *Student:faculty ratios.* This figure reflects in part the mix of programs and in part the staffing for basic arts and sciences courses. Accurate counts of faculty may be difficult to obtain because of large numbers of medical school appointments and part-time faculty, but self-reported data indicate the number of students per faculty member at public universities averages about 50 percent more than at privates. However, the faculty numbers are only part of the picture. Expenditures on nonacademic staff seem to be roughly parallel with faculty costs in both sectors, meaning that public universities have higher student-to-staff ratios as well.[55]

4. *Faculty salaries.* Faculty salaries at private universities were 25 percent higher than at publics in 2001.[56] This discrepancy again reflects the mix of

programs, but faculty in comparable fields were still better compensated in private universities. The implications for quality are obvious here: private universities have a decided advantage in competing for the academics they wish to hire. It is also possible to put a price on this factor: combining a 25 percent salary premium and a 50 percent difference in student-faculty ratios would mean that private universities pay 87.5 percent more per student in faculty wages. A similar calculation could be made for administrators and professional staff.

5. *Facilities and space.* In the intense competition for top students, physical facilities play a key role. Universities have invested all they can to make their splendid campuses even more splendid. Much of this investment is in amenities—new student centers, recreational facilities, and more commodious dormitories. Investments have also been made in educational facilities, including libraries and "smart" classrooms.

6. *Talented student peers.* Private universities tout the selectivity of their incoming classes, and this factor figures heavily in the annual rankings of *U.S. News and World Report* (see Chapter 3). The price of selectivity, as has been seen, is student financial aid. If high-cost institutions wish to enroll high-ability students, they must subsidize a good portion of them. In theory, even if a full-paying student subsidizes more-needy peers, a commensurate benefit will result from the better quality of fellow students.[57]

7. *Research.* Supporting a faculty active in original research and scholarship is directly associated with other cost factors such as doctoral programs and high salaries. It also implies more modest teaching obligations and provision for faculty research within departmental (that is, instructional) budgets. In addition, research universities consistently added and upgraded research facilities in the 1990s and have accelerated these investments since then.[58] In theory, such expenditures bolster the quality of instruction through enhanced faculty learning. These factors all relate to the scholarly reputation of university faculty, as established through peer ratings and noteworthy accomplishments, making the association between high costs and reputation fairly close. The volume of separately budgeted research expenditures is more loosely related to costs. Funds for this purpose come chiefly from external sources, and at many universities most such research is located outside of departments in separate centers and institutes (see Chapter 4). Research outside of academic departments (or in medical schools) has its own cost basis. Finally, highly rated departments are costly for universities to establish and sustain.

Quality is obviously a complex phenomenon, but these seven factors link it firmly with costs. Moreover, they roughly indicate the forms that increased spending will assume as additional revenues become available. The tendency among less research-oriented institutions to spend money on such features is often stigmatized as "academic drift." However, these universities cannot improve themselves as knowledge institutions without advancing in these areas. For established research universities, the pull is all the more powerful. Indeed, a study of costs at leading private universities ascribed the greatest portion of increase to the inherent dynamic of quality enhancement.[59] Thus the developments of the 1990s should, on balance, have been advantageous for bolstering quality in private universities, particularly the quality of the faculty.

The faculty represents the key factor price for higher education. Of course, universities purchase all manner of goods and services, but most of the unavoidable expenditures, like utilities, share three characteristics: universities have little control over prices; they prefer to minimize their cost and use; and prices are unrelated to institutional quality. Faculty, in contrast, embody the knowledge expertise that is the essence of universities, and institutions carefully weigh how much they can purchase and at what prices. Moreover, faculty salaries provide guidelines for the compensation of other professionals throughout the institution.

According to current economic thinking, the costs of faculty labor in conventional classrooms exhibit an inherent tendency to rise. As explained by William G. Bowen in the late 1960s, labor-intensive industries with fixed technologies that do not allow for productivity increase, like the performing arts or universities, will find their salary costs drawn upward by productivity increases elsewhere in the economy.[60] Their professional workers will expect their compensation to match the rising standard of living of workers with similar levels of qualification who enjoy the fruits of productivity gains. The degree to which this general effect operates in any given period will depend on a variety of market conditions, as well as the amount of revenues that institutions of higher education have to spend.

Because labor markets in higher education are highly segmented, it is not obvious how the Bowen effect operates. Faculty members in most disciplines seldom participate in labor pools for nonacademic positions, and do not compete directly with colleagues in different departments. Yet there are still internal and external influences that transcend such segmentation. If academic salaries become too low, some individuals will desert the university and other potential faculty members will eschew academic careers.[61] Under such conditions, new hires will have to be offered more attractive terms, producing "salary compression" between new and old faculty. However, prevailing notions of equity exert a considerable influence in universities and encourage them to diminish such discrepancies over time.[62]

In the era of privatization, the distance separating academic and commercial careers has narrowed in fields like molecular biology and computer science. The alternative of employment in industry has exerted real upward pressure on salaries. In theory, administrators tend to favor horizontal equity within the university, but balkanization and resource constraints make it difficult to defy the pull of these external markets. Law and business schools have long had their own salary schedules, and now faculty in other economically relevant fields also command premiums.[63] Such effects illustrate Bowen's point that the real economy exerts an upward pull on university salary costs, but in the 1990s these effects were far from uniform.

From the mid-1980s to the late 1990s, despite rising real salaries, higher education faculty lost ground to other highly educated professionals.[64] This growing gap should have generated pressure to raise academic payrolls. However, as in the U.S. economy, increasing inequality has prevailed in higher education. Faculty at doctorate-granting universities receive a considerable premium; those at the leading research universities are paid more; and those at private research universities more still.[65] Within these universities, divergence in compensation among fields is pronounced, and "superstar salaries" have extended the upper end of the scale.[66]

Faculty members at research universities have not suffered the relative deprivation that has afflicted the profession as a whole.[67] These universities appear to have protected the living standards of their faculty chiefly by limiting their numbers. This behavior is testimony of a sort to the existence of the Bowen effect, which probably works in several ways. Compared with the rest of higher education, research universities employ more faculty members who are closely connected with the commercial economy, and they also operate in a competitive environment for all faculty talent. Their limitation on faculty numbers has far-reaching implications.

Figures 11 and 12 show the restrained growth of faculty since 1980. In private universities, revenues that grew 78 percent in the 1980s brought a 13 percent increase in faculty. From 1990 to 1996, a 24 percent increase in revenues increased faculty numbers by just 1 percent. In the sample of public universities, revenue growth of 41 percent in the 1980s yielded 7 percent more faculty. From 1990 to 1996, a modest revenue increase of 10 percent funded just 390 additional regular faculty (+0.6 percent). Universities in both sectors used their budgets to retain more senior faculty and to try to

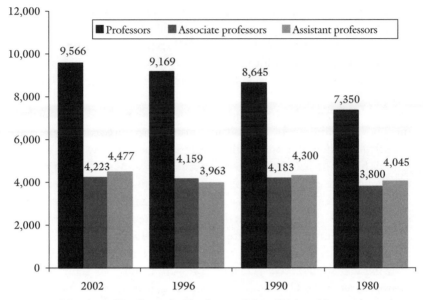

FIG. II. Number of Professors by Rank at 28 Private Universities, 1980–2002

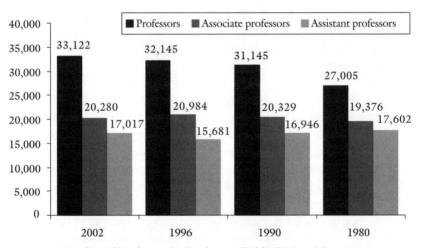

FIG. I2. Number of Professors by Rank at 64 Public Universities, 1980–2002

maintain competitive salary levels. But they did so at the expense of hiring junior faculty, particularly in the public sector. The increase in the number and weight of full professors in both sectors represents an upgrading of faculty expertise and experience, but this effect was more pronounced at private universities.

This fairly stagnant pattern changed around the turn of the century. From 1996 to 2002 the private universities continued to add full professors, but at a more subdued rate (approximately 400 for the period, versus 500 from 1990 to 1996). For the first time in decades, however, they also added junior faculty positions—more than 500. These increases produced a 5½ percent growth in faculty size in six years. In all likelihood, these universities continued to woo and hire star professors, but considering the bidding competition, better values may have been available among assistant professors. In perhaps the most significant change, the wealthiest and most highly rated universities took the lead in adding faculty positions, something they had conspicuously avoided doing during the previous period.[68]

Public universities also added junior faculty during these years, more than 1,300 positions. But they represented almost the entire growth in faculty for these years, probably because continued budgetary pressure caused senior vacancies to be filled with junior appointments. Conditions were naturally mixed across the states. The University of California, for example, went on a hiring spree at all levels, which more than restored its large faculty losses in the first half of the 1990s. However, the number of faculty actually contracted at the other public universities. Still, state universities that registered significant improvements in revenues tended to add faculty, and attrition appeared most severe in states where revenues did not expand. In a number of states there was no appreciable recovery between the recession of the early 1990s and the recession of 2001.

The faculty is the most critical input to the knowledge capabilities of universities. Yet the dynamics just reviewed do not suggest that faculty numbers or salaries by themselves have driven costs higher.[69] Rather, spending for faculty was restrained by budgetary limitations. For most universities, the need for more faculty to cover emerging fields of knowledge, for eminent professors to provide intellectual leadership, and for upgrading and equalizing of faculty salaries, all form part of the pressure to increase revenues so that universities might improve in their core tasks, and in the worst cases avoid decline.

Maintaining Quality, Accommodating Change

The years since 1990 have brought a few private universities unprecedented affluence, freeing them from the accustomed university condition of chronic scarcity. They have been burdened by the welcome yet serious challenge of expending their largesse in ways that are prudent for the long run, socially responsible, and unostentatious.

For most universities, though, including the entire public sector, preparing the annual budget still means wrestling with the realities of quality deficits, as identified in Chapter 1. Many strive to restore the support that eroded during the 1990s. Others wish to seize a propitious opportunity to advance their standing in the national hierarchy. And still others, despite notable progress, must cope with the rising standards set by affluent competitors. This latter category includes not only prestigious public universities that find themselves at an increasing disadvantage to the private sector, but also the less affluent members of the private university group. The problem of quality deficits is not simply one of status competition. The current era has witnessed a crescive expansion in the domains of academic knowledge.[70] No matter what the numbers of students or faculty, universities must grow intellectually or stagnate. They must adapt as well to changing conditions in society and the workplace. Their mandate is thus not only to aspire to quality, but also to adapt to the changing requirements of expertise.

The term "quality deficit" needs further elaboration. Universities are in some ways enormously resilient organizations. They accomplish their missions of teaching, research, and service with the means available at any given time, whether less or more than previously. And they cling tenaciously to traditions of excellence during stretches of fiscal stringency. They care intensely about the quality of their activities. Quality depends critically on the level of resources in two different ways. Internally, resources are invariably measured against accustomed standards; cutbacks can mean fewer teachers and larger classes, deferred maintenance, failure to replace out-dated equipment, and fewer books purchased for the library. Externally, declining or stagnant resources detract from the competitive position of the university. At stake is the ability to attract or retain top faculty, recruit excellent students, or compete effectively for research grants. These two facets are related, but in periods of contraction internal maintenance tends to be emphasized, while in expansionary times competitiveness can be more readily addressed.

Universities are normally able to tolerate considerable fiscal erosion without appreciable damage to institutional prestige. Somewhat larger classes may be less effective pedagogically, as is commonly believed, but the marginal effect is too subtle to measure. The impact of fiscal erosion on research is even more indirect because its funding comes overwhelmingly from external sources. University leaders have a fair amount of leeway even in bad years to protect and propitiate their most productive scholars. In such ways universities accumulate quality deficits incrementally as they adjust year after year to fiscal stringency. The effects become increasingly apparent within the institution, although often concealed from the outside. Measuring such deficits is always problematic, but per-student levels of core spending are a reasonable proxy (see Appendix A). Perhaps one-third of public universities and three-fifths of privates avoided this fate in the early to mid-1990s. They expanded spending at a comfortable rate that should have permitted academic improvement. For the rest, however, the experience of these years in all likelihood was to cling to the status quo, or worse.

For the universities fortunate enough to address the erosion problem during the boom years at the end of the 1990s, the path to follow was clear. If the general operating budget could be augmented, the first step would be to adjust the salaries of faculty and staff. Since salaries are the largest item by far in a university budget (about 75 percent), this step in itself absorbs a large portion of any increase in general funds. In much the same way, however, spending that was deferred on maintenance, equipment, libraries, and many other things should be brought back into line. Particularly important—and expensive—is restoring faculty positions that have been left unfilled. This whole process largely serves to address the internal dimension of quality loss by upgrading operations back to levels at which the institution is more comfortable. In order to remain competitive and contemporary, however, universities need to invest in improvement and change. This imperative creates challenges of a different dimension that cannot necessarily be addressed by conventional means.

In the 1990s, American universities were challenged as seldom before to update and amplify their activities. The upheaval in undergraduate education is the focus of the next chapter. Suffice it to note here that the negative clichés that abounded circa 1990 forced universities to demonstrate their concern for undergraduates and their education. This predicament also inspired the creation of programs that would highlight the advantages of education in a university active in research. The growing prevalence of merit aid provided further testimony of the value, the scarcity, and the rising cost of top students. The situation was similar with graduate students. The weak demand for doctoral education, and the ample resources of the major private universities, led departments to offer more generous graduate fellowships.[71] In these spheres universities were required to spend more just to maintain the status quo.

Information technology (IT) presented universities with an additional, costly necessity. Hardware, software, and support personnel have all become continuing and rising expenses. IT has changed the nature of libraries, administration, and research. And it has changed the lives of students. Savings have naturally resulted, but the law of technological advancement largely holds: far more can be accomplished but at greater total expense. The incorporation of IT into instruction is well under way, with consequences that are often more imagined than foreseen. Nevertheless, smart classrooms are becoming the standard, not the exception. What is certain for universities is that additional investments lie ahead.

The university's commitment to discovering, integrating, and disseminating new knowledge presents a never-ending challenge. The incorporation of new fields and the extension of old ones have challenged universities since their creation. The paradigmatic challenge of the 1990s, and beyond, has been the rapid evolution of the scientific base underlying biotechnology. This has affected far more than academic science, but the competition has provided universities with additional motivation to stay in the forefront of basic research.

Developments have been no less dramatic, if less notorious, in a host of other fields, including computing/informatics, microelectronics, and materials science; and the intellectual ferment has spilled over into fields with more traditional names, such as biochemistry and electrical engineering. For universities, such fields bring large capital requirements, the organizational challenge of creating multidisciplinary teams, and the need to compete with industry for scarce scientists. But these fields cannot be ignored. The university's claims to advance knowledge, train tomorrow's scientists, and translate new knowledge into economic growth all rest on their cultivation.

The imperative to be on the leading edge of discovery cannot await a surplus in the treasury. Universities have consequently endeavored to incorporate a capacity for accommodating change and expansion into fiscal administration. During the 1990s, four patterns were evident: conventional growth in base budgets, strategies for reallocation, entrepreneurship, and leveraging of private gifts. If all four could be found at most universities, certain institutions exemplified particular patterns.

Budgetary growth was the natural state of affairs for universities for a quarter-century after World War II. Enrollments and resources increased in fluctuating proportions as institutions hugely enlarged the scale and scope of their activities. Since about 1970, enrollment growth has been the exception, especially in the private sector, and hence no longer a source of additional resources. Universities had to find other ways to generate discretionary resources in order to address the imperatives of change.

As noted, the wealthiest private universities benefited most from the economic conditions of the 1990s. Although tuition revenues rose, their principal gains came from swelling endowments, the result of the bull market and munificent gifts. A market surge at the turn of the century produced for the leaders literally an embarrassment of riches.[72]

Some portion of the endowment must be spent each year. Although much of it may be restricted, the purposes for which it must be spent include faculty salaries and student aid that universities would fund in any case. Each university has its own spending rule for endowment funds, although they are quite similar. Typically, between 4 and 5 percent of a moving average of the market value for the previous three years is allocated for the next year's budget. When the market value rises rapidly, as in the late 1990s, the lagged moving average may depress spending below 4 percent of current market value. To spend any less, however, might invite legal challenges to their nonprofit status. Thus the most affluent private universities began deploying their remarkable wealth earlier in the decade.

As Yale's resources increased in the 1990s, it looked first to benefit the students of Yale College, whose predecessors were largely responsible for the university's prosperity. It built a thirteenth residential college—not to increase enrollment but to use as a spare. Each existing college has been scheduled in turn to occupy the spare college for a year while its old residence is refurbished. This investment was expensive, long-term, and focused on the university's most valued constituency. With the students taken care of, Yale began to add (or restore) faculty positions. Its approach here was to make clusters of senior or "star" appointments in prestigious departments such as political science, thereby bolstering or protecting top academic reputations. Yale's next commitment was to invest staggering sums in the biological and the physical sciences—$500 million each over ten years. Not since the Sterling bequest in the 1920s and 1930s has Yale invested so prodigiously in its future eminence as a research university.

Princeton has always focused even more intently on its undergraduate college, and its investment choices reflected that emphasis. In 1997 a special trustee committee was appointed to weigh strategic alternatives. Its recommendations were remarkable because they caused Princeton to break ranks with fellow COFHE members. Although most of these schools were prevented from collaborating in admissions by a federal antitrust suit, they continued to function as a tacit cartel.[73] They followed similar guidelines in calculating financial need, and the wealthiest schools at least remained faithful to need-blind admissions and full-need funding. They also refrained from more than marginal increases in enrollment: selectivity was paramount and the applicant pool was finite.

In 1998, Princeton broke the first commandment by altering the formulas by which it awarded financial aid. It increased its own contribution (institutional aid) to make more students eligible and to reduce their need for loans. This move particularly benefited students from middle-class families, where Princeton felt that cost of attendance was inhibiting recruitment. In 2001, Princeton took the further step of eliminating all loan requirements from its financial aid packages. These investments in student quality took a bite out of net tuition revenues, as expected. But it also forced Princeton's peer institutions to make similar adjustments, something most would have preferred not to do.[74]

In the spring of 2000, Princeton broke the second commandment by announcing that it would increase undergraduate enrollment by 500 students.[75] Princeton faced no difficulty recruiting the additional students, even with its rarified standards, but once again the impact was not welcomed by other schools in this sector, whose freshman recruitment pool thereby lost 125 of the bluest blue chippers.

The reasoning behind Princeton's decision to increase enrollment reflects the consequences of its meteoric revenue growth. Having consistently invested in faculty and facilities, Princeton judged that it already possessed an instructional capacity that could absorb 500 more students with no diminution in quality.[76] Further, these additions would restore a healthier weight to the undergraduate college after decades of creeping expansion in graduate education. Money would be no problem. The new students would cover their own marginal costs through tuition, and the capital budget could readily handle a new residential facility to house them. Expansion would make Princeton's extraordinary educational offerings available to additional talented students.[77] When setting priorities, the Princeton trustees turned first and foremost to bolstering the undergraduate college while in other respects continuing the course that had brought such remarkable prosperity.

For both these schools, and their few fortunate peers, revenue growth at the end of the century overwhelmed any pretense of scarcity or quality deficits. Although they still competed with each other, they also recognized the need to be circumspect in their spending to avoid driving up already inflated costs. Hence even the liberalization of financial aid undertaken by Princeton implied a manageable increment of spending among these peers—and not incidentally distanced them further from institutions where such measures would pinch.

But what do these super-affluent institutions do with funds that more than fulfill their needs? The simple answer is savings, but savings that take several forms. The endowment itself is the most conspicuous form of savings.[78] Traditionally it has grown through gifts and appreciation, but the super-affluent universities operated for several years with comfortable surpluses that contributed additional sums. A private corporation might call such funds profit, but here they are so commingled with donated funds as to obscure their nature.

Universities have engaged in another form of saving through extensive programs of building and renovation. New buildings become assets of the university, thus increasing net worth. Unlike endowment, buildings depreciate instead of appreciate, but their use value more than compensates. The extensive building programs provide for future needs of the university in times when capital may not be so readily available. Renovations do no less. Yale is rebuilding residential colleges built in the 1930s, which will meet the needs of Yale undergraduates for many decades to come. Yale's billion-dollar commitment to the sciences also includes numerous capital projects. Building cranes abound at private universities as these institutions use their current prosperity to create assets for the future.

Among public universities the economics of scarcity still prevail. The University of Michigan provides a salient example of budget growth in the public sector, but this growth typifies the era of privatization. From 1980 to 2000, real state appropriations rose by an annual average of slightly more than 1 percent. The university compensated by raising tuition revenues prodigiously. In-state tuition was raised to the top of the national range. Michigan was the first university to charge higher tuition to upperclassmen and graduate students, and it increased those premiums as well. With a huge demand from outside the state, Michigan was the only state university to set nonresident tuition at a level comparable to the tuition charged by private universities.[79] Its tuition policy resembles the high-tuition/high-aid approach of private universities, including a tuition discount rate of 13 percent in 2000. Michigan has a strong tradition of voluntary support, and in the 1990s it built the largest institutional endowment among stand-alone state universities. Only a handful of public universities derive significant revenue from endowments, but Michigan's potential annual contribution in 2000 approached $5,000 per student.[80]

The success of privatizing revenues, and continual disappointment with support from the state, led president James Duderstadt (1988–96) to suggest that this "privately financed public university" ought to be emancipated from public ownership. The state's role, he reasoned, had diminished to only a procurement relationship with the university, while the institution needed freedom from state-imposed constraints in order to fully develop revenues from tuition, research grants, private support, and auxiliary services. Such a university would be "privately supported but publicly committed."[81] Events did not follow this path, however. Although privatization in no way slowed, a full state treasury produced more generous appropriations, and Duderstadt's successor cultivated a more cooperative relationship with the state.

Private revenues have nevertheless allowed Michigan to steadily expand its core budget, with particularly strong gains at the end of the 1990s. At that juncture, Michigan was easily the strongest public university, financially and academically, outside of the University of California system. The key to Michigan's progress was the momentum it generated earlier. It was able to make substantial investments across a broad front.

Since the late 1980s, Michigan has been committed to an aggressive policy of promoting diversity throughout the university. In both faculty hiring and student recruitment this policy received substantial financial backing.[82] The construction of a Media Union was a pathbreaking initiative to bring new technologies directly to students. The university has been committed to enhancing undergraduate education, but without diminishing the importance of research.

In the early 1990s, when most major research universities saw their research share declining, Michigan grew to be the largest performer of academic R&D. This success was fueled by continuous investment. In typical fashion, Michigan in 1999 launched the Life Sciences Initiative, which aimed to position university scientists at the cutting edge of such emerging fields as bioinformatics and functional magnetic resonance imaging. At the University of Michigan a commitment to investing in change has been ingrained since the 1980s, and steady budgetary growth through privatization has permitted its realization.

Reallocation of resources to accommodate change became an increasingly pressing concern in the stagnant budgetary environment of the 1990s, but also one that raised fundamental issues of management. The traditional practice of incremental budgeting, it was long recognized, made it nearly impossible to take away significant sums from any unit.[83] Numerous approaches were touted, but the challenge was to accomplish this feat efficiently, effectively, and legitimately.[84] Usually, the faculty is assumed to be the problem: administrative systems therefore needed to provide faculty or departments with incentives to conserve or redistribute resources while also furthering the goals of the institution. Reallocation strategies consequently create a tension between decentralizing authority to the operating level and reserving a capacity to set directions at the center.

A fairly common approach to reallocation, consistent with old-fashioned incrementalism, is to impose a tax on the operating units. Units that are asked to reduce their proposed budgets by a small percentage each year are forced to make choices or become more efficient. The central administration can reallocate the resulting pool of funds according to its goals, typically for new projects or to supplement deserving units. For true believers in organizational panaceas, taxing is a pallid approach. It squeezes the units without changing their fundamental behavior, and the central administration remains under pressure to spread the supplements around.[85]

A stronger version of this centralized approach couples the strategic goals of the administration with carefully channeled initiatives from the operating units. The University of Wisconsin, Madison, employed this approach to induce greater collaboration across departmental lines. It reserved some twenty faculty appointments to be awarded to departments on the basis of proposals developed in collaboration with other departments. Like a foundation, the administration reviewed the proposals and awarded the positions to those deemed most meritorious.[86] This process produced interdisciplinary appointments that would have been quite unlikely using standard procedures.

The opposite approach, at least conceptually, is to decentralize fiscal responsibility so that resources (income) are linked directly to operations. "Every tub on its own bottom" has been Harvard's well-known motto for a century. The University of Pennsylvania and other private universities have adopted this principle in the current era, primarily as a way of containing or appeasing powerful professional schools. Applied to large state universities, this approach has been christened "responsibility-centered management," or RCM.[87] A partial measure at best, RCM allows the operating units to retain much of their revenues, but makes them responsible for their costs as well. The theory holds that units will thus have a pecuniary motivation to increase income and cut costs—to behave, in other words, like an efficient firm. But because some university units, such as libraries or central administration, do not generate any income, their funding has to be taken from those that do through a system of internal taxation or subvention—in itself a major departure from RCM principles.

Indiana University at Bloomington implemented RCM in 1990 and twice reaffirmed it, with minor modifications, after five-year reviews.[88] The Indiana system allocated all fee income to teaching units on the basis of student credit hours, balancing inequalities with subventions from the state appropriation. It then "assessed" each of these units in order to fund nonteaching units. RCM apparently achieved some of its expectations. Teaching units obtained greater control over their budgets and their futures, and departments became acutely sensitive to student preferences for class offerings.

The stagnation of state appropriations during the 1990s made this experiment somewhat painful, but there were inherent shortcomings as well. First, RCM put units into conflict with one another, whether for credit hours or assessments. It created a zero-sum situation in which gains could only be made at another unit's expense.[89] Perceptions were plentiful, although difficult to verify, that collegial relations suffered. Second, algorithms for the distribution of funds became all-powerful—and as difficult to alter as old-fashioned budget lines. Third, RCM as implemented deprived the central administration of the financial means for exerting leadership. This loss was auspicious because the system was driven by quantity (that is, student credit hours), leaving the administration with a burden of ensuring or enhancing academic quality. Support for research allocated by the Graduate School provided one qualitative counterweight, but more was felt to be needed. The first RCM review recommended a separate discretionary fund for the chancellor, and the second review asked that it be enlarged.[90]

RCM produced mixed reactions at Indiana, but in the reallocation of resources, one of its avowed goals, it appeared to have a muted impact. Resources migrated to some extent away from the dominant College of Arts and Sciences and toward professional schools. However, the burden of adapting to change lay more than ever with central administration.[91]

The RCM approach appears to have been more problematic at the University of Michigan despite more favorable circumstances. Michigan implemented its version of RCM with an expanding, rather than a flat, resource base. Perhaps more important, on a highly privatized campus, units tend to look outward for opportunities to expand income, rather than competing with their colleagues. But these conditions did not prevent rancorous disagreements among units. Moreover, RCM appeared to undermine the university's explicit commitment to interdisciplinary cooperation. After just two years, the RCM model was substantially diluted by incoming president Lee Bollinger (1997–2002). In particular, the central administration retained sufficient authority and resources to influence the academic units and to launch major initiatives.[92]

At Cornell, in contrast, the equivalent of RCM has been condemned by one close observer as inherently wasteful. The colleges at Cornell engaged in strategic behavior in order to attract or hoard valuable enrollments, heedless of the best interests of students or the university. The most successful (that is, the wealthiest) colleges, true to Howard Bowen's revenue theory of costs, spend all the income they can acquire, thus driving up total university costs.[93] Together, these examples seem to suggest that while RCM may be workable under some conditions, its efficacy as a strategy for reallocation is weak, perhaps even counterproductive. The "market" it creates is based on artificial prices, and the adjustments of participants are often unforeseen. The limitations of artificial internal markets are considered in Chapter 6.

Entrepreneurship has been a decentralizing strategy for stimulating change. By freeing and encouraging the initiatives of faculty and professional staff, universities forge additional links within their environment and gain the stimulus to adaptation that this brings. All research universities today must be entrepreneurial in many respects. However, for those institutions with stagnant base budgets, entrepreneurship becomes a possible strategy to remain competitive in research. Such an approach raises a number of subsidiary issues, most of which are variations of the question, who benefits more from these activities, entrepreneurs or the university?

Burton R. Clark's study of entrepreneurial universities in Europe suggests a framework for this phenomenon. Of key importance is the cultivation of a "developmental periphery" consisting chiefly but not exclusively of research centers or institutes. Such units provide a flexible infrastructure that reaches across academic departments within the university and establishes links with organizations outside. They stimulate the development of what Clark calls "third-stream income sources"—beyond base budgets and regular research grants—that diversify and augment funding.

Today, third-stream income comes largely from engagement with industry. Critically important for the organization is the integration of the periphery with the "academic heartland" and the "steering core" of academics and administrators.[94] Two conditions make these relationships crucial. Universities today face a "demand overload," where their many constituencies seek more services than universities can supply. Who determines which demands are met, entrepreneurs or administrators, will consequently define the institution. But these activities depend ultimately on the creativity and initiative of academics. Entrepreneurship will consequently depend on measures that grant these individuals freedom and incentives. The integration of the periphery with the academic heartland and steering core are thus inherently problematic. Centralized universities, and especially multi-university systems, are ill-suited to nurturing entrepreneurial activities.

American universities cultivated developmental peripheries throughout the twentieth century (see Chapter 4), but the degree of entrepreneurship in these endeavors is conditioned by several factors:

Centers and institutes: These entities vary from letterhead operations to multimillion-dollar laboratories, but each center is an actual or potential link with external patrons. The ease of forming centers and their freedom of operation will tend to facilitate this process.

Research faculty: Nondepartmental researchers, from postdocs to senior research scientists, can greatly expand the research capacity of a university. Where they are encouraged to apply for their own grants, rather than working only on those of others, research capacity can be enhanced.[95]

Indirect cost recovery [ICR]: How the so-called overhead on federal and other contracts is handled plays an important role in seeding additional research. Where units, including departments, are allowed to retain these funds for research purposes, both the incentive and the means for additional projects are fostered.

Entrepreneurial universities tend to regard the expansion of their research portfolio as an end in itself—a legitimate mission of the institution that need not be justified by links with instruction. They consequently welcome all respectable initiatives that will boost research grants and third-stream revenues. But such a posture can have drawbacks as well.

Entrepreneurship heightens inequality within the academic community. Faculty and researchers associated with centers often enjoy better facilities, greater staff support, and salary supplements. These advantages may stimulate more and better research, but also some faculty envy. The ties of the periphery to external patrons effectively diminish influence from the center. In a modern research university with multiple commitments such ties may hardly seem to matter, but they create a potential for problems. Universities have tenuous control over their faculty, and laissez-faire policies increase the probability that a few individuals will flout university rules. The most difficult locus to oversee has undoubtedly been university health centers, where researchers must bring in large sums to sustain their labs and third-stream monies abound.

The countervailing force should be the integration of peripheral units with the academic heartland and the cultivation of a unifying academic culture. But this process can be difficult for units that are distant from teaching and students. Hence in American universities there is no assurance that the academic heartland will be able to guide entrepreneurial activities. Units are more likely to respond individually to opportunities in their own spheres.

For universities with little possibility of finding the margins for change in their core budgets, entrepreneurship may be the most promising course. The University of Colorado, Boulder, receives the least state support in the sample, yet it was thirteenth in total research expenditures among public universities in 2000. It accomplished this feat through an extraordinary array of centers and institutes, chiefly in physics and environmental and space sciences, which account for two-thirds of the university's research grants (see Chapter 4). During a decade when tenure track faculty grew by just forty-seven, nonfaculty researchers increased by 327. Most of Colorado's research units have close relations with federal agencies and focus on basic research. These factors encourage academic integration. The university's policies also encourage entrepreneurial behavior. Institute researchers can write their own grants, and most ICR stays with grantees. Research thrives at Boulder while the academic departments, supported by general funds, continue to be squeezed.[96]

The University of Utah laments that it has a lower funding base than any public AAU (Association of American Universities) members with medical schools, but it too has sustained a vigorous research effort by giving free rein to its scientists. Until the late 1980s, the state claimed 70 percent of ICR revenues. The change in policy that allowed these funds to stay with the university, and with the units that generated them, has been credited with stimulating research. Utah now counts roughly 200 centers (although some have little substance). But the important point is that the university remains open to almost any means of enlarging its research portfolio. The medical school, with large fiefdoms and powerful patrons, epitomizes this spirit. Entrepreneurship has brought definite achievements. Utah has maintained its research share and reputation despite a stagnant revenue base. In addition, it has become far more integrated with the regional economy and, not unrelated, greatly increased third-stream income.

Leveraging private funds, the fourth way in which universities find the resources to adapt to cognitive change, is consonant with the current era of privatization. The practice of combining funds from several sources in order to finance a major project has existed in a variety of forms. Private universities have traditionally looked to private donors for major capital projects. Only recently have their burgeoning endowments allowed them to announce grandiose plans with the confidence that major donors will subsequently sign on.[97]

Foundations have long framed their giving programs with leverage, providing initial investments designed to stimulate additional funding from other sources. In the 1980s, governments employed this approach as well to foster university-industry cooperation. A number of state and federal programs provided grants that had to be matched by university and industry participants. By the end of the 1990s, leveraging had assumed a distinctive twist for public universities. Extraordinary state appropriations were made with the understanding that they would be matched by even larger sums from private sources.

The chief rationale for these newer initiatives has been to accommodate research relevant to economic development. Earlier in the 1990s, states were reluctant to appear to support anything not connected with undergraduate education, but by the end of the decade research was rehabilitated under this new guise (see Chapter 5). The leveraged approach avoids another ticklish political issue, rival claims from other state institutions. Only major research universities possess the ability to raise the millions of dollars in supplemental funding required for these major research facilities.

The University of Illinois at Urbana-Champaign has been an exemplar in combining public and private funding for huge projects. Having suffered through the 1990s with anemic state support for academic programs, the university's distinguished national reputation has become increasingly dependent on groupings of leading-edge research facilities.

The Beckman Institute for Advanced Science and Technology created a paradigm for public-private collaboration. Founded by the Arnold and Mabel Beckman Foundation in 1989 to stimulate multidisciplinary research, the institute now receives operating funds from the university, support for special programs from the foundation, and $30 million in federal research grants (1999).[98]

Similarly, in 1997 the W. M. Keck Foundation offered a sophisticated facility for genomics research if the university would provide matching funding for operations. The resulting Keck Center for Comparative and Functional Genomics provided Illini scientists with one of the most advanced facilities of its kind.

Two subsequent projects have involved state funding more directly. A $100 million quadrangle for information technology combines a major private gift, a similar sum from the National Science Foundation via the National Center for Supercomputer Applications, and a special appropriation of $42 million from the Illinois legislature.[99] A similar arrangement has been launched for a Post Genomics Institute.

Taken together, these facilities represent a significant augmentation of the university's research capacity and will pay dividends for decades to come, but in this day and age they only became possible through the strategic provision of private funding.

In the Illinois pattern, private funds have in a sense leveraged public monies out of the state. In California, the state employed some of its budgetary surplus to leverage nonstate funding. In 2000 a plan was implemented to provide $100 million over three years for each of three "Institutes for Science and Innovation" at the University of California. The rationale was to bolster the state's leading position in academic science and explicitly to contribute to future economic growth. The grants require two dollars of additional funding for each state dollar, yielding an initial investment of $900 million. Even for the University of California this sum represents a substantial increase in research capacity.

The picture that emerges for the 1990s is that only a few institutions were able to create a financial margin for adapting to the imperatives of knowledge growth through conventional budget growth. Reallocation strategies have an air of desperation about them, being applied in situations of stagnant or declining resources. They may make the best of these dire situations, but they ultimately depend on the skill of university leaders in shifting funds. The notion that efficient behaviors can be induced through artificial markets is probably naïve. Every tub on its own bottom may be an optimal approach for a compartmentalized institution with diverse external links. However, versions of RCM that depend chiefly on complex algorithms of taxation and subvention are both rigid and difficult to adjust— quite the opposite of market pricing. Once implemented, they tend to tilt the resource balance toward professional schools. Entrepreneurship and leveraging inherently skew resources toward those areas deemed relevant to the economy. For most of the universities considered in this study, securing adequate resources for general operations remains the dominant concern. This became all the more true as the economic malaise of the early 2000s persisted.

The beginning of the new century brought the same kind of economic weakness that scarred the start of the 1980s and 1990s. Despite two decades of privatization, public universities proved most vulnerable. Although they responded with the largest tuition hikes ever for the 2002 and 2003 academic years, their outlook quickly shifted from hopeful expansion back to internal maintenance. Suddenly strategies like leveraging became vulnerable too.

The University of Wisconsin, Madison, had achieved perhaps the most broadly beneficial example of leveraging in 1999. The Madison Initiative promised a $57 million increase to the campus's state appropriation over four years by pledging an additional $40 million from donors and the university's two foundations. After years of budget stagnation, the university finally convinced the state that academic excellence was a valuable asset for Wisconsin. Specifically, it had argued that the university's spending ought to be raised to at least the average for the Big Ten, but the arrangement could only be clinched with a substantial private contribution.[100] The first two-year installment brought the Madison campus 100 additional faculty appointments. However, when fiscal crisis struck the state, it reneged on its portion of the funding. Worse still, this default removed the matching obligations of private donors—a case of reverse leverage. With the Madison Initiative gutted, the university envisaged austerity budgets until at least 2005. Most public universities regard future prospects for state support as equally bleak.

In 2003, Stanford surprised the university world by announcing a salary freeze and other austerity measures for the next academic year. That such a fate could befall a university with an $8 billion endowment seems remarkable, to say the least. However, the basic strategy of budgetary growth was most likely to blame. Stanford not only competes directly with the wealthiest universities; it also had had to adjust to boom conditions in Silicon Valley. The plunge in the stock market and increased commitments for financial aid were cited as reasons for a $25 million shortfall, but liberal spending in the preceding years seems to have paved the way.[101] And Stanford has not been alone in announcing such measures. Still, the prosperity of the preceding years has left the wealthy private universities in much stronger financial condition than their public counterparts.

TO APPRECIATE the impact of changes in university finances during the current era one must distinguish long-range developments from the pressing concerns of the present. Over two decades, universities appreciably increased their levels of spending and wealth.

Conditions in the 1980s tended to lift all boats, while those of the 1990s induced increasing inequality. However, the way in which universities advanced their fortunes subjected them increasingly to market forces; and the marketplace constricted their independence of action. Quality paid increasing dividends in the current era in the form of better students, academic recognition, and fund-raising success; however, the challenge was finding the means to pay for enhanced quality.

Private universities used student financial aid to leverage huge increases in tuition revenues, although their relative dependence on tuition held steady. They nevertheless had to compete harder and pay premiums for top students. Public universities became more dependent on student tuition and consequently were drawn more deeply into this same competition.

The ramifications of this development are examined in the next chapter. Market forces shaped the same pattern of university efforts in the competition for faculty and research support. Universities today are physically larger and far better equipped than in 1980, for roughly the same number of students and faculty, but competition and inequality make their existence more precarious. Public universities suffer from a growing disadvantage to their private counterparts, and growing inequality among the latter exacerbates the insecurity of all but the wealthiest. As a result, the capacity of universities to support valued activities that produce little or no revenue stream has diminished. Markets have on the whole been generous to universities in the current era in providing an expanding volume of resources, especially resources for those things valued in the marketplace.

CHAPTER THREE

Undergraduates

THE EDUCATION of undergraduate students has been and remains the signature task of U.S. universities. Never mind if more dollars are spent for research or health centers, or if larger numbers of graduate and professional students attend; in the minds of the American public the principal purpose of universities is to transform young people into "college graduates." During the current era, that view has deepened despite stagnation in undergraduate enrollments and expansion of other university activities. This prominence in itself has powerfully affected the development of these institutions. However, the effects have differed for private and public universities.

Among private universities, market forces assumed paramount importance. The high absolute tuition price charged by these institutions accords each student considerable economic value. And the competition for status has made an institution's selectivity its foremost badge of prestige. Considerations of finance and prestige have in fact converged in the *selectivity sweepstakes*—the annual contest to enroll the nation's best and brightest freshmen. For these institutions, this contest is the most consequential factor affecting prestige and prosperity.

Among public universities, quite a different dynamic was at work. The well-worn refrain that undergraduates were a low priority at these giant, impersonal institutions was sung by a new chorus of critics in the 1990s, with a few new lyrics. As already seen, such charges compounded financial woes stemming from a weak economy. State universities consequently spent much of the decade in a defensive posture, addressing weaknesses and bolstering the prominence of undergraduate programs.

In consequence, there are two different stories for the undergraduate colleges at private and public universities, with only some common ground. On one hand, private universities were touched lightly by allegations that research universities were dysfunctional for undergraduates. In fact, their growing wealth allowed them to offer a multitude of embellishments to strong basic programs. The leading public universities, on the other hand, found themselves engaged willy-nilly in the selectivity sweepstakes. They too had to compete if they were to claim a share of the undergraduate talent pool. For both sectors in the 1990s, undergraduate education became the foremost priority.

The Selectivity Sweepstakes

The way American colleges and universities select their students changed markedly during the twentieth century. Until the 1920s, most universities accepted all "qualified" students. For the top private universities, which were by far the largest at the century's dawning, admissions were buffered in two ways. First, each had its own entrance examination, which narrowed the number of applicants, and they also raised standards periodically.[1] Second, the system produced a high degree of self-selection, based on a combination of social, religious, and educational factors. Admissions numbers were by no means set; students overflowed the campuses into the surrounding cities or towns, and schools had to ration coveted campus residences, often on the basis of seniority (rather than immaturity, as now).

Only after World War I were universities induced to practice a more systematic form of selection: the explicit rejection of otherwise qualified students. The number of applications ballooned in those years and university values changed. Institutions now wished to limit their growth as well as to mold the collegiate experience of their students. The two went hand in hand. If all students were to live in campus residences and participate in collegiate life, their numbers would have to be capped. As the leading private universities developed procedures to achieve this end, basic features of the American system of college selectivity emerged.

An initial consequence of selective admissions was to exclude applicants with the weakest academic records. This step in itself raised the academic profile of an entering class and was heartily supported by faculty. All the eastern schools agreed, though, that academics should not be the sole determinant of admission to college. They believed their role was to form character as well as intellect, and they were acutely concerned with fostering a social environment to promote extracurricular learning and socialization. Hence nonacademic criteria loomed large in admissions decisions.

In practice, private school graduates and alumni sons were favored, and outsiders, particularly Jewish applicants who sought admission in large numbers to nearby elite colleges, were to varying degrees screened out. The active recruitment of additional applicants of the preferred type was the last piece added to the interwar admissions system. At first alumni were enlisted to vet prospective applicants for the right social traits. In the 1930s, Harvard struck a new note when its president, James B. Conant, established competitive national scholarships explicitly for high-ability students.[2]

In the 1950s, after the enrollment bulge of GIs had worked through the colleges, the elite schools found themselves with a permanent surplus of applicants. Again it was Harvard that first grasped the implications. Its dean of admissions is credited with instituting a largely meritocratic system of admissions, including financial aid to meet the full need of less wealthy students, while preserving Harvard's links with its traditional clientele. When he retired at the end of the decade, he wrote a guide for his successor that encapsulated the emerging system of selective admissions. He considered, but ultimately warned against, the lure of a purely meritocratic approach that would recruit Harvard students from among the "top one percent." Too many such students were merely grade grubbers or, worse, "bearded types." Better that Harvard recognize the importance of personality and character, of potential contributions to extracurricular life, including athletics, and the institution's debt to the graduates and donors who had so munificently supported it. By this date, Harvard and similar schools had developed a policy on admissions that sought to enhance academic qualifications while at the same time valuing nonacademic dimensions of the collegiate experience.[3]

In practice, the American system of selective admissions meant choosing students from among a group of applicants with reasonably high academic qualifications. A given school thus depended on having a surfeit of applicants from which to choose. The evolution of selective admissions from the pattern of the late 1950s to the selectivity sweepstakes of the 1990s lies in this relationship: how universities enlarged their markets for undergraduate students; and how greater consumer awareness affected the behavior of potential students.

Beginning in the 1950s the market structure of the selective sector was formed through a process of integration.[4] The country's most prestigious universities and colleges broadened their recruitment, attracting strong applicants from beyond traditional regions and clienteles, and thereby displacing weaker ones. The academic profile of entering classes was ineluctably raised. This process was assisted by the development of the testing industry.

The College Board's Scholastic Aptitude Test (SAT), which had formerly been used only by member institutions, became generally available shortly after the war. The National Merit examinations were introduced in 1956, and the American College Test (ACT) followed in 1960.[5] Although each was somewhat different, they all aided institutions chiefly by identifying achievement levels among a broad population.

When the baby-boom generation reached college age in the early 1960s it provided a huge boost to selective institutions, with little effort on their part. Cohorts of aspiring students ballooned, many emerging from strengthened high school programs. With many more good students in the market, a college that modestly expanded its geographical sweep easily netted additional top applicants. Many selective schools increased their enrollments and raised tuition at the same time. Two other developments of the 1960s expanded the market further.

The civil rights movement transformed attitudes toward minority students. Previously rare on selective campuses, the recruitment of black students in particular became common.[6] This effort expanded the horizons of selective colleges beyond the usual private and suburban high schools and also required additional financial aid.

After mid-decade, this second development was assisted by the increasing availability of need-based aid from the federal government. By the early 1970s, selective colleges and universities had created separate offices for financial aid, and a consensus reigned that aid should be based on financial need rather than scholarship. The recruitment of minority students and the enhanced role of financial aid undoubtedly had an influence beyond those students directly affected. The perception of exclusivity that had inhibited many from applying to these selective schools diminished appreciably. In addition, institutions that had been all male began admitting women as undergraduates. Although women were not initially admitted in equal numbers, this step doubled the applicant pool.

The 1970s, nevertheless, were trying times in the selective sector. The academic attainment of high school graduates plummeted, and elitism carried a malodorous air. The pervasive cynicism toward established (or Establishment) institutions did not spare private universities, most of which had been scarred by student rebellion. But difficult conditions in this case spurred greater effort. Admissions offices throughout the private sector added staff and implemented new forms of marketing, including direct mail, which expanded the reach of selective institutions even further.

The use of more extensive and more focused marketing continued into the 1980s and has never ceased. And these efforts were considerably bolstered by the adoption of the high-tuition/high-aid policy described earlier. Selective schools further broadened their market by bringing financial aid to the middle class. By the 1990s, the traditional self-selection that had long given these schools their unique character was vastly diluted. A truly national market now existed for selective colleges and universities. This market reflected changes in the behavior of consumers as well as institutions, and that too had been a historical process.

Until the end of the 1950s, colleges and universities kept their admissions data largely to themselves. However, when the College Board began to release SAT results for institutions, high average scores became a point of pride. During the boom of the 1960s, *Barron's* and *Peterson's* published the first commercial college guides (the College Board *Handbook* appeared in 1959). Besides providing potential students with basic knowledge about many institutions, they also classified colleges and universities by broad levels of selectivity. In this manner, what had been tacit knowledge of relative reputations became broadly accessible to consumers. The proliferation of college guides during the 1970s reflected the progressive nationalization, or integration, of this market. However, a new dimension was added in 1983 when *U.S. News and World Report* published numerical rankings of colleges and universities.

Superficially, the *U.S. News* rankings merely put precise numbers (which changed every year!) on familiar reputations. More significantly, they powerfully reinforced selectivity as the most consequential feature of the private colleges and universities in this market. Originally an artifact of the market, the rankings soon began to define the market. The first two *U.S. News* rankings (1983, 1985) were based on surveys of college presidents. They thus reflected reputation, which almost by definition tracked closely with selectivity. At that point the magazine felt the need to legitimize the booming popularity of the rankings with a more objective methodology.

After 1987 the now annual rankings incorporated data on admissions, graduation rates, and resources, using a methodology described as opaque.[7] The results, however, principally reflected selectivity, particularly average SAT scores.[8] The admissions data—selectivity per se—carried a weight of only 15 percent in 2000, but the reputation survey (25 percent) and financial variables that correlate with selectivity constituted the majority of the weightings.[9] Thus the *U.S. News* rankings validated the existing pecking order; but by making that pecking order numerically explicit, they made small changes appear highly consequential.

Most academics deplore the *U.S. News* rankings because they crudely objectify a complex, multidimensional phenomenon. But for just that reason, people struggling with that complexity—certainly applicants—might find them useful. Even some academics use them to provide a handy list of the different types of colleges and universities. In fact, the rankings implicitly define the nebulous selective sector of the national market, which is the real subject here. They now contain a list of fifty "national universities" and fifty "national liberal arts colleges." For the institutions that compete for top students, a high ranking is a crucial qualification. Similarly, for borderline institutions to make these lists, and thus to become officially sanctioned in the national marketplace, can be vitally important. How important? One study found surprisingly direct effects. Slippage in the rankings for the top colleges and universities had an immediate impact on the next year's class. All measures of selectivity suffered, including average SAT scores. More ominous, matriculating students required more financial aid, which decreased net tuition.[10]

These findings reflect a market in which large numbers of consumers of necessity must narrow their choices for serious consideration to a manageable set of schools. Favorable rankings clearly attract attention and applications, as do basketball championships or other forms of welcome publicity. However, the fateful consequences of rankings highlight more fundamental features of this market: the tight connections between selectivity, costs, and perceptions of institutional quality.

The evolution of an integrated national market for selective higher education, characterized by a high degree of consumer awareness, has had the effect of stretching the natural hierarchy of American higher education. As economists have grappled with the unique features of this industry, a model has emerged that accounts well for the operation of the selective sector. Expressed most fully in the papers of Caroline M. Hoxby, this model emphasizes that market integration gave rise to qualitative competition, which became self-reinforcing for successful institutions.[11] For private colleges and universities in the selective sector, the feedback loop might be represented as shown in Figure 13.

Portrayed here as a positive feedback loop, these same processes can work in the opposite direction, as the example of sinking *U.S. News* rank-

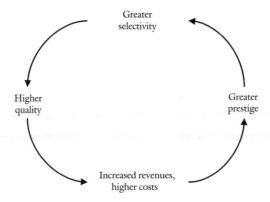

FIG. 13. Feedback Loop for Qualitative Competition among Selective Institutions

ings illustrates. In fact, it will be shown that these relationships are contingent on numerous circumstances. But the basic process underpins the Hoxby model and encapsulates the dynamics of the selective sector in the current era.[12]

The prime mover, according to Hoxby, was the change in market structure brought about by national integration. By itself, the enlarging markets of selective institutions should produce greater student segregation by ability level. As top students have more choices, they will tend to choose the greatest possible quality. This natural tendency produces a distinctive feedback in higher education, however, because students are not only the consumers of higher education; they are also a critical input. Because of their role in educating one another (peer effects), high-ability students have an incentive to cluster together.[13] Better students contribute to higher quality, which in turn attracts better students.

Universities recognize the value of such students and do all they can to attract them. Since the most effective inducement over the long run is high quality, they chiefly resort to qualitative competition. The alternative—price competition—in its cruder forms tends to restrict inputs and diminish quality. "Quality" is unspecified here since it could reflect the effects of bright peers, abundant inputs, or other attributes. In fact, the cumulative effects of such desirable inputs are the defining condition. In particular, increased spending for the enhancement of quality serves not only its immediate purpose; by also attracting more top students it has a multiplier effect that boosts quality further still.

Prestige ought to reflect quality, but far more is involved. As a function of consumer awareness, prestige is affected by the entire manner in which selective institutions market themselves and how they are treated in the media. Specifically, rankings advance their own definition of prestige, as has been seen. This aspect of the selectivity sweepstakes has been called a "positional market."[14] Institutions compete doggedly for relative position within their own particular strata, or for bragging rights about the company they keep (top twenty, top fifty, etc.). The positional markers in this competition (akin to positional goods in a true positional market) are measures of selectivity, costs, or rank. Prestige is vitally important nevertheless because it relates so closely to institutional wealth.[15]

Qualitative competition has apparently spurred universities to augment educational spending, principally through the policy of high tuition and high aid. The most prestigious institutions have been best able to make this approach work to their advantage. So in this respect, prestige helps to optimize tuition revenues. Prestige also appears to be a critical factor in attracting voluntary support. Prestige for these purposes comes in many flavors. However, academic distinction, particularly in undergraduate education, seems to be the most potent factor in unlocking the generosity of alumni. The discussion of costs in Chapter 2 underlined the spectacular financial success of the most prestigious private universities. High costs among private universities correlate closely with high selectivity, as measured by SAT scores. High levels of spending, in other words, appear to promote higher student quality. This pressure for ever more spending among the country's wealthiest universities is now conventionally called the "arms race."[16]

As described in Chapter 2, the wealthiest schools were able to raise tuition most aggressively in the 1980s, using both federal loans and institutional aid. But they also steadily expanded the subsidy they awarded to all students, the qualitative fillip that ensured their market dominance. This process was furthered by gifts from grateful alumni who clearly appreciate their alma mater's prosperity and celebrity. It is easy to see how the *U.S. News* rankings have contributed to this dynamic. They have been the mirror on the wall, reflecting the selectivity sweepstakes and faithfully declaring the most selective private colleges and universities to be the fairest of them all. However, this mirror contains a number of distortions.

Selectivity in Practice

The model just presented captures the basic dynamics of the selective sector, but social reality is more complicated. To better understand the clientele of American universities, and to appreciate the parameters of the selectivity model, the elements of that model should be critically examined: the consumer market for selective colleges and universities; the definition of selectivity forwarded by *U.S. News* and the private sector; the nature and significance of peer effects in the educational process; and the role of high costs and subsidies. For each of these elements there are significant differences between public and private universities.

At the end of the 1990s, out of nearly 4 million 18-year-olds in the United States, nearly 3 million graduated from high school and almost 2 million proceeded directly to college. Of this latter group, about 1.2 million enrolled as full-time students in a four-year college or university.[17] How many of these students attend selective institutions? No precise answer is possible for such an inherently imprecise category, but a rough estimate is possible based on the prevailing notion of selectivity. Using the *U.S. News* lists of fifty top "national universities" and "national liberal arts colleges" as a reasonable proxy, the selective sector would consist of roughly 145,000 freshman places: 64,000 in sixteen public universities, 56,000 in thirty-four private universities, and 25,000 in fifty colleges.[18] These enrollments represent fewer than one in five freshmen at private institutions and one in ten at publics. Membership in this group should mean, for example, that at least half of the freshman class scored in the top 10–15 percent of test-takers. This approach reflects an institutional definition of the selective sector. It does not indicate who attends these institutions.

The constituency that sustains the selective private colleges and universities of the country could be characterized loosely as belonging to one or more of the following groups: (1) Very high achieving students who, on that basis, are encouraged by their schools and others to pursue an ambitious educational strategy. Many academically talented minority students would be in this group. The reality today is that any student demonstrating very high achievement in high school is likely to be recognized and recruited by selective schools. (2) Children of upper-middle-class parents, typically well educated themselves, who care passionately about education. Such parents usually strive to give their children every possible educational advantage, and commonly try to guide them into the best possible colleges and universities. (3) Students whose parents can afford the cost of a selective private school or are affluent enough to reside in a top suburban school district. Economically and educationally advantaged, such students gravitate toward the private sector.[19]

This population can be characterized by the manner in which they shop for a college. These students undoubtedly consult *U.S. News* rankings and other college guides. They visit five or more campuses in the winnowing process. They take SAT examinations early and often, and may take special classes to boost their scores. Anyone employing a college counselor for assistance with the admissions process is a core member. And, by definition, they will apply to numerous institutions, principally private ones, or possibly seek early admission to the school of their dreams.[20] These students validate the prevailing notion of selectivity, and their parents provide the resources that largely sustain the selective private sector.

The students who shop so assiduously for a selective school are predominantly wealthy or well off. At the same time, they disproportionately obtain the high-quality schooling that helps to qualify them for admission. The system of high-tuition/high-aid at private universities is inherently dependent on these high parental incomes.

Only three principal sources of income support the basic educational enterprise: parental resources, external student aid (including loans), and endowment income. Except for a handful of universities with enormous endowments, parental resources must constitute the majority of that income. In 2000, perhaps 7 percent of families likely to have college-age children could afford or finance a private university education of $30,000–35,000 per year, including living expenses. Most of these families, in fact, sent their children to private institutions, but especially those with high costs. Of the ten nontechnical universities with the highest costs and selectivity, 45 percent of students received no aid—that is, they apparently could afford the approximately $150,000 that it cost a 2001 freshman to graduate in 2005. In addition, many of those who did receive aid were from families with above-average incomes who still paid a substantial portion of the bill.[21]

The evolution of the selectivity sweepstakes in the current era has undoubtedly enlarged the clientele shopping for admission to the selective sector. It has also, through the expansion of financial aid, allowed larger proportions of low-income students to enter the selective sector. But wealthy students have nevertheless been the chief beneficiaries. In 1981 about 25 percent of students from wealthy households (with income of $200,000 or more in 1998$) matriculated in the selective sector, and in 1998 this figure was 35 percent.[22] These positions were no doubt earned through academic attainments for the most part. If anything, the top institutions have probably become more meritocratic in their admissions. However, as the competition intensified, students with the cumulative advantages of wealth and excellent schooling appear to have captured a growing share of these places. For that reason, the apparent winners in the selectivity sweep-stakes are an amalgam of the brightest and wealthiest of American youth.

The very definition of selectivity favors the smaller institutions of the private sector. Commercial guides rate institutions on the difficulty of gaining admission as well as the quality of matriculants. Exclusiveness is judged by the percentage of applicants accepted for admission (the lower the better) and the proportion of admits who matriculate (the higher the better). Student quality is measured by average test scores and the proportion of students ranked in the top 10 percent of their graduating class. Size makes a huge difference for calculating these percentages and averages. State universities typically have entering classes of 3,000 to 6,000 students, but private universities enroll about one-quarter of those numbers. The top state universities might point to 1,000 of their students who could rival the freshman class of most leading private universities, but an additional 4,000 freshmen weigh down their averages. If selectivity were measured instead by the absolute number of top students, the private-public comparison would change considerably.

To depict the entire market for high-ability students, one would measure the number of such students at different schools rather than their percentages. Scores on standardized tests provide the only feasible criteria for making such a comparison, even though test scores represent only one dimension of academic ability and admissions criteria.[23] Students who score 700 or better on the verbal or mathematical portions of the SAT examination (recentered), or 30–36 on the ACT examination, constitute roughly the top 5 percent of test-takers. Tables 1 and 2 estimate the theoretical number of students who obtained such scores in the fall 1997 freshman classes of each institution. The number is theoretical because a math 700 and a verbal 700 would each count for half of a student, even when not the same person. Such students are highly sought after and have considerable choice of college. Their matriculation decisions consequently reflect the attractiveness of an institution irrespective of size.

Tables 1 and 2 show how many of these high-scoring students began studies at the thirty-five private and public universities enrolling the largest numbers.[24] Surprisingly, the total is virtually identical for both sets. Each set of universities claims about 30 percent of the national total. In comparison, the thirty-five most selective private colleges, with freshmen classes averaging fewer than 550, enroll only 8 percent of these students.[25] The four universities with the largest numbers are all public. Twelve private universities and seven publics enrolled freshman classes of 700 or more of these stu-

TABLE I

*Private Universities with the Largest Number of Students
Scoring 700 or Higher on the SAT*

Institution	Freshman class	Percentage of 700+ students	No. of 700+ students	Change in median SAT, 1995–2000
Cornell University	2,971	39	1,159	20
Harvard University	1,643	70	1,150	20
Stanford University	1,647	69	1,136	30
Brigham Young University	4,864	23	1,118	n.a.
University of Pennsylvania	2,349	45	1,057	70
Duke University	1,623	53	860	20
Yale University	1,307	65.5	856	15
New York University	3,257	25	814	55
Brown University	1,411	54.7	772	10
Princeton University	1,175	64.5	758	45
Massachusetts Institute of Technology (MIT)	1,064	71	755	25
Northwestern University	1,891	37.5	709	60
Boston University	3,867	18	696	35
Dartmouth College	1,093	56.5	618	10
University of Notre Dame	1,904	29.5	562	n.a.
Carnegie Mellon University	1,270	44	559	35
Georgetown University	1,393	38	529	n.a.
Columbia University	967	50	484	35
Rice University	704	64	451	(15)
University of Southern California	2758	16	441	115
University of Chicago	999	42.5	425	15
Tufts University	1,273	30.5	388	30
Johns Hopkins University	945	39	369	25
Washington University	1,231	28.5	351	90
Boston College	2,168	16	347	n.a.
Vanderbilt University	1,506	22.5	339	15
Tulane University of Louisiana	1,491	22	328	(40)
Emory University	1,170	22	257	65
Wake Forest University	975	26	254	15
University of Rochester	908	26	236	75
Saint Louis University	1,118	21	235	n.a.
Case Western Reserve University	739	31.5	233	0
George Washington University	1,716	13.5	232	0
Brandeis University	794	28	222	20
Syracuse University	2,587	8	207	25
Total (35 institutions)	58,778	34	19,907	31 (ave.)

n.a. = not available.

dents. Significantly, both groups of universities improved the apparent quality (average SAT scores) of matriculants from 1995 to 2000, although private universities outgained public ones.

This view of the market confirms that high-ability students tend to cluster together. However, unlike the prediction of the selectivity model, they

TABLE 2

Public Universities with the Largest Number of Students
Scoring 700 or Higher on the SAT

Institution	Freshman class	Percentage of 700+ students	No. of 700+ students	Change in median SAT, 1995–2000
University of California, Berkeley	3,573	37	1,322	15
University of Illinois, Urbana-Champaign	5,805	21.3	1,238	(5)
University of Michigan, Ann Arbor	5,458	22	1,201	15
University of Wisconsin, Madison	5,882	20	1,176	25
University of Texas, Austin	6,945	13	903	(10)
University of Virginia, main campus	2,903	29.5	856	5
University of California, Los Angeles	3,810	21	800	65
Texas A&M University	6,196	9.5	589	5
University of North Carolina, Chapel Hill	3,413	16	546	10
Ohio State University, main campus	5,852	9.3	544	n.a.
Georgia Institute of Technology	1,848	29	536	15
University of Missouri, Columbia	3,514	15	527	20
University of Maryland, College Park	3,960	13	515	80
Pennsylvania State University, main campus	4,244	11.5	488	(10)
University of Florida	3,699	13	481	(45)
University of Minnesota, Twin Cities	3,895	12.3	480	113
Michigan State University	6,815	7	477	· 20
University of California, San Diego	3,268	14	458	0
Iowa State University	3,954	11	435	85
Rutgers University, New Brunswick	3,900	11	429	n.a.
Purdue University	6,544	6	393	35
University of Kansas, main campus	3,555	11	391	70
University of Iowa	3,662	10	366	5
University of Oklahoma, Norman campus	2,800	13	364	30
University of Colorado, Boulder	4,349	8.3	362	0
University of Washington	4,505	8	360	15
University of Georgia	4,189	8.5	356	10
College of William & Mary	1,334	26	347	n.a.
University of California, Davis	3,540	9.5	336	20
North Carolina State University, Raleigh	3,620	9	326	15
Virginia Polytechnic Institute	4,460	7.25	323	n.a.
Louisiana State University, Baton Rouge	4,443	7	311	(40)
Arizona State University	5,191	5	260	10
University of Nebraska, Lincoln	3,200	8	256	115
University of Tennessee	3,890	6.5	253	15
Total (35 institutions)	148,216	13	19,273	23 (ave.)

n.a. = not available.

do not necessarily do so in the most selective institutions, as conventionally defined. This raises a fundamental question: if high selectivity is caused and reinforced by the peer effects of bright students and the high levels of educational spending, why do these state universities attract so many top students?

Theory and conventional wisdom posit that bright students concentrated together educate each other in ways not possible in more mixed settings. Institutions certainly act as if this were the case, but evidence of such positive effects has been elusive.[26] As a result, the exploration of this factor must be somewhat speculative.

There are two questions to consider. First, how do peers actually affect student learning (as opposed, for example, to providing connections useful for future employment)? And second, what arrangements are likely to encourage these effects? For learning, three pertinent processes would seem to be at work. A preponderance of high-ability students would have important *curricular* effects by allowing a more challenging pedagogy—more demanding classes, greater content, and a higher level of sophistication.[27] Bright peers might also have a *direct personal* effect by improving the academic performance of friends or roommates. A more generalized *cultural* effect should also result from a richer casual environment in which students would acquire from one another general knowledge and cultural sophistication. Isolating and measuring personal effects has proved difficult, and the results of such attempts seem at best suggestive.[28] The curriculum is more accessible, but deeply ambiguous.

Selective colleges and universities believe strongly in a rigorous curriculum when judging the fitness of applicants. However, when offering their respective curricula the prevailing approach has been to be inviting, not demanding. The reason for this has been the general unacceptability of negative sanctions. Selective schools face powerful incentives not to fail students, or even give poor grades. *U.S. News*, for one, bases 25 percent of its ranking score on retention measures. Institutions where the faculty persist in rigorous grading regard this, confidentially, as a problem. To actually fail students could have a devastating effect on both income and recruitment. As a result, grade inflation is notorious in the selective sector, and lackadaisical students can slide by with little application of effort.[29]

Selective schools, by and large, offer a rich and sophisticated curriculum designed to elicit the best efforts of students. The admissions process, in fact, is intended to identify high achievers and specifically to eschew applicants who might be slackers. Coursework at selective schools typically avoids textbooks and the presentation of codified knowledge in favor of long reading lists of academic studies. Students are seldom graded on objective tests, but given essay exams or papers where they can express their own ideas. Most students appear to learn a good deal in such an environment, motivated by some combination of intellectual stimulation and ambition to pursue postgraduate studies. The environment itself clearly depends on a preponderance of bright, motivated students who respond positively to a bountiful, nonpunitive learning environment.

Many of the same conditions might be found at a large state university, but there peer effects assume a somewhat different role. These institutions often create superior learning environments for a portion of their students by grouping together high-ability students. Honors programs have long been used for this purpose, and they have received renewed emphasis in recent years. However, positive peer effects in public universities result chiefly from a high degree of internal differentiation. Their large populations of high-ability students in fact can be expected to produce a critical mass in several areas.

The most important form of internal concentration of talented students occurs through choice of major.[30] Students studying pre-med, physics, or electrical engineering, for example, could expect to experience substantial positive peer effects, especially after the freshman year.[31] In fact, selective public universities appear to be particularly attractive in natural science and engineering; all have greater numbers of students who scored 700 on the math SAT than on the verbal. This disparity is possibly the chief distinction between public and private institutions in the recruitment of top students.

The second great disparity between public and private universities is institutional costs, which were seen to be 50 percent higher on average at private schools. If higher costs produce higher quality, the most able students should prefer private universities. Here too, averages and ratios may be deceiving. As an educational resource, for example, the size of a library is more important than the number of books per student. The leading public universities in fact possess tremendous learning resources, but far more students must share those resources than do in private universities.[32] However, this is less the case for those top students in rigorous programs. They are likely to have ample access to excellent faculty, facilities, and laboratories.[33] It has also been seen that high-cost private universities spend heavily for amenities and student aid. These expenditures contribute indirectly or, in the case of amenities, obliquely to overall quality.

Finally, public universities offer a relatively high level of quality at a far lower price. State universities possess a protected local market for state residents in spite of the integration of national markets. Total expenses for university study at state universities are less than half those at a private university. For middle-class students who qualify for little financial aid, education at a state's flagship university, or even an out-of-state public university, can provide high quality at a compelling saving.

High-ability students often have to overcome psychological barriers in order to rationalize studying at a state university.[34] Such students commit to an ambitious educational strategy early, and acutely feel the pressure to attend a high-prestige school. Hence reputation is an important consideration, which dovetails with a desire to attend a university with other high achievers. Because many expect to attend graduate or professional school, they care whether a university will be a pathway to prestigious postgraduate studies.

The stronger state universities have no difficulty demonstrating such qualifications, but prospective students deliberately seek reassurance on this point. A state university's advantage in price complements a long-term educational strategy. Students looking forward to extended postgraduate studies typically hope to avoid borrowing for their undergraduate degree. Merit aid plays a key role, often more symbolic than pecuniary. After being deluged with scholarship offers, high-ability students generally feel entitled to some aid. A modest offer of merit aid often cements their decision to attend a state university.[35]

The entire process of choosing a university is conditioned by the selectivity sweepstakes. High-ability students use the rankings extensively to sort and evaluate schools, and the bias against public universities directly affects them. They feel pressure from other students and from teachers to attend a medallion institution, and may defend their choice of a lower-ranked and less-expensive state university by emphasizing its special programs for the academically talented and the distinction of certain academic fields. Thus state universities need to evince some marks of prestige as a counterargument to the sweepstakes rankings, not least to reassure applicants from the selective market who may be already predisposed to attend.

The distinctive attribute of public universities for large numbers of top students is their reputation for research and scholarship, which is reflected in high ratings of research and graduate programs. The leading private research universities also have stellar ratings, but they rely more heavily on selectivity and ample educational resources. For the top public research universities, research reputation appears to be a magnet for attracting superior undergraduates.[36] The seven public universities with the highest numbers of high-ability students (Table 2) are among the most highly rated public universities for research and doctoral education. The others are generally strong research universities with eminence in certain areas. Their reputations, especially within their own states, may attract talented students. However, if one were to look very far beyond the academically strong public universities, ratings and reputation slump and the number of top students falls below the 5 percent average.[37] Put simply, public research universities with highly rated departments attract high-ability students, and those without them generally do not.

Public universities operate in the same markets as private universities, but their different structure subjects them to different dynamics. Specifically, the feedback loops that were observed for private institutions (see Figure 13) have different consequences in the public sector. The comparable share of academically talented students attending state universities contradicts the Hoxby model.[38] A portion of these students is recruited from the national market of mobile, selective-sector prospects, but another portion is derived from the protected market for state residents. However, state universities seem to be accorded less credit for the quality of their students. Peer effects certainly exist, as noted above, but they may be concentrated among only part of the student body. National rankings understate the prestige of these universities, although it is certainly recognized more generally. Given their large student bodies, places at these universities lack the scarcity value of the top private universities.

The largest problem for state universities is that feedback from quality does not produce high revenue rewards, as it does in the private sector. Prestige can translate into tuition revenues by attracting additional nonresidents, but most institutions face explicit or implicit caps on these students. And most state universities cannot raise tuition with impunity. Prestige greatly facilitates the attraction of voluntary monetary support, which plays an important role in bolstering quality and competitiveness. Gifts to state universities nevertheless tend to be for restricted purposes, and insofar as they provide general support, its impact is diluted among the large student body.

Still, politics is the chief impediment to rewarding quality. Most state legislatures resist higher university costs and were particularly vigilant in this regard during the 1990s. State legislatures simply do not reward quality or prestige with greater appropriations. Thus quality improvements are not reinforced through the principal source of revenue. The result is a curious pattern: differences in levels of expenditure in the current era have grown in the private sector, but have diminished among public universities.

This fundamental difference between the two sectors illuminates the predicament of state universities. They by no means forsook efforts to build quality, but in the absence of encouragement from the public fisc they sought resources from private sources. Hence the pervasive trend toward privatization was impelled in part by donor and patron appreciation of excellence. Similarly, public universities received positive reinforcement from their research role. Research largely generated its own resources, brought indirect cost reimbursements as well as valuable relationships with patrons, and enhanced prestige. Not surprisingly, public universities have favored increasing their volume of research, as well as their academic standing. Thus the marketplace appeared to provide little incentive for these universities to focus on the treatment of their most numerous clientele. Instead, nonmarket sources put pressure on public universities to give higher priority to undergraduate education.

Undergraduate Education at Research Universities: Critique and Reality

The notion that large state universities neglect undergraduate students has a venerable history. There was certainly some truth to it when the baby-boom generation reached college age in the 1960s. Few of these institutions were very selective, and the prevailing philosophy was "sink or swim." Certain introductory courses like chemistry and calculus were expected to cull the herd, diverting the less able to less demanding majors, or directly out the door.

Whether a student was deficient in preparation, application, or intelligence, little solicitude was offered: flunking out was an expected outcome for a portion of each class. Complaints about such practices were raised during the great student rebellion that stretched from the mid-1960s through the early 1970s, and student power played an indirect role in making it more difficult to fail. Classes, or at least some of them, were made easier, and new options, such as dropping a course late in the term or taking a course pass-fail, reduced the threat of bad grades or expulsion.

Probably more important in changing the culture of undergraduate education, faculty appeared to become less demanding of students or more generous in their grading. In addition, some universities became more selective and their students more capable. Retention became a stated institutional goal, and academic assistance more readily available, if students chose to seek it. In the mid-1980s, however, the familiar plaint arose once again: universities were neglecting their students. This time, it seems, they were not teaching students enough.

The critique of undergraduate education in the current era began in the 1980s and rose in a kind of crescendo to the early 1990s. Since then it has scarcely disappeared, but rather has been institutionalized in university practices and in advocacy organizations. The "critique," as defined for this discussion, consists of three propositions thought to be causally related: (1) undergraduate teaching was poor at large (chiefly public) universities; (2) a principal cause was faculty neglect; and (3) faculty neglected teaching in favor of research, either because of their own inclinations or in response to pressure from their institutions (the "reward structure"). Once these three propositions were joined, many permutations to the argument arose, and even more recommendations for improvement. Still, the verbiage spawned by these notions is more notable for redundancy and rhetoric than for originality. The critique itself represented no single movement, but loosely related efforts that shared some part of the central theme. It emerged in two venues that otherwise had little in common.

One line of attack on universities was a reprise of the culture wars of the 1960s, a riposte from Conservative America against the Left Academy. William Bennett was among the first and loudest critics. He originally sought to rehabilitate a traditional view of the humanities, and next, when he became secretary of education in 1985, consciously used his bully pulpit to chastise universities for their alleged curricular and moral shortcomings. Bennett's posturing no doubt tilled the soil for Allan Bloom's 1987 bestseller, *The Closing of the American Mind*. All the elements of the critique were presented by Bloom and Bennett, even though their main thrusts were aimed elsewhere. Namely, the professoriate was culpable, not just for left-leaning politics, but also for its preoccupation with specialization and research. And undergraduate students were the victims, not only being taught erroneous doctrines, but being taught badly as well (critics missed the irony of this juxtaposition).

A flood of books attacking universities ensued, most but not all by conservatives.[39] Political correctness was the principal target of Roger Kimball in *Tenured Radicals* (1990) and of Dinesh D'Souza in *Illiberal Education* (1991), but criticism of professors and research was part of the indictment. For Charles Sykes in *Profscam* (1988), Page Smith in *Killing the Spirit* (1990), and Martin Anderson in *Impostors in the Temple* (1992) it was the chief target. Whatever spleen the authors wished to vent, they invariably invoked concern for students, who were supposedly denied the education they deserved (or paid dearly for) by the failings of their teachers.[40]

A different form of the critique evolved from what might be called the superstructure of organizations that surround, support, represent, and advise the higher education industry. In the mid-1980s, following the call to reform K–12 education in *A Nation at Risk* (1983), three official reports sought to illuminate deficiencies in collegiate education.[41] The most comprehensive, *Involvement in Learning* (1984), specifically addressed the need for improvement in undergraduate education. It sounded a number of themes that would be reworked for the rest of the century. However, it did not single out universities (conditions seemed to be worse in other types of institutions); it did not blame faculty; and it did not hold research to be at fault.[42] The report did encourage the use of some form of assessment as a means of documenting educational attainments. Apparently encouraged by this spotlight, the American Association of Higher Education (AAHE), which represents administrators and publishes *Change*, embraced this cause and especially assessment.

Assessment was endorsed in a general way in *Involvement in Learning* as a way to give students more information about their performance so that they might improve on it (also called formative assessment). However, it soon was transmogrified into a movement inherently critical of traditional academic practice.[43] The assessment movement seemed to ignore that students are graded, or "assessed," on everything they do in class, and that a summary of these assessments is embodied in a college transcript. Instead, it sought alternative measures of learning that could be used as indicators of "outcomes." In particular, it sought to measure the acquisition of intellectual skills, such as critical thinking and analytical reasoning, rather than the mastery of mere knowledge.

Specifying and documenting such nebulous skills presented real challenges, whether for an individual, a class, a program, or a student's entire collegiate career.[44] Over time, the assessment movement assumed the qualities of a messianic movement, a boundless quest (there was always more to assess) for an unattainable ideal (perfect performance measures). In its advocates' hands, assessment shifted toward the notion that colleges and universities should be held accountable for the learning of their students through specific and comparable measures of attainment.

Were American collegians really learning less in the mid-1980s than they had in the 1970s—or the 1960s, or the 1950s? The question is largely unanswerable. Demographically, far more students from more diverse backgrounds were attending and graduating from college. Most of them were no longer taught many of the things expected of a college graduate a generation earlier (such as foreign languages).[45] Furthermore—and never acknowledged in these exchanges—American higher education had never in its history upheld rigorous standards across the majority of institutions. No matter. A plausible case was gradually built that college graduates were deficient in basic linguistic and arithmetical skills.[46] The superstructure organizations, which exist to provide services for the improvement of American higher education, were energized by this opportunity. As the assessment movement gained momentum, it shared more in common with the charges from conservatives.

A key element of the critique was supplied by Ernest L. Boyer, president of the Carnegie Foundation for the Advancement of Teaching. In his 1987 book, *College*, Boyer staked out two distinctive positions on the perennial question of the balance between teaching and research. At research universities, he conceded that "scholarship, research and publication should continue to be the central criteria by which faculty performance is measured," but he nevertheless argued that those institutions "must aggressively support good teaching." Other institutions, however, should not slavishly imitate the research standard, but should be open to recognizing other forms of intellectual accomplishment by their faculty. Boyer elaborated this second point in his next book, *Scholarship Reconsidered: Priorities of the Professoriate* (1991), which became the most influential text for the movement to enhance university teaching.[47] AAHE used it as a pretext to organize the first of its Forums on Faculty Roles and Rewards. The premise of these rallies was that the "problem" obstructing the improvement of teaching was a reward structure that privileged achievements in research but accorded scant credit for anything else, especially teaching. With this turn, the reformers embraced the same apocalyptic vision as the conservative critics: that the hegemony of research supposedly dictated the behavior of professors and prevented them from devoting the time and effort required for effective teaching.[48]

In the early 1990s, political correctness on campus became a nationally debated issue. The scandal over indirect cost reimbursements at Stanford, and similar allegations at other institutions, further tarnished the reputation of research universities, along with widely publicized allegations of fraud in research. In this atmosphere, a stream of tendentious publications belaboring the critique was credulously received. The chairman of the National Endowment for the Humanities likened research universities to "tyrannical machines"![49]

All told, perceptions of universities in the press and the polity turned more negative than they had been in two decades, since the aftermath of the student rebellion. These negative perceptions had a decided impact on higher education. The discomfiture of universities was a great stimulus for the assessment movement. Accreditation agencies enlarged their mission by requiring some form of assessment for reaccreditation. Universities themselves could hardly ignore this tumult. Most major universities conducted internal studies of undergraduate education and pondered actions that might respond to these charges. Perhaps most portentous for public universities, politicians developed a critical curiosity not just about how universities were educating undergraduates, but also about how preoccupied they were with research. In short, the critique of undergraduate education became a tangible force shaping university existence in the 1990s. Considering its importance, the particulars of the critique warrant a closer examination.

Fundamental to the critique was the contention that teaching and research conflict with each other rather than being reinforcing or joint-product activities. (The case for complementarity was presented in Chapter 1.) During the early 1990s, some effort was made to justify assertions of an inherent conflict. The Carnegie Foundation, for example, conducted an extensive faculty survey that implicitly juxtaposed teaching and research as competing alternatives. Efforts to characterize faculty proclivities for research in social scientific language found ready support and quick publication by AAHE in *Change*.[50] Such writings portrayed faculty in Pavlovian terms, conditioned to salivate in response to only one stimulus.

The role of a university faculty member in fact involves a multitude of tasks centered on expert knowledge. As professionals, faculty members are assumed best able to judge how to balance the requirements of those duties. The fulfillment of the faculty role depends heavily not just on professional judgment, but also on a willingness to perform seemingly optional tasks, from serving on committees to attending student social gatherings. The notion of altering this delicate balance through manipulation of the reward system, as critics persistently advocated, offends the sense of professional responsibility on which universities depend. Done crudely, it would certainly produce unintended and unwelcome consequences.

Perhaps more pernicious was the corollary that faculty at institutions where the primary mission is teaching should not engage in research. This argument found support among leading research universities, which feared for their share of federal research dollars. However, such a policy would be tantamount to deprofessionalization for the faculty of those institutions, at a time when their role in academic research was growing. Because of a lethargic market for new faculty, many capable young academics found positions at predominantly teaching institutions. At the same time, the Internet made it far more feasible for such scholars to remain active on the research frontiers. Preventing or discouraging scientists at these institutions from engaging in research would not only truncate their professional development; it would also diminish the potential of academic science.[51]

If the prescriptions that emerged from the critique were wrongheaded, it was chiefly because the diagnosis was wrong. But that does not mean that the patient—undergraduate education—was not ailing. Given the concern and consternation surrounding this issue, one might well ask, what underlying changes had occurred in higher education during the 1980s? Was there any tangible evidence that teaching and learning had declined?

For university faculty the 1980s was a period of accelerating activity. After a decade of relative stagnation, academic research doubled in the decade. According to the pendulum theory, a common-sense view of the current developments, the emphasis on research had swung to an extreme by the early 1990s. Self-reported data on faculty activity indicated marginal increases in the amount of time spent on research, but those figures most likely reflect considerable increases within certain research universities.[52] Circumstantial evidence may be more informative here. Growth in research and graduate education far outstripped the increase in regular faculty during the 1980s. In a trend less easily measured, specialized academic associations, conferences, and journals all proliferated during this era, expanding professional activity and claiming faculty time.

For junior faculty, in particular, the abundance of well-trained Ph.D.s and the paucity of new hires raised the bar for scholarly attainments. All indications are that more pressure was placed on the faculty role. This was not necessarily a bad thing. If engagement and high expectations are good for students, they ought to have positive effects on faculty too. However, there is no indication that these trends diminished in the 1990s, and thus no reason for the pendulum to swing back in the direction of undergraduate teaching.

An alternative interpretation, also based on popular impressions, holds that academic achievement eroded, chiefly because of the changing nature of students. "Generation X," according to anecdotal accounts, was steeped in the fantasy culture of the popular media and dismissive of rational inquiry and institutional authority. Its outlook shaped by consumerism, Gen-Xers felt entitled not only to their places in higher education, but to good grades as well. As students, Gen-Xers expected to be entertained in their classes. They were resistant to intellectual application and punitive toward teachers who challenged their narcissistic viewpoint.[53]

Behind these impressions lies a real concern about a fundamental shift in attitudes. David Riesman noted the ascendancy of student consumerism at the outset of the 1980s, and Clark Kerr called "this shift from academic merit to student consumerism . . . one of the . . . greatest reversals of direction in all the history of American higher education."[54] During the 1980s, the anti-intellectualism and postmodernism of Generation X may very well have exaggerated the impact of consumerism. A somewhat different argument holds permissive professors and institutions responsible for gutting the curriculum.[55] But this might also be interpreted as the institutional response to consumerism. Consider the testimony of a junior professor at an elite university: faced with shrinking enrollments and latent student hostility, he eventually dumbed-down his courses to an intellectual level more comfortable for students.[56]

Given the ascendancy of student consumerism and the aversion to negative sanctions, it is probably psychologically impossible for today's professors to maintain over the long run academic standards significantly at variance with student expectations. And such a stance would be suicidal if professors were held accountable for performance indicators such as enrollments, grades, and student evaluations.

However the research pendulum and Generation X may have affected student learning in the 1980s, the assessment movement itself represented a new fact of life. The assessment movement required the "problem" of undergraduate learning to justify its existence. The idea that some form of summary measurement ought to be imposed on the entire collegiate experience, rather than on individual students and courses, was raised in the first wave of higher education reports. This was an entirely new expectation in the American system of higher education. Its appeal to administrators and then to state governments was natural. As explained by one advocate, because "curriculum and program evaluation is by definition external to the educational process . . . responsibility for the assessment process lies as much with academic administrators as with faculty—a notion that, quite naturally, makes many faculty uncomfortable." In addition, assessment "automatically means asking whether obtained results are in some sense 'worth' invested resources," a notion that soon invoked the pecuniary interests of state legislatures.[57]

Well might faculty feel uncomfortable. No consensus existed over the content of a college education (at that juncture there was ferocious disagreement) or how it might be measured. The notion of performing cost-benefit analysis on so uncertain a basis, although intellectually chimerical, had much political appeal.

Assessment provided a means for both administrators and state politicians to gain leverage over the faculty—the supposed obstacle to reform. During the remainder of the 1980s state interest in assessment waxed and then temporarily waned. But the superstructure organizations aligned with administrators continued to champion this cause. The relevant historical point, however, is that a "problem" that served the purposes of so many interested parties was not about to disappear. Regardless of whether students were learning more or less or the same amount—and regardless of whether professors spent too much time doing research—student learning was a problem for the superstructure of American higher education. And that made it a problem for universities too.

Universities could scarcely avoid responding to this issue. During the years of this controversy they voluntarily undertook internal studies to gauge the state of undergraduate education, and in the spirit of outcomes assessment they measured what was measurable (such as retention rates and time to graduation). University presidents became outspoken champions of improving undergraduate learning. They, after all, represented the university to external constituencies and were virtually compelled to champion the students.

All these activities led universities to a position in which they had to respond to three imperatives. First, it became clear that there was room for improvement in undergraduate education. Universities are not easily changed, and the far-reaching measures associated with the critique, like changing the reward structure, would have been particularly difficult to implement. But universities were compelled to seek improvements in student learning. Second, they were also under pressure to respond to the terms of the critique. In response to these nonmarket pressures, they needed to make reforms that addressed the criticisms and sometimes the requirements imposed on them. Finally, student consumerism was still ascendant, and these consumers did not necessarily desire the same things as those who spoke in their name. Thus the imperatives of the market for undergraduate students were often at variance with the nonmarket strictures. Together these forces shaped the student-centered university of the 1990s.

Student-Centered Research Universities

SYRACUSE UNIVERSITY

In February 1992, just months after being installed as chancellor of Syracuse University, Kenneth Shaw announced a program of reforms intended to form a "student-centered research university." Coming at the critique's peak of notoriety, Shaw did not refrain from exploiting the negative clichés then being applied to research universities. Was the "student-centered research university" a clever marketing ploy? Camouflage for a program of draconian cutbacks? Or an effort to impose a unifying identity on an unwieldy conglomeration of schools and colleges? One could argue that it was all of those things. Syracuse University (SU) at the start of the 1990s was floundering in the competition for market position and was in dire need of a new strategy.

Syracuse University entered the current era in a relatively strong condition. During the 1970s it had overcome chronic budget deficits, bitter student protests, and the severing of research ties with the Pentagon.[58] By 1980, trends in higher education again favored what SU had to offer. Student preferences for vocational studies dovetailed with the university's large collection of professional schools and more than 200 majors. A more materialist student generation could appreciate SU's celebrity in big-time college sports, as well as its ingrained collegiate culture. But contemporary college guides noted an anomaly: the SU campus had the look and feel of a large state university.[59]

In 1981, SU had more than 20,000 students, 13,000 of them undergraduates. Its freshman class for that year exceeded 3,500, the largest in the country for a private research university. The units of the university varied widely in academic reputation and selectivity. Most prestigious was the Maxwell Graduate School of Public Affairs, which also taught social science to undergraduates. The Newhouse School of Public Communications was growing in prestige and popularity. Other highly regarded schools included architecture, engineering, and management. But with a freshman class as large as many state universities, SU could not afford to be selective in admissions. Its median SAT scores barely exceeded 1,000, and students generally believed that anyone who could pay the tuition would be admitted. And SU's facilities were not what one might expect at a private university. Classes were reputedly large and crowded, and the university's first student center was only opened in the mid-1980s. Typically, the first project in upgrading the campus was the 50,000-seat football and basketball arena, the Carrier Dome (1980).

Through mid-decade the SU formula proved effective. The university raised tuition almost as rapidly as other private universities and resorted to comparatively little tuition discounting. The budgets were so far in the black that a large "reserve plant fund" was accumulated. A capital campaign far exceeded its goal. SU also managed to strengthen research during the 1980s, more by exploiting public technology-transfer programs than by investing its own resources. It managed to win a state center for software engineering and eventually leveraged this into the Science and Technology Center, built with special state and federal appropriations. These funds stimulated research in areas linked with computer science, but overall SU became more marginal in the academic research system.[60] SU had largely deemphasized research during the troubles of the 1970s, and in the 1980s it continued to depend primarily on its student base. In clear recognition of this, the chancellor created a vice president for student affairs in 1986, and efforts to improve undergraduate education followed, much as contemporary national reports urged. SU had a decided student orientation even before the crisis struck.[61]

At the end of the 1980s the pressure of the selectivity sweepstakes began to be felt, and this was a contest in which SU was ill-suited to compete. The large size of its entering classes guaranteed that selectivity would be low, but even that level of selectivity required an applicant pool of more than 15,000. As conditions changed, this pool shrank (it was just over 10,000 in 1998). And it did not include many of the high-ability students that selective colleges craved. SU, in fact, offered few of the quality markers that distinguished more selective institutions, yet it sported a similar premium tuition. Despite the financial progress of the 1980s, relative per-student spending at SU slipped from twenty-sixth among the thirty-three private universities in this study to last in 1990. Participation in research, never the university's strong point, eroded as well. Its most distinguished academic departments, philosophy and geography, were not large draws. Numerous students still sought admission to the public communications and management programs, but few top students chose professional undergraduate majors. The university found itself with few means to bolster its prestige or to justify its premium price. When the recession of 1990 struck, these weaknesses directly affected admissions, as well as university finances.

At the same time that SU declared itself a student-centered research university it embarked on a radical downsizing designed at once to adapt to a much-reduced income and to conform more closely to the ascendant selectivity standards. In adapting to market imperatives, it faced a cruel predicament. Given its fiscal crisis, it could not become more selective by investing in quality, the normal path indicated by the Hoxby model. Instead it attempted to wring greater educational quality out of its faculty through a student-centered emphasis—and to achieve this by spending less, not more. Its chief investment, in keeping with the dictates of selectivity, was in the quality of students themselves.

In what came to be known as "the restructuring," SU chose to reduce enrollment rather than "becoming less selective in admissions and thereby damaging the institution's academic reputation."[62] From a high of over 12,500 undergraduates in 1989, enrollment fell to 10,000 in 1995, before stabilizing slightly above that level. Graduate enrollment dropped by about 1,000 over a slightly longer period. FTE enrollment declined more than 15 percent. At the same time, SU resolved to make a large investment in student recruitment, largely through merit scholarships. It began awarding "chancellor's scholarships" worth $6,000 to the top 15 percent of entering freshmen, and later added "dean's scholarships" of $4,000 for the next 25 percent. Awards based on financial need were augmented as well. As a result, the tuition discount rate increased from 10.5 percent in 1989 to 31 percent in 1996.

Fewer students and less net tuition meant a significantly smaller budget for the university. The payroll accordingly had to be reduced as well. Two hundred of the 950 faculty accepted inducements to resign. Ultimately, the number of faculty positions was reduced by 170, and staff by twice that amount. Those who remained endured a salary freeze followed by minimal raises. Overall, the fiscal restructuring eliminated $66 million in expenditures, or 33 percent of the base budget (1990–98).

In order to implement budget cuts of this magnitude, the student-centered university had to become a revenue-centered university. To some extent these objectives coincided. Student retention became a fiscal imperative. Numerous measures were taken to make students more contented and more engaged, at least in part so that they would remain at SU. Responsibility for covering costs devolved to the operating units in Syracuse's version of each tub on its own bottom.

The university's fifteen schools and colleges were required to generate two dollars of net revenue for each dollar of expenditure. The imposition of such a rigid formula naturally produced a reshuffling of resources. As usual with this approach, Arts and Sciences was a big loser: its credit hours fell by 16 percent and its budget was slashed by 14 percent. Engineering and Computer Science suffered a worse fate. Departments in the hard sciences have a higher cost basis and cannot operate effectively on the same credit-hour metric as softer subjects. These two units merged into a single college and absorbed a 41 percent budget reduction. The combined faculty fell from 120 to 70. This last development no doubt impaired SU's ability to attract research support and to retain active researchers on the faculty. But research was not accorded any special status in the student-centered university. Graduate degree programs that did not support themselves were eliminated, mostly in Arts and Sciences. New master's programs and continuing education were evaluated according to the net revenues they produced. The entire budgetary structure was thus designed to buttress units generating more tuition revenues and to starve those producing less.[63] In this way, the operating units were given ample incentive to be sensitive to student needs.

If the inspiration for a student-centered research university came from President Shaw, the task of articulating the details seemed to fall to Provost Gershon Vincow, who had been working toward this end since 1985. His 1994 report to the faculty presented the full model and discussed its implications. He was clear about the stakes for SU: by taking the lead in improving undergraduate education the university hoped "to improve our reputation for quality . . . [and] as a consequence, our 'market position' for attracting students."[64]

The overarching idea was to place learning at the center of the university's mission: "to promote learning through teaching, research, scholarship, creative accomplishment, and service," but to privilege student learning in all these activities. The challenge was to go beyond rhetoric to effective innovations. The student-centered research university was in this respect a process rather than a model. The steps that were taken or attempted at SU might be evaluated under three rubrics: room for improvement, student consumerism, and latent conflicts.

SU, like other universities, found much room for improvement when it examined educational practice. Some of the most obvious steps, which also aided retention, were aimed at the adjustment to college by first-year students. SU required all its schools to develop small "freshman forums" to promote close interaction with faculty as well as integration into the university. The size of most classes for first-year students was reduced for much the same rationale. Mid-semester progress reports were established as early warning systems for new students, and ample academic support was made available for those facing problems. Special measures were taken to improve academic advising, particularly for lower-division students. Graduate teaching assistants were given special training for their duties as well. The guidelines for establishing student-centered courses could hardly be faulted: achieve greater contact between students and faculty; employ active learning techniques, including collaborative projects; and provide prompt and meaningful feedback. The only question about innovations like these might be, what took so long? In fact, similar steps were being implemented at research universities across the country.

Vincow admonished his faculty to design courses from the learner's perspective rather than adhering to the assumed dictates of subject matter. As he interpreted this injunction, it placed student consumerism in a positive light: professors should understand the angst of today's students, and should appreciate their perspective on the courses they were taking. But the ultimate goal was to make students study longer and more diligently. Students who find course material interesting and relevant, he argued, will be more likely to attend class and do assignments. At no point did he insinuate any relaxation of standards. Rather, he urged his faculty to communicate high expectations to their students and to evaluate their learning with cumulative final examinations. The intention was for faculty to use the student-centered approach to inspire greater effort and thus induce greater student learning.

These directives might be taken for good practice in college teaching at any institution. But SU was insistent about its identity as a research university. It sought to emphasize the advantages of undergraduate study in just such an institution, and it encouraged professors to introduce examples of their research to their undergraduate classrooms. But by stressing student-centeredness so earnestly, the SU administration exposed a latent conflict that arose more from its own conflicting goals than from the activities of the faculty.

Vincow, himself a former scientist, offered the dubious injunction, "our principal rationale for research will be how it promotes learning by our students," and secondarily "[how] it advances our discipline."[65] He acknowledged that faculty working fifty or sixty hours per week could not put additional effort into teaching and advising without displacing their current activities. He suggested eliminating "low-priority activities" like committee meetings; and he offered the facile suggestion that faculty focus their reduced research time on quality rather than quantity. However, the bottom line was that "more time will have to be spent on improving teaching and advising and less on research." The administration had convinced itself, using internal and national surveys, that faculty would prefer to spend more time on teaching.[66] Thus it had reason to believe that the faculty would support such a shift in institutional culture.

The corollary was a shift in faculty rewards. Here the administration strongly asserted that teaching would henceforth be weighed equally with research. However, that seemingly simple equation raised an inherent difficulty: the teaching of most faculty was assessed as "good," but the evaluations of research ranged from "none" to "excellent."[67] In other words, most faculty members taught reasonably well, but the ability to contribute to one's field was a rarer trait. At the same time, suggesting that teaching and research are asymmetrical activities, and that they might play different roles in the evaluation of faculty (as they traditionally had), would have been heresy to the student-centered movement. Yet tensions produced by this reality persisted in the SU project.

By 1998 the restructuring of Syracuse University was complete. The student body was smaller but smarter, the budget was in balance, and the university could assess its own claim to be *the* leading student-centered research university.[68] There could be little doubt that SU had achieved a significant change in the climate and culture of the institution. Although the nature of the schools and colleges within the university varied widely, the predominant sense was that more emphasis had been accorded to teaching and that it was being evaluated more effectively. The reaccreditation team, which visited that spring, found the student-centered vision to be widely shared by faculty, students, and staff. College guides that had formerly noted student hedonism and the likeness to a state university, now remarked on the close interaction between faculty and students.[69] SU was rotated into the *U.S. News* top fifty, largely on credit earned for small classes.

There could be little doubt that SU was recruiting better students, treating them more attentively, and providing more educational programs and resources. In this respect, there was substance to the image that the university wished to project, but deeper questions remained. Was it possible to achieve greater quality while reducing costs? And, could a student-centered orientation be upheld without diminishing the institution's status as a research university?

Adoption of the student-centered model was facilitated at SU by its strong professional emphasis. Perhaps better described as a professional university than a research university, its most distinctive programs were all professional in nature. Only engineering and computer science competed in fields where research grants were essential, and their research requirements were sustained through several long-established centers. These circumstances help explain SU's increasingly marginal status in R&D funding (see Appendix B).

In the highly regarded Maxwell School of Public Affairs the faculty naturally needed to maintain a strong record of publication, if not grantsmanship, to uphold its reputation. This was less true for another of SU's well-respected colleges, Visual and Performing Arts. Other noted programs, including broadcast journalism, library science, and architecture, probably fell somewhere in between. Hence, "research" had a somewhat different connotation in many SU units, and student involvement and active learning were more readily implemented in the colleges just named. These factors no doubt predisposed much of the SU faculty to the student-centered approach. The evidence from the university's self-study nevertheless indicated that some danger points were near.

By 1998 the deans of the professional schools generally felt that more emphasis should be redirected toward research. Faculty too found that devotion to student learning did not eliminate the need to do research. Individual recognition in the disciplinary and professional communities still depended on contributions to knowledge. And even at home, certainly in the stronger colleges, there was no lowering of the standards for research in faculty evaluation. In fact, the reaccreditation team specifically recommended that SU stop paying lip service to the multiple forms of scholarship touted in *Scholarship Reconsidered* because such an emphasis could mislead or confuse junior faculty about expectations. Junior faculty, perhaps more than others, felt intense pressure. And, given the lid on salaries, there were no meaningful monetary rewards available for faculty with strong teaching records. The SU faculty as a whole genuinely seemed to embrace the student-centered mission, but over time they became an increasingly self-selected body, as individuals who disliked the perceived deemphasis on research migrated elsewhere.

The huge investment in students made by SU was paralleled by disinvestment in faculty and staff. Professorial salaries had roughly the same purchasing power in 1998 that they had in 1980.[70] During the restructuring the administration was committed to eliminating positions rather than cutting salaries, and to resisting the temptation to hire part-time replacements. In other words, a conscious effort was made to maintain faculty quality, but salary increases still barely matched inflation.

The reaccreditation team noted that faculty salaries were not competitive with those of other research universities, and specifically warned of problems retaining the best young faculty and recruiting scientists and engineers. In sum, the restructuring was accomplished to a large extent by drawing on the university's accumulated qualitative capital, but it now faced the need for replenishment. The reaccreditation team's advice was succinct: "the University's commitment to and investment in research needs to be as carefully and widely addressed during the next few years as the undergraduate experience has been."[71]

This message was taken to heart. In 2000 the university's new provost promised a "quest for excellence."[72] The university's restructuring by this time had finally succeeded in brightening the financial picture, chiefly by stabilizing enrollments and tuition revenues, but with some extra help from the bull market and a timely capital campaign. The faculty was growing instead of shrinking; and investments could again be contemplated. Above all, SU sought "advances in academic quality and stature" that would bring "increases in externally funded research."

The first area addressed was the recruitment and retention of faculty. An effort was launched to rectify the previous stagnation and compression in salaries. But SU also wanted to recruit "world-class faculty" who were "internationally renowned in research." For this purpose it earmarked funds to create an additional twenty to thirty endowed professorships over the next ten years. The hiring strategy would be to build a critical mass, preferably in interdisciplinary fields, to achieve recognized excellence. Doctoral education would receive similar attention, although there the strategy was to pare down in order to form fewer programs of greater distinction. In doctoral education too there was recognition that these objectives implied the necessity to be competitive in the national arena.

Reading between the lines of the new mission statement, one can perceive that the situation created by the restructuring of the 1990s was not viable for the long term. By vowing "to catapult itself into the next echelon of universities," SU acknowledged that it had not achieved a level of quality commensurate with its aspirations. Instead of claiming to be the leading university in a class by itself, it identified a dozen private universities with which to compare and measure itself.

As Syracuse University seeks to make this next transformation, the identity it has fashioned as a student-centered university will undoubtedly be a source of strength—an aid to student recruitment and a magnet for goodwill from alumni and benefactors. But if a moral can be drawn from the Syracuse experience, it would be that an institution that wishes to be a research university cannot long succeed by placing the learning of students in conflict with the intellectual accomplishments of their teachers.

UNIVERSITY OF ARIZONA

The University of Arizona (UA) rose to the stature of a major research university in the 1970s.[73] Being one of the few expanding universities during a decade of stagnation was an advantage, but much credit belongs to President John P. Schaefer (1971–81) and his deans, who pursued an activist strategy of building on academic strength. By 1980, UA could boast several programs of national distinction and a place among the top twenty-five R&D performers. Then the university's momentum dissipated. Recurrent state fiscal crises caused appropriations to stagnate, and low tuition set by the Arizona Board of Regents provided little additional revenue. Moreover, the board began to intervene directly in university matters, which encouraged bureaucratic ossification. The university nevertheless maintained its relative position in academic research. It performed nearly 1.2 percent of the nation's academic research during the 1980s and, indeed, throughout the 1990s. With fewer discretionary resources to work with, though, maintaining its stature in research became more of a struggle. In the 1990s, UA assumed the additional burden of becoming a student-centered research university.

This commitment resulted from a clear sequence of events, touched off by concerns identified by the visiting team for the university's 1990 reaccreditation review. The visitors found glaring deficiencies in the introductory and general education courses offered in the College of Arts and Sciences. These service courses had become "areas of low prestige and attendant neglect . . . a remedial operation," run with leftover resources. The unavailability of these courses for students who needed them was callously regarded as "routine" in the university. Overall, undergraduate education was alleged to be underfunded relative to the other major components of the university.[74] In other words, UA seemed to resemble the caricature of research universities then being pilloried in the critique literature. However, these problems were only partly of the university's own making.

Budgetary difficulties had been severe in the early 1980s, but finances improved considerably later in the decade. Among public research universities in this study, UA's relative financial position slipped just three places, from twenty-seventh to thirtieth. But the late 1980s also brought an increase in the number of undergraduates, some with weak preparation, but few additional faculty members.[75] The university was cramped for space for all purposes. According to the (perhaps generous) guidelines of the Arizona Board of Regents, UA had only half the space recommended for educational use. At the same time, as a newly arrived research university, units competed for resources to bolster graduate programs, sustain the momentum of rising departments, and improve lagging ones.

President Henry Koffler (1981–91) supported the university's drive for distinction as a prominent research university, but much of the evolution of these years could be characterized as drift. Certainly the interests of students were not a priority when the position of vice president for undergraduate education was abolished for budgetary reasons.

The reaccreditation report undoubtedly helped to reverse this outlook, and may have influenced the choice of the next president, Manuel Pacheco (1991–97). Pacheco had mainly been associated with undergraduate institutions in his career, and although his was a low-key presidency, he made undergraduate education his signature issue. He immediately appointed a task force on undergraduate education, which in May 1992 returned a set of feasible recommendations. For the curriculum, it urged a reformulation of general education, the establishment of freshman colloquia, and a capstone experience in the form of a senior thesis or project. Student advising, another blighted area, was designated for improvement, and the university infrastructure was to be expanded with the educational mission uppermost in mind. Perhaps the only controversial recommendation, although trumpeted throughout the country at the time, was that excellence in teaching, "rigorously assessed and fully documented," should be accorded greater value in promotion, tenure, and recognition.[76] At this juncture, the issue was raised to an even higher level at UA.

The Arizona Board of Regents, spearheaded by Phoenix lawyer Andrew Hurwitz, assumed the mantle of champion for undergraduates at the University of Arizona. Coincidentally or not, the new governor of the state had advocated abolishing the board and letting the universities manage their own affairs. Energized by its new cause, the board made a series of acrimonious charges of student neglect, which were countered by the university with combinations of rebuttal and reform.

A kind of cease-fire was negotiated in 1994: to meet board requirements the university proposed "measurable goals for linking faculty teaching effort to the improvement of the quality of undergraduate education." These so-called Hurwitz goals consisted of seven broad goals with thirty-five measures, and two specific outcomes with seven specific measures—in form a reflection of both the prevailing distrust of universities and the mania for performance measures. However, the goals did identify UA's problems.

A comparison of itself with peer institutions revealed that UA had low retention of freshmen and low graduation rates.[77] Students took too long to graduate (4.9 years) and earned more credits than they needed. Freshmen and sophomores had limited contact with regular faculty (barely one-half of lower-division courses were taught by full-time faculty) and experienced difficulty scheduling courses. The university also optimistically promised to improve outcome measures such as standardized test scores (which were not bad) and employer/alumni satisfaction (where no data existed), but chiefly it sought to improve the logistics of undergraduate education. A new advising system—an obvious need—was devised, giving all students advisers and clear plans of study. More regular faculty members were promised for teaching lower-division courses, and more courses were to be made available. As recommended, commitments were made to develop freshman colloquia and capstone experiences.[78] These steps were taken under some duress, with the threats of the board hanging over the university's head. But reforms of this nature were clearly called for, with or without forty-two performance measures. The changes made over the next several years signified an unequivocal commitment to undergraduate education.

In 1995, UA declared itself a student-centered research university. The year began with a conference on transforming the university, where Syracuse University's vice president for undergraduate studies expounded the new gospel. The University of Arizona's provost, Paul Sypherd, followed with a position paper signaling UA's conversion.

UA nevertheless remained wedded to its eminence as a nationally recognized research university. There would be no rhetoric disparaging research. Instead, the university committed itself to investing in undergraduate education. The vice presidency for undergraduate education was restored. New construction established the Freshman Center and eliminated the classroom deficit. If a symbol of the new commitment was needed, it took the form of an enormous excavation and construction project: the very center of the campus was clogged for years while the below-ground Integrated Learning Center was built.

The huge College of Arts and Sciences was broken into four separate colleges, and decentralization was greased further by extra funding for these colleges. General education, largely the responsibility of these colleges, was overhauled from 1995 to 1998. In addition, the honors program was greatly expanded, part of a larger effort to be competitive in the market for top students.

The one investment not made to advance student learning, just as at Syracuse, was in hiring additional regular faculty. Instead, the faculty received a carrot, in the form of awards for excellence in teaching, and a stick, in the form of post-tenure review that included annual assessments of their teaching. However, resources were found to create permanent programs for faculty development.

These steps, in addition to the previous reforms, substantially aided undergraduate education at UA. They addressed deficiencies and provided organizational and physical structures to better accommodate learning. Perhaps it was inevitable that such progress brought greater bureaucratization. An entire unit, for example, had to be created to monitor the Hurwitz goals. In 1997 a new president, Peter Likens, endorsed the notion of a student-centered research university. And the end of the decade brought another North Central Association reaccreditation review.

The University of Arizona was able to report this time that it had largely attained the goals set for undergraduate education. Both availability of courses and satisfaction with advising had improved. The proportion of lower-division courses taught by regular faculty had risen to the target of two-thirds. Classroom space goals had been met or exceeded. Students still did not know faculty very well, but the number participating in research experiences exceeded expectations. Teaching (again, much like at Syracuse) did not appear to be a problem: 80 percent of the faculty received strong evaluations, and the number deemed incompetent was infinitesimal (less than 1 percent). However, the outcomes that all these steps were meant to improve barely budged. Retention of freshmen actually dropped; six-year graduation rates moved in the right direction, but nowhere near the goal. The average time to degree remained the same, as did the excessive number of credits that graduates accumulated.[79] Could it be that student-centeredness was not the correct prescription for the malady afflicting UA?

Retention and graduation rates reflect the characteristics students bring to college more than what happens to them on campus. The notion that these measures can be altered by making classes easier to schedule or plans of study clearer is certainly naïve. However, to recognize this is an argument against the simplistic use of performance measures, not efforts to improve the student experience. In fact, it might be easier for universities to do the right thing if they were not required to prove they were doing so to a higher authority. In this case, a salient reality is that half of UA freshmen ranked below the top quarter of their graduating classes in Arizona's none-too-rigorous secondary schools.[80] The belief that 60 percent of these students needed a research experience before receiving an undergraduate degree (a Hurwitz goal) may have been ambitious, to say the least. More pertinent, the agreement with the board to abolish remedial classes in favor of freshman colloquia may have been shortsighted. Even the assumption that less-gifted students would be better taught by regular faculty may deserve closer scrutiny. Above all, someone might have pondered the unpleasant truth: if expectations for student learning are increased, fewer students are likely to meet them.

Merely raising this issue invokes the other side of the learning equation: the differential motivation, application, and capacity of students to learn. President Likens seemed to recognize this problem when he acknowledged the student-centered research university as well suited for the motivated, well-prepared student. But UA had, in his words, "a very heterogeneous student body, especially at the undergraduate level. It is a challenge for us to help all students reach full potential."[81] Two difficulties emerge from this view, one anchored in reality and one of the university's own making.

If a student-centered research university presupposes motivated, well-prepared students, then the logical course of action is to increase selectivity in admissions. This was the course that Syracuse took, reducing the size of entering classes and investing heavily in merit scholarships. UA has also sought to attract more students of the right sort through such steps as tripling the size of the honors college and enrolling more students from outside the state. However, UA still enrolls almost one of every ten Arizona high school graduates. Its selectivity barely improved over two decades.[82]

Although it has reached what it hopes will be the limits of growth, it bears an inescapable responsibility to educate a cross section of Arizona's young people. It obviously needs an approach that will work for students of middling abilities and ambitions. This task, after all, is one that the majority of universities face every day, but the rhetoric of student-centeredness at UA would seem to make it more difficult to face this task squarely, as the vagueness of president Likens's language belies.

Syracuse at least recognized this to be an issue and encouraged faculty to demand greater effort from students. The UA documents, in contrast, seem wholly uncritical. The phrase "a preeminent student-centered research university" is repeated like a mantra. The premise seems to be that enough welcoming, caring, involving, and mentoring by the faculty will lead to the achievement of the university's student learning goals. But just in case, the university promises to maintain "a program of extensive and focused assessment that *makes sure* all these aims are *really* pursued and accomplished" (emphasis added).[83] It is ironic that an institution that employs empty rhetoric aspires to teach critical thinking to its students. The real danger is that the overuse of slogans and feel-good language interferes with critical thinking about managing a research university.

While individuals at both SU and UA believed with pure motives in the idea of a student-centered research university, rather different rationales existed for adopting this strategy. Syracuse faced a marketing crisis. Invoking the new image gave a positive cast to a restructuring process intended to overcome serious weaknesses. Arizona, for its part, largely faced a political challenge from activist members of the Arizona Board of Regents, who climbed on the national bandwagon by posing as champions of the students against an uncaring research university. UA, in reaction, sought not only to neutralize this criticism by accepting a demeaning form of monitoring, but also to erect a more permanent defense by becoming officially student-centered.

The Syracuse strategy succeeded internally and externally. By all accounts, the faculty and staff largely embraced the student-centered identity. Several factors may have helped. The university was already heavily committed to teaching. More important, the university community undoubtedly appreciated the precariousness of the situation, particularly as it witnessed long-time colleagues being terminated. The leadership may have helped by presenting the restructuring as a process—a work in progress— and encouraging faculty participation. Externally, this strategy diverted attention to the new identity until the university's competitive position began to improve.

In contrast, a substantial portion of the Arizona community always saw the policy as a ploy to placate the board. The aloofness of the administration, the locus of student-centered initiatives in the bureaucracy, and the overindulgence in rhetoric all tended to distance this effort from the rank and file. But UA's research was never overtly threatened by the new emphasis. At Syracuse the chancellor was not above disparaging other research universities for student neglect in order to place his institution in a more favorable light. And the provost talked openly of cutting time for research. At Arizona, the university's national reputation was based primarily on research. The official line was that teaching and research were *not* zero-sum activities, but rather complemented each other; and the research university identity was as vital as being student-centered.

Arizona thus seems to have avoided the bind that Syracuse fell into by first deemphasizing research and then feeling compelled to rebuild. Instead, UA maintained its position in the academic research system with minor slippage (see Appendix B). Nearly 60 percent of research is performed at centers and institutes, distanced somewhat from undergraduate education. Perhaps for this reason research appears to have taken care of itself at a time when administrative energy was obviously focused elsewhere. Still, the relative inattention took a toll. At the end of the 1990s—a decade of feverish construction—research laboratories had the largest space deficits. Still, the chief threat to research at UA was simply the scarcity of resources.

If UA's conversion to a student-centered university was intended to generate political favor, the policy failed. Appropriation increments in the late 1990s remained as miserly as before and became worse after 2000. A lid placed on tuition by the board precluded fiscal relief by that means. Then the necessity of preserving the university's research prowess, and the economic benefits it brought to the state, became the chief argument against the board's budget cuts.

The university claimed it absorbed a revenue shortfall of $30 to $40 million per year in the 1990s and that its revenues were $60 to $90 million behind those of peer institutions.[84] Costs had risen inexorably. Besides the expense associated with becoming student-centered, instructional technology claimed an additional $500 per student, and debt service on the building boom close to $1,000 more.[85] These items alone represented more than 10 percent of available revenues.

The years of financial strangulation placed the greatest pressure on the competitiveness of faculty salaries. UA suffered a continual loss of valued faculty to institutions offering more generous compensation. To defend itself from these raids, it had to reallocate the salaries of departed faculty members to counter offers made to others. Hence the faculty continued to shrink, and the student-faculty ratio to rise, at a preeminent student-centered research university.[86]

Syracuse University and the University of Arizona were both prompted by unusually severe pressures to adopt a nomenclature that suggested a change in mission, a placing of greater emphasis on undergraduate education. But the concrete measures they took were hardly unique. Most research universities during the 1990s responded to market and political pressure by increasing institutional priorities for recruiting, instructing, and generally accommodating their undergraduate students.

The Competition for Students

Being student-centered has become a fact of life for virtually all research universities. It carries great weight in institutional policies, and not necessarily to the detriment of academics. Somewhat paradoxically, the academic distinction of the faculty remains a sine qua non for a university's reputation. It is the ticket of admission to the exclusive club of research universities, the class of institution to which most top students apply.

Institutional concerns for undergraduate students thus lie in somewhat awkward juxtaposition to the imperatives of the research mission, implicitly in competition but more deeply united in a common interest. But within this domain, the heightened concern for students has a logic of its own. For private universities especially, admissions are primary.

Most battles for prestige, financial well-being, and academic distinction are decided in the admissions process. Factors bearing on the competitive position of a university assume much of their importance in relation to admissions. High on this list are student amenities, which ensure that students will enjoy a high level of comfort. Also prominent are extracurricular activities: gratification for the body, the spirit, and also the mind. And then there are academics, the ostensible content of a college education. In this context, the academic curriculum also serves as a showcase for competitive purposes, tempting young people with promises of what college can offer.

Admissions, amenities, activities, and academics thus are the chief arenas in which the competition for the hearts, minds, and tuition of students takes place. For private universities this competition is a struggle for their very existence. As competition intensified, public universities responded too, partly by becoming more like their private competitors and partly by seeking their own competitive advantage.

THE PREVIOUS DISCUSSION has detailed the principal drivers in the selective admissions sweepstakes: the importance of peer effects in education and institutional prestige, and the reliance on qualitative competition to attract high-ability students. Despite the apparent stability of the elite hierarchy, there is no reason to believe that it represents a lasting equilibrium. Rather, market forces themselves have affected institutional behavior in ways that threaten the current system. Indeed, Michael McPherson and Morton Owen Schapiro have suggested that the end of the current era of selective admissions may be at hand.[87]

For some time, the weaker schools in the selective sector have resorted to merit aid in order to enroll more academically able students. Sometimes offered as outright scholarships, but more often mixed with need-based aid as "preferential packaging," such aid represented, from the institutional view, a more effective use of financial aid resources, or from an economic perspective, price competition.[88]

Over time, merit aid has ascended the selectivity hierarchy. Now most of the wealthiest and most selective universities offer merit aid in some form. Many award generous scholarships regardless of need to truly outstanding applicants, students who could attend any institution in the country.

Clearly, universities want the very best. At the same time, these institutions have retained their basic policy of meeting full financial need. But this practice has been shaded as well. The elite universities have departed from standard practices of estimating need in ways that favor wealthier families, and they have become "flexible" in matching offers from other universities. Princeton has twice rocked the cartel by unilaterally liberalizing its aid formulas, thereby lowering its real price. Although Princeton possessed the largest per-student endowment, its thinning ranks of peers were forced to match this raise or fold their hands, conceding Princeton a price advantage in the selectivity sweepstakes.[89]

At least four factors would seem to lie behind the drift toward price competition. First, a powerful social restraint was eliminated by a quixotic federal action. Until 1991, twenty-three of the most selective private colleges and universities in the East met regularly to share information about financial aid offers. Known as the Overlap Group, these institutions were all committed to meeting the full demonstrated need of students they admitted. They cooperated by coordinating information on a student's expected family contribution, using a shared methodology. This collusion ensured the integrity of the financial aid process and, in effect, made the price of attending any of these schools roughly the same. While participation was voluntary, association with the nation's most prestigious institutions was a powerful motivation not to break rank. In 1991 the Department of Justice challenged the Overlap Group under the Sherman Antitrust Act. This monumentally myopic action, occurring at the height of conservative attacks on the university, may well have owed more to the broad mistrust of elite universities than to the tenuous legal and economic pretexts. Nevertheless, the Overlap Group immediately dissolved. Only MIT fought the government claims in the courts, and it eventually prevailed. But this victory was too late to save the system. The most selective universities henceforth assumed that any attempt to cooperate on policies of tuition or student aid would face the threat of federal lawsuits. Instead of the most prestigious universities presenting a united front against price competition, laissez-faire reigned.[90]

Second, the competition for the most desirable students intensified. Evidence for this trend includes the fact that selective sector aspirants are applying to more institutions. The logic of merit aid is an even more powerful confirmation of greater competition. Merit aid is intended to induce enrollment by students who might otherwise attend more prestigious institutions. Thus competitive pressure is exerted upward, from less selective to more selective institutions, up to the very peak of the pyramid.[91] In addition, competition from public universities, which were already seen to attract large numbers of top students, has increased. They have bolstered their inherent price advantage by also becoming more aggressive recruiters. Princeton seems to have confirmed this competition when it justified expanding aid to middle-income students as a means of attracting more of these students away from public universities.

Third, the growing affluence of leading universities in the late 1990s increased the stakes in admissions competition. Previously, all of these institutions were conscious of the potentially ruinous effects of price competition. By 2000, however, the calculus had changed. Princeton may be the extreme example, but its first extension of student aid cost less than $1,000 per student, and the second only slightly more. Together, these commitments would claim just 4 percent of its endowment income. Elsewhere, the generous scholarships that many of these institutions now offer are fully endowed. Above all else, private universities have invested in their undergraduate students.

Fourth, one can infer from these investments that the value of high achievers is increasing for these universities. Peer effects on student learning have already been reviewed. With the increasing prominence of college rankings, the allegedly beneficial influence of high-achieving students has become one of the chief advertisements for institutional quality. This kind of publicity might be likened to a second multiplier effect. A third multiplier occurs when these students become high-achieving adults. Universities expect outstanding alumni to be continuing assets to the institution. In addition, a special value seems to be accorded to la crème de la crème. They garner national awards, which schools can proudly display in viewbooks and on their websites. These poster students convey the unmistakable message that this university's students are among the very best.

The cumulative effect of these four factors seems to be a shift in the admissions process toward greater weighting of academic prowess. As explained earlier, selective admissions in the United States have always given ample weight to nonacademic factors. Often, character and extracurricular activities were given equal consideration with academics for students who exceeded certain cutoff points. Harvard, for example, has long assigned applicants separate grades for academics, activities, athletics, and personality.[92]

With SAT scores becoming the most visible marker of student-body quality, universities may be weighting them more heavily in their calculus of virtue. From 1995 to 2000 both public and private research universities increased median SAT scores, but privates boosted their already high averages most (see Tables 1 and 2). Although other criteria are often given greater weight for demonstrating superior academic preparation (SAT sub-ject tests and Advanced Placement, for example), this evidence may still sig-nal a trend. Perhaps it is significant as well that intercollegiate athletics, for all its manifold faults, was castigated in 2001 for unduly distorting the ad-missions process at selective institutions.[93]

In light of all these developments, the trend seems clear. Intensified competition for high-achieving students, and greater appreciation for aca-demic distinction in particular, have exerted pressure on other facets of the university to assist (and certainly not to hinder) the admissions process.

Food and shelter, the necessities of life, have become chips in the bid-ding for the favor of potential students. Perhaps nothing epitomizes the consumerism of this era more than the "arms race" over what students con-sume. While most of the increasing costs are passed through to student consumers, a portion of those expenses must be paid by institutions them-selves as part of unmet financial need.[94] A more direct financial burden to universities is the capital cost of erecting ever-grander structures for the creature comforts of the young scholars. The escalation of expectations is particularly evident in student centers. As places for students to meet, eat, and procure essential services, centers perform a necessary function. How-ever, a new standard has emerged for combining all these things in an ar-chitecturally imposing structure, often resembling a suburban mall not only in design but also in the availability of upscale shopping and choice of co-mestibles. A similar story might be told about the escalating standards for recreational facilities.

Dormitories are perhaps the arena where universities feel greatest pres-sure to keep pace in the amenities race.[95] These universities require all first-year students to live on campus, and living accommodations clearly make an impression on potential students. Dorm rooms and food are even rated in the college guides. In addition, by fostering learning communities and sponsoring intellectual activities, the living units are intended to provide an additional dimension to learning. If any single factor epitomizes the trans-formation in student living style, it is dormitory food. A generation ago, jokes about the lamentable offerings of dormitory kitchens were ubiquitous and nearly identical across campuses. Today's students can eat as much or as little as they like and choose from a staggering variety of cuisines (includ-ing, of course, fast food). To achieve a competitive advantage here requires some imagination. Cornell, for example, periodically flies in chefs from fa-mous restaurants to prepare gourmet meals — a factor no doubt in winning a "best food" rating from Princeton Review.[96]

Still, capital costs are paramount. Universities with insufficient dormitory space, the case for most urban schools, have felt compelled to build new, attractive residences. The historic dormitories of many older campuses need to be entirely retrofitted (as at Yale) to meet current standards. It is unlikely that these projects will cover their true economic costs through future revenues. The last boom in dormitory construction occurred in the 1960s, propelled by very low-interest federal loans. In the current era, institutions would prefer to finance these projects through major gifts. However, there are opportunity costs to such an approach—the forgoing of other projects that such gifts might have funded.[97] The importance of these investments to universities is derived chiefly from the competition for student favor.

Student activities may not invoke nine-figure investments by universities, but they are another area in which the university mission and competitive pressures conspire to multiply offerings. Given the emphasis placed on activities in the admissions process, the selective schools enroll classes filled with joiners and leaders, students with wide interests and multiple talents as well as conspicuous achievements in single fields. Appropriately, one of the chief recruitment themes is the abundant opportunity proffered to these students to pursue and develop their interests. Typically, one moderate-sized university invites prospective students to contemplate joining some 200 special-interest organizations or, if need be, to form new ones.

At least some student organizations contribute to the rich intellectual life that these institutions wish to be their hallmark. Then too, students involved with extracurricular activities form closer bonds with their institutions, and as a group they become the most consistently generous graduates. Universities typically go to great lengths to socialize students to campus life as soon as possible. Most offer special programs for new admits immediately after admissions announcements. Dartmouth initiates its new students to college life with a class retreat in the White Mountains. In sum, student activities make multiple contributions to attracting the attention of prospective students, accommodating the diverse talents of students, fostering learning beyond the classroom, and forging closer bonds with the institution.

Intercollegiate athletics play a surprisingly prominent role at selective institutions. Only a handful of private universities (nine of thirty-three) court national celebrity through participation in Division IA athletics, and they struggle constantly to remain competitive with larger, less selective schools. Most selective institutions do not award athletic scholarships, and sports on these campuses are more for participants than for spectators. But these same schools often sponsor the largest number of teams. Universities in the Ivy League, for example, average 50 percent more varsity teams than schools of the Big Ten and the Atlantic Coast Conference. As a result, a sizable proportion of their students are varsity athletes. These programs impose high costs on institutions. The panoply of teams in minor sports results from tradition, reinforced by small but influential alumni constituencies that protest any proposed cutbacks. And, since the 1970s the requirements of Title IX have caused a parallel set of programs to be created for women. The essence of sports is competitiveness, and controversies over support for these activities invariably invoke the necessity of keeping up with peers.[98]

Students and their parents ultimately choose a university chiefly for the education it offers. Thus academics are of paramount importance as a competitive factor. But the academic side of the university can be intimidating as well. It encompasses a realm of adult activities, such as graduate education and research, that are vital to the institution and its reputation but are largely beyond the ken of prospective freshmen and most of their parents. Compared with the fun and games just discussed, the unknown rigors of the classroom can loom as a source of apprehension. Institutions thus face the challenge of portraying academics in an attractive light for prospective students. In part, this too becomes an exercise in marketing. But in other respects it affects the shape and content of the curriculum.

Most private universities specifically seek to dispel the negative images that have been attributed to research universities. Typically, they claim the advantages of a small college combined with the resources of a great university. The faculty, they aver, are dedicated to undergraduate teaching and take a personal interest in students. The earnest but friendly faces of recipients of teaching awards are displayed in brochures to buttress this point. Assurance is usually given that teaching assistants, the pariahs of undergraduate education, teach few or no classes.

Small classes are another bragging point, especially since they have been given the *U.S. News* seal of approval.[99] Freshman seminars have achieved wide popularity, perhaps in part as a selling point. Originally introduced at unselective institutions to develop coping and academic skills for at-risk students, first-year seminars are now employed under various rubrics by elite universities to provide relevance, mentoring, or intellectual stimulation in a freshman course load that (this is not stated) often lacks those elements.

The undeniable strength of the private universities is their rich array of academic programs. Still, the competition seems to require that they be augmented in conspicuous ways to enhance their appeal. One leading private university, for example, vows to "intensify undergraduate learning." To this end it offers up the full menu of fashionable promises: creating a learning community; student ownership of education, including customized coursework; close work with faculty; mastery of core competencies; development of intellectual and artistic passion; intensive small-group learning and exciting lecture courses; more specialized interdisciplinary programs; foreign study and outside internships; senior theses and junior tutorials.[100] Intense indeed.

Most universities boast special packages emphasizing focused attention on the environment, social issues, globalization, and even liberal arts. Such programs advertise cross-disciplinary approaches (a current summum bonum) and frequently include impressive excursions or foreign travel. Another popular theme is independence—allowing students to shape their own course of study, to design their own major, or to earn interdisciplinary degrees. In addition, universities have expanded programs that involve undergraduates directly in research. A minority taste, perhaps, research can nevertheless play a key role in attracting the most able students.

The private universities endeavor to offer something for every special interest and taste, while also providing everyone with personal attention and a solid liberal education. Such commitments make large claims on faculty time. The cost of offering small classes, in particular, would seem to be disproportionate to the pedagogical benefits. The wealthier institutions, with lower student-faculty ratios, are more able to deliver such classes, but all feature them prominently in the admissions showcase.

In sum, the private universities are locked into a fierce market competition in which they must meet two significant tests. First, they must convince chiefly parents that the value of the education they offer is worth an investment of some $150,000 for a bachelor's degree (before discounts). Passing this test requires promising a level of quality that justifies the price, despite the presence of other suppliers offering substantially the same product at lower prices. Remarkably, even considering the country's fin-de-siècle prosperity, a substantial number of buyers have existed for these selective schools at the full or a somewhat reduced price. But at those prices buyers have abundant choices. Hence the second market test. The private universities must capture the hearts and imaginations of sufficient numbers of talented 18-year-olds to maintain, at once, their prestige, selectivity, and cash flow. This challenge, as has been seen, requires the careful crafting and presentation of student amenities, activities, and some aspects of the curriculum. Unlike in previous generations, when students were expected to conform to the requirements of their colleges, today universities go far to conform to the tastes of their student consumers. The private universities, for the most part, are admirably equipped to compete in this market. The chief liability is that the cost of competition continues to mount.

In the arms race that private universities now find themselves in, any new innovation that contributes to the attractiveness of the undergraduate program will achieve only a temporary advantage. Other institutions will feel compelled to do much the same thing because the alternative—falling behind or becoming noncompetitive—is unacceptable. That is, failure to keep pace will lead to falling prestige in the national market, enrolling students with lower average abilities, and deteriorating financial strength—an unequivocal decline in the welfare of the institution. Hence the mounting commitments to student centers, dormitories, or recreational facilities. Student activities, other than athletics, are less expensive, but for that reason every school can boast of similar offerings.

Many curricular gimmicks can be implemented at little cost; but those that encumber significant faculty time are more burdensome. Still, the most destructive weapon in the arsenal is price competition. It may have been initiated by the weaker selective institutions, but actions like those taken by Princeton ultimately define the superpowers of this arms race.

Arms races by their nature tend toward two results. They generate a constant pressure for increased spending, and the wealthiest usually win.[101] Both results are visible among private universities in the twenty-first century. It has already been seen that the rich have gotten richer, not by a little but by a lot. Despite having to cope with increased competition at the margins, their domination has probably never been greater. But the case of Syracuse University suggests that, even for weaker players, it is far better to be in the race than not. Still, increasing competition in the selectivity sweepstakes aggravates the steepness of the private university hierarchy.

The other consequence of arms races is more difficult to evaluate. Some economists regard them as provoking spending that is inherently inefficient, and beyond a certain point that would undoubtedly be true.[102] But universities have multiple missions, usually constrained by finite resources. From this perspective the pressures of the selectivity sweepstakes do seem to have shaped the spending priorities of private universities. By becoming decidedly more student-centered in the 1990s, they have directed a lion's share of incremental investments to attracting and pleasing students. The same market forces have affected public universities as well, but with somewhat different results.

Public universities have also faced a double test in the current market for students. They first had to dispel the negative stereotypes about undergraduate education in large public universities that gained currency from the critique literature. Second, they needed to capitalize on their real academic strengths as research universities. Both these challenges have an internal and an external face—the necessity for real innovation in university practices and the need to publicize innovations to potential students and external supporters (or critics). In addition, these steps had to be taken with far fewer resources per student than were common in the private sector.

For the many reasons described, the sixty-six public universities in this study are in some ways more diverse than the thirty-three privates. Politics and markets differ in each state, but all of these universities meet and discuss their common problems in national and regional forums, which exist for all administrative functions of the university. They also gather data on peer institutions for comparative purposes.[103] These universities know one another very well, and word of innovations travels fast. Although the timing, circumstances, and receptivity of innovations has varied from campus to campus, it is possible to depict a general pattern of steps toward a student-centered orientation from the late 1980s to the early 2000s. Every public university, it is safe to say, confronted similar issues; and each responded in its own distinctive manner.[104]

External pressures on public universities first and foremost affected the highest levels of leadership—university presidents, boards of trustees, and other academic officers. Presidents provide the interface between their institutions and interested constituencies, including alumni, donors, and state legislatures; presidents also serve directly under boards of trustees, who approach academic affairs chiefly as interested outsiders.

Under the president, the provost or chief academic officer communicates university policy throughout the institution. From the late 1980s onward, the cadre of presidents and provosts who had ramped up academic research gradually ceded their positions to a new generation of leaders for whom the litmus test of appointment was unequivocal solicitude to undergraduate education. Some new leaders no doubt adopted this posture out of necessity, recognizing that these issues had to be addressed if other parts of the university were to be protected. Still others were true believers, accepting the critique and aiming toward fundamental changes in the traditional mode of operation. In either case, concern for strengthening undergraduate education rose to the highest institutional priority.

Presidents, whether new or sitting, were forced to deal with the "problem" as the critics had defined it. Considerable bluster was aired about the supposedly negligent faculty and the nefarious lure of research. Promises were made to "change the reward structure" in favor of teaching, in spite of inherent obstacles. Pressure was exerted on colleges and departments to require faculty to spend more hours in classrooms, and in some cases it may have brought the desired result. Certainly the drift toward fewer classroom hours was arrested. The vigilant assessment of tenured faculty was also promised, occasionally through post-tenure review but more often through more rigorous annual evaluations. Faculty teaching awards were created as one conspicuous step toward changing the culture. Rhetoric on these matters may have blunted the offensive against the universities, but where it threatened the faculty it engendered hostility as well. Universities soon moved to redefine these issues.

When universities examined the state of undergraduate education on their own campuses they often found, as Arizona did, that poor classroom teaching was not the problem. But they did find discouraging evidence of low retention and graduation rates. Too many students, including those with demonstrated academic ability, failed to return after their first year. And graduation in four years was the exception rather than the rule. Part of the problem seemed to lie in the freshman experience. As at Arizona, advising seemed to be weak everywhere. Graduate teaching assistants were a particular grievance in the sciences, where the poor English of a few stigmatized the many. In this context, too, complaints about the difficulty of scheduling required courses were inflated into a major failing. In part, these "problems" were a product of the very process of self-scrutiny and external assessment.

Universities were now being held, and were holding themselves, to a higher standard than ever before. However, these were matters that universities could address within their existing mode of operations. Furthermore, once these "problems" had been documented and measured against benchmarks and projected goals, corrective actions became imperative.

The period from the early 1990s through mid-decade might be labeled the corrective phase of the student-centered movement, a time when most public universities identified and attempted to redress weaknesses in undergraduate education. Concern for freshmen blossomed into a minor industry.[105] Most efforts focused on making the introductory curriculum less stultifying and affording first-year students some opportunity to take small classes and interact with regular faculty. Advising was improved or overhauled on most campuses, and steps were taken to limit and simplify graduation requirements. For example, one of the reasons used to justify responsibility-centered management at Indiana was to compel departments to make classes more readily available. Programs for faculty development and instructional support, long a fixture in most universities, were expanded and given a greater role. They were specifically charged with improving instruction by the perennial whipping boys, the graduate teaching assistants. In a sign of the changing times, doctoral students began to seek out such programs as they realized that pedagogical training was becoming an asset for securing an academic position in a horrendous market.

Virtually every university revised its formula for general education during these years. These efforts were partly an attempt to deal with tepid student interest in existing menus, and partly a reflection of perennial faculty frustration in seeking this holy grail. As a curricular issue, general education is both inherently prescriptive and quintessentially a faculty matter. Faculty have long debated what knowledge and skills a college graduate ought to possess. Differing views over prescribed courses had already given rise to the battles between proponents of multiculturalism and Western heritage. In the mid-1990s, the prescriptive inclinations of faculty confronted triumphant student consumerism. The trick became devising a choice of courses that would instill the desired intellectual qualities and also pique the curiosity of students born in the current era. It is probably testimony to the growing concern for students that faculty committees applied themselves so assiduously to this challenge.

Instead of offering a convenient menu of choices, some universities proposed ambitious new courses in the fashion of the times: interdisciplinary, issue-focused, with active learning and small-group interaction. UCLA, for example, incorporated all of these in one of the most ambitious new general education options: it featured year-long (a scheduling nightmare), specially designed (requiring extraordinary faculty effort), interdisciplinary clusters on broad intellectual themes, delivered in team-taught lecture-seminar combinations.[106]

The actions taken during the corrective phase did not necessarily require a great deal of additional expenditure. These were years in which public universities faced stagnant or declining levels of resources. Particularly challenging was the goal of promoting more faculty contact with freshmen or undergraduates with fewer faculty. Nevertheless, the emphasis on students certainly influenced university investments in these years, as seen at Arizona.

But even these clearly needed measures were insufficient by themselves. When most public universities monitored their market position, rather than their internal vital signs, a much larger challenge loomed. Merely correcting weaknesses did little to enhance their position in national rankings or attract the caliber of students for which selective schools competed. By the late 1990s, many public universities took steps to enhance their position in the selectivity sweepstakes.

As at private universities, these initiatives were taken from a variety of motives. Genuine concern with promoting student learning was no doubt uppermost in the minds of those most involved, even if a marketing angle suggested itself to others. Thus freshman seminars were justified primarily as a means of improving retention. However, they also could be advertised to dispel the image of the huge, impersonal State U. The University of Colorado inverted the logic, reasoning that seminars for seniors would make a more significant contribution to intellectual development, but the advertising value was the same. The grouping together in special dormitories of students with similar interests (in living-learning units), along with faculty residents, separate classes, and special programs, had wide appeal. Once again, enhanced quality of learning should be the principal benefit, but these offerings also helped to recruit serious students.

Research opportunities for undergraduates are an innovation that has benefited public universities in numerous ways. Long practiced at elite research universities like MIT, the practice has now spread throughout American higher education, blurring the definition of research in the process.[107] The pure programs offered at Wisconsin and Colorado provided summer stipends for several hundred undergraduates to work with faculty on sponsored research. These programs are popular with faculty and students, and have even been applauded by state politicians. But the payoff is larger than that. They project a positive role for research in undergraduate education and emphasize a distinct advantage of research universities. The research reputation of the university is thus directly enlisted to appeal to undergraduate students.

The admissions office still plays a critical role in enrolling top students. Public universities have rather belatedly concluded that they must compete vigorously for their share. Perhaps that is less true at the University of California, where demography and reputation conspire to attract the best and the brightest California students.[108] But elsewhere competition has required concerted efforts, including investments in merit aid. In a few states these funds have come from state programs—the famous Hope scholarships in Georgia and the Bright Futures Scholarships in Florida. These full-tuition awards make study within the state so attractive for qualifying students that they have elevated the entire profile of entering classes at the flagship universities. Research universities across the South have adopted other stratagems for recruiting high-ability students, motivated by the wish to both enhance their own reputations and keep talented young people in the state for the benefit of the local economy.[109]

Elsewhere, public universities cobble together endowments and general revenues for scholarships. To a remarkable extent, these funds have been used to recruit nonresident students. This behavior is not unlike that of private universities: a relatively small scholarship may induce a student to attend who will still pay a substantial amount in out-of-state tuition. Public university admissions offices too have both enrollment and revenue targets.

Public universities have also emphasized honors programs as an inducement to top students. Honors programs in their current form date from the 1950s, but they received little attention during the 1980s and early 1990s. During years of budgetary constraint it was difficult to justify extra spending on programs that by their very nature could be called elitist. However, public universities in their current drive to recruit top students have embraced this form of elitism, and honors programs provide an ideal vehicle. Arrangements vary widely across universities on a scale from inclusive to exclusive.[110] Inclusive honors programs set relatively modest standards for acceptance, and students who miss the mark can sometimes enroll in honors sections upon request. Benefits too are somewhat more diffuse. Honors students must compete for limited scholarship awards, and honors housing may be optional. This approach has the virtue of appealing to a fairly large number of very good students, particularly those within the state.

Indiana, for example, includes about 10 percent (650) of entering freshmen in honors, and Arizona in the 1990s tripled its honors cohort to near 20 percent (1,000) of freshmen. More recently, Penn State adopted the opposite approach, converting its previous program into an Honors College that accepted just 300 entering students, all with exceptional academic credentials who receive scholarships for partial tuition. In addition to the advantages of special classes and advising, honors students reside in a special, refurbished residence hall. The aim of such an exclusive program is to recruit the very top students to a state university.

The two phases of student-centered developments at public universities, correction and enhancement, have been responses to different stimuli, even if some of the measures taken would apply to both. The corrective phase may or may not have been initiated by external criticism, but the process itself focused attention on internal weaknesses, which then had to be addressed. The severity of external pressure may well have conditioned the degree of internal response—the extent to which programs and promises were designed to mollify critics. Politically, however, it is difficult for universities to gain credibility through these measures: publicizing corrective measures tended to validate the charges of external critics.

Internally, the calculus of benefits and costs was rarely tallied. Any gains in student learning and achievement, although difficult to demonstrate, would obviously be considered pluses. If they were achieved through increased expenditures or investments, this may have been money well spent. But forming or expanding administrative units to perform redundant exercises in assessment may not only be costly but also have a stultifying effect on academic life. And unrealistic statistical targets (performance indicators) may take a toll on a university's credibility.

Most delicate of all is the issue of academic standards. Although the goal of student-centered reforms was always to raise standards and enlarge student learning, the fixation with quantitative measures tends to work in the opposite direction. Grade inflation, after all, has a positive effect on student retention, faculty teaching ratings, and the satisfaction of student consumers.

The enhancement phase of student-centered concerns developed out of an increasing sensitivity to market forces. Public universities too had much to gain by increasing their selectivity. Given the fixation with statistical goals, the most feasible means of increasing retention, graduation, and average student achievement was to eliminate the least-prepared students. This could only be accomplished by attracting additional applicants. The increased national competition for strong students, in addition, compelled public universities to compete more strenuously just to retain their existing student base. To do so they had to transcend entirely the old, negative stereotypes and project a positive image of the advantages of undergraduate education at a public research university.

As already seen, owing to internal differentiation, these large, multipurpose institutions have always provided superb educational opportunities in demanding programs. Public universities augmented these opportunities with well-publicized programs for honors, living-learning communities, and undergraduate research. Such programs emphasized enhanced opportunities for learning. In contrast to outcome measures like retention, all the incentives pointed in the same, positive direction. However, given large and diverse student bodies and limited funds, these programs succeed by furthering internal differentiation. Although this can also happen in private universities, public universities have the means to offer enhanced learning opportunities to only some, not all, of their students. Efforts to reach everyone—to raise the level of learning through efforts such as improved general education—seem unlikely to reverse this drift. But selective programs nevertheless accomplish the broader goal of bolstering the image and market position of a university.

In the current era, market forces have become far more important to public universities, even though they operate individually in relatively autarkic markets. Prestige, nevertheless, is the common coin. Prestige is a factor in attracting sufficient applicants from within a state and indispensable for competing in the national marketplace. Perhaps more significant, prestige is the key to attracting private gifts, to meeting the goals of the huge capital campaigns that most of these institutions have conducted. Thus even middle-range public universities now look to the rankings in *U.S. News*.

These schools have little chance of reaching the top national list, which is tilted in any case toward selective private universities. They aspire to a place on a separate list of the top fifty public universities. Failing that, a respectable or improving rank in the "second tier" of universities may suffice. The visibility of the *U.S. News* rankings gives them an importance that overshadows the more prestigious National Research Council ratings or the National Science Foundation rankings of R&D. Since the *U.S. News* rankings are heavily based on selectivity, these measures become critical factors for state universities.[111] Their campaigns to gain stature as research universities consequently include pointed efforts to improve the statistical profile of the undergraduate student body.

The top public universities face a stiffer challenge. They compete directly with private universities in the national market for high-ability students. The competition here, as in the private sector, has required universities to increase student aid, for merit and for need. The University of Michigan epitomizes this situation: its nonresident tuition approximates that of a private university, and it awards the largest amount of institutional aid in the public sector.

Other leading public universities have been drawn in this direction. Public universities may lack the resources to join the arms race with the private universities, but they are affected nonetheless. In part, they appeal to undergraduates with their vast educational complexes and their worldwide reputations. But they also are lured by the market to promote the attractions of private universities. Thus their spending on student aid is pushed inexorably higher, and they offer enhanced programs to a minority of their students. Insofar as possible, they attempt to support such quality-building initiatives with donated funds. But their resources are finite and fungible. The forces that have impelled public universities toward a more student-centered orientation have also placed greater demands on their stretched financial base.

CHAPTER FOUR

Academic Research

SINCE WORLD WAR II, university research in the United States has been in the forefront of international science. Whether measured by publications, citations, or international awards, American predominance has been overwhelming and consistent. Even as other countries have strengthened their scientific efforts, the international scientific community has increasingly shifted the center of gravity toward the United States. English has become the lingua franca of science, and advanced training in the United States as indispensable as study in Germany was in the late nineteenth century. Several factors are usually invoked to account for this: a massive federal investment in science, a large array of world-class universities, and a huge community of academic scientists sustained by both. But size alone cannot account for the most impressive aspect of this achievement—the persistence of American leadership through decades of political, economic, and intellectual transformation.

Few scholars have probed the adaptive process that has facilitated the continual renewal of American science. Joseph Ben-David, examining U.S. science late in the heyday of its 1960s growth, found an explanation in the decentralized, competitive structure of the university system, which fostered and rewarded innovative and entrepreneurial behavior. Two decades later, Burton R. Clark emphasized the internal organization of the "graduate department university," which nurtured research and graduate study through a vertical division of labor.[1] A more comprehensive picture of the dynamics of innovation, incorporating factors discussed by both Ben-David and Clark, might distinguish three organizational fields that define this process: the financial supporters of academic research; the universities as institutional actors; and within universities, the multiple departments and units in which research is conducted. Every grant or contract for sponsored research represents a link across these three fields: funds given by a sponsor to a university to support a researcher in a particular unit. These myriad links connect organizational fields that are each inherently competitive and decentralized.[2]

For funds to support research, universities compete not just among themselves, but also with other performers of research. Close, sustaining relationships have developed over the years between the university sector and funding agencies such as the National Science Foundation and between universities and private foundations; but supporters of research are primarily interested in results. Scientific agencies may work with scholars in the field to identify cutting-edge topics, but they ultimately determine for themselves what areas to support. Industry and mission agencies of the federal government look to scientists who can best meet their needs, regardless of institutional locus.

Universities provide the settings for academic research, but they are far more than intermediaries. As institutions, they largely determine the potential for given types of research. That is, universities ultimately make decisions about providing or not providing the faculty, research facilities, and centers or institutes that conduct and accommodate research. Competition among universities is characterized by differentiation of research roles and, above all, hierarchy based on provisions for advancing knowledge.

Units that conduct research, whether departments or institutes, compete with one another within a single university for resources to augment their research role. And they compete with comparable units elsewhere in the research system for direct support for research projects. At this level the process is truly Darwinian. Units that succeed will increase in size or status (or both); those that fail to keep abreast of the intellectual frontiers will wither or languish, at least as far as research is concerned.

The sections that follow explore some of the dynamics of these organizational fields in order to illuminate recent developments in academic research. The first places academic research within the ecology of knowledge in the United States, demonstrating the necessity for universities to adapt to a shifting constellation of research supporters. Research within universities is examined next in several organizational contexts. The third section focuses on academic research and the private universities, and the fourth addresses the public sector. The final part identifies trends shaping the current system.

Universities in the Ecology of Scientific Research

Universities play a large role in the intellectual life of the nation, well beyond their educational mission. They harbor poets and artists, social critics and business consultants; they employ most of the professionals who seek to understand the past as well as seers who probe the future. Their largest and most organized intellectual role in the generation of knowledge lies in the domain of scientific research. This endeavor, whether in the social sciences, natural sciences, or engineering, typically requires special arrangements and external support. It thus constitutes a distinct economic activity, part of a much larger national effort (see Table 3).

Since its creation in 1950, the National Science Foundation has been charged with record keeping for American science. It classifies all national research and development activities as basic research, applied research, or development.[3] The last category, development of actual products or processes, is by far the largest, comprising more than 60 percent of R&D. It is also the most volatile. Gigantic national commitments like the Apollo Program in the 1960s and the Strategic Defense Initiative (Star Wars) in the 1980s created upward spikes in development expenditures. And the decline of federal R&D in the 1990s occurred disproportionately in development spending for defense. Despite these fluctuations, the dominant note in R&D spending has been relative stability: roughly one-fortieth (2.5 percent) of the national economy has been devoted to research and development not just since 1980 but back to 1960. In the 1980s and 1990s, most notably, R&D kept pace with and made relative gains within a robust economy.[4] Its apparent stability also masked two remarkable changes.

The first was the powerful expansion of R&D supported by industry and, concomitantly, the relative decline of federally supported R&D. Since 1980, real spending for R&D increased by less than 20 percent from federal sources and by 200 percent from industry. Moreover, this long-term trend reversed the situation of the mid-1960s. In those years the federal government provided 70 percent of R&D, and industry less than 30 percent. Interestingly, the character of federal R&D has shifted: basic research support grew by 50 percent in real terms during the 1980s and remained roughly level in the 1990s, while development plummeted. Industrial R&D, in contrast, consisted of 6–7 percent basic research throughout most of this period, with an upturn at the end of the 1990s. Together these developments underpin the second secular shift: the relative expansion of basic research.

Basic research kept pace with the growth of R&D in the 1980s and then

TABLE 3

Trends in Research and Development (R&D), 1980–2000

Total U.S. R&D	1980	1985	1990	1995	2000
Billions of 1996$	114.9	160.1	178.2	187.2	247.5
Percent of GDP	2.32	2.78	2.67	2.49	2.59
Percent federal	47.3	45.9	40.5	34.5	26.3
Percent industry	49.0	50.7	55.0	60.7	68.0
Percent basic research	13.7	12.7	13.9	16.1	18.1

expanded its share in the 1990s (see Table 3). When viewed as a share of GDP, basic research grew from 0.32 percent in 1980, to 0.40 percent in 1990, to an estimated 0.48 percent in 2000. The implication of this trend is clear and important: the high-technology economy of the United States seems to demand increasing inputs of basic research. This conclusion is underlined by the fact that the growth of the 1990s came from industry to meet its own needs. That said, industrial requirements for basic research vary greatly. The percentage of industry R&D devoted to basic research is actually a composite of firms employing large amounts of basic research, such as biotechnology companies, or little basic research, such as automotive corporations. A rising percentage is thus as likely to represent a changing composition of industries as changing R&D practice within an industry.

The boom in high-tech industry at the end of the 1990s seems to have had just this kind of effect. With capital being showered on start-up and newly public companies, the basic research component of industrial research shot above 8 percent.[5] Even without this last spurt, the secular growth of basic research has been a favorable trend for universities.

Some fundamental elements of academic research have exhibited remarkable stability (see Table 4). Since the 1960s, the essential scientific role of universities has been to perform approximately half of the nation's basic research—the drop in 2000 notwithstanding. Basic research has consistently accounted for about two-thirds of academic research, and this figure holds as well for academic research supported by industry. Nevertheless, given the large role of professional schools in academic research, it is hardly surprising that universities perform a significant amount of applied research (14 percent of the national total), as well as a small amount of development (less than 2 percent). But even in more applied fields academic research inclines toward basic or theoretical subjects. American universities are truly

TABLE 4

Trends in Academic Research and Development (R&D), 1980–2000

Academic R&D	1980	1985	1990	1995	2000
Billions of 1996$	11.4	14	19.5	23	28.2
Percent of GDP	0.23	0.24	0.29	0.305	0.303
Percent federal	67.0	62.0	59.0	60.0	58.0
Percent industry	4.0	6.0	7.0	7.0	8.0
Percent basic research	67.0	68.0	66.0	67.0	69.0
Percent U.S. basic research	48.0	47.0	48.0	51.0	43.0

the home of basic research, but they have no monopoly. The other half of basic research is located in federal laboratories, federally funded centers, and private nonprofit laboratories (roughly 10 percent each) and a growing portion (20 percent or more) in industry.

What has changed in academic research are the sources of support. Federal funds supplied about two-thirds of support during the 1970s, but then slid to roughly three-fifths during the 1980s. Industry doubled its relative contribution from a low level. Universities supplied the other relative increase with their own funds (not shown). University research grew as a part of the total economy: during the late 1980s it captured a larger share of GDP, and even during the boom of the late 1990s, academic research largely kept pace with economic growth. Three one-thousandths of a percent may not sound like much, but it is the highest level ever attained for academic research, and as a portion of a $10 trillion economy it is a daunting sum. More remarkable than the absolute amount of academic research is its relative growth. Through two decades of rapid change, universities have managed to increase their contribution to American science and to the American economy by adapting to the changing demands for science rather than the other way around.

The role of American universities in the market for scientific research has always defied simple characterizations. At the outset of the postwar period, Vannevar Bush had argued for federal support for academic science by invoking the premise that basic research was the fount from which technological advancement flowed. The National Science Foundation took this premise as its birthright and widely propagated this view.[6] However, by the time NSF was created in 1950, federal commitments to academic science were already dominated by the requirements of national defense and, to a lesser extent, public health.

After the Soviet launch of Sputnik in 1957, the exploration of space would be added to these federal rationales for supporting science. The discourse concerning the merits of basic versus directed research, especially in universities, persisted into the 1970s and tended to obscure the foremost reality of the situation: federal support for academic science was always dominated by the programmatic needs of mission agencies. To use later terminology, technology transfer for defense and health care was the principal goal of the vast federal investment in university research.

In the current era, the so-called Bush paradigm became a straw man for attacking the simplistic view of basic science and suggesting that the nature of academic science had been or was being transformed. Critics wished to convey two ideas about contemporary scientific research that were undoubtedly important but perhaps not as novel as claimed. First they sought to replace the "transmission belt" metaphor, which connected discoveries of basic research with the spawning of applied research, technology, and the eventual development of products. In its stead they posited a reciprocal relationship whereby technological development in itself yields basic discoveries, or raises problems that inspire basic science. From this perspective, the rationale for basic research assumes somewhat different form. Instead of arising purely from scientific paradigms, research questions may also arise from technology and thus be consumer driven. This view has implications for supporting research as well. Instead of relying on scientists in the field to initiate proposals for basic research, science might better be managed in ways that would recognize and incorporate consumer demands.

In fact, the need for basic research as a byproduct of technological development has long been recognized. Large development projects of the Department of Defense in the past seemed to devote about 5 percent of their funds to basic research, although in the 1990s this figure shrank to nearer 3 percent.[7] Industry, with perhaps less interest in knowledge for its own sake, increased its own investment in basic research from the 4–5 percent range before 1980 to roughly 8 percent of R&D in 2000. Given these ranges, the feedback effect by which applied research and technology generate demand for basic research might be estimated for recent years to be at least 6 percent. For the year 2000, when applied research and development totaled nearly $220 billion, such an effect would theoretically account for $13 billion of basic research, more than one-quarter of the total. This calculation suggests that roughly three-quarters of basic research is inspired by different considerations.

The second objection to the Bush paradigm promoted the notion that the distinction between basic and applied science had been transcended. The key development, National Academy of Sciences president Frank Press explained in 1992, was the increasing prominence of "research-based technologies," or areas of fundamental scientific inquiry that were linked to obvious and important technologies.

This description sounds a good deal like "targeted basic research," which had been the dominant form of federal investment in defense- and health-related research. But by the 1990s, it was argued, the distance between basic science and applications had lessened appreciably, and with this change the attitudes of scientists had changed as well. Instead of expecting to remain aloof from technology, many sought opportunities to maintain close contact with industrial research and to see their discoveries developed into products.[8] The examples of research technologies offered by Press clinched the argument: advanced materials, especially those developed for superconductivity; optoelectronics and sensor technology; and the most spectacular scientific revolution of the era, biotechnology.

Press's notion of research technologies resonated with the most conspicuous current scientific developments. Soon more succinct terms were being used to invoke this same idea: generic research, strategic research, precommercial research. In 1994, Michael Gibbons and associates argued that the production of knowledge in contemporary societies had assumed new characteristics, which they dubbed "Mode 2." In the traditional patterns of science, or Mode 1, the definition of problems and validation of discoveries in their view was dominated by the academic disciplines. Mode 2, in contrast, exhibited many of the features just mentioned: knowledge production occurred in a "context of application," through the interchange of science and technology, and it was "transdisciplinary" in nature. The authors explored numerous ramifications of the new production of knowledge, but on the whole they found them to work against universities. Mode 2 implied a deconcentration of expertise and greater social distribution of the production of knowledge, largely to the detriment of universities: "disciplinary-based sciences, institutionalized largely in universities, and driven intellectually by internal considerations" seemed unlikely to contribute to economic performance, and therefore unlikely to prosper under these new conditions.[9] However, judging from developments in the United States, that scenario seems mistaken.

In the United States, as just seen, the proliferation of research technologies, the migration of R&D toward industry, and indeed an increasing demand for economic relevance in research, have all been accompanied by trends toward greater basic research and more research in universities. The new production of knowledge, perhaps more than the old, includes an indispensable role for academic research. Two fundamental reasons, rooted in the nature of the research system, account for this. First, research by its very nature draws on previous research and raises questions that stimulate further research. (A standing joke chides academics for concluding every study with calls for additional research.) Closely related is the increasing interconnection of different fields and subfields of inquiry, which fertilize one another. The research process generates an expanding demand for additional knowledge. For good reason, basic science doubles every fifteen years (see Table 4).[10]

Second, by virtue of their distinctive role in the research system, American universities have played an irreplaceable role in meeting those knowledge demands. Universities serve as vast repositories of intellectual capital. Their role of harboring knowledge is inextricably linked with the missions of disseminating and advancing knowledge. They nurture this process through investment in the expertise of their faculty. By hiring and supporting the development of experts in specific fields of study, universities cultivate and sustain an enormous range of the most advanced forms of knowledge.[11] This expertise is complemented by equipment and facilities for advanced investigations as well as by young apprentices developing their own expertise. This combination offers a powerful and uniquely valuable resource for tapping into advanced, esoteric knowledge. Organizations that develop technologies, in contrast, whether in government or industry, largely limit long-term investments to their specialized areas of interest. When they need additional knowledge or expertise of a complementary or more general nature, they can and do turn to universities. Hence the more research conducted in these "contexts of application," the more interaction is likely with academic research. However, the efficiency or efficacy of this process is by no means automatic; it assumes a large degree of effort and accommodation on the part of universities (the subject of the next chapter).

This depiction of the place of universities in the ecology of knowledge points to the challenge faced by universities in the current era. If they are to maintain their relevance for the research economy, and continue to perform half of the nation's basic research, universities must continually adapt to the advancing frontiers of science. This means maintaining a fruitful interchange with commercial technology. To do so universities must often reconfigure themselves to accommodate tasks remote from their academic focus and to become actors in the realms of commerce and economic development. At the same time, they must fulfill their traditional roles in teaching and research, for which they are held to an exacting standard. Thus the universities' dilemma in the current era: to accommodate the demands of the new research economy without compromising their basic mission.

Research in Universities

Research is one part of the basic mission of U.S. universities, along with teaching and service. This venerable trio has implicitly been regarded as what economists call joint products—natural and compatible outputs of the underlying intellectual resources. In this respect, the development of research in a given university reflects to some degree the level of resources accumulated for academic purposes.

The university as an organization plays a key role in this process through the number and quality of the teacher-scholars it employs, the students it recruits, the collections it sustains, and the physical facilities it commands. However, research has long existed as an end in itself, complementary to but largely autonomous from other academic ends. This situation typically occurs when patrons demand research in magnitudes that exceed the possibilities for joint production. Universities have responded by creating separately organized research units (ORUs) to fulfill those demands.[12]

A special case of excess demand for research developed in medical schools after World War II and now constitutes a large and distinctive part of academic research. The research portfolio of a university might consist of the joint product of its academic core, dedicated ORUs, and the specialized activities of a medical school. These categories are by no means mutually exclusive, but each represents quite different conditions for conducting academic research.

Looking first at separate research units, universities have often confronted demands for research that far exceed any corresponding educational tasks, and they have responded by devising organizational arrangements to accommodate these demands. Such arrangements have not been without controversy, but over time they have tended to assume forms appropriate to their tasks. This *autonomous research role* has played a key part in shaping the university research system, specifically permitting its large scale and varied scope.

This was true as early as the nineteenth century, when American colleges and universities haphazardly incorporated astronomical observatories, museum collections, and agricultural experiment stations—all intended for what is now called research. In the 1920s and 1930s the great foundations bestowed research institutes on leading universities to advance knowledge in chosen areas. The most decisive thrust in this direction occurred during and after World War II, when the federal government enlisted the universities to perform indispensable investigations for national defense. Given the magnitude of the tasks involved, they tended to be housed in laboratories of unprecedented size. Although the support for all these endeavors came from outside of universities, the institutions themselves played a crucial role in accepting these units, housing them, and sometimes letting them go.[13]

The configuration of defense-related research after World War II illustrates how autonomous research accomplished tasks that academic units would find difficult.[14] Several features of defense research were at odds with university norms and procedures. The requirements of secrecy, exacerbated by Cold War conditions, violated a cherished value of the scientific ethos. Much of this research was applied in character and evolved toward the development of products and weapons systems. The scale of these undertakings, involving large numbers of professional scientists, engineers, and technicians, dwarfed academic departments in related areas. In practice, these incongruities were muted through various degrees of separation from main academic units.

The largest laboratories, including the Jet Propulsion Laboratory at Caltech and the Applied Physics Laboratory at Johns Hopkins—both bigger than their host institutions—became separate federal laboratories under university management.[15] Another class of laboratories remained under the university tent, but encapsulated apart from the rest of the campus. Some were heavily applied in character, like the Navy's water tunnel at Pennsylvania State University; others conducted the most basic kinds of research, like the Lawrence Laboratory at Berkeley and other nuclear physics laboratories. MIT and then Stanford were particularly receptive to this type of government laboratory, applied or theoretical. At most such units a select group of faculty and graduate students conducted research in conjunction with a professional staff. Laboratories that forged links with academic departments, in particular, contributed materially to the development of their respective universities.

The legacies of these early laboratories are still present. The science may change, but where the mission endures the chances are that the laboratory will too. Numerous new laboratories have joined these early creations, many sponsored by the National Science Foundation. Unlike some defense-related labs, these later units often provide unique scientific instruments for fundamental investigations. As such, they have been enormous assets for the host institutions, providing a magnet for scientists working in these specialized areas.

In awarding these prized laboratories, federal agencies ideally seek the most effective locus for scientific purposes. The presence of eminent scientists naturally becomes a prime consideration, and one that favors the leading universities. But geography can also be pertinent, not to mention politics. More recently, the financial contribution of the institution itself has loomed large in placement decisions. As a result, large federally funded facilities are found throughout the university research system. They advance the scientific reputation of universities and swell R&D expenditures, but impose financial obligations as well. And they are but one manifestation of the autonomous research mission.

Organized research units exist in a bewildering variety of forms. The large laboratories just mentioned are probably furthest, organizationally and culturally, from the academic core. Nevertheless, a continuum can be hypothesized between such ORUs and academic departments. Many centers and institutes fulfill a dual role, to enhance knowledge of a particular topic and to facilitate work within academic disciplines.[16] Other ORUs are designed (and funded) primarily to serve external clientele. Among the latter group, centers for encouraging university-industry research relationships and technology transfer were a notable area of growth in the 1980s, as Chapter 5 describes. University research centers—ORUs—helped make this relationship feasible by encapsulating and resolving interorganizational tensions. These centers enhanced the economic relevance of academic research and linked it with commercial technology, the most rapidly expanding portion of the national research economy.

A second organizational pattern, produced by the demand for research exceeding educational needs, occurred in medical schools. Before World War II medical research was concentrated in a handful of universities. The immediate postwar expansion, although large as a percentage, occurred from this narrow base and largely favored the same institutions. In the mid-1950s, the National Institutes of Health began a massive expansion of grants for medical and biological research. Support for research facilities and the training of biomedical scientists soon followed.[17] Research grants alone grew fifteenfold in a decade. By the late 1960s the abundance of support for research was one of the factors that had transformed American medical schools.

Federal largesse created an autonomous research role for medical schools even as the schools themselves were being enveloped in huge academic health centers. Medical departments assumed the features of research institutes, especially in the preclinical or basic science field. Faculty routinely spent most of their time on research and received most of their salary from grants. The academic nature of these departments was strengthened as they enlarged Ph.D. programs and added postdoctoral fellows to assist in research and train additional researchers. At the same time, the ties between medical schools and their universities were attenuated. Growing responsibilities for health care virtually required that academic health centers be separated financially, if not organizationally, from the parent universities. These developments gave medical research a structure and dynamic all its own.

Ever since the revolution that brought medical education and research firmly into the university early in the twentieth century, all of the country's major medical schools were linked with leading universities.[18] By 1970, though, links with the National Institutes of Health (NIH) and the health care delivery system took precedence over those with universities. This allowed the emergence of new kinds of "research universities" in which virtually all research was produced by a medical school. Freestanding medical universities appeared, which was nothing new, but now they were among the largest performers of academic research.[19]

These same institutions attained lofty ratings for the quality of their programs. Given the abundance of resources in the evolving biomedical universe, the rise of new kinds of institutions did nothing to diminish the stature or productivity of the traditional leaders, affiliated with leading research universities. However, with financial bases quite different from those of universities, medical research powerhouses might be found as separate parts of top research universities, connected with regional campuses (such as the University of Alabama at Birmingham), or even liberal arts colleges (Wake Forest), or as parts of autonomous campuses (University of California, San Francisco; University of Texas–Southwestern Medical Center; Baylor College of Medicine).

The special, separate character of medical research was further exaggerated by the development of faculty medical practice, which occurred after the original ramping up of NIH awards.[20] The opportunities for lucrative faculty practice were greatly enhanced by the creation of Medicare and Medicaid in the 1960s. Still, it was not until the 1980s, after years of pinched funding, that faculty practice became a staple of medical school finance. The availability of income from clinical practice largely justified the addition of any number of clinical faculty. Medical schools added more than 18,000 in the 1970s and a like number in the 1980s, compared with an additional 7,000 full-time faculty in the basic sciences. Revenues from faculty-practice plans nearly quintupled in the 1980s. This income contributed greatly to the financial well-being of medical schools, including subsidies for research. But as a result, according to historian Kenneth Ludmerer, "the rationale of the medical school as part of the university was forgotten. Medical schools grew rich, but they lost connection with their [university] roots."[21]

Beginning in the 1980s, pressures for cost containment began to alter the market conditions that had fueled these developments. The market for patient care in this case consisted entirely of third-party payers, government and insurers, and they spearheaded the revolution of managed care that swept the health care system in the 1990s. Up to that point, some 28 percent of clinical income had been used to subsidize medical education and research, but those lush margins were squeezed out of existence.[22] The full ramifications have yet to be seen, but two consequences have become obvious. With respect to patient care, clinical faculty must now perform far more services, more efficiently, to obtain the revenues to support themselves. Medical research, after enduring an initial shock, seems to have become more dependent on the resources of the NIH and, to a lesser extent, industry.

Despite the recent turmoil, medical science has been the largest and the fastest-growing field of academic research. From 1979 to 1997 it gained 5 percent of the total (23.2 to 28.2 percent)—an increase greater than the total research funding for academic physics or social science. Yet its ties to the academy are paradoxical. Intellectually, medical research is now more tightly integrated with biological science as a result of the revolutions in molecular biology and genomics.[23] In this respect, biomedical research shares more basic science with investigators in biological and agricultural fields. But organizationally, medical research has become a world of its own, an autonomous research mission shaped by the unique environment of academic health centers.

Because of their large, anomalous presence, medical schools deserve special consideration in any discussion of academic research.[24] They are depicted here, together with ORUs, as manifesting university incorporation of and adaptation to an autonomous research role. In both these situations, academic science or expertise appears to be the fixed point, the desired object of external demands. But over time, the conditions imposed by external patrons tend to shape the institutional contours of the units they support.

A similar relationship exists between university research and commercial technology, where institutional arrangements are still developing and fundamental terms of the relationship are still under negotiation (see Chapter 5). Yet judging from the national trends reviewed in the previous section, commercial technology will be a major source of future research growth, one moreover in which the demand for research far exceeds the capacities of the academic core.

The *academic core* of research universities ideally embodies the principle "that enlarging and disseminating knowledge are equally important activities and that each is done better when both are done in the same place by the same people."[25] This statement underlines not only that teaching and research are joint products, but that together they enhance their respective value. This ideal may not actually describe contemporary research universities since, as just seen, they also include units containing individuals devoted solely to research, as well as others in which people teach without doing research. And service commitments, however valuable in themselves, are probably more marginal for those who both enlarge and disseminate knowledge. Without disparaging any of the other things research universities do, the degree-granting programs that jointly engage in teaching and research can be identified as the academic core.

To be more specific, this notion of the academic core suggests a model in which the individual faculty member is the organizational unit for the production of both educational and research outputs. Implicitly, departments employ faculty in order to fulfill their teaching requirements and to cover the intellectual domain of their subject. The faculty then engage in research on topics of their choosing, based largely on the paradigms of their respective fields. The scale of any individual's research depends on supportive resources, some of which are provided by the university and some of which would be secured through external grants. The researcher might, for example, lead a group of graduate research assistants, postdocs, and staff. Only when permanent organizations become necessary—when an ORU is needed—is this individual model transcended. Otherwise, it matters not whether the investigator initiates her own topics or responds to requests from others; nor does it matter if she collaborates with colleagues or works alone. The individual faculty member is the node that engenders the research process.

Research in the academic core can be decomposed into four inputs: the number of faculty, the time devoted to research, support from facilities and assistants, and productivity or quality. All of these elements are critically dependent on institutional resources. Resource-rich universities are able to attract the most productive scholars to their faculty and support an optimal number of them. They can provide facilities and assistance to enhance productivity, and through low teaching obligations they allow the faculty to devote a significant portion of time to research. Large universities can assemble large numbers of faculty-researchers, and through the division of academic labor can ensure an adequate resource base for many of them. The challenge for any university is to allocate and arrange these resources to best accomplish the research and teaching missions, but also to interact with the system of external support for academic research. Because research in different fields requires vastly different arrangements, conditions are likely to be more uniform in the same disciplines in different research universities than across disciplines within a single university.

This model raises interesting questions when applied to academic research in the current era. The most remarkable feature is that research more than doubled while expansion of the academic core was far smaller (see Table 5). Part of the explanation is the expansion of the autonomous research role, in which medical research was the most rapidly growing sector. The employment of doctoral scientists in nonfaculty positions more than doubled in these decades. Even so, they were outnumbered four to one by faculty scientists.[26] Clearly, developments in the academic core, and particularly the role of faculty, must have played a role in the mushrooming of academic research.

Perhaps the least understood element of research in the academic core is the allotment of faculty time. Dedicated time for research is provided by two sources: the university itself and outside funders. A portion of the faculty workload is explicitly or implicitly devoted to the advancement of knowledge and the enhancement of the individual faculty member's expertise. The defining features of a research university, in fact, are the relatively large portion of the workload devoted to this purpose and the expectation that personal enhancement will produce knowledge in the form of scholarly publications. The commitment to research is built into a faculty position in the form of limited teaching responsibilities as well as sabbatical leaves. It is an investment by the institution in the intellectual capital of the faculty. Outside funders award grants that "purchase" time for research by reimbursing the university for a portion of a faculty member's salary. Such funds may purchase time during summer vacations, buy out time designated for teaching courses, or displace some of the institution's own investment. Often ORUs play a role in this process by administering grants. Nevertheless,

TABLE 5

Changes in the Academic Core and Academic Research in
33 Private and 66 Public Universities, 1980–2000

	Private	Public
Enrollment		
1980	335,378	1,391,422
2000	390,827	1,593,873
Change (percent)	16.5	11
Faculty[a]		
1980	15,195	63,983
2000	18,266	70,419
Change (percent)	20	10
Research (billions of 1996$)		
1980	3.25	6.03
2000	6.65	14.54
Change (percent)	105	141

[a]28 private; 64 public universities (see Figures 11 and 12).

TABLE 6

Faculty Time Spent on Teaching and Research, Research
Universities, 1987–1998 (percent)

	Private	Public
1987		
Teaching	40	43
Research	29	30
1992		
Teaching	35	40
Research	36	32
1998		
Teaching	42	46
Research	26	29

Source: National Survey of Postsecondary Faculty 1988; 1993; 1999.

research undertaken in conjunction with a faculty position and intended to enhance intellectual capital belongs within the academic core.

The portion of faculty work devoted to research or scholarship represents some combination of internal and external funding. This figure became a bone of contention in the controversy over undergraduate education at research universities. Surveys of faculty allocations of time, which depend on self-reporting, are difficult to compare. The faculty surveys of the National Center for Education Statistics indicate some fluctuation over time (see Table 6). These data appear to show a shift toward greater research during the boom of the late 1980s, and then an even larger reaction toward teaching in the 1990s. Anecdotal evidence seems consistent with such a pattern. But because self-reported data tend to exaggerate socially preferred activities, the pattern might well reflect shifting expectations as much as time at the bench. Furthermore, this distinction is in some degree arbitrary; advanced teaching and research usually blend as a true joint product.[27] But the distinction is real in the accounting for sponsored research; and it is no less real for faculty members who must free up blocks of time in order to complete major research projects.

A second perplexing element, quality, is inherent to the advancement of knowledge. In its most basic form, new knowledge takes the form of publications, chiefly scientific papers; but another component is the formation of new scientists or scholars, the doctoral graduates of Ph.D. programs. Where knowledge is concerned, considerations of quality assume paramount importance. Universities are judged not only on the volume of knowledge they produce—the number of publications—but on the putative significance of those contributions as well. It would be hopelessly difficult for a single university to make such judgments. Instead, quality in academic research and doctoral programs has been monitored in the current era by decennial assessments of academic departments conducted under the auspices of the National Research Council. Quantity can be measured more readily through the annual expenditures for sponsored research by individual universities. And quality and quantity powerfully interact. Since patrons of research generally seek the highest attainable quality, the amount of research a university performs reflects quality to a large degree. But academic research is also subject to capacity constraints. Without resorting to organized research units, the joint production of teaching and research in the academic core would in theory have an optimal level. This same relationship between quality and quantity, size and constraints, governs key inputs: highly rated departments on average are larger than those with lesser ratings; and because students too seek quality, the best departments tend to have the largest doctoral programs as well.

The inherent size constraints of the academic core actually make academic research a remarkably decentralized industry. The largest performers account for only 2 percent of the expenditures, and that figure has been declining since World War II. If research were a profitable undertaking, it is doubtful that this would be the case.[28] Rather, most research is joined in a complicated way with the academic core and thus consumes finite institutional resources. The changing contours of the research system are thus produced by the complex interplay between quality and quantity—the scarcity or abundance of internal and external resources.

The gold standard for measuring academic quality has been the NRC-sanctioned ratings of research-doctoral programs. These elaborate and costly studies are based on the ratings by academics of the faculty quality and program effectiveness of departments in their discipline.[29] They continue a long line of reputational, or peer-rated studies, predicated on the principle that only scholars in a field have the expertise to judge the relative merit of their peers. These studies have nevertheless been controversial.[30]

Two substantive lines of criticism have been directed against reputational ratings.[31] First, owing to their raters' limited knowledge and subjective impressions they are inherently conservative, giving undue recognition to traditionally distinguished departments at prestigious universities. A "halo effect" thus exists that may reward past or assumed accomplishments more than present ones. Without denying the presence of such tendencies, one could also argue that they do not obviate the value of such an exercise. Academic quality is a major concern of large numbers of academic scholars and scientists, especially those involved with hiring decisions; and their collective judgments should not be casually dismissed.

The second criticism is epistemological: namely, that the frontiers of knowledge have become so fragmented into specialties, subfields, and interdisciplinary hybrids that they can no longer be captured under the rubrics of single disciplines. The biological sciences have been completely recategorized for this reason, but the latest scheme is far from ideal. Some universities, for example, have more than one department in the same field. Standard disciplinary identities, such as anthropology and political science, conceal a congeries of subjects that have little relation with one another. Such fragmentation makes it difficult for "peers" to rate quality across subfields and calls into question the meaning of summary ratings of an entire department.

Both these criticisms reflect the fundamental difficulty of aggregating quality for comparative purposes. Academics know quite well what they mean by quality in the context of their own work. Indeed, judgments about quality remain fundamental to the operation of the academic enterprise. However, the ineffable nature of academic quality should be borne in mind when peer ratings or other qualitative indicators are aggregated for comparative purposes.

The 1982 *Assessment of Research-Doctorate Programs* and the 1995 report permit a comparison of the system of academic research at the start of the 1980s and in the early years of the 1990s. Although economic conditions were poor in both these periods, the intervening years were propitious for both economic growth and academic development. The most striking change in this interval was the substantial rise in the quality ratings of departments.[32] In all but one discipline, average quality rose. Scores increased two- to three-tenths on a five-point scale for each major area. More interesting is the pattern of increases. In almost all cases, the size of the rating improvement increased from the first to the fourth quartile. That is, the weakest departments made the greatest absolute gains in their numerical ratings. Clearly, a ceiling effect operated here: that is, departments found it harder to advance from a rating of strong (4) to distinguished (5), than from marginal (1) to adequate (2) or good (3).

Although ratings improved little among the top departments, there was no evidence of backsliding. In fact, a separate rating for improvement over the previous five years (1987–92) showed just the opposite pattern—greatest strengthening among the most highly rated departments.[33] The chief message about the evolution of the academic research system to be drawn from the 1995 report is that the quality of academic departments grew during the 1980s, and by implication, so did the quality of the academic core, particularly in the intermediate and lower ranks. This conclusion appears consistent with major trends in research expenditures.

A study of the changing institutional distribution of academic research during the 1980s revealed a curious, nonlinear pattern. The largest and the most highly rated universities experienced a marked decrease in research share. The most significant gainers of research share belonged to the tier of universities below the leaders, but institutions that were still weaker academically for the most part fared poorly.[34] The gainers in that middle group (second tier) were initially substantial performers of research with good to strong departments. Besides enlarging their research share, most of these gainers also improved their departmental quality ratings. Numerous factors affected both measures. Academic research grew by nearly 70 percent in constant dollars during the 1980s, but growth was especially strong in engineering (+99 percent) and medicine (+89 percent). Most of the gainers had a significant presence in one of those areas. Internal factors nevertheless seemed paramount. Institutions that gained research share, compared with those whose share declined, on balance showed greater growth in faculty and full professors, doctorates awarded, and funding from NSF—all changes associated with a strengthening of the academic core. They also employed far more of their own funds for research, an indication of institutional commitment. Why were these universities able to grow in the research system when most higher- and lower-rated institutions were not?

Besides experiencing a robust expansion of funding for academic research, the 1980s also produced a surfeit of potential university scientists. Levels of doctoral production declined only slightly after 1975 when American higher education ceased to expand. Doctorates in the natural sciences and engineering grew significantly in the 1980s, with highly rated departments leading the way. These conditions produced an abundance of well-trained scientists, far in excess of academic posts.[35] At the same time, institutional finances improved during the decade (see Chapter 2), although this factor did not seem to be directly related to changes in research share. The result nevertheless was a buyer's market that allowed weak departments to shore up their competence, as reflected in rating improvements at the lower end.

Second-tier institutions too had an opportunity to upgrade their faculties, but they also possessed the research infrastructure to capitalize on the abundance of research funding. Unlike the departments at more highly rated universities, they had room for improvement and expansion. Most top-tier universities seem to have been operating near optimal levels for research. They increased their research appreciably during the decade, but not as rapidly as the research system as a whole. Second-tier institutions, at least those willing or able to make the effort, faced conditions that encouraged them to move from suboptimal toward optimal levels of research performance.[36] Moreover, greater growth during expansionary conditions should allow for greater adaptation to shifting demands for research, which seems to have occurred.

The qualitative and quantitative trends of the 1980s produced an undoubted enhancement in the capacity and the efficacy of the academic research system. Going into the 1990s, conditions changed. Young, well-trained scientists remained in oversupply relative to academic posts. But institutional finances weakened notably in the first half of the decade, especially in the public sector.

For many universities, merely sustaining the academic core was a challenge for most of the decade. The growth of funds for academic research slowed to a halt after mid-decade, and no one could foresee its resumption. Engineering and defense-related research particularly suffered after the end of the Cold War. And industrially funded research was not able to sustain the momentum of the previous decade. Commercial technology boomed, but hard-pressed firms often cut back on R&D; and public subsidies for university-industry cooperation shrank. Medical research enlarged its share of academic research, at least until confronted by the crisis of managed care.

These new realities shaped the context of academic research through the mid-1990s. However, the capacity or inclination of individual universities to adapt to this new environment was decisive in shaping their research roles.

Institutional Patterns of Research

Getting ahead seems to be an obsession in higher education no less than in American life. With their multiple purposes, universities can usually highlight some category of accomplishment to demonstrate progress and virtue, or to obscure underperformance elsewhere. Where only research is concerned, the situation is no different. It has already been argued that research depends heavily on disparate developments in ORUs, medical schools, and the academic core. For any given university, research is likely to be advancing to new triumphs in some fields, while perhaps stagnating in others. Extrapolated to the ninety-nine universities, this would suggest a kind of Brownian motion of short, unpredictable change, cumulatively signifying nothing. Such an image might reasonably portray the situation of many universities. And it would not signify futility.

Solid accomplishments and a high degree of competence are required just to sustain the same relative position in an ever-advancing research system. Nevertheless, some institutions register significant movements with respect to research, either forward or backward. They reflect in some combination the market forces acting on the system as a whole and endogenous factors at individual institutions (see Appendix B).

Although no single factor could account for the totality of developments in research, different aspects of the research role ought to be reflected in different measures of research activity. Perhaps the most obvious relationship would be between developments in a medical school and expenditures for medical research. On one hand, the doubling of NIH budgets from 1997 to 2003 provided an enormous impetus to biomedical research. On the other hand, cutbacks in defense research in the 1990s dampened growth for engineering research.

Developments in the academic core are more central to a university's entire operations. Increases in the level of expenditures should in most cases be associated with improvements in the academic core. But those improvements would not necessarily increase research activity. Given the preponderant importance accorded to undergraduate education, as seen in Chapter 3, universities might well decide to allocate additional revenues for that purpose. Enlargement of the faculty tends to be associated with advancement of research capacity in the academic core, and vice versa. In addition,

TABLE 7

Change in Research Share by Sector in the 1990s

Universities	Research share, 2000	Change, 1990–2000	Medical share, 1999[a]	Change 1989–99	Faculty increase, 1900–98 (% change)	Average cost per student, 2000[b] ($)
33 private	23.6	–3.0	9.5	0.9	375 (2.0)	24,115
66 public	51.5	–2.4	12.5	1.9	106 (0.15)	14,917
11 medical[c]	6.6	0.5	4.4	0.2	n.a.	n.a.
National total	100	0	29.5	4.0		

[a]Share of total academic R&D
[b]See Appendix A.
[c]Medical universities in top 100 of academic R&D expenditures.

certain areas of research possess strategic importance at particular junctures. Such has certainly been the case with genetics and molecular biology in the current era. As revolutionary advances swept through all levels of biology, this area claimed additional research funding. Extraordinary exertions were required for a university to keep pace with these advances. At the same time that scientists in these areas became most sought after, molecular biology became Big Science, or Big Biology, performed with teams of researchers in multiple laboratories equipped with costly, sophisticated instruments. A university's efforts in biological research during these years probably indicated its seriousness about advancing the research role.

The data in Table 7 provide clues to understanding the relative change in the research roles of American universities. The changes themselves, if properly understood, ought to be consistent with the major institutional trends of the current era, which can be summarized as follows.

A shift in research share to public universities. Although the academic eminence of the leading private universities has been undiminished, private universities have over time performed a shrinking portion of the nation's academic research. They ceded 2 percent of their share in the 1980s and 3 percent in the 1990s. Public universities gained 1 percent in the 1980s, and their somewhat smaller losses in the 1990s were spread over twice as many institutions (see Appendix B). This persistent pattern indicates some fundamental differences in the research role in the two sectors.

The curse of the academic leaders. The nineteen most highly rated universities in the 1982 *Assessment* all lost significant research share sometime during the period 1980–2000.[37] Some public institutions departed from this trend in the 1990s, as will be seen, but dispersion continued to affect most of these academic leaders, which shed 3.5 percent of their research share from 1990 to 2000 (see Tables 7 and 8).

TABLE 8

Private Universities in the 1990s: 10 Leaders in Academic Research (percent)

Institution	Average rating, 1995	Research share, 1999	Change, 1990–2000	Medical share, 1999[a]	Change, 1989–99	Faculty change, 1990–2000	Cost per student, 2000 ($)[b]
Massachusetts Institute of Technology	4.62	1.55	-0.62	0.05	0.05	-17	31,582
Harvard University	4.51	1.21	-0.33	0.42	-0.01	49	45,459
Stanford University	4.32	1.58	-0.49	0.75	-0.06	49	29,412
California Institute of Technology	4.29	0.78	0.05	0	0	2	34,192
Princeton University	4.28	0.46	-0.14	0	0	3	50,621
University of Chicago	4.27	0.60	-0.20	0.27	-0.05	78	24,689
Yale University	4.13	1.01	-0.21	0.58	0.04	44	37.850
Cornell University	3.97	1.46	0.64	0.46	-0.03	-24	26,545
Columbia University	3.84	1.03	-0.14	0.36	0.11	-22	24,071
University of Pennsylvania	3.78	1.42	0.21	0.65	0.04	-70	25,787

Note: Faculty totals from AAUP surveys, published annually in March issue of *Academe*. Medical faculty not included. Minnesota totals from university Office of Institutional Research and Reports, 1991–2000.
[a]Medical research in total share.
[b]1996$.

The growing weight of medical research in the academic research system. Medical research grew from 23 percent to 25 percent of the national total in the 1980s, and then rose to almost 30 percent in 2000. Medicine's gains in the 1990s, which belonged almost entirely to medical schools, strongly influence any numerical comparisons, and all the more so for private universities, where the proportion of medical research is nearly 40 percent.

The academic core and performance in research. Great differences exist among universities in capacity for research, as well as apparent differences in their willingness to use available capacity in ways that would optimize research. The strengthening of academic cores generally boosted research in the 1980s, but in the 1990s results were more variable. That is, the policies and actions of individual universities most likely played a greater role in the loss or gain of research share.

RESEARCH IN PRIVATE UNIVERSITIES

The thirty-three private universities in this study performed about 24 percent of academic research at the end of the 1990s. That figure was 3 percent less than a decade earlier, and 5 percent less than at the end of the 1970s. Put another way, in twenty years the principal private research universities ceded one-sixth of their relative research role, an amount that in 2000 represented roughly $1.5 billion. Compared with the public universities in this sample, average research expenditures at privates were only slightly lower. However, in private universities 38 percent of these funds were concentrated in medical sciences, compared with only 26 percent in the publics. During the 1990s the private universities maintained their activity in this growing segment of the research economy.

The erosion of research at private universities occurred outside of the medical centers. In fact, they steadily gave up 1 percent of the nonmedical research share every five years from 1979 to 1999. This was a curious development in a period of growing financial strength among most of these same institutions. Even more curious is the fact that erosion of research share was most severe among the academic and financial leaders.

The underperformance of private universities is confounded with the curse of the academic leaders. The institutions listed in Table 8 account for almost all of the share loss during the 1990s. The curse afflicted different leaders at different times. Caltech alone was stable throughout the 1980s and 1990s; but the University of Pennsylvania, the outlier for the 1990s, ceded one-quarter of its research share during the 1980s. Harvard experienced pronounced losses in the early 1980s; MIT, Columbia, and Penn in the late 1980s; Stanford, Yale, and Cornell in the early 1990s; and Chicago in all of those periods.

Given the wealth of these institutions, it would be difficult to attribute these losses to financial stringency, although belt-tightening occurred in the early years of each decade. For another set of institutions that experienced losses—Syracuse, RPI, and Rochester—financial constraints would appear to be a likely cause. No doubt internal factors could be isolated for each of these campuses that would help to explain these changes. Both Stanford and Yale, for example, experienced internal turmoil during the years of the most precipitous declines. But such factors occurred within a context where research performance and prestige were near optimal levels and universities found other missions more compelling. Princeton provides one example of shifting priorities toward research.

During the 1980s, Princeton faced the challenge of rebuilding departments in both biology and biochemistry.[38] It also resolved to establish a presence commensurate with its accustomed status in the key field of molecular biology. President William Bowen committed the university to major investments in both faculty and facilities. He advocated this cause to alumni donors, who normally had little appreciation for research, in order to garner the funds to construct the Lewis Thomas Laboratory. With this facility, Princeton was able to build the kind of accomplished team needed for cutting-edge genetic research. Still, according to their leading geneticist, the Princeton team and its new facility constituted the minimum scale needed for advanced genetics research.

Undertaking this kind of Big Science was uncharacteristic for Princeton.[39] Princeton also invested its own resources in improving its capacity in materials science and took advantage of state funding to construct a laboratory for photonics. These efforts were quickly reflected in Princeton's research share, which grew by 17 percent from 1984 to 1989. By the early 1990s, however, efforts of this kind were decidedly out of favor. Princeton leaders thought it inconceivable that similar initiatives might be contemplated given the new outlook. Princeton's research share accordingly drifted lower during the 1990s, ending the decade below its level in 1984.[40]

The early 1990s were the years of public attacks on university research, but probably more important was the rise in importance—for prestige and for financial health—of undergraduate education. Given this atmosphere, and the crucial significance of the selectivity sweepstakes for universities like Princeton, the fact that research was becoming less attractive financially may have been a secondary consideration. In the wake of the Stanford debacle, the federal government lowered the rates at which it reimbursed universities for indirect costs. Indirect cost reimbursements (ICR) play a crucial role in sustaining research at many universities, especially private ones, where these rates were highest.

The 1990s also saw hard-pressed federal agencies require more matching funds from universities for research projects.[41] In addition, the start-up costs for establishing and renovating scientific laboratories escalated. Furthermore, initiatives of the kind taken at Princeton chiefly benefited graduate students in the sciences (another expense) but had less visibility for enriching undergraduate education. The calculus of research includes many considerations beyond cash flow; but outside of the medical sciences it became less favorable in the early 1990s. Looking forward, planners could see only a massive federal deficit and a shrinking federal commitment to academic science.[42]

Of course, the leading private universities had no intention of abandoning research. Academic leadership was a point of pride and a necessity for upholding their international stature. But in the academic core, reputation was more vital than the amount of research dollars. The leading universities could continue to operate their scientific departments at something like their existing levels. When necessary, they had the means to hire the very best scientists to fill open slots. Thus they employed a strategy of hiring stars—paying ever-higher salaries to ensure eminent appointments—rather than enlarging departments and expanding research. For the dozen academic leaders in the private sector, professorial salaries were 22 percent higher in 2000 than salaries of their public counterparts. Moreover, full professors constituted fully 60 percent of the regular faculty at private universities, 54 percent at the publics.[43] This approach to hiring and salaries seems to have prevailed throughout much of the private university sector during the 1990s.

Developments in university health centers had little connection with the academic core. The private universities that gained research share during the 1990s did so principally in the field of medicine.

Duke is an interesting example. During the 1980s it invested heavily in its academic core and brilliantly magnified the impact of its new appointments by creating special research centers and institutes. It augmented its research share by 30 percent in the 1980s and then again in the 1990s. The growth in the latter period, however, occurred almost entirely in medicine.

Duke in the 1990s, unlike Princeton, sought to sustain at least some of the dynamism of its previous advance, but fear of looming financial con-

TABLE 9

Largest Research Gains by Private Universities, 1990–2000
(percent)

Institution	Research share, 2000	Gain, 1990–2000
Duke University	1.21	0.28
Washington University	1.22	0.26
University of Pennsylvania	1.46	0.21
Emory University	0.69	0.18
Vanderbilt University	0.58	0.10

straints caused it to assume a defensive posture. A comprehensive planning document drafted in 1994 for the new president, Nannerl O. Keohane, foresaw support for basic research declining even as the costs of science were growing. Accordingly, it recommended targeting efforts and resources on areas of "strength and programmatic opportunity" identified by an earlier task force.

In a more strongly worded recommendation, the report declared, "undergraduate education will have to become a demonstrably central concern." This restrictive stance toward research pertained to the academic core but did not apply to the Duke University Medical Center. There a vigorous program of applied and basic research was deemed necessary in order to participate in advances taking place in medical therapy. The report particularly advocated new forms of interdisciplinary research to probe "biological questions at the molecular and cellular levels." Also notable was an explicit commitment to technology transfer, "to enhance research funding [and] to bring the results of research directly to the market place."[44]

The development of research at Duke for the remainder of the decade was entirely in keeping with the university's stated intentions. It also well represented the divergent approaches adopted by private universities for their academic core and their medical centers.[45]

Elsewhere in the private sector only a handful of institutions increased their research share outside of medicine, largely in the biological sciences. In this highly competitive area the private universities held their own during the 1990s, performing just under one-quarter of the national total. Washington University in St. Louis and the University of Pennsylvania took the lead in this area, surpassing perennial leader Harvard. Washington University had viewed the financial landscape of the early 1990s much as Duke had, and drew many of the same conclusions. Its principal policy toward research was that tight funding would require the sharing of facilities.[46] Still, biological research grew vigorously on its medical campus, and the university by 2000 was more prosperous than it could have dreamed. But on the main campus undergraduate education remained the top priority.

Penn experienced similar financial prosperity, although its academic core appeared to shrink during the 1990s. Like Washington U., biological research was concentrated in Penn's enormous health complex. Unlike other private universities, Penn resolved in 1995 to "aggressively seek greater research opportunities," and specifically "to attract an increasing share of the available research dollars." It largely succeeded in meeting this strategic goal. It was the largest gainer of research share among the academic leaders (see Table 8), and almost all its gains accrued in the last half of the decade. The biological sciences (that is, without medicine) accounted for the entire increase. Its four health schools (medicine, dentistry, nursing, and veterinary science), as well as the School of Arts and Sciences, participated in this research thrust, which targeted genomics. The School of Medicine nevertheless made the greatest progress. Responsible for half of the university's research awards in 1990, it boasted two-thirds in 2000.[47]

With these partial exceptions, a general pattern is apparent. Private universities in the 1990s tended to be reluctant to expand their academic core, or at least to do so for the sake of enlarging scientific research. And, outside of medicine and biology, they apparently were reluctant to expand their research portfolio in areas very far removed from undergraduate instruction.

RESEARCH IN PUBLIC UNIVERSITIES

During the last two decades of the twentieth century the public universities in this study consistently performed just over half of all academic research (see Table 7). Medical research left a large footprint in the public sector too. During the 1990s the amount of medical research rose from 10 to 12 percentage points of its 51 percent share. But aside from this similarity, the dynamics of research appeared somewhat different from that in private universities. Outside of medicine, a tighter link seemed to exist in the public sector among research performance, financial condition, and developments in the academic core.

The curse of the academic leaders had less impact on the public universities. This was a change from the 1980s when the leading state universities of the Midwest and West either lost share or at best held their own.[48] In the 1990s, as many of the leaders gained significant amounts of research share as lost it (see Table 10). However, no single number can represent the roller coaster ride that these institutions experienced during the economic slump of the early 1990s and the subsequent recovery. When state politics and the

TABLE 10

Public Universities in the 1990s: 9 Leaders in Academic Research

Institution	Average rating, 1995	Research share, 2000	Change, 1990–2000	Medical share, 1999[a]	Change, 1989–99	Faculty change, 1990–2000	Cost per student, 2000[b]
University of California, Berkeley	4.52	1.75	0.23	0.23	0.14	–61	$20,522
University of California, San Diego	4.08	1.75	0.19	0.67	0.06	124	17,380
University of California, Los Angeles	3.92	1.80	0.17	1.04	0.18	143	19,357
University of Michigan	3.92	1.87	–0.16	0.59	0.03	129	21,205
University of Wisconsin	3.92	1.87	–0.18	0.57	–0.04	–209	16,346
University of Washington	3.78	1.79	0.18	0.77	0.29	–62	15,495
University of Illinois	3.75	1.26	–0.25	0.02	–0.03	–172	13,751
University of Texas	3.72	0.92	–0.53	0.03	0.01	–214	13,605
University of Minnesota	3.60	1.39	–0.50	0.55	–0.07	–134	20,285

Note: Faculty totals from AAUP surveys, published annually in March issue of *Academe*. Medical faculty not included. Minnesota totals from university Office of Institutional Research and Reports, 1991–2000.
[a] Medical research in total share.
[b] 1996$.

movement for student-centeredness are factored in, numerous individual stories emerge. In general, though, financial constraints early in the decade produced cutbacks in the academic core through mid-decade, which had negative effects on research performance.

The four universities that endured the largest loss of research share during the 1990s—Minnesota, Texas, Wisconsin, and Illinois (Urbana)—all experienced a prolonged erosion of their fiscal base. The early 1990s may have been the worst period, but these campuses seem to have been squeezed for resources throughout much of the 1980s and 1990s. The University of Texas calculated, for example, that its general funds budget grew in constant dollars by only 2.6 percent from 1985 to 2000.[49] The University of Minnesota deliberately reduced its undergraduate enrollment by 20 percent, a move that boosted revenues per student but did nothing for total revenues supporting the academic core. Under the kind of year-in and year-out pressure that these universities experienced, investments in academic strengthening become problematic, especially maintaining the quality of the faculty. The toll on the academic core was evident at these four schools in the loss of 729 regular faculty positions during the 1990s.

By 2001, all four institutions had frankly acknowledged this problem and were attempting to address it. The University of Illinois was able to augment its research capacity with several new facilities, built with combinations of public and private funds. It planned to augment its faculty as well. The university's research share hit a nadir around the mid-1990s, but was rising by decade's end.

For Wisconsin too, the leveraging of public and private funds produced an infusion of new investment capital in 2000, the first substantial increase in twenty years. That same year Wisconsin led the country in total research expenditures. Both Texas and Minnesota acknowledged their slippage in research strength and committed to plans for the new decade to reverse these trends, including significant additions to the faculty. In all these cases, the projected new hires were carefully targeted, in many instances for cross-disciplinary collaborations. This approach to the rebuilding of the academic core implies some degree of reshaping as well. By 2003, however, state budget deficits had put optimistic plans such as these on hold. The plans themselves spoke eloquently to the needs of public universities to rejuvenate sagging research roles; but increasingly they concluded instead that academic upgrading would have to be supported with private funds, particularly student tuition.[50]

The fiscal roller coaster of the 1990s had the steepest slopes at the University of California. The impact of the recession on state revenues caused the state's contribution to be cut by some 20 percent from 1990 to 1993. The total shortfall was estimated to be $900 million when measured against projected expenditures. Student fees were raised substantially and salaries were frozen. Still, half of the shortfall was met with permanent budget cuts, including a reduction of 5,000 employees across the nine campuses. Berkeley lost 245 regular faculty positions by 1995, and UCLA 164; both campuses also experienced a decline in research share. Beginning with the 1995–96 budget, these cuts began to be restored. Over the next six years, increasing state appropriations raised the base budget of the university (even as tuition increases were rolled back), and special appropriations provided additional funds for targeted programs.[51] The result was a surge of new blood into faculty ranks. Berkeley restored almost 200 faculty positions, and UCLA added more than 300. These new hires included both junior and senior scholars. This growth in faculty corresponded with notable increases in research share: 0.34 percentage points for Berkeley and 0.44 for UCLA in just six years (1994–2000).

The experience of the University of California demonstrates a strong link between research performance and the vitality of the academic core. This is particularly true at Berkeley, the undisputed academic leader of the public sector. The operative philosophy there has long been to build academic excellence first and then to allow faculty initiatives to determine the course of research.[52] Berkeley may epitomize the connection between the academic core and research. Indeed, this is a notable pattern for the birthplace of ORUs. In fact, the centers and institutes at Berkeley tend more to serve than to structure the research interests of faculty. Conversely, the establishment of new centers depends principally on faculty research agendas. Although half of research expenditure at Berkeley is funneled through ORUs, research ultimately depends quite heavily on the initiative of the regular faculty.[53]

In retrospect, the fiscal crisis of the early 1990s at the University of California had a more salutary outcome than the persistent erosion of funding had in other states. The early retirement of senior faculty created openings for new talent when budgets again began to rise.[54] And well-chosen new faculty apparently proved a tonic for research and scholarship. The pattern of erosion found in other states, in contrast, caused small losses each year, met more often than not through coping strategies and budgetary juggling. All too often these tactics meant appointments postponed and investments deferred. The cumulative effects could be just as grave as the California crisis, but did not seem to carry the implicit obligation to redress at least some of the damage caused by the dramatic cuts there.

Underlying the circumstances of these two patterns, however, is a more fundamental issue of a state's commitment to academic quality. This commitment has remained extraordinarily strong in California, where citizens and politicians expect to have the nation's best public university, and where higher education was partially protected from the budget crisis of the early 2000s. In most states the feedback loop for reinforcing quality stops in the state legislature. This general lack of public support for academic quality highlights the significance of private sources of support. The University of Michigan, with comparatively little help from the state, has generated the private resources to buttress both academic quality and research.

During the 1990s the University of Michigan seized the leadership mantle in academic research. After 1990 it was the only university able to claim 2 percent of total research, and it began the next decade with its research share again approaching that level. Neither great size nor high quality has been a curse in Ann Arbor. This was not accidental. Michigan has pursued one of the most proactive policies in expanding its research capacity.

The explanation for Michigan's research performance must begin with its notable financial strength, which is based on aggressive privatization. In the mid-1980s it resolved to compensate for depressed state appropriations by tapping private sources. Tuition revenues, which were half of state appropriations in 1980, exceeded them by 40 percent by 2000. Michigan implemented a high-tuition/high-aid strategy, but by shifting much of the financial burden to out-of-state students it raised net tuition revenues per student far above the in-state sticker price. In addition, the university accomplished the first billion-dollar campaign by a public institution. Michigan attained the highest per-student spending level in the public sector (see Appendix A), with 56 percent coming from tuition and endowment.[55] Moreover, Michigan used its wealth to bolster its academic core. It has maintained a vital and productive faculty through four consistent practices: insisting on academic excellence in faculty appointments; paying the highest salaries in the public sector (outside of the University of California); steadily expanding the faculty by consistently filling vacancies and selectively creating new positions; and reallocating faculty positions on the basis of both teaching needs and research opportunities.[56] The academic core at Michigan has been admirably equipped for research and scholarship, but the research role has been stimulated further by an emphasis on interdisciplinary centers and institutes.

Michigan's tradition of interdisciplinary ORUs dates from the postwar period, but it resolved in the 1980s to create more such units to accommodate the increasingly interdisciplinary drift of academic research. A $5 million grant from the Kellogg Foundation in 1986 established the permanent Presidential Initiative Fund to seed research in emergent, high-risk/high-reward areas, with particular emphasis on cross-disciplinary collaboration. This original initiative elicited an outpouring of faculty initiatives, and was soon supplemented by the larger Strategic Research Initiatives program under the vice president for research. Together, these programs provided between $5 and 10 million each year to seed and stimulate innovative research. Some of the most conspicuous results were the founding of new research units—"hubs for collaborative work," as they were dubbed. By 2000, Michigan counted some 160 such research units, more than half established in the 1990s.

In that decade the university also adopted, and then modified, a form of decentralized budgeting that in effect allocated income to the units generating it. Quite simply, this system put research units under great pressure to get grants. They may have received assistance from the president, provost, or vice president for research when established, or for special needs, but to persist and to thrive they must successfully compete for external support. These units are allowed to keep their indirect cost reimbursements (ICR), further enhancing incentives and providing resources for internal initiatives. Research at Michigan thus depends heavily on ORUs, which provide extraordinary resources and opportunities for core faculty to collaborate. The Michigan structure combines the advantages of central direction in guiding and stimulating research, faculty determination of actual research projects, and the entrepreneurialism of resource-dependent research units.

The Michigan scheme seeks to integrate the research role in two areas: across colleges and disciplines, and with the educational enterprise. A recent example of this approach is the Life Sciences Initiative. Although many universities have reorganized to cope with the revolution in biology, Michigan's approach combines planning, strategic investment, and integration in a distinctive way. In 1998, President Lee Bollinger appointed a Life Sciences Commission to determine how the university might secure a leading position in the revolutionary developments that were transforming this field. In accordance with their recommendations, the Regents committed $200 million to form the Life Sciences Institute, the centerpiece of the new initiative. The institute focuses on pathbreaking areas in which Michigan can establish leadership: biocomplexity, biotechnology and translational research, complex genomics, chemical and structural biology, and cognitive neurosciences. The institute is intended as an intellectual and institutional bridge between the medical school and departments in the College of Literature, Sciences, and the Arts. Each of the thirty new faculty has a 50 percent appointment in an academic department, and all are expected to develop undergraduate courses in their fields. The initiative also includes the Program in Life Sciences, Values, and Society, which aims to focus the attention of nonbiological scholars on issues arising from the biological revolution. In total, the initiative represents a large investment in future biological and medical research, structured to have an impact on the entire university.[57]

Michigan's remarkable success in fostering research is ultimately attributable to deliberate administrative leadership. The president for most of this period was James Duderstadt (1988–96), probably the most radical leader of a major university in the 1990s. Trained as an engineer, Duderstadt became convinced that the modern university ultimately needed to be reengineered to adapt to changing times. With this posture, he was not reluctant to implement reforms. He apparently approved of his leadership style being characterized as "fire, ready, aim."[58] He presided over the aggressive privatization of the university's finances and foresaw that trend carrying much further. He tinkered with the Presidential Initiatives Fund until it worked properly. And he introduced responsibility-centered management, which also required subsequent adjustments. But he believed in adaptation. In his most visionary statement, he described the university as "*a loosely coupled adaptive system*, with a growing complexity as its various components respond to changes in its environment."[59] This vision, however, may have been too far ahead for some—and quite possibly wrong. He was pressured into resigning in 1995 (effective June 1996) and a turnover of the top administrative leadership ensued.[60] The rhetoric became more subdued, but the operating principles remained intact. As the Life Sciences Initiative would indicate, the university continued to be a very dynamic adaptive system, committed to the several goals of its multiple missions, especially research.

The cases described thus far suggest a causal link between the prosperity of the academic core and growth in research. These universities can all be counted among the academic leaders, who must spend heavily to maintain the quality of their faculty and conditions conducive to research. They also maintain multiple centers of research, which collectively may reflect the financial health of the institution more than developments in the research system that might buffet smaller performers. The example of the University of Michigan clouds this clear link somewhat because of its extensive use of ORUs to broaden and invigorate the research role. An examination of UC San Diego most likely would have detected a similar pattern. Thus there can be no assurance that incremental changes in the academic core and research performance are closely related at all universities, or that research performance cannot be enhanced by other means. The variety of patterns elsewhere in the public sector indicates the subtlety of the interaction between academic units and organized research.

For most public universities the 1990s brought prolonged budgetary pressures. Not until the end of the decade was it again possible to contemplate a significant advancement of the university mission. As a consequence, few universities were able to strengthen the academic core appreciably before 1996 (see Chapter 2) or, by implication, further research by the same means. Accordingly, public universities often looked beyond the academic core to bolster the research role.

The pattern seen in private universities of expanding medical research masking stagnation or decline in research elsewhere in a university was present in the public sector as well. Among the leaders, the University of Washington exemplified this situation, with share gains in medicine accounting for more than the entire gain for total R&D (see Table 10). During the 1980s, UW exhibited all the symptoms of the leader's curse, consistently ceding research share. However, in the 1990s it managed to stabilize its research role, and particularly augment federal funding. UW received the largest amount of federal funding throughout the decade. In FY2000 nearly two-thirds of those funds were from NIH. Internally, more than half of all research awards belonged to its health-related departments. UW also strove during the 1990s to strengthen ties with industry and economic development. A relatively late starter in technology transfer, it nevertheless achieved notable success, largely in health-related industries (see Table 11). By the end of the decade UW was sixth in research funding from industry and eighth in income from patent licenses. It also claimed credit for spawning 100 new companies.[61] Yet funding for the academic core remained a problem, largely due to legislative preferences for tax reduction, punitive performance measures, and low tuition. Adjusted for inflation, spending per student was lower in 1999 than in 1991, and the size of the faculty declined during the decade as well.[62] A similar pattern of development was evident at the University of Pittsburgh, where tight budgets and a steady state for most of the university did not preclude robust expansion of medical research. As in the private sector, the research role at some public universities was increasingly confined to the medical school.[63]

The University of Colorado at Boulder (UCB) presents a stark example of the research role thriving despite precarious conditions in an underfunded academic core. The largest source of revenue for the university, after federal research grants, is tuition from nonresident students. The state not only provides the most meager appropriations to a public university of any in this study, but it applied a fiscal tourniquet in the form of the Taxpayers Bill of Rights, which caps increases in revenues while adjusting appropriations so that any *decreases* become permanent. The state has contemplated changes in governance that might give the university more autonomy—and more leeway to further privatize its sources of support.[64] However, UCB's funding base has been the weakest among public members of the Association of American Universities (AAU): its accreditation evaluation in 2000 found the "dire status of basic state support" to be the greatest risk to UCB's continuation as an outstanding research university. This penury particularly threatened the recruitment and retention of excellent faculty. Maintaining competitive salaries meant cutting corners elsewhere. Most new hires, for example, are made at the junior level; and UCB had the highest percentage of part-time faculty among AAU publics.[65] How then did the university manage to increase its academic rating and expand its research share?[66]

The UCB houses a complex of federally supported laboratories that study the sciences of the earth, the air, and the sky—from environmental studies to astrophysics. The largest of these cumbersomely named units are the Cooperative Institute for Research in Environmental Sciences, supported by the National Oceanic and Atmospheric Administration; JILA (originally the Joint Institute for Laboratory Astrophysics) sponsored by the National Institute of Standards and Technology, one of four institutes dedicated to the physics of atmospheres, planets, and space; and the NASA-sponsored Center for Limb Atmospheric Sounding. The units in the earth-air-sky complex by themselves account for half of the research funding at UCB. In addition, the university has distinguished research programs in the biological sciences, psychology, and engineering, as well as more centers and institutes to accommodate them. Most of these ORUs are interdisciplinary in nature and report to the vice-chancellor for research. Most also look to the federal government for their funding.[67]

Directly or indirectly, 90 percent of research funding at UCB is derived from federal sources. Dependence on federal agencies has generally been antithetical to growth in research funding in the era of privatization, but UCB has worked on expanding fields. The opening of NASA's Limb Center in 1997 by itself accounted for half of the increase in research share. Moreover, the agencies that support these centers are scientific patrons, dedicated to furthering understanding of scientific questions of immense complexity. The laboratories conduct basic research that is readily integrated with academic departments.

At Berkeley, ORUs function largely to further the research agendas of the faculty, but at UCB this relationship tends to be reversed. The laboratories have the resources and the personnel to set the research agenda, and this welter of scientific activity stimulates and enriches the academic core. There are several key features to this relationship. Although the university is bedeviled by state interference, the ORUs essentially enjoy free rein. They are allowed to retain their ICR, and their research personnel can be principal investigators on grants. These units thus have the freedom and the incentive to seek additional research support. Conversely, institute faculty members have appointments in academic departments where they can teach or buy out their time. The result is a mutually advantageous reciprocal relationship between ORUs and departments—the institutes providing excellent facilities and support for research and the departments supplying graduate students and faculty to complement these scientific endeavors. The federally funded laboratories provide UCB with far more research and academic quality than the citizens of Colorado have been willing to support.[68]

In neighboring Utah, the flagship university has faced similar financial limitations, for different reasons. With half the population of Colorado, and less than half the economic base, Utah was still able to provide the University of Utah with an appropriation 150 percent larger than UCB's, for a comparable number of students. But competitive conditions have kept tuition low at the Salt Lake City campus. As a result, the tuition ratios are mirror opposites: 71 percent tuition at UCB versus 30 percent at Utah. But the end result is similar: Utah laments that it has the lowest funding base among AAU public universities *with medical schools*. It has nevertheless maintained its research share in the 1990s, largely by relying on ORUs.

Organized research at the University of Utah presents a stark contrast to UCB. Instead of large federally funded laboratories, Utah has a myriad of mostly small centers and institutes, perhaps 200 in all. This pattern seems the result of a laissez-faire policy toward research that began in the 1980s. Until then, the state of Utah claimed 70 percent of ICR. When this practice was ended, these funds stayed with the university and were used to enhance the research mission. With greater incentives and explicit encouragement from the president, the Utah faculty became more entrepreneurial. In particular, they sought research opportunities in the private sector, which tended to breed a panoply of targeted ORUs, largely outside the academic core. Many of these are located in the medical school. Others have a decidedly practical slant, like the Energy and Geoscience Institute, which studies petroleum basins and reservoirs and geothermal energy, or the Center for the Simulation of Accidental Fires and Explosions ($1.7 million in FY1999).[69]

The research mission at Utah appears more distant from the academic core than at the universities already discussed. It plays a crucial role, of course, in the university's nationally oriented graduate programs.[70] And undergraduates too are offered opportunities to participate in research. However, the university's research portfolio seems to be chiefly oriented toward bringing income to the institution, outlets for faculty expertise, service to the community, and economic development. Pursuit of these worthy goals tends to encourage relationships with the private sector. In the 1980s and 1990s, Utah became far more closely integrated with the Salt Lake City community and economy. Its research park is one of the oldest and most successful in the country.[71]

A state program to stimulate university-industry research was established in 1986, and a decade later it was providing support for eleven centers, although the vast bulk of funding came from industry. Links with industry accelerated in the 1990s in the form of spin-off companies, patents and licenses, and considerable growth in industrial support for research.[72] This closer involvement with the economy has in all likelihood aided the university's fund-raising efforts. It has been unusually successful, considering its economic base, in garnering donations, most of which have been designated for capital purposes.

In sum, faced with at best stable levels of enrollment and base funding, the University of Utah has sought to expand in the relatively unfettered areas of research and economic service. By fostering such opportunities through the formation of ORUs, and encouraging entrepreneurial activity on the part of faculty, the university fashioned an autonomous research role. This approach was not without problems. Giving faculty a free hand and encouragement to make external connections has meant ceding some university control over faculty activities. The payoffs are nevertheless clear in the form of research activity, private support, and contributions to economic development. For this reason, Utah's path may be the more common one in the public sector, where the majority of universities have wrestled with the incubus of financial constraint and the responsibility for public service.

Trends in Academic Research

The preceding discussion has somewhat artificially resolved developments in academic research into three foci—the academic core, organized research units, and medical centers. In any actual university these organizational pieces interpenetrate one another. Medical schools have academic cores as well as institutes; core faculty members are usually crucial figures in the operations of ORUs. However, this trifocal view brings greater clarity to a disorderly subject by isolating parts of the university that operate according to quite different dynamics. The academic core is linked with the teaching role and the base funding of universities. An autonomous research role is beholden to external patrons. And medical centers are driven by one unique segment of the research economy as well as by the financial imperatives of health care delivery. The university, to which they all feign obeisance, wisely treats each differently.

When individual institutions are considered, as the preceding examples show, the picture begins to blur again. Context plays a large role in determining how each institution reacts to conditions affecting research. Substantial differences were noted between private and public universities, between academic leaders and the rank and file, between the wealthy and the impecunious. Thus "trends" may have quite disparate impacts. It may be more accurate to think in terms of "vectors," that is, forces pushing in particular directions. Vector forces may or may not affect research on a given campus: countervailing forces may be stronger, or exposure may be minimal. Hence, although vectors represent fundamental movements in the shaping of academic research, their impact may only be perceptible in certain types of institutions.

The joint production of teaching and research—of student and faculty learning—defines the essence of the modern university. Accordingly, more than one administrator interviewed for this study suggested that the most direct way to increase research was to hire more faculty. New faculty, presumably of the right sort, ought to invigorate and expand an institution's research performance. Through most of the 1990s, however, this course was seldom taken. In the first part of the decade there were good reasons: neither student numbers nor financial conditions warranted expansion. But in the later years both of these conditions changed. Yet the total number of faculty at research universities scarcely budged.[73] At private universities, the number of regular faculty grew by less than 1 percent from 1990 to 1996; at public universities the sliver of growth was smaller (0.6 percent; see Figures 11 and 12). Yet the explanations are different for the two sectors.

Private universities by the mid-1990s had the financial means to expand their faculties, but consciously chose not to do so. Apparently, their intense preoccupation with undergraduates did not include providing these students with more teachers. In fact, market forces largely encouraged this behavior, as seen in Chapter 3. But this restrictive posture was most likely related to their failure to expand research share. The only private universities to augment their research role significantly did so almost entirely in their medical schools.

Public universities, in contrast, faced financial constraints, often severe, that did not abate until near the end of the decade. Their fluctuating fortunes suggested at least circumstantial evidence of a relationship between financial health, faculty numbers, and research performance. Universities that were able, with improved funding, to enlarge the academic core generally gained research share as well. For the majority, however, this course was not feasible. An alternative was to expand research in health centers or organized research units. Ironically, as conditions improved in the public sector, competition seems to have heated up, with some unwelcome consequences. During the most difficult years of the 1990s, maintaining faculty salaries in the public sector became an increasing problem. Salary compression (the failure of salaries of continuing faculty to match market increases) and the widening disadvantage to private universities made public faculties more vulnerable to outside offers. But few faculty were hired in those years. By 2000 that situation had changed. Although faculty payrolls were healthier, public universities now found the competition real and damaging. At times they had to cannibalize positions in order to free funds with which to match outside offers. The challenge to maintain faculty quality became more difficult, especially for universities that were still struggling to regain their financial bearings.

Political pressures for student-centeredness did nothing to enhance the academic core. Academic leaders like the Universities of California and Michigan seemed able to transcend these pressures. Michigan, in particular, stayed ahead of the curve, implementing student-centered reforms on its own initiative and its own terms.[74] Elsewhere, though, the student-centered orientation of the 1990s claimed its share of scarce resources. Administrative energy and institutional investments were skewed toward these ends. Furthermore, new living-learning communities and teaching and advising centers were staffed with nonacademic appointments. Such developments were but a small part of an apparently implacable trend in employment that made the academic core an ever smaller portion of the university organization. Even less welcome has been the burgeoning use of part-time and off-tenure-track teachers, driven largely by budgetary pressure. The creation of a separate cadre of instructors who only teach further separates teaching and research.[75]

The reluctance of universities to hire regular faculty appears so pervasive that it must have deeper causes. In all likelihood, expense and flexibility, as well as current trends, are factors. The faculty payroll may be the most inflexible portion of a university budget (save debt). Hiring costs are considerable, particularly in the sciences, where start-up costs have risen exponentially. But more daunting is the commitment to tenure, which usually means that an individual will propound his or her specialized field for another two or three decades. The granting of tenure, which was once a formidable barrier, now appears to have become far more routine, although for good reasons. Candidates for junior faculty positions have been well trained and are in abundant supply. Beginning junior faculty members now typically arrive with publications and postdoctoral research experience to their credit. In addition, universities have established mentoring programs and other forms of assistance to make the achievement of tenure more likely. In 1998, 78 percent of regular faculty at universities in this study had tenure, up from 74 percent in 1990.[76]

Put simply, if additional classroom instruction is needed, adding regular faculty positions is an expensive solution—and one that could jeopardize the future adaptability of the institution. However, keeping a static academic core has liabilities too. It requires the same number of faculty to bear the burdens of conducting and coordinating the university's expanding knowledge-based activities. Such is certainly the case with research.

In a crude sense, the increasing separation of research from the academic core would seem to be an indisputable trend. Sources of funding in the university research economy have come increasingly from patrons interested in usable knowledge, be they congressmen or industrialists. The volume of research has continued to grow relative to the academic core, just as the number of researchers has increased more rapidly than university faculty. Organized research units have proliferated, and, where this figure is reported, they typically perform half or more of an institution's research. The more closely this type of research is scrutinized, however, the more difficult it becomes to characterize it as a dichotomy. ORUs serve as vehicles to advance an individual faculty member's research agenda; as captive laboratories of external sponsors; as providers of scientific services for faculty and nonfaculty researchers alike; as administrative structures for huge scientific instruments; and especially recently, as repositories of research technologies. Three kinds of ORUs are characteristic of the current era: interdisciplinary centers, which are intended to enhance and channel faculty research, in part by appealing to patrons; scientific institutes, which have been created to house important research technologies; and consumer-oriented centers, which chiefly serve the needs of sponsors. Each embodies somewhat different facets of the autonomous research mission.

Large numbers of ORUs, often bearing the name of centers, are intended to serve the research needs of faculty. The prototype for these might be the area studies centers established in the postwar era.[77] The current driver for the establishment of such centers is a similar desire to bring together faculty members from different disciplinary backgrounds for collaborative work. Universities have become much more proactive in pursuing this end. They recognize that funding for research has increasingly favored cross-disciplinary investigations and that departments or schools, left on their own, do little to foster such projects. The general approach has been to encourage the formation of interdisciplinary organizations, particularly by linking them with new appointments. The University of Wisconsin, for example, as it restored lost faculty positions, sought to create "clusters" of faculty who would focus on topics from different disciplinary perspectives. Proposals for potential clusters originated with departmental faculty, and the university chose the most promising of them for funding.[78] Similar approaches have been implemented at many universities.[79] Although not all universities establish dedicated research centers, some formal structure is required to provide continuity for such work. The striking feature of this pattern is that the research economy—developments at the frontiers of science and the demand for such knowledge—has injected cross-disciplinary topics into the curriculum and the academic core.

A second stimulus for the creation of ORUs has been the enormous advances in the technologies that undergird research. The increasing scale, cost, and sophistication of scientific instrumentation now often requires separate structures and dedicated staff.[80] This phenomenon is not new. The federally funded particle accelerators in high-energy physics, for example, created a similar situation in which the instrumentation determined what experiments could be conducted and what questions could be answered. Big Biology encompasses a much larger scope of activities, and a wider funding base as well. Universities seriously committed to this field nearly all boast a genomics institute in some form. It typically provides services to researchers in all departments of the life sciences.

Such units go far beyond the routine testing and measuring that the notion of service function used to imply. The technology now drives research by defining the possible. These institutes often appoint their own faculty, who are charged with extending the technology as much as utilizing it. The W. M. Keck Center for Computational and Functional Genetics at the University of Illinois, to take one example, is expected to lead rather than follow the research questions of biologists throughout the university. In keeping with these new realities, the Life Sciences Initiative at the University of Michigan has defined its objectives around "core technologies" rather than subject matter.[81]

Big Biology may be the most spectacular manifestation of technology leading research, but hardly the only one. In a somewhat analogous development, centers for the study of nanoscale science and engineering have been constructed or planned at universities across the country. The federal government promoted the enormous long-range potential of these related fields through the National Nanotechnology Initiative. Nanoscale research and engineering requires expensive facilities that include clean rooms, vibration-free buildings, and scanning-tunneling electron microscopes. Universities possess the expertise and facilities to dominate this field, garnering roughly two-thirds of nanotechnology grants.[82]

These research units constitute enormous investments that require special efforts to finance. A pooling of public, private, and university funds seems to be the most feasible approach, particularly in state universities. In the case of nanotechnology, several states have made investments as well to ensure that their universities will benefit from the National Initiative. But leveraging has been employed in many fields.

Illinois successfully pooled funding sources to enlarge an already well equipped infrastructure. The $80 million Post-Genomics Institute was made possible by economic development funds from the state, special faculty lines from the state Board of Higher Education, and funds raised by the university. In similar fashion, a $100 million facility for information technology was funded nearly equally by the federal National Center for Supercomputer Applications, an alumni donation, and a state contribution. Both of these facilities are closely associated with separate research parks—one for IT and one for biotechnology—so that the research technologies will not only stimulate academic research, but results will be translated into firms and products as well.

The Life Sciences Initiative at the University of Michigan is another recipient of public, private, and university funding in excess of $100 million. The University of Wisconsin too has rejuvenated its research infrastructure through leveraged public and private funds. In one of the largest of these initiatives, the University of California in 2000 announced state funding of $100 million each, with a required 2:1 match, for three institutes focused on research technologies important for the state's economic development (nanoscience, biotechnology, and wireless technologies).

These colossal projects have several implications for academic research. Paradoxically, they are manifestations of an autonomous research mission, in that their impetus comes from harnessing an emerging research technology and their justification invariably includes economic development. Yet they are essential for keeping both research and instruction abreast of advancing scientific frontiers. In this respect, once again, the research mission appears to be leading the academic core. The National Nanotechnology Initiative aims to inspire curriculum in this area at participating universities; more locally, the Duke Center for Advanced Photonics and Communications Systems includes an undergraduate certificate program in photonics and cross-disciplinary courses in communications.

Financially, large facilities for research technologies are beyond the reach of most universities. A few private universities have undertaken projects of this magnitude, but for public universities the only feasible means of accumulating sufficient capital is to combine public, private, and often university resources. But this arrangement affects the character of the projects. Attracting private capital, and even more so selling the economic development rationale to the state, requires that these facilities promise payoffs through technology transfer.

Finally, these state-of-the-art facilities should occupy a dominant position in their respective fields for years to come. Barring radical changes in the research economy, the scientists at these institutes will possess superb settings to advance their fields; and they should likewise be able to win the grants needed to support this research. Does this mean that a concentration of academic research is likely to ensue, perhaps reversing the dispersion that has been the dominant pattern? This development has been predicted for molecular biology.

Three forces have been hypothesized as driving a concentration of research. First is the inherent nature of Big Biology. Large teams of researchers are needed for gene sequencing, gene expression, proteomics, and bioinformatics. In a science like biology there will always be a place for descriptive projects on a smaller scale, but the cutting edge of the revolution in all likelihood will occur in large-scale operations—megacenters of biological research. Second, the financial requirements, the limited number of patrons, and the competition for top scientists all dictate that only a few megacenters are possible. Third, increasing returns to scale in Big Biology will ensure that private capital gravitates to the megacenters where the cutting-edge science is being done. In the new era of patenting, spin-off firms, and other deals, these would not be trifling sums. Hence the megacenters, in addition to substantial grant money from NIH, should have ready access to private capital. Enhanced creativity in such settings might also bring increasing intellectual returns to scale. The intellectual ferment produced by this conjuncture of academic and industrial talent ought to provide fertile spawning beds for the most significant—and profitable—new ideas.[83] These organizational effects are discussed in the next chapter, but recent data seem to support the notion of concentration.

Biomedical research data indeed support these hypotheses. Megacenters are not only growing larger, but also growing faster than the rest of the field. Table 11 combines funding for medical and biological sciences. Together they constituted 49 percent of academic R&D in 2000, up 4 percentage points from 1996. Academic R&D, against which these shares are measured, grew by 30 percent in current dollars during these years, so a university that maintained its share would actually have expanded research even more. Yet the eight of nine universities with shares of biomedical research greater than 1 percent of total academic R&D ($300 million) all exceeded this pace. Institutions in this group on average increased their share by 12 percent. Of the five that exceeded this rate, four registered larger gains in the smaller sector of biological sciences, which probably means they are leading advances in the new biology. This development is particularly noteworthy in light of the trend of dispersion of research share at the expense of large performers. Moreover, all of these institutions appear to be active in

TABLE 11

Universities Performing More Than 1 Percent of Biomedical Research, 2000

Institution	Medsciences share	Biosciences share	Change, 1996–2000	Licensing, 1999 (million $)	Percent of licensing $ in the life sciences
University of California, San Francisco	1.25	0.20	0.11	80.9[a]	66.0[a]
Johns Hopkins University	0.87	0.33	0.00	10.5	99.7
University of California, Los Angeles	1.05	0.18	0.19	80.9[a]	66.0[a]
University of Washington	0.81	0.38	0.11	27.9	80.0
University of Pennsylvania	0.67	0.45	0.19	3.1	85.3
Duke University	0.78	0.23	0.15	1.6	
Washington University	0.56	0.52	0.24	7.1	
Baylor College of Medicine	0.54	0.58	0.29	12.5	98.4
University of Wisconsin	0.61	0.41	0.09	18.0	75.1

[a]University of California system totals.

the commercialization of biotechnology. All except Duke were among the top twenty-five recipients of income from patent licenses, and Duke was the largest recipient of research funding from industry, chiefly from clinical trials.

Biomedical sciences encompass all manner of investigations, including large amounts of clinical research. The trend toward concentration nevertheless suggests that pathbreaking research associated with molecular biology has become increasingly capital intensive. Universities traditionally sought capital principally through donations or resorted to borrowing only for revenue-generating projects, but the flow of revenue from the commercialization of research is relatively small in comparison with these needs.[84] Raising the large sums needed for new, state-of-the-art institutes necessitates institutional commitment. Universities that made such commitments, notably, Duke, Penn, and Washington U., each of which resolved to enlarge biomedical research, registered some of the largest gains, particularly in biology.

The ability of universities to incorporate into their structure institutes for the most advanced research technologies—or conversely, the choice of American society to place these facilities in its leading universities—is a key development of the current era. It is also a partial answer to the question posed earlier in this chapter: how can research universities keep pace with the changing character of the research economy? The existence of large, capital-intensive centers for the most sophisticated research technologies is a crucial factor in keeping academic research intellectually vital, and vital to the scientific needs of American society. Moreover, having these facilities attached to universities guarantees that society will have access to their findings, commercialization notwithstanding. This condition in fact provides another part of that answer. Universities have greatly modified their practices in the current era to meet the needs of the users of research. This consideration relates to the third dimension of the autonomous research mission, that of serving the consumers of research.

The autonomous research mission in its contemporary form developed after World War II primarily to serve the requirements of research for the federal government, more specifically the defense establishment. These agencies wanted the access to academic expertise they had enjoyed during the war, often on a permanent basis. ORUs were the institutional form that accommodated both parties. Faculty members might lead and participate in these units to varying degrees, but permanent research scientists performed the bulk of the research needed by the agencies. The graduate students of participating faculty might also benefit from the facilities and the research opportunities they presented. Institutes of this type became a common feature of research universities, not only for defense research, but also for agriculture, natural resources, and transportation, to mention only the more generic areas. Overall, universities derive somewhat narrow academic benefits in the form of research equipment and research opportunities for selected faculty and students at the sponsors' expense.

The distinguishing feature of the current era has been the proliferation of this kind of consumer-oriented ORU linked with industry. Such arrangements have long existed, but privatization and policies designed to encourage technology transfer caused them to multiply. This topic is part of a much larger subject, the complex of relationships between universities and the private economy that have developed since 1980. University-industry research centers are accordingly discussed in that context in the next chapter. They have been a salient feature of university research in the current era and one broadly consistent with larger developments.

The central paradox of research universities in the 1990s was the relative stagnation of the academic core and the burgeoning vitality of the research mission. The first was aggravated by the preoccupation with undergraduate education and a suspicion, bordering on disdain, of academic research. Breathtaking advances in science and technology impelled academic research forward, most conspicuously the revolution in molecular biology, but also transformational advances in information technology, medicine, and materials science. While this paradox suggests a separation between teaching and research in universities, the realities have been far more subtle.

The stagnation of the academic core had different causes in public and private universities. For public universities, state fiscal constraints were combined with an inherent reluctance of state legislatures to invest in academic quality. Private universities faced market disincentives to increase undergraduate or graduate enrollments, and thus tended to cap their faculty size. Public universities possessed considerable incentive to overcome their situation, both because they favored expanding research for its own sake and because they did not want to lose ground to their private rivals. Privatization has been the most feasible escape route from this predicament, best exemplified by the University of Michigan. The generation of private revenues became the means for building the academic quality that states refused to support. The path to a revitalization of research was no different. The large investments necessary for leadership in research were only possible by leveraging public, private, and institutional funds. Thus the academic core remained somewhat constrained in comparison with the demands placed on it, but the research mission was able to prosper on campuses where this took place.

Private universities, enjoying unprecedented prosperity, seemingly faced less need for major additional investments in research. However, to stand still in the dynamic scientific environment of the 1990s meant falling behind. Medical schools felt this pressure acutely; and a few private universities consciously sought to gain even more ground. The means for furthering research turned out to be much the same as in the public sector: investing in new technologies that would complement existing capabilities in the academic core. Funding arrangements varied, but the economic boom of the decade's end produced enormous fortunes and generous donors. Most important, by the end of the 1990s, many private universities had made renewed commitments to their research missions.

The changed orientation toward research was most evident among the academic leaders. Nearly all of the leading public universities either began major enhancements of their research role or announced the intention to do so. Among private leaders, Yale began the new millennium with the most spectacular commitment: $1 billion in new buildings, renovations, and appointments to be divided evenly between the medical school and science and engineering. Planners at Duke now saw research technologies as a top priority, intending to leverage "several hundreds of millions of dollars" of university funds for "strengthening such high-priority areas as photonics and genomics."[85] When Princeton in 2001 chose Shirley M. Tilghman, the director of the Institute for Integrative Genomics, to be the university's new president, one could only conclude that Princeton was no longer chary of initiatives in science.

One reason for these developments was the remarkable advances in science and the increasing competition for leadership. However, it is also relevant that the economics of investments in research technologies became more attractive as well.

The new institutes for research technologies that were built or promised have the potential to reconfigure research on campus. Perfecting and advancing these technologies is a scientific challenge in itself, requiring the specific assignment of faculty, postdocs, research staff, and graduate students. But the technologies themselves have ramifications in two directions. They will be used by and interact with basic research in other fields in the university, thus powerfully aiding academic development. And they will have applications to commercial technologies that may take the form of spin-off companies, patent licensing, or research partnerships. Such units consequently promise a future upstream income in the form of research grants, as well as downstream revenues from successful commercialization. Relations with the private economy are thus inherent to the planning, financing, and operations of these research facilities. In this light, the relationship of the contemporary university with industry is not a separate issue: it is central to its current development.

CHAPTER FIVE

Universities, Industry, and Economic Development

T HE SURGE IN research relationships between universities and industry that began around 1980 passed through several phases.[1] It was originally propelled by an ideological interpretation of the existing economic predicament. The persistent weakness in the economic competitiveness of American industry coexisted with a strong system of academic research that allegedly failed to convey its findings to the commercial realm. To remedy this, steps were taken at the federal level to encourage greater interaction between academic and industrial R&D—to facilitate what began to be called technology transfer. One of the most fateful of these steps was the Bayh-Dole Act of 1980, which gave universities ownership of patents arising from federally funded research grants. The blending of academic and commercial realms was swept along by the cresting wave of the biological revolution. Nevertheless, within universities opponents of ties with industry fiercely denounced this trend, raising fears of secrecy, conflict of interest, distortion of research agendas, misuse of graduate assistants, and more generally apprehension about the proper separation of private and public resources and benefits. These serious concerns required clarification. However, even as policies began to be formulated for the more tractable of these matters, university-industry interaction accelerated in the mid-1980s.

On campuses, it soon became clear that critics of industry were not the same individuals who had research ties with firms. The debate became increasingly disconnected from actual developments. The most decisive influence probably came from government. Programs to encourage and, more important, to subsidize technology transfer were enacted by the National Science Foundation and by many states. The most important of these supported the establishment of centers for cooperative research. Given such an unambiguous signal, university leaders leaped onto this bandwagon. By the end of the decade, nearly every major research university had established or reorganized an office to patent discoveries emanating from campus research; and most developed formal channels to encourage university-inspired businesses with business incubators, research parks, and equity participation. All these efforts had a palpable effect: during the early 1980s rising levels of industrial R&D were the direct cause of growth in industrially sponsored academic research, but after mid-decade proactive policies by states and universities increased the share of industrial research awarded to universities.[2]

In the early 1990s, nevertheless, the dynamism of this relationship appeared to ebb. Academic research came under a cloud, and political backing for technology transfer either waned or looked beyond universities. Industrial R&D stagnated as well amid confusing crosscurrents buffeting the old and new technologies. Industry's contribution to academic research leveled off at its high-water mark of 7 percent, and few new initiatives were taken to nudge it higher. The national dialogue on research during these years was equally trendless, exhorting academic science to both increase its relevance and decrease its size. Beneath the surface, however, the groundwork created in the 1980s supported advances of profound significance for both academic and industrial science. When the technology boom of the late 1990s arrived, collaboration between universities and industry again appeared in a favorable light.

Two signal developments define the latest phase of this evolving relationship. First, the transformation of bio- and medical technology has produced a fusion of academic and industrial science into complementary, and sometimes competing, parts of a single system of innovation. Here, faculty involvement in commercial endeavors is no longer the exception but the rule; and what is true for faculty is also true for their universities. Large amounts of money are at stake, and universities, whether they wish to or not, have become actors in the marketplace. Second, universities have become significant agents of economic development. They are no longer concerned only with transferring technology to the commercial sector; they now feel compelled to foster conditions for generating regional wealth. With these two roles thrust into prominence, universities again have the opportunity to leverage economic expectations into academic advancement.

In some ways, the expectations for university-industry links have been more volatile than the links themselves. There has been no shortage of boosters or detractors. However, in their contest to influence the policy agenda each side has attempted to impose a monolithic characterization of this relationship. At the same time, a growing body of scholarship has illuminated the multiple ways in which academic research and industrial technology interact. The path to understanding this relationship lies in an examination of the parts.

The Two Cultures

In university-industry research relationships (UIRRs) universities are the sellers and commercial firms the buyers. The behavior of sellers can greatly affect the nature of these transactions, but the initiative still lies with the buyers. For that reason, understanding the logic of UIRRs requires seeing them from the perspective of industry. Firms purchase research from universities to aid in developing goods and services to bring to market. They make judgments first about the role of research (if any) in the development of products, and next about how and where to procure that research.[3]

Firms that use research meet most of their needs internally. Nationally, 94 percent of basic and applied research financed by industry was also performed in industry, and the percentage is higher for development. Compared with academic research, industrial research is considerably more volatile. Real industry spending for research rose steadily from the mid-1970s until 1986, but then remained on a plateau until the mid-1990s. From that point it shot upward by 50 percent by 2000. But the forces driving research varied widely across industries. Real spending from the mid-1980s to the late 1990s was flat in chemistry, doubled for electrical equipment, and grew by 150 percent for medicine and drugs. Spending by individual firms varied even more. A share analysis like that done for universities in the last chapter would show wild swings from year to year. Among the 100 largest performers in 1997, the annual change varied from +100 to −20 percent.[4] Among those same companies, the portion of sales devoted to R&D varied from 50 percent to less than 1 percent. Industry spending on research is sensitive to the state of the economy, relative opportunities for investment, and government policies, as well as the waxing or waning of high-tech industries. The role of universities in this effort is much less volatile. In the 1990s it hovered around 4 percent of industry spending for applied and basic research.

A rich literature has grown up describing how academic research contributes to technological advance in industry.[5] The conclusions have been summarized succinctly by Nathan Rosenberg and Richard Nelson: "What university research most often does today is to stimulate and enhance the power of R&D done in industry, as contrasted with providing a substitute for it."[6] This characterization, however, best applies to the traditional relationship between these two realms that prevailed through most of the twentieth century. The situation changes in important respects when commercially valuable inventions emerge from academic laboratories, something quite unusual in the traditional relationship, but now an expected outcome in biotechnology (which is examined in the final section of this chapter). First, there is much to learn about traditional relationships.

The cultures of industrial and academic research are fundamentally different.[7] The goal of industry in utilizing research is to obtain an economic return from some technological advantage. A technological advantage allows a firm to produce something new or different, or to make it faster, better, or more efficiently than its rivals. When such advantages are based on proprietary knowledge, they are embodied in trade secrets, first-mover advantages, or patents.[8] In all cases the firm has a powerful interest in not disclosing the knowledge in question before it can fully exploit or protect it. A second feature of industrial culture is the process of transforming proprietary knowledge into salable products. No matter how fundamental the original discovery or breakthrough, subsequent investigation and refinement will move it inexorably toward application. Research in industry thus possesses an inherent inclination toward applied research and nondisclosure.

Universities, in contrast, have a mission to advance and disseminate systematic knowledge, and these goals permeate the culture of the faculty. For academic scientists the advancement of their field, duly shared through publication, results in recognition and reputation. Scientific recognition takes place through professional channels and rewards. Universities, in turn, reward such achievements with promotion, tenure, salary, and the intellectual freedom to pursue further professional recognition. Moreover, recognition is greater for more theoretical contributions—those pertaining to a larger class of phenomena. Faculty research is thus inherently inclined toward theoretical topics and open publication.

How do UIRRs overcome this cultural divide? The actual overlap between academic and industrial research is quite small (4 percent). But in this territory arrangements are negotiated that meet the interests of both realms. Firms may wish to engage university scientists with high academic reputations as the most promising source of advantageous new knowledge, but

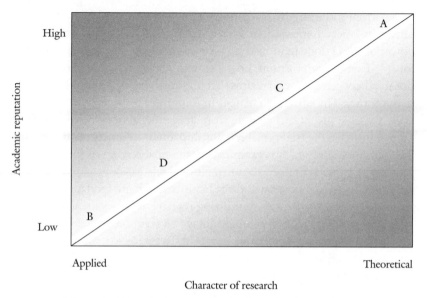

FIG. 14. Theoretical Frontier between Academic and Industrial Research

they also need to find scientists who will focus on their particular problems. Faculty may wish to engage in reputation-enhancing basic research, but they also need support for their laboratories and students. The various arrangements that are negotiated thus constitute a frontier defined by compromises acceptable to both sides.

The diagonal line in Figure 14 represents a frontier at which acceptable trade-offs could be negotiated between the quality of the academic scientists and the character of the research. That is, eminent scientists, who can presumably obtain research grants for their own theoretical investigations, would be expected to have little interest in more applied industrial research. And conversely, scientists lacking a reputation for theoretical contributions should be willing to accept the terms offered by industry for research support. For purposes of illustration, the frontier is depicted as a straight line. However, an abundance of federal support for basic research, for example, would cause it to sag toward the lower right corner, while a paucity of same would bend the frontier toward the opposite corner. A study by Lucien Randazzese on faculty involvement with industrially supported research validated the existence of such a frontier: "based on . . . statistically significant results, academic research quality, manifested in terms of reputation and eminence, is the principal factor affecting the tradeoff faced by faculty between the conduct of academic research and the patronage of industry."[9] Hence locations along this frontier represent research relationships with different characteristics, represented by the points A, B, C, and D.

The notorious contract between the Novartis Corporation and the UC Berkeley Department of Plant and Microbial Biology would be located at position A. Novartis wanted access to basic research of the highest quality and was willing to support that research on terms acceptable to the Berkeley scientists. In fact, the agreement was between two research organizations, the UC Berkeley College of Natural Resources and the research arm of Novartis.[10] The performance of applied research was not an issue, since the role of moving ideas from basic research toward product development belonged with the industrial laboratory. If anything, the research grants from this arrangement afforded greater freedom to the Berkeley scientists, since the in-house approval process omitted the elaborate documentation and evaluation required for federal grants. Predictably, disclosure of findings was the most sensitive point, and the one most emphasized by critics. Essentially, the company was given a "first look" at all findings by participating faculty, with the right to license ensuing patents through regular procedures. Ultimately, the interests of the company and faculty scientists were aligned: both sought significant scientific advancements. For faculty, this was the traditional goal of academic research; but for the company, pathbreaking findings might provide a technological edge for successful new products.

The Georgia Tech Research Institute (GTRI) would be located at position B. Descended from the Engineering Experiment Station, its avowed mission is to be the "applied research arm" of Georgia Tech. Its chief client has long been the Department of Defense, but it offers the same kinds of services to industry, which in 2000 contracted for more than $20 million of R&D. GTRI is wholly dedicated to meeting the needs of its clients and providing them with immediately usable results. Basic research and academic reputation are irrelevant here. Research is not conducted by tenure-track faculty, but by a permanent staff of researchers, most of whom hold master's degrees. This level of qualifications would tend to affirm the view that applied science and engineering largely employ "off-the-shelf science."[11] Years of experience working in specialized fields have nevertheless given the GTRI staff considerable technological sophistication. Furthermore, the Georgia Tech faculty are close by for consultation should fundamental scientific questions arise. GTRI is the largest university-sponsored applied research organization, but many other universities have analogous units to provide technological services; and like GTRI their distinguishing feature is the employment of researchers who do not hold regular faculty appointments.[12]

Points C and D in Figure 14 are meant to represent generically the relative benefits to industry of local versus national research partners. Firms that value the generation of new knowledge most highly tend to seek research partners with high academic reputations, represented by C. Usually this means shopping in the national marketplace, although not necessarily looking only at peak institutions. In thousands of highly specialized technological niches, academic expertise is spread fairly broadly among research universities. The more prestigious research units indeed produce more academic publications, but are less likely to provide "downstream" research assistance in the form of product development, new processes, or patent disclosures.[13]

For such assistance, or applied research generally, firms apparently sacrifice prestige in research partners, which makes local alternatives more attractive (point D).[14] Local partners have the additional advantage of promoting closer interaction with company researchers and greater ease in hiring students.[15] Many factors come into play. Firms that locate their research investments at C rather than D may place paramount value on new knowledge. For them, the input of university research may be fairly remote from the downstream development of products.[16]

Figure 14 at the very least suggests that industry investments in university research lie along a continuum, not just in the character of the research that is purchased, but also in how that knowledge is integrated into the innovation cycle of product development in firms. Industry can find most anything it searches for among the more than 100 research universities in the United States, or, more precisely, among their multifarious units. Accordingly, a much more textured picture of UIRRs can be had by viewing these interactions with the various parts of a single university.

Industry-Sponsored Research at Pennsylvania State University

Pennsylvania State University has a long tradition of research with practical orientations. Early Penn State researchers devised ways to measure calories in food and R-values in insulation. They have improved concrete for highways and turf grass for golf courses. The university is known for its contributions to making ice cream, growing geraniums, and cultivating mushrooms. Even some basic discoveries have a tangible quality: Penn

State scientists were the first to see a single atom and the first to discover planets beyond the solar system. In 2001, Penn State was eleventh in total R&D expenditures, and many of its projects had a practical bent. Not surprisingly, it has a history of working with industry. During the 1980s and 1990s, Penn State performed more industrial research than any other public university.[17]

To view the full extent of industry-sponsored research, a snapshot was obtained of all industrial research grants in effect in the fall of 2001 at the main University Park campus. This picture excludes the medical school at Hershey and includes virtually no research in biotechnology. What it illuminates, for the most part, is traditional research relationships of the kind described by Rosenberg and Nelson, located largely in engineering and the physical sciences. In total, this snapshot recorded 938 entries worth $46 million.[18]

The category of industry-sponsored research contains far more than actual research projects supported by private companies. A good number of awards were from trade associations and a few from public or not-for-profit organizations. National and independent research laboratories also sponsored projects, often as subcontracts. And not all grants support research per se. Some provide general support for a laboratory or for students. A relatively large number of supporters invest, usually modest amounts, in consortia that seek research-based information. These types of quasi-research support account for most of the awards outside of the natural and applied sciences, where one would not expect to find much research for industry. As a whole, they represent a large number of grants, but mostly for small amounts. So, despite a good deal of noise in these data, the broad patterns stand out rather clearly.

The bulk of this research was performed by two of Penn State's colleges, the College of Engineering and the College of Earth and Mineral Sciences, and four large ORUs (Table 12). The College of Science played a smaller role, and less of its support came directly from industry. For the other units, though, direct support from industry for research projects was the predominant form. These grants represent the true core of research interactions with industry at Penn State. While one might surmise from some project titles whether the research were basic, applied, or generic, such identifications are largely beside the point. The relevance of these investigations for industry is revealed in their subject matter. In most cases, the projects were located in units devoted to studying applied fields with unmistakable relevance for the economy, and thus for industry as well.

TABLE 12

Industry-Sponsored R&D at Pennsylvania State University, Fall 2001

	Grant Amounts (in $1,000s)						
	Total	Percent of total	Industry	Trade associations	Research institutes	Consortia	Other
Colleges: Academic Department							
Earth and Mineral Science (excl. Energy Institute)	7,459		5,194	608	888	105	664
Engineering (excl. Pennsylvania Transportation Institute)	7,898		4,424	890	1,234	593	757
Science	3,663		1,342	126	2,047	0	148
Subtotal	19,020	41	10,960	1,624	4,169	698	1,569
Organized Research Units							
Applied Research Lab (ARL)	9,255		4,608	1,397	3,030	101	119
Materials Research Institute (MRI)	3,338		2,141	144	250	784	19
Energy Institute	2,427		1,716	172	328	212	0
Pennsylvania Transportation Institute	2,033		1,700	150	183	0	0
Subtotal	17,053	37	10,165	1,863	3,791	1,097	138
Other units	10,289	22	3,881	2,719	436	667	2,587
Total	46,363	100	25,006	6,206	8,396	2,462	4,294

Like most ORUs, Penn State's large institutes represent unique configurations of research capabilities. Their general character can be sketched, but the full range of their activities defies summary. The Applied Research Lab (ARL), the oldest and largest of these units, was established at Penn State by the Navy after World War II. Originally centered on the Garfield Water Tunnel, it still performs most research for its chief patron, the Office of Naval Research. In a half-century, research at ARL has expanded in many directions. In 2001 it advertised sixty-four areas of expertise, ranging from routine to world-class.

Firms that manufacture products for the Navy naturally take an interest in this work, and the inherent utility of these fields attracts other companies as well. These specialties typically encompass activities ranging from basic research to development and manufacturing. Electro-optics, for example, probes fundamental spectroscopy while also seeking to develop technologies for manufacturing applications. In acoustics, ARL, in conjunction with the College of Engineering, has fashioned probably the premier program in the country. But other units are more mundane. For example, the Gear Research Institute is an independent nonprofit consortium with seventeen corporate members that performs all its investigations on hardening, lubrication, and durability at ARL—more than $1 million worth of the projects in this list.

Although ARL has close ties with the College of Engineering, its research prowess stems largely from an experienced staff of researchers and specialized facilities. Its reputation attracts research ties with firms throughout the world, as well as subcontracts from national laboratories. ARL represents a well-established node in a vast network for the creation and dissemination of technological innovation centered on the Office of Naval Research. And judging from its numerous contracts, it also fulfills a useful function for corporations and other laboratories. At the same time, ARL provides research opportunities for students and faculty at Penn State.

The Materials Research Institute (MRI) has a much different character from ARL. As an ORU centered on research technologies, its chief function is to connect and administer research activities of faculty in the general area of materials. Although there is a Department of Materials Science and Engineering in the College of Earth and Mineral Sciences, the more than 200 faculty associated with MRI also come from chemistry, physics, engineering, and other units, including ARL.

The Penn State programs in materials science have the greatest research expenditures and are consistently rated among the leaders. Although the bulk of MRI's $50 million in annual research expenditures is derived from federal sources, a few of its programs are tailored to industrial needs. The Center for Innovative Sintered Products, a state-subsidized consortium, has some seventy-five industrial members. The Center for Dielectric Studies, focused on the next generation of electronic components, is an NSF University/Industry Cooperative Research Center with twenty major corporations as members.

Beyond these units dedicated to technology transfer, materials science represents a collection of interdisciplinary specialties, and research there tends to have generic significance for present and future technologies. In this respect, it is not unlike molecular biology. For example, the study of surfaces at the nanometer level, a specialty of MRI, relates to myriad phenomena. A scientist who studies the interaction of fluids and surfaces reported, "even at the most fundamental level [she] can envision applications for the work."[19] Firms consequently have good reason to want to be connected with such research.

The two other ORUs listed in Table 12 focus on areas of application and contain units specifically oriented toward consumers. The Pennsylvania Transportation Institute has grown in more than three decades into a locus for faculty research on road-building, road networks, and vehicle safety. These activities (like those of ARL) are pertinent to contractors in the industry. However, unlike defense contractors, road builders perform no research themselves. The Energy Institute differs somewhat in being aimed primarily at aiding industry in ways that foster economic development. It maintains two consortia with large memberships in the areas of carbon technologies and products, and other research groups study catalysis, combustion, and fuel technologies.

From the titles of projects, it would seem that both these institutes perform testing services for industry, capitalizing no doubt on the highly sophisticated equipment possessed by the university. Research in the Energy Institute, in addition, appears to shade into fundamental investigations in materials. Much, though not all, of the research at both institutes might fit the characterization of Rosenberg and Nelson as "a substitute for industrial R&D."[20] This pattern occurs in industries where firms lack a capacity for internal research, which would be true of road builders and some extractive industries. It would also pertain to fields like environmental technologies, where a single firm would have difficulty capturing value from investments in research. Once established, these institutes tend to persist in serving their respective industries, even if such activities are peripheral within universities. The Transportation and Energy Institutes substantially fit this mold, although both also utilize faculty as researchers and interact with some firms having internal research efforts.

Industry-sponsored research in the three colleges listed in Table 12 substantially overlaps with the ORUs just described. Engineering faculty, in particular, figured prominently in all four, while faculty members from the other colleges were more likely to be associated with MRI. Penn State engineers and physical scientists in fact interact freely and frequently in ways that are determined more by scientific interests than by administrative units. The role of industry should also be placed in perspective. It played the largest role in the College of Engineering, but other colleges look chiefly to federal agencies. Patterns of research funding vary by department.

The investigations performed for industrial supporters can be characterized as three ideal types:[21]

1. *Basic projects*: A relatively small number of grants sponsored self-contained projects intended to yield defined research findings. Such projects were more prevalent in biology, were more likely to be subcontracts from

national laboratories, and were found in MRI as often as in departments. While the object of such grants may have been to produce "useful new knowledge," the literature suggests that enhancement rather than new findings is the principal benefit firms derive from such academic research.[22]

2. *Description*: A large number of grants promised essentially descriptive work, although of a highly sophisticated nature. The titles of these awards contained language like: "measurement of"; "characterization of"; "determination of kinetic parameters"; "acoustic analysis"; "molecular simulation"; and "parametric geometry modeling." Motivated by specific needs in the sponsors' own R&D, grants for such research services took advantage of the university's particular analytical capabilities.

3. *Monitoring*: Numerous awards were designated simply as support for a scientist and his or her research or laboratory. Others supported graduate students or donated equipment. The aim here could be monitoring research in a given laboratory in order, on one hand, to learn of any breakthroughs relevant to corporate R&D or, on the other, to cultivate an ongoing relationship with an expert in a relevant field. Thus monitoring grants, like consulting relationships, formed part of a larger effort that many writers consider the principal means by which university research stimulates and enhances industrial R&D.[23]

These ideal types might also be characterized by their relationship to the frontier of negotiated research relationships (Figure 14). Basic projects are naturally most compatible with the theoretical orientation of academic scientists. Given the difficulty of appropriating results from such investigations, they tend to be funded by firms with high levels of internal R&D. They would most likely represent positions on the high-reputation/theoretical portion of the frontier.

Descriptive studies, being applied and firm-specific, would tend to fall toward the opposite quadrant (lower reputation/applied). Certainly many descriptive studies are performed in Penn State's ORUs. A slightly different rationale may apply to those located in departments, however. Graduate research assistants under the oversight of the principal investigator likely perform much of the actual work for such projects. In this sense, the nexus between less reputation and a more applied focus would hold. Such activities also provide excellent training opportunities for students, most of whom will find careers in industry. Pure support for a faculty scientist's laboratory would likely subsidize theoretical research. Thus monitoring grants are generally used to establish relationships with researchers with high reputations.

Other considerations play a role as well. In engineering and the physical sciences such relationships depend heavily on individual specialties. In addition, where consulting is the major consideration, firms prefer faculty who are willing to address their particular research problems. The logic of the negotiated frontier seems to hold, even though the pattern of grants has great variety. The same might be said about academic units.

The College of Earth and Mineral Sciences is the most highly rated of Penn State's colleges. Outside of the Energy Institute, most of its interaction with industry occurred in the Department of Materials Science and Engineering. It received support for each of the three types of activities outlined above. Except for monitoring, these grants have no discernible difference from those received by MRI. Elsewhere in the college, basic science projects were the rule, often in the form of subcontracts from national laboratories.

Industry support for research in the College of Engineering was heavily weighted toward descriptive studies, much like awards to the ORUs. And for good reason. In many cases the principal investigators were the same, and the college itself housed more than twenty-five centers and institutes of its own. Such grants were particularly evident in the department of Engineering Science and Mechanics. Electrical Engineering, with close links to MRI, harbored a number of basic projects, and Chemical Engineering received general grants of the monitoring type. Service to industry was highly developed in this college and took place through many channels.

The College of Science, in contrast, was focused on academic research. Most direct support from industry supported the research and laboratories of individual scientists. However, many chemists and physicists conducted their research at MRI. For them, support from industry was more likely to be channeled through MRI and to utilize its sophisticated instrumentation.

Overall, these departmental patterns were not very robust.[24] Research at Penn State, as at most universities, resembles a matrix in its organization. Individual researchers frequently belong to an academic unit and one or more ORUs. Most likely, the placement of individual grants from industry depended heavily on where relevant equipment or faculty laboratories happened to be located. These data nevertheless suggest some larger patterns.

The two most salient features of this sample of grants are the large number of firms sponsoring research at Penn State and the relatively small size of each award. Roughly 250 different firms sponsored research projects, and at least 200 more (with some overlap) contributed to consortia. Many smaller companies were connected in other ways. Forty-three trade associations sponsored research of some form and presumably passed the findings on to their members. Penn State also participated in the state's Ben Franklin Program, which arranges university research projects for small firms ($1.08 million), as well as a program of free technical assistance not included in this sample.

The university's laboratories are undoubtedly accessible to industry, and industry has taken advantage of that access, but mostly through moderate investments. The median grant was $30,000, and the middle quartiles stretched from $10,000 to $65,000. Just 112 grants equaled or exceeded $100,000, but they brought almost 60 percent of the revenues in the sample (not including consortia). Few firms looked to Penn State for new products or processes.[25] Rather, the picture that emerges is one of many firms forging research ties with Penn State in order to keep abreast of critical fields and to complement their internal R&D.

The vast majority of UIRRs are in areas that Herbert Simon called "the sciences of the artificial." That is, these fields seek understanding not of nature (as in natural science) but of man-made artifacts. This domain includes all areas of engineering, but also computers, some aspects of materials, and much more. At Penn State it would comprise nutrition and agriculture as well. Lumping these fields together under the rubric of "applied sciences" is misleading. Academic research here seeks a fundamental understanding of process and design. These endeavors are some distance removed from applied research and development, the tasks of incorporating such understanding into actual products.[26] But they are nevertheless relevant to industrial technology. Hence there has always been much ambiguity in characterizing the relationship between academic research and industrial innovation.

The Penn State data suggest a relationship that would reflect the following dynamics: a large participation of industrial firms in monitoring research findings in these "artificial sciences," combined with some efforts to obtain specific results. But the level of investment by most firms was quite restrained, suggesting that product innovation (which would justify large investments) was preponderantly pursued through internal R&D. In other words, these firms did not seek "inventions" from university science. In fact, invention disclosures were less likely to result from industry-sponsored research than from federally sponsored basic research.[27] The relationship between industry and Penn State exemplifies the traditional model of university-industry research ties. However, the model itself needs further explication.

Enhancement of Industry Research

The traditional model holds the contribution of university science to proprietary outputs ("deliverables") to be less significant economically than the intermediate contributions to stimulating and enhancing industrial R&D. This last sphere of activities may be called the *enhancement function* of industry-supported academic research. This function is far more subtle and multidimensional than direct contributions to product development. In purpose it poses the same issue of why firms engage in basic—or academic—research.[28] Comprehending the enhancement function, however, requires an understanding not only of what contribution these investments make to industry, but also of the factors that discourage industry from making such investments.

The classic economic analyses of the role of basic research in industry posit that a capitalist economy does not provide adequate incentives for firms to invest in knowledge production.[29] The chief impediments are, first, uncertainty: the more basic the research, the less certainty that it will produce economically valuable results and the longer the time frame for those results to appear. The second is appropriability: since knowledge once created becomes freely available, producers have difficulty obtaining proprietary control. While hardly insuperable, these impediments discourage firms from investing in basic research. The result, other things being equal, is a depressed private rate of return to such investments and consequently a less-than-optimal social rate of investment.

In the real world, several factors can mitigate these problems. Historically, one of the most prominent has been market power. Firms that dominated their industries were able to support the uncertainty of long-range investments in knowledge because they could be confident, with a dominant market share, of appropriating the lion's share of whatever benefits emerged. The storied industrial laboratories of IBM and AT&T sustained technological leadership even as their scientists garnered Nobel Prizes. In the 1990s, however, complex forces in the economy, including deregulation and globalization, eroded dominant market positions, with Bell Labs being perhaps the foremost casualty.[30]

Industrial laboratories continue to play an indispensable role, but under more competitive conditions they no longer are supported by the comfortable overheads of market-dominating firms. This drift of events actually favors a more interactive mode of research, which draws especially on the expertise of universities. Firms in high-tech industries can hardly forgo the knowledge needed to drive innovation. If basic research is uncertain, the absence of research leads to the certainty of obsolescence. The challenge for firms is thus to manage research investments strategically for productivity and cost effectiveness.

The problem of appropriability is simple in theory but subtle in reality. The three standard ways in which firms appropriate, or establish proprietary control over, new knowledge have already been mentioned: trade secrets, first-mover advantage, and patents. Different industries and technologies employ these approaches according to their circumstances.[31] However, these methods are more pertinent to final products or processes—to inventions or their components. A somewhat different set of considerations pertains to industrial use of academic research.

Advanced scientific or technological knowledge is scarcely a free good. Unlike "off-the-shelf science," it can be used only by those with a sophisticated grasp of its nature and context—by those, in short, who are participants in the research process. As Nathan Rosenberg put it: "the performance of basic research may be thought of as a ticket of admission to an information network."[32] A technological firm must be plugged in to the network of scientific communication in order to keep abreast of advances relevant to its technologies. Furthermore, it must support an internal capacity for research in order to know how to use such advancements. This internal capacity has also been described as "tacit knowledge." Whereas "codified knowledge" is freely available through scientific publications, firms rely on tacit knowledge, cultivated through the experience of internal staff and academic experts, to translate new and codified knowledge into product innovation.

Basic research is but one complex input into the process of technological innovation, but for most industries characterized by rapid technological advance it is indispensable. Rosenberg has described it as "a peculiar kind of intermediate good that may be used, not to produce a final good, but (perhaps) to play some further role in the invention of a new final good."[33] This characterization is fully consistent with the enhancement function of industry-sponsored academic research. Its justification, in other words, lies not in the new knowledge produced, but rather in the contribution of the entire process to eventual innovations. These complex processes touch on the entirety of industrial innovation, but for present purposes the enhancement function can be characterized as consisting of four kinds of interaction.

1. *Field-intensive knowledge.* Firms that operate in delimited scientific fields are interested in academic research in those same fields, and academic findings are likely to prove relevant to the firm's R&D. Being plugged in to

(monitoring) the largely university-based scientific community is thus essential to keep internal R&D on the cutting edge. This link is particularly important for science-based technologies, or for "generic" basic research.

2. *Field-extensive knowledge.* Firms in many industries seek to develop complex technological systems that touch on many areas of expertise. Because it may be impossible to cultivate internally the range and depth of expertise to deal with all the problems that arise, they may draw on academic expertise to overcome unfamiliar difficulties.[34] Of these two kinds of knowledge-seeking, the literature suggests that ties with academic research are more critical for bolstering existing expertise than for compensating for an absence of expertise.

3. *Personnel enhancement.* Many firms value their university contacts most highly as a source of future researchers, and contact with university researchers and their students can be justified for the purpose of hiring alone. Those contacts are also important for internal industry researchers, who must continually renew their expertise. Codified knowledge is helpful, but personal contacts are more effective. Hence the importance of being plugged in to information networks connected with academic research.

4. *Instrumentation.* Universities have traditionally been a source of valuable new instrumentation that has been incorporated into industry.[35] University scientists often devise instruments for their own needs that later prove to have far wider application. This phenomenon is actually part of a larger process through which techniques of academic research are learned by and shared with industry. In addition, university laboratories possess costly instruments of great sophistication uniquely capable of performing certain experiments. This capacity may be integral to science-based technologies, where academic and industrial science tend to converge.

These activities enhance the effectiveness of industrial R&D and thus have real value for firms. But since these activities produce intermediate goods, there is no way to assign them a monetary value, or an appropriate price. How then do firms decide how much to spend?[36] The Penn State data suggest one partial answer. Since three-quarters of the grants from industry were for less than $65,000, not including consortia, firms seemed to hedge their bets by restricting the size of single investments. Where uncertainty is high, as in monitoring, broad coverage through token grants might be the most effective strategy. Conversely, where firms make larger investments, the certainty of relevance can be assumed to be much greater. Underlying all of the transactions just described, the most important feature of the economics of university-industry research relationships may well be subsidization.

Enhancing Enhancement: Subsidies and University-Industry Centers

Public subsidization of basic research compensates for socially suboptimal levels of investment by industry. Public investments operate on the macro-level to expand the stock of science and technology available to industry. On the micro-level, public subsidies encourage greater private investments by industry by lowering the cost of the potential benefits, thus diminishing the impediments discussed above.

Looking only at the forms of subsidization that involve universities, three levels can be discerned. First, public support for academic science is largely responsible for creating the vast informational network to which industrial laboratories can connect. The volume and nature of this public investment has significant consequences for different fields and industries. The massive funding of biomedical research by the National Institutes of Health (NIH) is the most notable example. Second, universities, by assuming a large share of the costs of sustaining research, make it available to industry at what amounts to a subsidized price. For example, indirect costs for research at independent laboratories are considerably higher than in universities.[37] The difference amounts to an indirect subsidy, or price discount, for industry. Third, since at least 1980, government policies have devised several forms of direct subsidization of university-industry cooperation in order to encourage the generation and transfer of technology. These policies are consistent with the framework for enhancement just depicted, and they have had a major impact on expanding research relationships between firms and universities.

The factors needed to create state-supported programs for joint university-industry research coalesced in the early 1980s. Interest in such endeavors emerged in the late 1970s, but only one federal program was created (the Industry/University Cooperative Research Centers [IUCRC] Program).[38] Most states possessed some programs to promote economic growth by assisting industrial technology, but beginning in 1982 several states took singular initiatives to create partnerships between industry and universities. By mid-decade these had gained wide popularity.[39] One stimulus was provided in 1984 when federal legislation exempted industry research consortia from punitive antitrust laws. The following year the NSF launched a major program to create Engineering Research Centers. The greatest activity was at the state level, however. By 1990, 22 states with diverse programs had created 144 university-industry technology centers. In keeping with this spirit, NSF created an additional program for joint NSF-state supported IUCRCs.[40]

Collectively, these research units represented a distinctive social invention—publicly supported university centers designed to foster collaborative research with industry and technology transfer. As products of public policy, these centers are a more coherent group than the university ORUs that have ad hoc research relationships with firms, but their arrangements with the state and federal funders nevertheless vary widely.[41] The federal programs at least (and many states mimic them) are awarded on a competitive basis. Universities submit proposals that are rigorously evaluated according to scientific merits and technological significance. All programs require the participation of regular university faculty and prearranged membership and financial support from firms. In addition, all have a marked educational component, since one of the avowed purposes is to train scientists and engineers accustomed to working in this culture. Finally, the federal programs all have sunset provisions for the termination of federal support. With all possible renewals, eleven years is usually the longest a center can receive support. The goal of these sunset provisions is not to close a center, but for it to become self-sustaining.

The aims of these centers might be situated on a continuum of activities from technology development to technology assistance. Most programs aim chiefly for technology development; that is, their purpose is to further generic technologies in areas of economic significance through fundamental research. But they are committed as well to seeing these technologies utilized by firms and conduct a variety of activities to achieve this end, such as collaborative or proprietary research, workshops, and consulting. Most centers are not designed to provide the more basic kinds of technical assistance often needed by smaller companies with limited internal capabilities. Such services are in great demand, and most states have other, nonuniversity programs for this purpose. Centers nevertheless often feel pressured to move toward that end of the continuum.

Industrial participants in most centers pay membership and annual fees. Industry members usually belong to an advisory board that plays a large role in selecting research projects, which consequently match the interests of industry. Collaborative research is encouraged. The literature reviewed earlier finds that research interactions between university and industry scientists are far more fruitful than one-way knowledge transfers, and academics believe that such exchanges are an important benefit for them. In addition, most centers encourage participating firms to contract for additional research projects. In the IUCRCs, for example, 60 percent of member companies sponsored additional research tailored to their specific needs.[42]

Although public subsidization is a basic feature, the level of subsidy varies greatly and strongly affects the nature of the centers. Engineering Research Centers (ERCs) receive the most generous public funding—a base grant of approximately $2 million per year. In 1995, twenty-one of these centers were in operation and they had 708 industrial partners:[43]

Amount	Source and type of ERC funding
$51.7 million	NSF funds from the ERC program
$37.7 million	Industry: grants, contracts, and in-kind contributions
$36.7 million	Other federal, state, and university funds
$37 million	Industry memberships: cash
Total: $178.9 million	

The cash contributions from individual industrial partners, which averaged only $24,000, purchased access to engineering research of far greater value, as well as a good deal of interaction with center researchers. These centers are driven by the technological possibilities foreseen by universities and vetted by NSF. Firms are invited to partake of this feast according to their respective appetites. Still, the cost is minimal if the fare suits their taste.[44]

In the IUCRC Program the leverage operates in the opposite direction. NSF acts almost as a facilitator for far smaller cooperative centers with grassroots support. University professors take the initiative (often with an NSF planning grant) to organize a group of firms to support investigation in a particular area. A full NSF grant originally provided $100,000 (later $70,000) of annual support for five years, but the minimum industry support had to be $300,000. In 2000 these centers received just $5.2 million from NSF and $68 million from other, chiefly industry, sources. Clearly, despite the public subsidy, these centers have to meet real needs of industry. The public subsidy in this case serves a largely organizational purpose: encouraging and providing means for the formation of centers, as well as a strong managerial framework through NSF procedures and evaluations.[45]

The state version of IUCRCs, which was discontinued, was structured more like the engineering research centers. The NSF grant had to be matched once by the state and a second time by the industrial participants. Industry thus supplied only one-third of the funds supporting core research projects—those determined by the advisory board. Firms were also encouraged to support additional projects through direct grants and contracts. When members of both types of centers were asked to compare the benefits and costs, approximately equal numbers said benefits were (1) much greater, (2) greater, (3) equal to, or (4) less.[46] These predominately favorable responses nevertheless suggest that firms were sensitive to price. Public subsidies thus appear to be an important factor in increasing industrial investment in generic research.

These programs and the individual centers have all undergone rigorous evaluations by NSF, but there has been no attempt to assess their collective impact as public or private investments. The continued participation of firms and the successful debut of additional centers seems testimony to their general cost-effectiveness for industry, at least at the subsidized price. The benefits reported by firms conform quite closely with the enhancement function outlined above.[47]

By far the largest number of participants reports benefiting from "access to new ideas or know-how." One noted gaining "access to worldwide information in the fields of our interest"; and another that "ideas from the ERC . . . translate into development programs in our department." Some 40 percent of ERC members and 33 percent of IUCRC members hired students or graduates from the centers and reported high levels of satisfaction with these hires. Access to university instruments and learning research techniques were also reported as benefits. For many, receiving direct technical assistance was clearly an important result, but very few (10 percent) directly used intellectual property through patents or licenses. One somewhat unanticipated benefit, reported by over half of ERC members, was "increased interaction with other firms participating in the same ERC."

These results are the product of a reciprocal relationship between the centers and their members. Hence the percentage of firms experiencing particular benefits does not fully reflect the value of the centers. For example, one factor most strongly related to satisfaction was the organizational receptivity within the firm to center research—a phase of technology transfer that was by no means automatic. On average, one of six memberships was discontinued each year for various reasons. Conversely and not surprisingly, benefits from membership were strongly associated with the length of participation and degree of active involvement in center research. Those that stayed no doubt were among the 30–40 percent reporting that participation in the centers increased their competitiveness and contributed to the development of new products or processes.

Government satisfaction with these same programs has been more equivocal. The wave of enthusiasm in the 1980s ebbed. At NSF no new Engineering Research Centers were established between 1990 and 1994, and in the latter year it conducted an evaluation of the entire program. Since then, however, support has rebounded. University-industry cooperation again became a policy focus, and NSF chose to emphasize the kind of interdisciplinary, collaborative research that the centers exemplified. Five new centers were opened in both 1996 and 1998, and four more were added in 2000. In the states, though, the politics of university-industry centers became on the whole less favorable.

The difficulties of the now moribund state IUCRC program exemplify the situation.[48] States found it difficult to justify the expenditures for these programs despite matching funds from NSF and industry. The implicit issue seemed to be the problem of targeting investments to stimulate economic development for the state rather than for the nation. To this end, the state program explicitly sought to attract smaller firms, which were more likely to be local. Indeed, some 45 percent of in-state members met this criterion.[49]

However, smaller firms fit less well into the center paradigm. The limited scope and scale of their internal research is less amenable to the enhancement function. They often need definite and speedy results, which is not the forte of academic research. And many need technical assistance to produce proprietary products.

States seemed to conclude that their own economic interests, at least in the short run, were better served through programs of technical assistance than through support for technology development. Through most of the 1990s, most state programs turned away from the university centers established in the preceding years and invested instead in outright technical assistance through nonuniversity programs.[50] To appreciate this drift of events, the role of centers should be viewed from the larger perspective of university-industry research relationships.

As at Penn State, much traditional industrial sponsorship of university research takes place through centers.[51] And for good reason. Centers tend to be formed in areas where research is demanded, often to accommodate unique capabilities, and separation from the academic core minimizes friction. Centers also have the visibility to attract firms and the administrative capabilities to address their requirements.

The federal and state programs that were created to encourage and subsidize centers built on this proven model. Explicitly intended to enlarge this sphere of interaction, they also sought to alter the culture of engineering research by making collaboration and technology transfer routine and valued activities. There can be little doubt that these goals were in some measure achieved—that these investments in technology development enhanced the stock of productive technology available to U.S. industry or, from a more theoretical perspective, lessened society's inherent underinvestment in generic research.

However, the retreat from state support for these programs may be a symptom of another set of economic factors. Just as firms face the problem of capturing the returns from their investments in fundamental research, so too do states and localities face the challenge of capturing returns in the form of economic development from public support for research. Presumably, this situation also inhibits a socially optimal investment in discovery.[52] Given greater assurance of economic payoffs, states and localities would have more incentive to subsidize, and hence stimulate, greater investments from industry in cooperative research with universities. Aggregate investment in technology development would thus be further enlarged.

Enhancing Enhancement: Regional Economic Development

When the links between research, technology, and economic development are considered, the example of Silicon Valley is invariably invoked as the most admired and studied case of high-tech innovation driving frenetic economic growth. Observers have identified the components of this formula, including military and industrial investments in applied research, venture capital, entrepreneurship, institutional networks, and human and social capital, as well as proximity to three of the country's outstanding research universities.[53] But the inputs in this case cannot by themselves explain the outcome; rather, the crucial factor seems to be how they all work together. This process has been likened to a separate economy: a *creative infrastructure* that translates the technology and ideas of entrepreneurial teams "into the basis for an operating company with products and customers."[54]

Research may be only one of the inputs to such an economy, but its relation with the creative infrastructure is the focal point of this discussion. Such an infrastructure captures a large portion of the spillover from investments in research.[55] Policymakers who would have universities play a larger role in economic development wistfully contemplate the Silicon Valley miracle. Research universities have undoubtedly boosted growth in Ann Arbor, Atlanta, and Austin, to mention only conspicuous examples starting with A. However, the key to optimizing the local economic impact of research lies outside of universities in the creative infrastructure.

Local and national links both have important roles to play. The importance of being plugged in to national or international networks has already been stressed. The significance of local ties results chiefly from personal in-

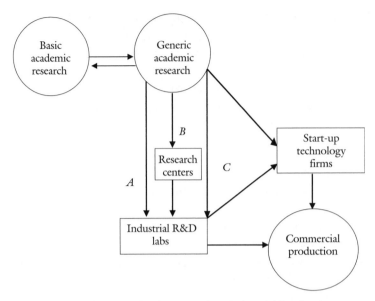

FIG. 15. Pathways from Academic Research to Industrial Production

teractions. The greater the density of interactions among university and industry researchers and entrepreneurs, the more vibrant and creative an infrastructure is likely to be.[56] And the character of those interactions is critical. Hans Weiler has suggested that Silicon Valley has been distinguished by the affinity between university and industrial actors, and a resulting reciprocity in their exchanges.[57] Another study of regional innovation systems found that strong R&D regions, besides interacting with other strong regions, drew a larger proportion of their learning from interactions with local universities. Such a region, the authors conclude, must be "a good learner—that is, it learns extensively from other important regional sources as well as locally."[58]

The role of creative infrastructure adds a dimension to the understanding of university-industry relations. When combined with the arrangements previously described it suggests the processes depicted in Figure 15. The figure first assumes a reciprocal relationship between basic and generic academic research. Generic research serves to enhance industrial research chiefly through industrial R&D labs. The pathways A, B, and C represent the processes associated with the traditional model. Each leads to interaction that is mutually beneficial to universities and industry. For universities, these relationships bring additional support for research and education as well as intellectually valuable interactions between academic and industrial scientists. Industry benefits chiefly through enhancement effects that allow it to produce new and improved products. The difference in these pathways is the mode of investment and the appropriation of economic returns.

Path A represents the traditional research relationship between universities and firms. Firms purchase access to university research according to their own estimates of cost effectiveness, and the benefits largely take the form of enhancement of internal R&D, or, less frequently, substitution for internal R&D.

Path B represents a net addition to academic R&D through public subsidization of technology development. The lower cost of research in subsidized centers, as well as the industrially relevant focus imposed on these centers, stimulates additional research investments from firms, but benefits from these technologies tend to be industrywide rather than local.

Path C represents creative local infrastructures. Here the density of interactions is increased by the presence of and the propensity to form new technology-based firms. These firms perform the same intermediate function as industrial labs at established firms since a good deal of R&D is usually required before they have products to sell. In Silicon Valley such firms tended to emerge chiefly from industrial labs, but spin-off firms are also formed by academic entrepreneurs. Given affinity and reciprocity, learning will occur in all directions, increasing the likelihood of commercial spin-offs. Most important, the economic spillovers are cumulative and largely retained in the region. These economic returns create an additional source of investment and stimulation for university research.

All three pathways can operate simultaneously, and most universities participate in some measure in just such interactions. For universities at the dawn of the twenty-first century, pathways A and B are relatively mature. That is, pathway A can be expected to expand in line with the economy, and pathway B with extensions of existing public subsidization of centers. Hence the most attractive, unbounded alternative beckoning universities has been pathway C, tapping the potential synergies of an expanded research role harnessed to regional economic development. The Silicon Valley model may be impossible to replicate, but that "miracle" rested on a foundation of strategic initiatives undertaken decades earlier.[59] The more ambitious research universities throughout the country have been exploring and testing possibilities for blazing their own path toward this goal.

The current strategies for generating "Silicon Valley effects" are in part an extension of the means employed to stimulate technology transfer in the 1980s. These were chiefly the establishment of university-related research parks and business incubators. Universities also created or revamped offices for technology transfer and intellectual property, but these units were designed to process internal discoveries and were not necessarily oriented toward local economic development.[60]

University research parks epitomized the technology transfer bandwagon of the 1980s. The first research parks dated from a much earlier era. The Stanford Industrial Park was launched in 1951, partly to utilize the university's embarrassingly vast land holdings. Research Triangle Park was created in 1959 as a deliberate effort to stimulate economic development in the state of North Carolina. These two were the largest and the most conspicuously successful of a small population of parks that numbered thirteen in 1969 and twenty-four in 1979.[61] With the technology transfer boom of the 1980s, however, the number of parks mushroomed. A dozen were opened in 1982 alone, and this pace of foundings was sustained for the next six years. By the end of the decade, 80 percent of university-related research parks were less than ten years old.

Research parks are multimillion-dollar real estate developments, and the many ways in which they are financed and managed reflect the practices of that industry. Some were organized and developed by universities themselves, university foundations took responsibility for another set, and government or corporate bodies sponsored others. These arrangements, and the resulting nature of the parks, strongly affect the degree of interaction with the university. The underlying rationale for the parks, of course, is that the juxtaposition of university and industry will produce interaction—particularly involvement with faculty—for the mutual benefit of university, firm, and local economy. The operating principle is thus *propinquity*—spatial proximity will cause these fruitful interactions to occur.

Since few faculty are likely to have ties with research park tenants, faculty involvement is highly variable. It nevertheless occurs with regularity and contributes to research park effectiveness. However, one expectation dear to park planners and managers has not been borne out. Research parks seem to do little to stimulate faculty entrepreneurship through patenting or forming start-up companies. Rather, the relationship between faculty and tenants is predominantly the traditional one of transmitting generic knowledge through research and consultation or, more broadly, the roles encompassed by the enhancement function.[62]

Propinquity in most cases failed to create the affinity and reciprocity that characterized Silicon Valley. Although the most effective research parks have been closely associated with research universities, the real source of economic growth in these situations seemed to be the university itself. Certainly in the absence of other favorable conditions, research parks by themselves are capable of generating little economic impact. Although their overall role seemed to be a positive one, in most cases adding to local employment,[63] such incremental job creation is a far cry from spawning a regional technopolis.

The situation for business incubators is little different.[64] These units are formed to provide assistance to start-up companies, which may or may not be linked with university research. The units themselves have low capital requirements, often starting out in unused buildings. Such arrangements serve the vital objective of keeping costs as low as possible for tenants. Incubators' ties with universities are likely to be more tenuous than those of research parks; and tenants are not likely to share technology with each other. But given the low investment, the economic gains are almost purely additive. Here too, universities are able to make an incremental contribution to the local economy.

As the technology transfer boom began to ebb at the end of the 1980s, a degree of disillusionment became evident. The most thorough study of research parks held that far too many parks had been created and implied that many of them should be considered failures.[65] Openings of new parks slowed to five per year from 1990 to 1996, and these were largely the result of projects initiated in the 1980s. The pessimism was undoubtedly overdone—a product of unrealistic expectations as well as the cloud overhanging university research. Soon, appreciation of the nexus between academic research and economic development began to revive, along with more critical thinking about the potential contribution of parks and incubators.

At the end of the 1990s, the Internet boom provoked amazement once again at the fecundity of a few fortunate regions. Clearly, something greater than propinquity and additional jobs was at work. Economic geographers attributed this phenomenon to the economics of *agglomeration*. They meant that, owing to dense interactions among numerous producers, productivity tends to rise at the same time that gross output expands.[66] Firms extract resources from their surroundings more easily than they develop them internally. This was true as well for the kinds of knowledge produced from generic research: cutting-edge, research-based knowledge is far too vast to internalize within any but a monopolist firm, but the more dense and multivalent the external transactions, the greater the likelihood of extracting valuable information.

University planners had no need for such theory. They were mesmerized by the same models as economic geographers. They sought means to transcend the pattern of piecemeal additions to the local economy and to induce synergistic interactions among universities and their partners (path C, Figure 15). They envisioned a kind of takeoff into self-sustaining development that would benefit all concerned, but that particularly would bring additional resources to universities. Accordingly, the late 1990s witnessed new departures in the harnessing of technology transfer for economic development.

CENTENNIAL CAMPUS

The new Centennial Campus at North Carolina State University has radically advanced the notion of integrating industry and academe. Unabashedly aspiring to create a "technopolis," the Centennial Campus is also part of a strategy to make NC State one of the country's leading land-grant universities.[67] In the 1980s the university was fortunate to acquire an enormous parcel of land close by its cramped and aging main campus. The space was needed for academic expansion and also provided the opportunity to create a research park. Over time, these two objectives merged into a new vision of a partnership between the university and knowledge consumers.

The most difficult obstacle during the initial stages was enticing industry to participate. NC State began to develop the campus by employing state building appropriations. The first structure housed the College of Textiles, and the next major installation was for the Engineering Graduate Research Center. Both units had ties with industry and further extended their research interaction with federal grants for a National Textile Center and three NSF University/Industry Research Centers. The state then assisted these efforts by authorizing the university to float self-financing bonds for further development, making it possible for the campus to develop research space for private tenants. Buildings constructed on this basis had to generate income to cover these costs, whether occupied by companies or university units.

A threshold of sorts was passed when major corporations opted to locate on the campus. First the Swedish firm ABB, then Lucent Technologies and Red Hat, constructed buildings of their own for corporate offices and research laboratories. In these cases, the crucial factor for the location decision was the opportunity for close interaction with students and faculty. Their presence made the campus all the more attractive to smaller enterprises.

The university too gradually relocated academic units to the campus.

The College of Engineering will be fully ensconced on the Centennial Campus by 2005. As of 2002, the campus accommodated sixty-five corporate and government entities and seventy research or departmental units of the university. When fully developed it is projected to accommodate 12,500 corporate and government employees (five times the number in 2002) and a like number of NC State students, staff, and faculty (three times the number in 2002).[68]

The symmetry of these projected figures suggests the equivalent status accorded to the mostly industrial tenants. For example, tenants are accorded the same campus privileges as faculty and students. Indeed, interaction is the foremost principle. Negotiations with prospective tenants, or "partners," begin with roundtable meetings to discuss how they foresee interacting with the university and establishing complementary relationships. Tenants are assigned their own "partnership developer," who oversees and facilitates these contacts. The campus's Partnership Office also helps facilitate connections between tenants seeking expertise and scientists seeking contacts with industry. The entire design of the campus is intended to facilitate formal and informal contacts. It is organized into four R&D neighborhoods: advanced materials, advanced communication technologies, biosciences/biotechnology, and environmental technologies (not yet built). University classrooms are interspersed with industrial offices and labs. In addition, lectures and social activities are intended to augment interaction.

From industry's point of view, the Centennial Campus maximizes the enhancement benefits of academic research discussed earlier. Of course, access to field-intensive or field-extensive expertise is close at hand, and the partnership developers can assist in making such connections. Probably even more valuable is the potential for human capital or personnel enhancement. Industry researchers can enrich their learning through formally arranged courses or through informal contacts. And tenant firms can employ students, graduates, or postdocs. As an additional benefit, they have access to all of the university's sophisticated instrumentation. The university encourages them to take advantage of all of this—no special negotiations required.

For its part, NC State appears to have benefited considerably. Although such an embrace of industry would not be well received at all universities, given its regional proximity to academic leaders Duke and UNC Chapel Hill, NC State has had little recourse but to emphasize its land-grant heritage and culture. It has developed strong programs in engineering and computer science, as well as food and veterinary science. It has traditionally been oriented more toward the private consumers of research than toward academic ones.

The old campus is enclosed by the city of Raleigh and ripe for renovation. The Centennial Campus not only provided the space for expansion, but a rationale for reinvigoration too. The public-private partnership used to develop the campus has proved effective. Financially, the campus supports itself to a substantial degree through income from tenants and, for the university's space, indirect cost reimbursements on sponsored research. NC State is one of the few universities without a medical school that has consistently gained research share in the current era, and the Centennial Campus of late has made a large contribution (one-third of the total). Believing so strongly in the efficacy of this model, in 2002 the university announced a master plan to replicate it by developing a separate Centennial Biomedical Campus centered on the Veterinary College. A similar combination of borrowed and private funding will be employed, and research is expected to expand significantly.[69]

Centennial Campus, through construction and new employers, has undoubtedly contributed to economic activity in and around Raleigh. The university's larger aspiration has been to stimulate a creative infrastructure with an entrepreneurial culture that would generate sustained growth. To this end it has sought to create a critical mass of creative scientists and to provide the appropriate conduits for their interaction. The campus includes a business incubator and a venture capital fund to facilitate these possibilities. These initiatives have vaulted NC State into national recognition for technology transfer and particularly for spawning start-up firms.[70] Its working model for university-industry collaboration generates more technological innovation and technology transfer than piecemeal efforts existing elsewhere and challenges the widespread notion that close relations with industry compromise academic integrity.

According to Vice Chancellor Charles G. Moreland, an architect of the Centennial model, there is no question of compromise on matters of academic freedom or intellectual property. The university deals with industry from a position of strength; the only viable policy is to uphold academic standards consistently and uniformly. Moreover, this model could not possibly succeed without the cooperation and support of the faculty, who appreciate that the campus is not a real estate development reflecting the values of business. It is a true campus where academic mores predominate.

Industry too seems to want it that way. All indications are that firms value the academic atmosphere and above all the enhancement benefits that they derive from the richness of the academic surroundings.[71]

There may be one point of agreement between critics and boosters: the degree of close collaboration posited by the Centennial model requires a large input of faculty time and effort. Supporters—faculty members who thrive in this culture—find these exertions intellectually and professionally stimulating. Scholars more interested in making contributions to their disciplines would feel differently and would not likely be content in such a setting. Thus the Centennial model may not be easily replicated at other universities. However, even if NC State represents one extreme on a spectrum, it has blazed a path for both university and economic development.[72]

YAMACRAW

Georgia has taken a different but no less novel path. The state has furthered university-industry collaboration with the intent of promoting economic growth, chiefly by capitalizing on the expansion of greater Atlanta and the region's desire to develop high-tech industries. Equally vital has been the presence of the Georgia Institute of Technology, a unique technologically focused institution without which those aspirations could scarcely be realized.[73]

Like many states, Georgia adopted measures to boost university research in the 1980s. The Governor's Research Consortium supported the creation of several specialized university centers from 1986 to 1990, usually by providing buildings and equipment. As this project expired, a group of Atlanta businessmen sought to sustain the effort, and also to rekindle the state's interest. They created the Georgia Research Alliance (GRA) as a nonprofit corporation, directed by the CEOs of twelve Georgia corporations and the presidents of the state's six principal universities.[74] With the governor's backing and state appropriations, the GRA made strategic investments in the research capacity of member universities. By 1999, over $300 million in state (79 percent) and private (21 percent) funds had been expended to create chairs for "eminent scholars" and support for research infrastructure. That year a grander coalition of state, university, and industrial partners announced a more ambitious undertaking.

For much of the previous year a group of scientists, consultants, and university and civic leaders had met secretly to devise a strategy for a focused development of high-tech industry and employment. The group's code name was Yamacraw, which the project has retained. The group concluded that the design of broadband telecommunications systems, devices, and chips was the critical technology in which Atlanta and Georgia might develop a comparative advantage and international leadership. The industry was booming, Atlanta possessed a large industry base, and design engineers were in short supply. If Georgia universities could supply technology and human capital, they speculated, the industry would develop around these resources. The state committed $100 million over five to seven years, and Yamacraw began operations in 2000.[75]

The state universities are the key element in this elaborate scheme to create high-tech jobs. The bulk of the funds are designated for the creation of eighty-four faculty chairs at the eight participating institutions. These positions are intended to attract outstanding researchers who, together with students and staff, will develop and enhance technology in three crucial areas: broadband access hardware, embedded software, and system prototyping. Industry affiliates are attracted to the project to gain access to this technology, with different terms of membership for small and large companies. To join, firms must promise to create a specific number of jobs for Yamacraw graduates (100 for full members; 20 for emerging members) and pay a nominal annual fee ($25,000 and $5,000). The universities, for their part, foresee increasing the number of graduates in the three fields from 400 to 1,000 per year. To do this, they have added Yamacraw-inspired courses to the curriculum, a step that goes well beyond most economic development projects.[76]

The project's original objective was the creation of 2,000 additional positions for design professionals, but after two years 1,000 new jobs had been filled and another 2,000 pledged. At the halfway point in the project, 64 Yamacraw faculty and more than 200 researchers were in place. Half of those positions were created at Georgia Tech, where the Departments of Electrical Engineering and Computer Science were ideally suited for this opportunity, and where special ORUs of this type were routine.

Yamacraw faculty and researchers present and publish their research through regular academic outlets. However, findings of potential proprietary value are unveiled at closed meetings of affiliates, where they are expected to lead to patent licenses or start-up ventures. A venture capital fund also assists the formation of start-up firms. In sum, in a short time the Yamacraw project created a large, extremely talented, interactive scientific community focused on specific areas of technological innovation.[77]

The planning, design, and execution of the Yamacraw project provide a textbook case of successful economic development policy. Ugly reality nevertheless began to intrude in 2001 when a deep depression engulfed the telecommunications industry. By 2002, the state was holding back funds for the remaining professorships, and the hiring targets of some member firms were deferred. Still, compared with the devastation throughout the industry, Yamacraw was comparatively unaffected.

Two lessons seem evident. First, the wild card in economic development strategies is the economy. As universities commit themselves to economic development and harness their activities to particular industries, they expose themselves to increasing risk from the vagaries of the economy. Second, the Yamacraw strategy avoided much potential vulnerability by concentrating on cutting-edge research and the training of experts. Yamacraw, in other words, was not a job-training program, but rather an investment in human and intellectual capital. That capital retained its value despite the temporary glut of telecommunications equipment. Furthermore, the investment has been extremely productive for universities, precisely because it extended and exploited what universities do best.

Georgia Tech may have been the chief beneficiary of Yamacraw, but there was also a considerable trickle-down effect. Regional public universities were able to attract far better faculty and students in computer sciences than they had formerly. Still, Georgia Tech is the locus for the project, most of the research, and the permanent building for the Yamacraw Design Center. For Georgia Tech, Yamacraw was another building block in a quest to fashion the country's foremost public technological university. Georgia Tech prides itself on its engineering mission, and more than half its faculty are in the Colleges of Engineering and Computer Science. That mission has always encompassed a commitment to economic development.[78] The institute aims not only to develop new technologies, but also to ensure their utilization by industry. Georgia Tech's units for this purpose are intertwined with those of the state, and its development has in turn been furthered by state policies.

The University System of Georgia funds its institutions on a credit-hour basis that works against higher-cost research universities. The latter have benefited instead from the state's desire to nurture high-tech industry. For these purposes the state has been willing to invest in quality. Hence GRA and Yamacraw have allowed Georgia Tech to add centers of academic excellence that base funding could never cover. Moreover, these additions were strategically chosen for their contribution to technology development.

Georgia Tech also benefited in a serendipitous way from another state investment in higher education, the HOPE Scholarships. The lure of free tuition dramatically affected the attendance of high-ability Georgia students. For many of those opting to study in Georgia, Tech was the natural choice. The institute has become one of the most selective public institutions, attracting talented applicants from the national pool as well as its home state.

Still, much of the credit for Georgia Tech's efflorescence belongs with the institution itself. It has fostered an entrepreneurial culture among its faculty and relies on their initiatives to develop and disseminate technology. Administration is largely decentralized, allowing units to retain much of the revenue generated from their research to recycle into new projects. Moreover, such funds can be leveraged to hire additional faculty. By any reckoning, the state of Georgia has reaped a generous return from its investments in Georgia Tech.

Georgia Tech aspires to "define the technological university of the 21st century," a goal even loftier than that of NC State.[79] Both universities represent paradigms for interaction with industry that far transcend earlier models. The growth of commercial ties by universities in the 1980s was explained at the time as a form of "opportunism," designed to take advantage of the occasional discovery with commercial value.[80] Most university efforts were designed to systematically identify and exploit such opportunities; they were less apt to create new ones. The Centennial and Yamacraw models, and the universities that fashioned them, are designed to do exactly that—to build the ties and the culture that will expand the opportunities for technology development. They deliberately aim to generate the effects of agglomeration where a heightened level of interaction between researchers and engineers in universities and industry will significantly magnify both the scale of university research and the amount of technological innovation conveyed to industry. And unlike the earlier, passive university models, which were then regarded with justified skepticism, these new paradigms really work: they fostered both academic and economic development.

They have also shaped, or perhaps greatly enlarged, a new academic role, that of more or less continuous, as opposed to sporadic or serendipitous, technology transfer. This development, for all its benefits, represents an extension of university-industry collaboration beyond the role of enhancement and closer to that of commercialization.

Biotechnology and the Commercialization of Technology Transfer

The outstanding scientific revolution of the last quarter of the twentieth century occurred in biotechnology. Scientifically, this development was comparable to the unlocking and harnessing of atomic energy from the

1940s to the 1960s. Economically, however, the consequences were rather different. Atomic energy led to giant, government-dominated industries to produce weapons and electric power. Although still in existence, both these endeavors are limited in scope and have long been contracting. In contrast, biotechnology holds enormous promise for the fundamental industries of agriculture and human health. With potential applications that have only begun to be tapped, biotechnology is inextricably linked with these spheres of economic activity. Although the principal commitment of universities has been to the advancement of biological science, it has not been possible to isolate this endeavor from the vast industries it affects.

The term *biotechnology* is an apt rubric for the revolution in understanding of life processes at the molecular level. Basic research in this field has depended on novel techniques for manipulating genetic and other molecular material. The initial breakthrough occurred in 1973 when Herbert Boyer and Stanley Cohen perfected the technique for splicing genes: recombinant DNA. When they patented their discovery, it became doubly paradigmatic for the field. Subsequent discoveries and developments are far too numerous to recount. Their effect was not merely to expand understanding, but to open vast scientific terrain for both further investigations and potential applications.[81]

As the twenty-first century opened, biological scientists were active on multiple frontiers, including isolating the expression of single genes (functional genomics) and determining the actions of proteins whose production they control (proteomics). As a scientific revolution, biotechnology has focused on the common bases of life, thereby making the previous divisions of biology passé. The most thoroughly researched organisms have included yeast, e-coli, drosophilia, and zebra fish. However, the greatest scientific prizes and the greatest economic payoffs lie with human biology and the health care industry. Symbolically, the full human genome was decoded in 2001—simultaneously by a corporate project and an academic one.

Biotechnology is the most dynamic component in the enormous enterprise of biomedical science. This field is dominated on one side by the National Institutes of Health and on the other by large corporations of the health care industry. NIH, after comparatively small budget growth early in the 1990s, saw its appropriations double in five years to over $23 billion in 2002—a 15 percent growth rate reminiscent of the golden age in the 1960s. The majority of these funds support research projects, primarily in universities and university-affiliated medical centers. Additional programs aid biomedical research and training in other ways. Universities are thus the principal recipients of NIH funds.

Industry spending for biomedical R&D is even greater—an estimated $30 billion in 2001—and has been growing more rapidly.[82] The largest spender, Pfizer, alone allocated $5.3 billion for R&D in 2001 (compared with less than $2 billion in 1996). After Pfizer are ranked a long list of pharmaceutical giants, based in the United States and elsewhere, several maturing biotech firms with $1 billion or more in sales, and various medical supply firms and health care conglomerates. Still, small and medium-sized firms also play important roles in this immense industry, including a steady stream of university-based start-ups.[83] With health care expenditures exceeding $1 trillion in the United States, any useful innovation might earn a share of the lucre.

University biotechnology, and biomedical research more generally, thus lies at the confluence of a scientific revolution of huge import and a dynamic, profitable, high-tech industry. The scientific potential of the field has ensured ample support for research, not just from the federal government but also from industry, states, philanthropy, and universities themselves. And its obvious potential for commercial development has drawn universities ineluctably into commercial relationships.

The most significant feature of biotechnology in the shaping of those relationships is the direct connection between basic research in molecular biology and potential commercial applications. This seemingly inherent condition is powerfully affected by social and legal factors. Most fateful is the large role of patents in defining and controlling intellectual property. Hence patents occupy a critical point in relationships between the academic and commercial wings of the biosciences.

These relationships represent a second fundamental feature of biotechnology: instead of a clear division of labor between academic and industrial scientists, the field has evolved into separately organized parts of a single scientific community. Scientific cooperation and competition flow across both sectors. This fluidity has a number of consequences, but it particularly facilitates the commercialization of the field.

A third fundamental feature has been the drift of biotechnology toward Big Science. Almost from the outset, biotechnology required teams of researchers to link molecular biology with specialties such as genetics, immunology, and virology. The development of the field has incorporated larger and more complex instruments, as well as advanced computation. At the cutting edge, biotechnology research now requires large teams, extensive interaction among teams, and large capital investments. Taken separately, none of these features is unique to biotechnology, but together they have created a set of conditions that represent a special case for academic science.[84]

PATENTS AND LICENSING

Universities have long engaged in patenting on the infrequent occasions when valuable inventions emerged from their laboratories. The Research Corporation was established in 1912 to assist them on such occasions, and in 1925 the lucrative patent for vitamin D donated by a University of Wisconsin scientist became the basis for the Wisconsin Alumni Research Foundation. Before 1970, fewer than 200 patents were awarded annually to universities, less than 0.5 percent of the total. By the 1990s, however, academic patenting was a major preoccupation of research universities, although still less than 2 percent of the national total. Academic patenting differs in character from industrial patenting, and it has come to be dominated by biomedical sciences.

A patent confers to its owner exclusive rights to utilize an invention for a period of twenty years. It thus allows an entrepreneur to exclude imitators in order to develop and sell a new product. This simple description, however, belies both the limitations and the complications of the role of patenting in the economy. Patents are most effective for protecting innovations that are discrete and readily defined. They also tend to be more effective for products than for processes. Accordingly, patenting is most dominant for chemicals and drugs, where these conditions obtain. Nevertheless, the largest classes of patents nationally are electrical and mechanical, fields where patents play multiple roles.

Besides preventing copying, patents are used to block the development of related products, to establish positions for negotiations, to preclude infringement suits, and to earn licensing revenues. A study by Wesley Cohen and colleagues found that "firms that patent the most are disproportionately concerned about prevention of suits and the use of patents in negotiations"; and that "using patents to earn licensing revenue is the least important reason for [firms] applying for patents."[85] For universities, however, licensing revenue is easily the foremost reason for patenting.[86] For them patents are not a means to produce a product; patents are the product.

The number of patents awarded in the United States began to rise unevenly in the mid-1980s, after two decades of stagnation. By the late 1990s the total had doubled to nearly 150,000. The majority of these patents were awarded for mechanical or electrical inventions; drugs and medical patents constituted less than 10 percent. The number of academic patents grew far more rapidly, rising from roughly 500 to 2,500 in the same period. Drug and medical patents were the chief drivers of this growth, rising from 18 to 46 percent of academic patents, but these figures understate their importance. Drug and medical patents provide far and away the bulk of licensing revenues for the major participants. For the twenty universities that garnered the highest royalties in 1997, 81 percent of the income came from life sciences patents (see Table 13).[87] Without these windfalls the current scale of academic patenting could not be supported.

The trend toward greater academic patenting was discernible during the 1970s at a handful of precocious institutions, including Stanford, MIT, and the University of California.[88] However, the new developments of the 1980s soon engulfed the majority of research universities. In addition to the biotechnology revolution, greater funding for biomedical research, and the general enthusiasm for technology transfer, changes specific to patenting made it far more attractive for universities. The Patent and Trademark Amendments of 1980 (Public Law 96–517), popularly known as the Bayh-Dole Act, was the opening wedge.

The act allowed universities to retain property rights for discoveries made through federally funded research, which at the time supported two-thirds of academic R&D. It thus enlarged the potential scope of university patenting and also invited universities to become more active. The prevailing belief was that lack of patent protection inhibited the development of new technologies, thus depressing the potential for economic growth. This belief continued to be translated into public policy through a series of measures that strengthened intellectual property rights and encouraged the commercialization of university discoveries.[89]

Of particular importance for biotechnology was a 1982 court decision (*Diamond* vs. *Chakrabarty*) that upheld the patenting of engineered life forms, later extended to genetic material. This drift of events made active patenting virtually irresistible for universities. Besides the lotterylike lure of royalty jackpots, this form of technology transfer was engraved in public policy as a duty to the economy. Furthermore, the legal bolstering of intellectual property rights permitted the patenting of more general concepts—the kind most likely to arise from basic academic research.

Universities responded to these cues chiefly by establishing their own intellectual property or technology transfer units. Whereas just twenty universities possessed such units before Bayh-Dole, fifty-nine established an office in the 1980s, including most universities in this study; and another fifty-three did so in the 1990s.[90] These later entrants had previously referred invention disclosures to the Research Corporation or other patent management organizations, but the new technology transfer offices (TTOs) encouraged scientists to seek more patents. They are responsible for soliciting and evaluating disclosures from faculty inventors, on one hand, and shepherding inventions through the maze of the patent system on the other. Their skill and the extent of their resources directly affect the propensity of faculty to disclose potentially patentable discoveries as well as the profitability of a university's patent portfolio.[91] Not surprisingly, well-established offices proved more adept at these tasks than neophytes; but both new and old hands contributed to swelling the annual number of academic patents awarded to 1,000 by the end of the 1980s.

Many analysts greeted the boom in academic patenting of the 1980s skeptically.[92] Patenting on the small scale of most universities is an expensive sideline and difficult to do well, which is why patent management organizations had been used for this task. A separate office represents a substantial overhead cost, and fees for a single patent application averaged nearly $14,000 in the 1990s. A blockbuster patent might bring huge returns, but since the best ideas are acted on first, it seemed unlikely that filing more patent applications would produce more big hits.

Critics may have been right on at least two points, but they missed two other factors of considerable importance. One was the enormous potential for royalties from biotechnology. Largely owing to the earnings from biomedical patents, licensing revenues in the 1990s increased at roughly twice the rate of university patenting. Critics also failed to foresee how TTOs would adapt to the calculus of patenting. Increasingly, they placed licensing above all other considerations when deciding when and what to patent. Standard practice was adjusted so that arrangements for licensing were made before applying for a patent. This practice was greatly abetted when the U.S. Patent and Trademark Office introduced provisional patents in 1995. These allow inventors to protect intellectual property for one year at a modest cost.[93] Provisional patents were ideal for universities, which used the twelve months of protection to find licensees willing to cover the costs of a regular patent. At the end of the 1990s licensees were reimbursing universities for more than 40 percent of the $100 million bill for obtaining patents.[94]

The foresight of critics was sound on two other matters. First, the increased rate of university patenting did not seem to increase the number of important academic patents, but it did greatly expand the number of marginal patents. Before 1980, academic patents were on average more important and more general than corporate patents, judging from citation patterns, but by the end of the 1980s that difference had disappeared. The overall quality of patents from leading universities declined somewhat, but the patents of newcomers were for the most part of less value.[95] Thus increased patenting did appear to yield decreasing returns.

TABLE 13

16 Universities with the Most Licensing Revenue, Selected Data, 1999

University	R&D rank, 2000	Licensing revenues ($ millions)	Percent Life Science	Patents issued	Total active licenses and options	Industry research ($ millions)	Start-up companies
Columbia University	25	95.8	85.7	77	706	3.4	5
University of California System	a	80.9	66.0	281	1,078	177.6	13
Florida State University	92	57.3	97.0	5	20	0.7	1
Yale University	29	40.8	98.7	37	237	14.4	3
Stanford University	8	40.1	81.9	90	872	41.3	19
University of Washington	5	27.9	80	36	207	57.4	n.a.
Michigan State University	42	23.7	99.6	63	134	11.2	1
University of Florida	26	21.6	98.8	58	124	34.9	2
University of Wisconsin	2	18.0	75.1	79	346	16.1	4
Massachusetts Institute of Technology	12	17.1	69.9	154	565	83.1	17
Emory University	46	16.2	58.2	44	82	7.5	4
State University of New York System	b	13.6	95.5	53	298	17.5	3
Harvard University	23	13.5	94.9	72	388	12.2	2
Baylor College of Medicine	24	12.5	98.4	25	221	17.6	0
New York University	55	10.7		30	30	7.7	2
Johns Hopkins University	1	10.5	99.7	111	370	46.9	7
Total, all universities		675.5	80	3,079	15,203	2,178.2	275
16 universities' share of total (percent)		74	84.8	39.5	37.3	25.2	30.2

Sources: *AUTM Licensing Survey: FY1999*; Life Sciences percent from *AUTM Licensing Survey: FY1996*; R&D$ from NSF, 2000 data; Johns Hopkins data include APL.

[a]UC campus R&D rank: Los Angeles: 4; San Diego: 6; Berkeley: 7; San Francisco: 9; Davis: 17; Irvine: 67; Santa Barbara: 88; Riverside: 108; Santa Cruz: 128.

[b]SUNY campus R&D rank: Buffalo: 53; Stony Brook: 63; Albany: 109.

n.a. = not available.

Second, only a few of the newcomers were able to replicate the success of the existing patent leaders. Institutions that did vault to the top—Columbia (TTO in 1982), the University of Washington (1983), and Emory (1985)— owed their success to biomedical patents. Others will probably follow.

The distribution of virtually all measures associated with patents has nevertheless remained highly skewed. For example, in 1999 the top twenty universities for licensing income received 74 percent of all such income; the twenty with the most active licenses and options had 61 percent of the total; the top twenty patenters were issued 46 percent of all academic patents; and the twenty largest TTOs employed 44 percent of licensing professionals.[96] The universities in each of these categories are not identical, but they overlap substantially. Table 13 lists the leaders in academic patenting and those with the strongest commercial ties.

The patenting and licensing revenues of universities are sometimes used as indicators of economic involvement. From the data in Table 13, it appears doubtful that they represent anything other than patenting and licensing. Two factors account for this. First, by their nature, patents are exceptional byproducts of academic research, even after the great expansion.[97] Other outcomes, such as large licensing royalties and start-up firms, are more exceptional still.[98] Second, these outcomes are highly localized in certain fields — engineering, biotechnology, and areas of medicine such as surgery and pharmacy. The comparisons portrayed in Table 13 thus reflect parts of universities that have developed quite differentially as well as commercial valuations of technologies that are determined entirely outside of universities.

Table 13 depicts universities that earned more than $10 million in gross licensing revenues in 1999. This measure is the most skewed, because of the enormous payoffs of a few blockbuster patents, predominantly in the life sciences. Columbia owes its top status to the Axel patent for a gene-transfer process used in the commercial production of proteins. Harvard in 1996 received the majority of its royalties from a heart-imaging contrast agent. The University of Washington owes its patenting payoffs to technologies for producing hepatitis B vaccine and interferon. Such big winners are all the more conspicuous at universities with smaller patenting efforts: the anticancer drug taxol developed at Florida State and antitumor agents at Michigan State, for example.[99]

Beyond the impact of blockbusters, the skewed nature of academic patenting seems to reflect the existence of an elite group of active and successful universities. These institutions consistently rank among the top ten in patents issued, and appear to be extending their cumulative advantage in quality and quantity. These institutions — the University of California (which reports its nine campuses as one system), MIT, Stanford, Columbia, and Wisconsin — were early to establish patenting offices, develop a campus culture favorable to the patenting process, and build a strong presence in biotechnology.[100] They also have been able to invest in hiring professional staff for their patenting offices. Indeed, even disregarding the multicampus University of California, the consistent dominance of the patenting leadership by this handful of institutions is notable.

Of all the factors contributing to patenting success, the organization of the TTO seems to be the most readily replicated. Indeed most major universities have established such offices, and the greatest growth in patenting has been generated by institutions that ramped up their TTOs. In 1999, fifty universities obtained twenty or more patents, and twenty received forty or more. The comparable numbers of institutions for six years earlier were eighteen and five. The continuing advantage of the patenting elite is evident in the most prized outcomes—licensing income and start-ups. A study of this phenomenon by Jason Owen-Smith credits the experience and expertise of TTO professionals with fashioning a patenting process that is in harmony with faculty interests and culture. Smaller and less-experienced TTOs, in contrast, tend to operate like bureaucracies, resulting in delay, inconvenience, and rigid decision rules. Most important, Owen-Smith concluded, an efficient and effective TTO made patenting *more* compatible with academic science than did more bureaucratic offices, which were narrowly focused on generating income.[101]

The patenting leaders in Table 13 spawned by far the most start-up companies. Although such companies are more exceptional than patents, they form one of the most fruitful connections between patenting and economic development. Start-ups are one manifestation of a larger nexus between university patents and small business. The Bayh-Dole Act actually contained a stipulation that small businesses would receive preference in developing university inventions. This preference has never been incorporated into university policies, but most licenses for university patents are executed by small businesses or start-ups.[102] This phenomenon, by its very nature, is likely to generate economic activity that would not otherwise have taken place. The reasons for this illuminate several aspects of academic patenting.

One survey of academic patents found that "more than 75% of the inventions licensed were no more than proof of concept (48% with no prototype available) or lab scale prototype (29%)."[103] Several consequences follow. First, the value of most such inventions is initially indeterminate; it emerges only later, if at all, through subsequent development. For this reason, most academic inventions need to be marketed rather deliberately to potential licensees. The most effective TTOs depend on faculty inventors and their networks to establish such contacts. Most patent licenses are then negotiated with a single interested firm rather than auctioned to eager bidders. Second, universities report that small businesses are more amenable to this situation; that is, they are more willing than large firms to invest time, effort, and resources in an unproven invention in the hope of developing a proprietary product.[104] Hence small businesses provide the most direct conduit to the economy. Third, the theoretical nature of these inventions creates a condition in which the continued involvement of the faculty inventor is virtually required for the eventual development of a product.[105] This last fact has implications universities cannot ignore.

Faculty start-ups naturally combine the commitment of a fledgling company with the involvement of the inventor, but all this comes at a price to the university's most valued resource. During the first biotech boom, Stanford president Donald Kennedy complained that the university was losing "parts of people."[106] Universities had little choice but to tolerate this situation, since attempts to prevent it would probably have meant losing all of those people. More recently, however, patent leaders seem to have concluded they have more to gain than to lose by facilitating start-ups. By providing assistance to a faculty entrepreneur in organizing a company and securing funding, the university can simultaneously minimize the portion of the faculty member's effort that is lost and improve the chances for the company's success. At MIT the possibility of forming a start-up is considered from the initial evaluation of disclosures, and about 10 percent of inventors choose this route. Such arrangements now represent best practice and figure prominently in the economic development strategies of NC State and Georgia Tech, among others. Commonly, invention disclosures are analyzed by TTOs to devise the best strategy for commercialization. If a start-up company is the alternative chosen, the university provides assistance for organizing, financing, and managing the enterprise.

In addition, universities have increasingly structured licensing agreements in ways that enhance the viability of a new company. In practical terms, this usually means accepting equity instead of royalties. For TTOs that need to generate immediate revenues to support their own operations, such an approach holds little attraction. Once again, patent leaders have the flexibility to take a longer view, and perhaps to make arrangements more beneficial for the new firm and the university.[107]

Finally, one might infer from Table 13 that there is little or no relationship between academic patenting and industrial funding of academic research. (Of the universities with large numbers of patents, about half perform considerable research for industry and half do not.) Such a conclusion highlights the dichotomy between the traditional model of university-industry research relations and the emergent pattern for biotechnology. Appropriately perhaps, such a conclusion also seems only half right.

The patenting of academic discoveries serves rather different purposes in the physical and the life sciences.[108] In both areas scientists patent to protect their discoveries and to use them as leverage for gaining more resources. In the physical sciences, however, patents usually have less monetary value.

Scientists and engineers are content to use patents much like bargaining chips to build relationships with industrial laboratories. These relationships bring benefits primarily for a scientist's own research: access to relevant industrial research, donations of sophisticated equipment, and research grants and support for graduate students. The effects of patenting in the physical sciences are thus consistent with the traditional division of labor between industrial and academic research. In the life sciences, where patents are more lucrative, patents produce financial capital to propel the research process. Patents are crucial to obtaining venture capital or large industrial investments in a line of research. Size matters. Life scientists with access to these forms of support are able to expand their laboratories and research staff, to publish more, and to compete more effectively for NIH grants.

The different behavior of physical and life scientists is particularly telling in the creation of start-up companies. Physical scientists and engineers acknowledge the existence of the two cultures. When they are enticed into spin-off firms they often take a leave of absence from academic responsibilities to devote themselves wholly to their commercial role. Life scientists, for whom this is a more common occurrence, almost always retain their academic post and simultaneously pursue both roles.[109] These different approaches reflect the different realities of these fields. In engineering and the physical sciences the traditional model still holds. Academic research, whether basic or generic, serves as a source of enhancement for industrial research, but the two realms are fundamentally separate. Industry prefers to develop products in its own laboratories whether patenting is involved or not. Both sides have much to offer each other, contributions that complement their respective tasks.

In biotechnology, in contrast, the science is largely the same in academic and industrial laboratories.[110] The best brains *may* be in the universities, but they are available for hire. The financial resources of industry nevertheless allow some scientific tasks to be performed more effectively there. The relationship is not just complementary, but cumulative—the wider and deeper the research networks, the more fruitful they are likely to be. Under these circumstances it becomes difficult to internalize knowledge generation in the way that other industries employ trade secrets and first-mover advantages. Rather, access to multiple external knowledge resources becomes indispensable for discovery, whether to win the approval of the National Institutes of Health or of the Food and Drug Administration.[111] This distinctive feature of biotechnology, more than the large role of patenting, helps to explain the curious development of the field.

BIOTECHNOLOGY AND BIOCAPITALISM

The commingling of academic and commercial science is scarcely unique to biotechnology. In other high-tech fields industry has for a time seized primacy in research (for example, microelectronics in the late 1970s). The perplexing feature of biotechnology has been the absence subsequently of the emergence of a clear division of labor—of respective spheres of endeavor. Instead, the close interaction of academic and commercial science has persisted even as the industry has matured. Recent studies have shown that distinctive factors shaped biotechnology as it developed.

When the basic techniques of recombinant DNA were developed in the 1970s, relatively few scientists possessed the tacit knowledge, as opposed to codified knowledge published in scientific papers, to engage in biotechnology research. Studies by Lynne Zucker and associates have demonstrated that the expertise of these few scientists, the "stars," was the critical input for both commercial and academic development of the field.[112] Star scientists were distinguished by outstanding publishing productivity. They were also heavily involved in commercialization through patenting and ties with biotech firms. Because of the esoteric nature of this breakthrough technology—a product of new techniques, tacit knowledge, and complexity—their knowledge was vital to advance academic understanding, to train additional practitioners, and to develop commercial products. Most of them did all these things, retaining their academic posts and also establishing ties with new biotech firms.

One interesting result is that this expertise remained highly localized. New biotech firms tended to be founded in the same places as the academic stars. Consequently, the largest industry clusters developed around Cambridge, Mass., the New York metropolitan area, Baltimore/Bethesda, and the San Francisco Bay Area. Second, this pattern of development produced true synergies, for both sides. Biotech firms with star collaborators tended to be more successful; and stars with commercial ties also had greater academic success—publishing more, having more collaborators, and receiving more citations to their work. These synergies apparently created the unusual situation where the leading scientists in a field dominate the transfer of technology to industry (see Figure 14). But there appears to be a good reason for this. The additional resources that these stars garnered from their commercial ties apparently allowed them to perform more and better work.[113]

After 1990, biotechnology was still a youthful and dynamic industry, but no longer in a fledgling state. The techniques of recombinant DNA could now be learned in any major university. Yet the confounding of academic and commercial science described in the Zucker study became more, not less, prominent. Now, though, the cause was somewhat different. According to a study by W. W. Powell and associates, biotechnology firms were led by the nature of the knowledge base to form increasing numbers of R&D alliances and contacts. These "learning networks" were necessitated by the rapid expansion of the knowledge base and its distributed nature. Because firms could not contain and control all of the vital, relevant knowledge internally, they had to depend on networks to sustain active learning.[114]

The same was true for academic biotechnology. Given the advanced level of science in biotech firms, collaboration contributed to network learning on both sides. The density of network contacts of this kind also promoted commercial activity by academic scientists. Close interaction with their counterparts in industry virtually ensured that potentially valuable discoveries would be quickly identified and advanced toward commercialization. As a result, university-industry ties no longer result from a scarcity of expertise, but rather from the dense interconnections in the biotechnology complex.

In one sense, biotechnology has probably set the pattern for commercial involvement for all biomedical scientists. In particular, direct ties with medical or pharmaceutical companies became the rule rather than the exception in many departments, even without the scientific interdependence that characterized biotech fields. Perhaps most significant has been the continued involvement and financial interest of life science faculty in the development of commercial products. The vague nature of most academic patents virtually requires the continuing involvement of the inventor, and the most effective way to ensure this is by tying financial incentives to the successful development of a product.[115] In this way, biotechnology faculty in particular, and life sciences faculty more generally, evolved a pattern, now widely accepted, of holding a financial interest in commercialization.

The pattern of technology transfer that has evolved in biotechnology is represented in Figure 16. Superficially, it resembles the patterns depicted in Figure 15, but the differences are fundamental. In the former scheme—the traditional pattern—the knowledge transferred was an *intermediate good*. As such, it possessed no intrinsic value. It acquired tangible value only after first being transferred to industry, and then being combined with industry's own stock of intellectual capital to develop marketable products. This was true whether the conduit was an industrial R&D laboratory or a start-up company; and whether the knowledge in question was broadly generic or a commissioned piece of research targeted for a specific need.

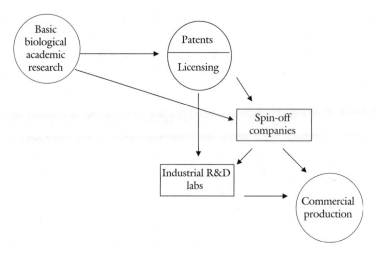

FIG. 16. Biotechnology: Pathways from Academic Research to Industrial Production

In biotechnology, in contrast, the knowledge transferred from universities to industry takes the form of intellectual property. In most cases the knowledge is patented and licensed to either an established or a start-up company. Because the knowledge, or discovery, is still most often in an intermediate state, further work is required in an industrial laboratory or spin-off company to develop a product. In biotechnology, however, the academic interests in this process are different. In the traditional pattern, universities benefit by expanding their research activities and contributing to economic development, outcomes that contribute to both prestige and the service mission. Individual faculty members derive similar benefits by expanding their own research and learning, in addition to gaining support and opportunities for students. These same benefits exist in the biotechnology pattern, but here there are monetary incentives as well. In comparison, the traditional pattern of technology transfer operating through personal contacts, grants, and gifts resembles a barter economy. Biotechnology represents the efflorescence of capitalism, but in a distinctive form that might be termed "*biocapitalism.*"

In biocapitalism, economic roles are shaped by the principal sources of capital: investments in the research system, principally but by no means exclusively from the National Institutes of Health; venture capital for start-up firms; and the gargantuan revenue streams of multinational pharmaceutical corporations, which support massive investments in R&D. The fecund discoveries of academic science are made possible chiefly by the great public investment in biomedical research. This enormous subsidy makes the fruits of academic research relatively abundant and inexpensive, the fuel that drives biocapitalism. To some extent, corporations tap directly into this rich lode of upstream academic research (consultants, research contracts, licenses), but as is usually true with academic research, additional R&D is often required to move discoveries toward utilization.

Venture capital has facilitated this step by financing a multitude of biotech start-ups. In fact, these firms were the fastest-growing segment of this dynamic industry at the turn of the century.[116] Although a few of these firms have grown into major corporations, the vast majority form a distinctive type of organization that serves chiefly to transfer technology.[117] These firms take the fruits of academic research, protected with patents, and fashion them into intermediate products that are most often developed further in collaboration with large corporations.[118] Observers have long marveled at the resemblance of biotech firms to academic settings. In fact, they are truly an extension of the upstream academic innovation system, and thus inextricably linked with academic science, largely through academic entrepreneurs. However, these biotech firms serve as vital intermediaries (see Figure 16). In their absence the pressures on universities and their faculty for commercialization might well be greater.

These two sources of biotechnology discovery, universities and biotech firms, produce a cornucopia of potential innovations. However, given the extremely sophisticated nature of this knowledge, corporations must invest huge sums in internal R&D efforts in order to evaluate these discoveries and to select those with potential value for further development. Thus these firms too perform large amounts of fundamental research and participate in larger networks.[119] Biocapitalism, then, depends crucially on the transformation of academic knowledge into intellectual property, well upstream, so that discoveries can be capitalized as they move downstream toward becoming potential products. Economically, the distinctive feature of biocapitalism is the enormous subsidization of this upstream research—from public and nonprofit support for university research and venture-capital funding of biotech firms. These funds generate far more innovation than normal capitalist arrangements could possibly generate.

Universities benefit from biocapitalism through the "backflow" of commercial revenues, industrial support for research, and public investments for economic development. Moreover, these revenues are obtained with little risk. True, an initial investment is needed to establish a TTO; and patenting inevitably brings legal challenges, which are sometimes lost. But established TTOs generate revenues to pay some or all of their own expenses, and some produce a surplus for the university. Entrepreneurial biologists are in an analogous situation: conducting research with other people's money, yet potentially participating in the profits from any lucrative finding.

One should not underestimate the energy required to launch a start-up company, or to develop an invention to the stage that it finally generates income. The point is rather that academic entrepreneurs can do these things while still receiving a comfortable salary. Both universities and their biologists occupy advantageous positions in biocapitalism, sharing in the income but bearing little of the risk.

From the time that biocapitalism began to take shape in the early 1980s, however, critics have warned that the noneconomic costs of these benefits were unacceptable. They deplored the commercialization of academic research generally, arguing that commercial motives are incompatible with the university's role as a disinterested purveyor and arbiter of knowledge.[120] The ineffectiveness of this critique in slowing the trend is testimony, in part, to the power of the economic forces driving biocapitalism. Critics largely failed to grasp the dynamics of the phenomenon they opposed.

One of the most persistent laments has been that commercialization will ultimately stifle disinterested research: for example, "as the university is bought and parceled out, basic science in the university will increasingly suffer."[121] However, the evidence already presented shows just the opposite taking place. The most recognized biological scientists have disproportionately engaged in commercialization, and they have used their commercial ties to enlarge and advance the scope of their research.

The concern for secrecy has been persistent and legitimate, particularly where it threatens to delay publication or restrict student theses. Practical guidelines have been developed to address these concerns, not always without difficulty, and the basic problem of protecting the right to publish has proven manageable. More serious seems to be the deliberate withholding of information by life scientists. Commercialization would seem to bear only part of the blame. A thorough study of this phenomenon concluded, on one hand, "data withholding may . . . occur most commonly during extremely rapid progress, since scientists are generating large numbers of new findings that stimulate much jockeying for scientific priority"; but on the other hand, "having engaged in commercialization of university-based research was significantly associated with increased likelihood of data-withholding."[122] The phase of research during which secrecy might be desirable is in most cases fairly fleeting: a decision must be made before too long to patent or publish.

In the larger picture, furthermore, incentives have been seen to operate in the opposite direction: against secrecy and for cooperation. All the studies of biotechnology research stress the crucial value of interconnectedness, networking, and interaction—the antithesis of secrecy. Life scientists clearly have more to gain in this complex field by communicating widely and frequently.[123]

Conflict of interest is the bugbear of this entire field. Critics fear that the lure of pecuniary advantage will corrupt the professional standards of university scientists. Some publicized cases have prompted new requirements for broader disclosure when reporting research that could affect the valuation of companies. This problem is most acute for clinical trials, which are not research at all, but product testing. Critics invariably point to the same well-publicized scandals.[124] Although the same standards of academic integrity should prevail in clinical trials, they represent an inherently commercial activity, quite different from academic research.

Conflict of interest in research may be more an issue of human frailty than of corruption by commerce. The role of a faculty member requires adherence to professional standards of conduct toward students, colleagues, and the field. These standards are powerfully upheld by the external grants system, by colleagues, and by the reward system of science generally. Given the generous amount of commercial involvement that is tolerated without transgressing those standards, pushing the envelope would seem foolhardy. Professors who place pecuniary motives above their professional responsibilities are usually happier outside the university and sooner or later emigrate. Caltech president David Baltimore probably expressed the consensus view when he stated that the commercial implications of the biotechnology enterprise "have worked themselves out. They produced very deep conflicts of interest that many have been able to resolve very comfortably."[125]

But many critics still raise a fundamental and ultimately normative objection: that engagement in commercial activities is incompatible with a university's fundamental commitment to the objective pursuit and dissemination of knowledge. The American university today would never deny the noble mission of advancing knowledge in a disinterested manner, but it would be forced to deny any incompatibility.

Universities fulfill a multitude of roles. Their embrace of technology transfer and enhancement of economic development has committed them to links with the economy. The nature of those links depends on the characteristics of given industries. In biotechnology, the links occur through the commercialization of intellectual property. In this respect, biotechnology forms a special case of university-industry interaction, but it is consistent with the general transformation of university research since 1980.

IN THE DECADES of the 1980s and 1990s, American universities literally transformed themselves. Responding to changes in federal policy, exhortations from national reports, and the lure of the marketplace, they emphasized generic fields of research, sought to recruit companies into university ventures, and made forays into the private economy by commercializing their own discoveries. A large portion of academic research is now conducted in areas closely linked with the economy, although research relevant to the interests and activities of government has by no means been displaced. Moreover, the obstacles to transferring technology from universities to industry, which originally dominated discussion of this issue, have virtually ceased to exist. Ample arrangements for universities to share their expertise and discoveries are now in place. If any obstacle persists, it would be found in the capacity and willingness of firms in some industries to take advantage of the fruits of academic research.

Universities in these decades increased their contributions to economic development by intensifying the traditional pattern of interaction with industry. They strengthened the underlying enhancement function by creating research units specifically intended to work jointly with industry. Subsidization of such centers by state and federal policies tilted the economics of such arrangements, lowering the costs to industry and encouraging their greater participation. When it soon became apparent that concentrations of university-industry research interaction multiplied economic payoffs, new efforts were focused on achieving agglomerations of academic and industrial research. On the whole, these efforts seem to have borne fruit. Research universities by themselves are nodes of economic activity, and all the more so those most closely linked with industry. But to pursue this strategy universities have had to follow the money—to allow their decisions about growth and investment to be shaped by the marketplace.

The path to commercialization led universities ever more deeply into market relationships. Universities first had to gain some measure of control over internal processes—keeping entrepreneurial biologists in the fold and establishing procedures to secure intellectual property. Soon, the patenting leaders traced a path toward more aggressive commercialization. When their success became apparent in the 1990s, the number of imitators swelled. The patenting paradigm has spread from biology to other fields, with consequences that are not yet evident. Furthermore, the impressive revenues that some universities have generated from commercializing activities are largely channeled into existing or additional commercial ventures. The larger technology transfer offices, of course, operate more effectively; and an internal source of capital encourages further commercial investments.

Success begets success. The achievement of American universities in stimulating economic development, for their regions and for themselves, has not yet reached its limits. This is still another realm in which markets have increasingly shaped the course of university development.

CHAPTER SIX

Universities and Markets

THE FOUR SPHERES of activity of contemporary American univer-sities examined in the previous chapters—finances, undergraduates, research, and relations with industry—do not encompass the full range of university responsibilities and operations, but all are important and each has changed substantially in the current era. Potent market forces have been central to the nature and direction of these changes. Hence the recurring metaphor of the marketplace. This chapter aims to provide some deeper un-derstanding of these processes by considering the advantages that market relationships have brought, which are for the most part more immediate and apparent, and the real or potential costs, which may be longer term and less direct.

The "age of privatization" has been accompanied by an apotheosis of free-market ideology.[1] The extension of the market economy around the globe has been paralleled by a kind of functional extension, actual or advo-cated, of market relationships beyond the for-profit realm of the economy. However, the operation of markets depends on contextual factors that reg-ulate, constrain, or otherwise influence the economic forces of capitalism. Such factors play an even larger role in sectors that lie outside the for-profit sector, notably education. Economist Charles E. Lindblom has offered such an encompassing view in *The Market System*. Although he does not discuss higher education specifically, his critical perspective on markets offers in-sight into these issues.[2]

Markets in essence perform the task of social coordination. Market co-ordination is the antithesis of central or government coordination. It has the virtue of being noncoercive since it proceeds largely through processes of mutual adaptation. But it is far from being the only form of social coordination. Considering just higher education, the distribution of opportunities for postsecondary instruction is a ubiquitous concern in modern societies and hence invites a large degree of central coordination. Everywhere, the coordination of educational opportunity is heavily influenced by government decisions about the availability of places and the terms of attendance. In the same way, one might consider the coordination of the multiple social roles of universities. Market coordination certainly plays an important role here, but so do the actions of government, philanthropy, and voluntary associations of universities themselves. From this perspective, the question becomes, what is the role of market coordination in the social coordination of universities, and how has it changed during the current era?

A second set of considerations requires closer scrutiny of the supposed benefits of market coordination. Market coordination ought to move social coordination in the direction of greater efficiency, but such movement occurs within a constraining structure. The domain of market coordination is limited by prior conditions and numerous contextual factors. In particular, in areas where large spillovers exist (that is, where benefits or costs are not reflected in prices) prices are relatively arbitrary. It has already been seen that this was true for the price of undergraduate education. Other factors also constrict the domain of market coordination, and "its limited domain is a limit on its capacity to achieve efficient allocations."[3]

Governments have a large influence on market systems, affecting social coordination in three ways: they make significant purchases of goods and services; they penalize some activities through taxation; and they encourage behaviors they favor through subsidization. The result is not a free market, but rather an administered market system—one, moreover, in which the values of the polity play a large role in affecting approved and disapproved activities. It is chimerical, Lindblom argues, to believe that unalloyed market coordination can achieve economic efficiency. Rather, a mix of factors, including values and legal systems, determines at any moment the balance between market coordination and other forms of social coordination.

In the current era, for example, the United States made numerous choices that affected that balance. Policies were enacted at both the state and federal levels that channeled public funds to students rather than institutions in order to help pay the costs of higher education. The federal government brought legal action to prevent universities from cooperating instead of competing in the award of institutional student financial aid. The

1980 Bayh-Dole Act was the most conspicuous of several pieces of legislation that encouraged the commercialization of the results of academic research. And in the 1990s, the federal government decreed that the special facilities and treatments offered by university health care centers would no longer be exempted from the pricing system for managed health care. Each of these actions introduced an element of market coordination in areas that had, in Lindblom's words, very limited "capacity to achieve efficient allocations."[4] Yet they also represented values that favored voluntary choice and distrusted institutional determinations of the social good.

The discussion that follows invokes some of the fundamental properties of markets suggested by Lindblom. Most basic is the opposition between market and other forms of social coordination. Next is the role of pricing and the choices it effects. Finally, there is the realm of incentives—the stimulation of motivation for participants to seek benefits, or avoid harm, in the market system. This perspective highlights the paradoxes of market aggrandizement—the real gains achieved versus the actual and potential costs.

Private Universities

Although the system of independent colleges and universities in the United States may appear to possess many of the characteristics of a free market, the institutions have often eschewed competitive behavior and sought the shelter of voluntary coordination. The industry is itself highly segmented, and participants have formed associations for purposes ranging from sharing information to outright collusion. The College Board was an early effort by top schools to coordinate admissions. The Consortium for Financing Higher Education (COFHE, founded in 1975) later facilitated a kind of mutual coordination among many of the same institutions. And the formation of the Ivy League permitted the coordination of athletics. Coordination in these instances allowed private schools to control with whom they would compete and on what terms.

Voluntary coordination, in particular, achieved a crucial consensus over student financial aid. Beginning with the establishment of the College Scholarship Service in 1954, the leading universities sought to promote the understanding that student aid would be awarded solely on the basis of financial need. It probably took two decades, but after the federal government fashioned a need-based system of aid in 1972, this principle was firmly accepted across the selective sector.

The following quarter-century appears in retrospect as the "student aid era."[5] Highly selective universities and colleges agreed in principle that price should be eliminated insofar as possible as a factor in student choice. They specifically accepted a common formula for determining the expected family contribution and an implicit obligation by the institution to cover a student's "unmet need." Of course, a single price system inherently favored the top institutions since, given equal prices, the most highly sought-after students would naturally prefer schools with the greatest resources and highest prestige. But less-affluent institutions nevertheless benefited by being associated with the academic elite. The process of queue and overflow, described in Chapter 1, assured them of highly qualified students as well.

The incipient decline of the Student Aid Era was signaled by the Department of Justice challenge of the Overlap Group in 1991. When the leading institutions could no longer cooperate on setting financial aid awards, overt voluntary coordination had to be abandoned. Actual practice was slow to change, no doubt because of the advantage of these arrangements for participants. However, the consensus of the student aid era, which had been formalized in the Overlap Group, merely served to suppress for a time powerful forces being generated in the admissions market.[6]

The market conditions of the 1980s, as explained in Chapter 2, encouraged private universities to raise quality by spending more and to raise their prices as well. The secular trend toward an increasingly integrated national market advanced markedly in these years, and with it the competition for high-ability students.[7] Universities that were able to enhance their quality were also able to increase their selectivity and prestige. They increased income as well, through escalating tuition (list and net) and the generosity of their benefactors. This form of qualitative competition was the most important economic consequence of the student aid era, although it was obscured somewhat by the veneer of voluntary coordination. Moreover, it persisted and intensified as the student aid consensus began to crumble. Perhaps its most striking characteristic was the inherent advantage possessed by institutions that already enjoyed high quality and wealth. The phenomenon of the rich getting richer was the natural result of qualitative competition. These competitive forces also produced increasing market coordination in the selective sector, and as this occurred market power migrated from universities to prospective students.

During the student aid era, the renunciation of price competition accorded leading universities a form of "rent" (or unearned profit); they matriculated high-ability students without paying the full market value for those students' contribution to educational quality through peer effects.

But even before federal intervention, market forces were eroding this form of market power. Less selective colleges offered merit aid in lieu of qualitative competition, and even the less wealthy cartel members bent the rules for financial aid.[8] By the late 1990s, such rents were disappearing: a competitive market began forcing even the most highly selective institutions to pay additional "wages" for talented students. The taboo against merit aid persisted among the most prestigious institutions, but they found other ways to bid for students.

The system of qualitative competition with voluntary coordination was roundly criticized for boosting tuition prices, but in retrospect it may have been preferable to the form of market coordination that succeeded it. With respect to prices, net tuition rose far less than list tuition, and as universities increased general subsidies, quality in theory rose faster than net tuition. More fundamentally, this system created conditions in which institutions were motivated to enrich educational opportunities for highly able students, and those students obtained greater choice of institutions to attend. This process produced greater segregation of students by ability level through the hierarchy of institutions, a pattern that also likely produced a more efficient distribution of students for purposes of optimizing educational benefits. Still, market coordination has had problematic consequences for (1) social stratification, (2) price competition, (3) institutional trust, and (4) what economists call the arms race.

Qualitative competition, combined with increasing returns to selective college graduates, attracted more potential students to these institutions. This high-stakes competition for places naturally favored those students with the cumulative advantages of high social background and privileged schooling. More precisely, the more competitive admission to high-quality colleges becomes, the greater the effect of social attributes, acquired from privileged social backgrounds, and the less the effect of innate intelligence (however defined).[9]

Elite universities are not only aware of this situation; they ostensibly work to counteract it in the name of diversity and democracy. The recruitment of underrepresented minorities and financial aid mitigate these forces to some extent, and assuage institutional consciences far more; but the dominant effect can scarcely be reversed. The places at highly selective universities, and the presumed subsequent earnings advantage, have increasingly been filled by high-achieving, wealthy students.[10] Furthermore, the system would be unsustainable if this were not the case since, as was seen in Chapter 2, tuition income has provided the principal fuel for spending growth.

Market coordination has brought a subtle yet profound alteration in the role of pricing. High-tuition/high aid was originally intended to generate revenue without impeding access for those who could not afford to pay high prices—in other words, to achieve price neutrality for the prospective student. In the new market for selective private universities, the mix of tuition and aid reflects the "wage" that highly desirable students can command, irrespective of need.[11] Of course, need-based financial aid remains a large part of the mix; but universities now often pay an additional wage for sought-after students.[12] This situation—and the specter of "ruinous competition"—is precisely what universities originally sought to avoid through voluntary coordination. Perhaps no private research university is likely to be ruined in this way, but the cost of such wages still must be borne. These wages purchase the input that is now most highly valued: high-ability students and the peer effects attributed to them. For all but the wealthiest universities, however, these expenditures must substitute for other inputs to the learning process.

Market coordination has produced another troubling consequence in differential pricing. During the student aid era differential prices were determined by the single criterion of financial need. Now the price a student pays reflects a combination of financial need, merit wages, and how well or poorly she games the system. Prevailing notions of strategic aid or enrollment management justify institutional practices for maximizing the revenue derived from each student.[13] Yet the classic justification for the nonprofit status of educational institutions is asymmetry of information between buyers and sellers. Because consumers cannot adequately monitor the quality of educational services, they prefer dealing with institutions they can trust not to take advantage of them to realize a profit.[14] But maximizing revenue now looks a good deal like making a profit. Private universities now engage in such deceptive practices as awarding less aid to early-admission students or front-loading the first year of aid packages.[15] Students in the aggregate may gain greater wages through these arrangements, but each student must fend for herself. Trust in this relationship can no longer be assumed.

The final negative feature of market coordination has been termed the arms race among selective schools, meaning the tendency to spend ever greater sums ostensibly for educational quality, but more accurately to avoid losing position in the steep institutional hierarchy.[16] This phenomenon has affected the entire selective sector, but for the wealthiest institutions spending has reached seemingly ridiculous levels. For them, surely, the point of diminishing returns to university costs was passed some time ago.

The arms race makes sense for the actors involved, though. For consumers, particularly devoted parents who seek the best possible education for their children, a college cannot offer too much. They are motivated by the prestige of the institution, which depends in turn on its exclusivity. Prestige is presumably enhanced as the bundle of services becomes larger and more lavish. For universities, the admissions process has assumed a higher priority than classroom instruction (see Chapter 3). The foremost challenge is to enroll the prodigies of those devoted parents in order to sustain and bolster peer effects and status. Hence the imperative to meet or exceed the service bundles offered by their most immediate competitors.

But from a social perspective, the arms race is inefficient or downright wasteful. Educational opportunities for society would be more optimal if high-cost institutions would offer a superior educational experience to far more students. Would not two students being educated for $25,000 per year yield a greater social benefit than one being schooled for $50,000? The question is obviously moot, since the incentives for universities and consumers under market coordination are otherwise—so much so that any institution attempting such a course would be severely penalized by the market.[17]

In sum, the extraordinary expansion of resources for private universities has undoubtedly bolstered quality across the sector, but has especially favored the leaders since the 1990s. Moreover, this growing affluence has been accompanied by greater dependence on wealthy students, erosion of trust as nonprofit fiduciaries, predatory pricing practices, and seemingly unbounded spending to bolster selectivity.

Public Universities

The flagship universities of most states have historically been centrally coordinated. Before the current era almost all their income came from their respective legislatures, and with this support often came directives on how funds were to be spent. Many of these universities operated with considerable autonomy, but their purview extended little beyond their state borders. Their horizons widened with the rise of federally sponsored research after World War II. Large performers of research were less beholden to the state capitol, at least for some departments. Soon, a different form of coordination emerged. Statewide coordination became widespread in the 1970s, in part through federal urging. The major state universities now had to balance various state controls with the open competition of the national research system. These institutions also sought voluntary cooperation among their peers, but central coordination far outweighed the impact of such links. Since 1980, market coordination has increasingly intruded into this mix. For state universities in the twenty-first century, perhaps the biggest challenge has become balancing the forces of central and market coordination.

States support universities in the belief, explicit or implicit, that these institutions generate positive externalities—that they provide social benefits in addition to the private benefits for students, and that in the absence of public support fewer such benefits would be produced.

This premise has engendered a distinctive form of production. State universities are large enough to accommodate substantial numbers of resident students, access must be provided on an equitable basis, and the institution is expected to serve the state economy in ways that go beyond training educated workers. On the whole, universities are remarkably free to determine the academic details. But states are vigilant about enforcing their specific interests. They monitor and sometimes dictate tuition prices, and they frequently insist that sufficient places be reserved for state residents. They typically feel strongly about equity, among students and institutions, sometimes to the point of failing to recognize the special needs of research universities. And, invoking their budgetary authority over appropriations, state legislatures occasionally intervene directly in university operations. For states the basic questions to be addressed are: How much state support should be given? How much should students pay? What level of quality is desirable or affordable, and at which institutions? Remarkably, there are fifty sets of answers.

For state universities the perennial challenge has been to acquire the resources to support a high level of academic quality. Their research roles are coordinated to a large extent by the national research economy, which distributes research funds on a competitive basis. But the academic competitiveness of universities reflects the quality of the personnel and infrastructure at individual institutions, and the willingness of states to make such investments varies enormously. In the 1990s, many states hesitated to support academic quality and occasionally criticized the research role. With the erosion of state support, universities were left to their own devices to augment their spending base. Their alternatives were tuition increases and voluntary support.[18]

A high-tuition strategy became increasingly attractive to public universities as state support faltered during the 1990s, and especially after the recession of 2001. But unlike privates, they could not leverage high tuition with extensive institutional financial aid. Since tuition covered only a portion of cost, education at public universities was substantially underpriced. For most schools, higher prices would have little impact on demand.

State policies nevertheless varied widely. In most states the impulse toward higher in-state tuition collided with state coordination. Where state boards set tuition, as in Arizona, tuition hikes were sometimes rejected in the name of protecting students from "greedy" universities. Some legislatures froze tuition outright, and others imposed deals that linked tuition with appropriations. In all these cases, universities were precluded from charging more nearly what the market would bear.[19] Perhaps one-quarter of public research universities can be placed in the high-tuition category, which for the 2001 academic year meant charges of more than $4,800 for in-state students.[20] These prices represent only one leg of a successful high-tuition strategy.

In order to boost tuition revenues significantly, public universities also need to attract higher-paying out-of-state students. To do this they must enter the national market for undergraduates where, as described for private universities, market power has shifted from universities to students. How can they compete against more affluent private institutions? They start with a price advantage. Tuition for out-of-state students in 2001 was about $10,000 less than at private universities: $12,000 to $15,000 in most cases, with some as low as $10,000 and only Michigan and Colorado approaching private levels. Thus state universities are able to compete in the middle band of tuition pricing identified in Chapter 2. Moreover, most offer some wage or subsidy from their state appropriation. And they have a great deal to offer in terms of quality—but it is configured differently from their more exclusive and homogeneous private competitors.

Market coordination in the private sector was seen to produce vertical differentiation, through selectivity and spending, and horizontal differentiation through special offerings.[21] The typical large state university accomplishes these same effects through internal differentiation. That is, students sort themselves out by college and major to produce more homogeneous groupings of peers. But state universities can no longer assume that high-ability students will matriculate close to home. Traditionally, flagship campuses in most parts of the country laid claim to a large portion of high-achieving students in their states. Now, the advent of student market power has plunged them into qualitative competition in the national marketplace.

The increasing emphasis on capital campaigns and voluntary support plays a crucial role for public universities in this competition. Building endowment for private universities is fundamental to the financing of the institution; but in public universities endowment income tends to be earmarked for specific qualitative improvements. The income per FTE may be paltry, but it is targeted to produce maximum effects.[22] Capital campaigns typically have focused on attracting better students and better scholars through scholarships (wages), endowed professorships, and new facilities.

Public universities participate to varying degrees in the national market dominated by student power and qualitative competition. In this respect they have become more like private institutions, maximizing tuition revenues through strategic use of financial aid and seeking gifts and endowment to bolster quality. At the same time, they preserve as a base of operations the services traditionally offered to their respective states. The former orientation reflects market coordination, and the latter central coordination, although these forces are weighted differently for each institution.

These divergent tendencies represent an incipient paradox for public universities. Those institutions with sufficient autonomy from state coordination are best able to adapt to the national market by enhancing their quality and competitiveness. Responding to these incentives, however, may detract from their direct service to state citizens. Universities that are hindered from adapting to the national market by state controls may remain focused on their state roles, but will perform them less effectively.

Internal Coordination

The coordination of activities within universities, as described in Chapter 1, is balanced between the top-down activities of fiscal and administrative control and the bottom-up academic authority of the faculty over teaching, learning, and activities stemming from the university's knowledge base. University administrators, in theory, face the challenge of optimizing three activities: (1) the flow of revenues to the university; (2) the distribution of those revenues among units to accomplish the multiple missions of the institution; and (3) the efficient utilization of those resources by the constituent units. In practice, these tasks are performed serially and incrementally, starting from the existing annual budget and organizational structure.

On the other side, the operating units exemplify the revenue theory of costs. They receive annual allocations of funds that largely define what they can, and often must, spend. External income, such as research grants, is usually designated for specific purposes, and hence by definition must be spent. For units, then, the challenge is to increase revenues, if possible, but particularly to optimize the mix of activities given the income available. The growing influence of the marketplace in the current era has had an impact on both administrative and academic coordination.

By any measure, the capacity of universities for administrative coordination has been extended greatly in the modern era. Management information systems, institutional research, and permanent planning units have all provided administrators with an avalanche of quantitative data about every facet of their institutions. This capacity together with an abundance of organizational theories for improving university performance falls under the rubric of managerialism. A long-standing trend, the growth of managerialism in the current era should have provided academic managers with the tools to rationalize and lead universities into the new century.

Contemporary universities are undoubtedly run more tightly than those of preceding generations, yet managerialism probably deserves little of the credit. Despite inflated claims, universities largely persist in their accustomed state of internal incoherence. That is, managers coordinate the fiscal and administrative structure—chiefly task 2 above. But the real work of the university remains with the knowledge workers and is not easily coordinated by managers (task 3). Moreover, with respect to task 1, the thrust of managerialism has not always been consistent with the market forces that affect university revenues.

Many of the management schemes transposed from business to universities were predicated on the need for cost containment and efficiency, given limited or shrinking revenues.[23] Strategic planning was enthusiastically adopted as a panacea for the fiscal woes of the early 1980s; responsibility-centered management (RCM) was intended to introduce resource-conscious decision-making by operating units; and performance measures promised to introduce greater efficiency. However, these approaches were all implemented at a time when the marketplace was rewarding colleges and universities for spending more, not less, on their students and professors. Of course, universities were not blind to this reality. Private universities especially, and many publics as well, enthusiastically sought to expand revenues; and some fiscal discipline had to be imposed on units through administrative coordination no matter how affluent the institution. But managerialism tended to work at cross purposes with this trend.

Responsibility-centered management provides perhaps the best example of the confusion of managerialsim and markets. Inspired by the ascendancy of market ideology, RCM sought to introduce marketlike incentives at the level of operating units, chiefly by having them earn income through student credit hours. Making academic units responsible for their own income and instituting a system of real prices would create an incentive structure for adaptive behavior, thus encouraging efficiency. By creating an internal market, RCM claimed to shift the locus of coordination from the central administration to the academic units.

Predictably, the first complaint about RCM was the loss of capacity for central leadership (Chapter 2). RCM in practice was nothing like a free market where units could control their revenues and expenditures. Rather, it was an administered system with set prices more closely resembling the planned economy of the Soviet Union. Units, as rational actors, tended to engage in strategic behavior. While units had an incentive to reduce costs, this could best be accomplished by minimizing the purchase of university services or ducking university taxes. The greater incentive, however, was to increase revenues. Larger course enrollments were achieved more readily through coercion (required courses) than through qualitative competition. Beyond the administered system, external revenue might also be gained through entrepreneurship.

In either case, results were likely to be different from original expectations. RCM exacerbated internal inequality, facilitated greater spending by affluent units, weakened central leadership, and did nothing to promote quality.[24] It provided a workable framework, one especially congenial to powerful autonomous professional schools, but results scarcely justified the large informational and managerial efforts it demanded.

The idea of using market coordination within universities had several laudable objectives. It sought to decentralize decision-making to the operating units and provide them with incentives for greater effectiveness (in this case defined as raising demand for their services) and efficiency (reducing costs). In any university the effectiveness and efficiency of academic units should be a paramount concern, and one that virtually mandates a substantial degree of local control. However, internal markets take this form of coordination away from academics and concede it to students. Academic coordination, through control of the curriculum, is supposed to structure student learning. In a market based on student demand, student choices will coordinate the curriculum. For example, in any university students may choose to take "gut" courses, but departments do not have an incentive to offer them.[25] Consequently, schemes like RCM probably work best in situations where little competition exists between units (and thus are least marketlike), as has always been true for the Harvard tubs.

More generally, the increasing immersion of universities in external markets tends to work counter to managerial efforts to assert greater control. As market coordination assumes greater importance for institutions, the scope of administrative coordination is likely to diminish.

Enrollment management provides one example. What first appeared to be a managerial technique actually ceded decision-making power to market forces. Enrollment management is intended to manipulate the admissions process in order to optimize financial outcomes. The goal is to enroll the best possible class that will meet a given revenue target. Although a university with surplus applicants would have a certain amount of leeway, at some point in the admissions process the potential income from an admitted student becomes the deciding factor. When this occurs, the market coordinates the admissions process.[26]

The consequences of artificially induced internal market coordination are more perverse than paradoxical. The supposed benefit of greater efficiency is illusory, but far worse is the intent to encourage departments to optimize expenditures rather than academic tasks. Such systems provide little incentive for quality, and even less for cooperation. They promote unwelcome forms of internal competition, as well as encourage the trend toward student consumerism.[27]

Undergraduate Education

Undergraduate education remains the most conspicuous and consequential activity of universities. In Chapter 3 it was seen that no fewer than four powerful sets of forces contend in this arena: (1) the national admissions market for high-ability and (mostly) affluent entering students; (2) the ascendancy of student consumerism; (3) the critique of teaching at research universities and the attendant advocacy for pedagogical alternatives; and (4) the fundamental values, practices, and dynamics of the academic fields. Each is a complex and perhaps not entirely consistent phenomenon. Each can also be represented at least in part as resulting from market coordination. And largely for that reason, each exerts a vector of influence over developments in undergraduate education.

The national market of prospective students exerts a huge influence on institutions in the selective sector. The financial implications have already been reviewed, but market coordination extends much further. The operation of this market has been described as a queue-and-overflow process.

The most preferred institutions would thus appear to be in enviable positions—and they are. Yet they still have to compete among themselves for the most coveted students. Beyond the top twenty institutions, the pecking order becomes more muddled and the competition more diffuse. Degrees of prestige among these very good institutions depend heavily on the quality of each entering class, which in turn affects the well-being of the university. Under these conditions, the admissions process assumes paramount priority. Of course, only after students matriculate does the real work of the university begin. However, the priority of admission means that certain aspects of that work, such as fashionable academic programs, will be tailored to enhance the admissions profile. Certainly the pressure is great for universities to avoid any actions that might detract from factors that matter in undergraduate admissions.

The influence of the national market has been so pervasive among private universities that the behaviors it has molded might be taken for granted. Its effects stand out more clearly for universities that are closer to the borders of the selective sector. Syracuse University had to invest more heavily in student quality and was rewarded for its sacrifice. A similar investment in students occurred among the private universities of the South as they sought a more diversified, national clientele. The impact of this form of coordination has become increasingly visible among some leading state universities. To attract lucrative out-of-state students from the national market, and to avoid losing home-state talent, they were compelled to compete on similar terms.

Student consumerism and the national market are mutually reinforcing, which can produce disquieting consequences. Consumers, Lindblom points out, "swim in an ocean of information and misinformation." Yet the efficiency of this market depends on the intelligence of their choices.[28] Students begin choosing a college by narrowing the multitude of choices down to some semblance of a manageable list. Prospective students may include schools for bizarre reasons at this stage. Most important for institutions is the cultivation of a "brand name" to increase the likelihood that students will give them serious consideration. At the next stage, prospective students exhibit considerable rational behavior in identifying and matching their own goals with institutional capabilities; and they are sensitive to whether an institution is a likely route to postgraduate educational or career aspirations.

Students also manifest price sensitivity, especially when personal loans are at stake. The proclivity of students to seek the most selective college that would have them is economically rational according to the Hoxby model.[29] And most high-ability students choose a research university; but many institutions can usually fulfill such criteria. When it comes to choosing among these worthy alternatives, other consumer desires may intrude. Here amenities and activities become significant factors in quality competition. And since they play a salient role in all-important final decisions, they become part of the arms race as well. However, consumerism may play a more dubious role in the curriculum.

Critics and reformers sometimes promote the idea that students are the customers of colleges and universities and ought to be treated accordingly. Traditionalists try to deflect this notion by pointing out that students should be regarded as clients. What is the difference?

In retail trades the well-worn motto holds that "the customer is always right"; but clients seek professional services in the belief that professionals are "right" and provide valuable services with their expertise. Universities have traditionally accorded control over the curriculum to the faculty with the understanding that it knew best what students ought to learn. Scarcely a hard-and-fast principle, this matter has been negotiated ever since the elective system displaced the classical course at the end of the nineteenth century. In the current era, however, the market power of students has consistently shifted the balance in the direction of "customers."

In the period preceding the current era, student power and administrative appeasement loosened the curriculum by eliminating required courses, attenuating the threat of failure, and permitting courses demanded by student activists. The beginning of the current era actually witnessed curricular stiffening as some past excesses were rectified and as universities, in keeping with their growing selectivity, sought to project images of academic excellence.

But the pervasive market power of students continued to transform the curriculum from within. As student satisfaction became a more highly valued goal, the assumed forms of student expression became more consequential. Student course evaluations, for example, which can provide useful feedback to instructors, were incorporated into assessments of faculty job performance. Factors such as student retention became performance indicators that might have budgetary impacts. RCM, as mentioned, allowed students to vote for school budgets with their course elections. When students objected to actual course content, as in the protests against Western heritage and material written by "dead European white males," they often had their way.

Perhaps the most pervasive changes were least visible: universities became increasingly averse to the traditional negative sanctions of college—not just bad grades and the threat of failure, but everyday matters like mandatory attendance, pop quizzes, and comprehensive final examinations. Grade inflation, whatever else its cause, is consistent with this reluctance to coerce, as opposed to cajole, effort from students. Academic traditionalists have long and loudly deplored such trends. The highly selective schools, in contrast, find these concerns to be minor or irrelevant to their model for undergraduate education.

The ideal in the selective sector is to assemble a relatively homogeneous (but demographically diverse!) class of bright, well-prepared, energetic, and highly motivated achievers. Such students may be trusted to respond enthusiastically to the rich educational opportunities arrayed before them. The positive pull of intellectual interests, stimulated by teachers, fellow students, and structured activities, will guide their learning. Negative sanctions? A gentle prod perhaps for those temporarily disoriented (all these schools offer extensive psychological services); but this is a model of positive inducements for students who are ready and eager to learn. And it is not caricature.

At the most selective colleges and universities, students who are carefully chosen to behave in this way by and large seem to do so.[30] However, the distribution of ideal students is a market phenomenon. As one descends the pecking order for universities (and the rest of higher education) student bodies on the whole possess relatively less brightness, preparation, energy, and motivation. As these qualities attenuate at the margins, the impact of student consumerism becomes incrementally more pernicious. Student consumerism, on balance, detracts from student learning even as universities seek formal measures to bolster it.

The critique of undergraduate education emanated from self-appointed spokesmen rather than market forces, but over time its effects became assimilated with student consumerism. The original impact of the critique brought pressure for outcomes assessment and performance measures—in essence, forms of administrative coordination. In the main, such metrics were influenced more strongly by the quality of the students than by how they were being educated, as the critics implied.

Universities nevertheless undertook a corrective process to address alleged weaknesses. These steps probably improved student satisfaction, if not academic performance. When it came to enhancement, however, public universities in particular were compelled by the market to bolster their tarnished images and compete more effectively for talented undergraduates. The reforms that ensued—honors programs, living-learning arrangements, undergraduate research—all held promise of appealing to high-ability students and specifically enriching *their* learning. The consequence of such programs was seldom acknowledged: greater internal differentiation in the treatment of students.

Despite a disparity in resources, it should probably not be assumed that the benefits conferred on this talented minority detract from the educational experience of the majority. Still, in the age of student consumerism it has become monumentally difficult to impose any requirement on the entire student body. Curricular initiatives are presented instead as choices. These developments suggest that even pedagogical reform tends to find the path of least resistance—a form of market coordination resulting from individual adaptation.

This last pattern appeared in somewhat different form in the experiences of "student-centered research universities." The market forces to be contended with in these cases were those that confer faculty distinction and academic standing. Proponents of student-centeredness attacked the value of research and advocated changing faculty reward structures, as if an individual institution could defy the forces that coordinated the systemic distribution of academic prestige. Thus from the outset, student-centered universities experienced deep contradictions.

At Syracuse University, research and academic standing were consciously sacrificed to the new image and its fiscal demands. Unable to compete in the markets for both students and research, it opted to invest in students. After the university was restructured, however, it became apparent that academic distinction would have to be rebuilt for the institution to attain the prestige it sought among its peers.

At Arizona the initial fiscal situation was not so dire, and the university sought to become student-centered without eroding its reputation for research. Walking this tightrope was nevertheless a trying experience. Arizona at best sustained its position in the markets for both students and research, without advancing in either. And it failed to mollify its external detractors.

Market coordination of undergraduate education has probably risen as precipitously as tuition, but with paradoxical results. The increasing segregation of undergraduates by ability level has largely worked in favor of research universities. Some universities have appreciably raised the quality of undergraduate entrants in the current era, and all have probably made marginal improvements. This matching of better students with richer educational settings should work to the advantage of both. At the same time, the admissions market and powerful accompanying cultural trends have accentuated student consumerism throughout American higher education. The consequence is diminished influence of institutions over student learning and an underlying anti-intellectual drift. Ironically, this situation has frustrated attempts to force improvements in student learning through administrative coordination.

Markets for Research

Academic research constitutes an administered market with unique characteristics. When viewed as a part of national R&D, it dominates the subsector for basic research. In this market, university scientists are the sellers of research; outside funders are the purchasers. The service for sale—research—is priced at cost, direct costs in this case being defined by conventions, with a mark-up allowed for indirect costs. The crucial element in these transactions is the quality of the research proffered. Purchasers seek to maximize the quality of the investigations they support; scientists compete for this support chiefly on the basis of the quality of the research they propose.

The research market is beautifully efficient. It is nationally integrated, with units of the federal government independently purchasing 60 percent of research. At the same time it is highly decentralized, with no unit buying more than a small portion (2 percent) of the total. Buyers and sellers know one another extremely well, exchanging visits, attending the same meetings, and cooperating in evaluations. There is considerable latitude for negotiations between the parties over the terms of work. Forms of contracting are flexible as well.

Agencies that wish to advance a scientific field typically invite investigator-initiated proposals. Those with predilections for the direction research should follow issue "requests for proposals" that specify those interests. Funders seeking research on particular topics can draft appropriate contracts with university scientists. Each arrangement represents a different combination of buyer interests and seller interests. By mutual adjustment these complementary goals are fulfilled. At the end of the day (or fiscal year) the market clears. The highest quality and most apposite academic research is supported by the funds available for these purposes.

Academic scientists who endure the tribulations of grantsmanship may regard this process as neither beautiful nor efficient (although many would). The continual preparation and evaluation of proposals represents a kind of friction consuming (although not entirely wasting) scientific energy. Other kinds of difficulties arise. The 1990s witnessed occasional examples of fraud; problems of secrecy or vested interest; a congressional penchant for pork-barrel funding; and as always, criticism of peer review.[31] However, the indignation with which these matters are aired is testimony that the system rests on a solid foundation of strongly held normative values. The market for academic research has not only effectively coordinated the distribution of academic research over half a century; it has also shaped American universities.

University accommodations to the research market go much further than the offices that report to the vice president for research. Basic operations have been adapted to the requirements of sponsored research. Teaching schedules, for example, are malleable enough to permit professors receiving grants to buy out courses, in effect privileging externally supported research over instruction. More fundamental is the development of the autonomous research role, most conspicuous in organized research units (ORUs), but generated by the demand for more or different research than can be provided through joint production. The current era brought significant alterations in the relationship of the university to the academic research market.

As was seen in Chapter 4, research in this set of universities more than doubled in the 1980s and 1990s while the academic core grew by barely 10 percent. This change in the balance of university activity was brought about by a significant expansion of autonomous research, but also by enhanced productivity from the academic core. Specifically, a significant number of middle- and lower-rated universities advanced toward optimal levels of research activity. Intuitively, one can envision such a change, but the notion of optimum begs a more precise definition.

In a 1972 paper on tuition pricing, economist Marc Nerlove incidentally proposed a model of possible trade-offs between research and graduate education on one hand and undergraduate instruction on the other. He hypothesized that at the extremes (nearly all teaching or all research) the alternate activity could be obtained cost-free as a by-product of the primary activity. In between those extremes, teaching and research were substitutes, although at varying price ratios. And at some point the marginal cost of the two activities would be equal:

> Thus, if society subsidizes the higher education sector to produce research in a socially optimal way, the sector will always operate at a point . . . where teaching

and research are substitutes in the sense that for a given level of resources devoted to higher education more research [and graduate education] can only be obtained by providing fewer undergraduate educational services, and conversely.[32]

Nerlove was not referring to anything as tangible as faculty time. Rather, he posited research and undergraduate education measured in "quality-adjusted units," so that the amount of either represented some combination of quality and quantity. Although he envisioned an optimum for society, the same principle might be applied to a university, a department, or a single faculty member. In fact, universities routinely and intuitively make such adjustments, and they apparently have done so to adjust the balance of activities in the current era.[33]

This process presupposes certain conditions. Research subsidies and also research students are scarce goods, rationed according to academic quality. The ability to perform valuable research is in scarce supply as well. It is doubtful that the average faculty member operates at a point where greater value could be had by substituting research for teaching.

However, after 1980 conditions in this research market changed. Universities for the most part were able to enlarge their core costs, placing more resources at their disposal. The abundance of well-qualified Ph.D.s made faculty appointments opportunities for improvement. And social subsidies for research were rapidly rising. Universities were able to displace less-productive faculty researchers with more-productive ones; and funds were available to support their research. These universities had the capacity and the opportunity to move toward a mix of activities with relatively greater research. This movement was evident in the dispersion of academic research as well as in the average improvement in academic ratings. But what happens when an institution approaches its optimal balance, where the marginal value of each activity is the same?

An optimal mix for a high-quality institution would imply that units of undergraduate education were also quite valuable. At this point, research should not be increased in relative terms because it would then be more costly than instruction. Research might still be increased by expanding the academic core, but doing that would require adding similarly valued units of undergraduate education. Given the inelasticity of that market, universities were loath to increase enrollments.[34] Most were content to maintain a stable academic core. Optimality in this sense is a wonderful condition, but it discourages further development. These considerations, however, do not affect autonomous research.

Centers and institutes, and medical schools too, have important links with the academic core. They exist to some extent because external patrons wish to connect with university scientists. And their volume of research depends more on external than on internal factors. Thus MIT saw its research share shrink as large defense research projects were phased out; and the University of Colorado gained research share as its federal centers were enlarged.

In general, state universities feel a greater obligation than privates to provide the kinds of services that much of this research entails. Outside of medicine, the largest performers of research are public universities with numerous autonomous ORUs. For private universities, medical research has provided the chief form of autonomous research, which could be expanded without affecting optimal conditions in the academic core. Hence the observed pattern of stable academic cores and burgeoning expenditures for medical research. Universities faced variable inducements to participate in the research market, and these had consequences for supply, demand, and costs.

When academic research was under siege by its critics in the early 1990s, it was sometimes alleged that sponsored research actually cost universities more than the revenues brought in. Never mind that research was a mission of these universities; if it could be shown (or not disproved) that student fees were subsidizing research for sponsors, the institutions would indeed be embarrassed.

This issue prompted evaluation specialist Lawrence Mohr to attempt to determine all of the impacts of sponsored research on universities using available empirical data, and thus to simulate issues that universities face in deciding to pursue such support.[35] The study was significant for what it did not find. No discernible effects from federal grants were detected on student tuition or expenditures for instruction. Nor was any impact found on endowment growth, voluntary support, or the quality of incoming undergraduates. Data indicated that research grants did have a positive influence where it might be most expected: faculty quality and working conditions, professional standing (National Research Council ratings), and quality of incoming graduate students. More speculatively, Mohr concluded that the impact would be positive on the content of undergraduate learning and graduate teaching. In sum, the spillovers from sponsored research were all positive: better faculty, greater prestige, stronger graduate education, and possibly more effective undergraduate teaching as well. Other factors, most importantly costs, appeared unaffected. Mohr thus provided a rational explanation for the observed behavior of universities in the current era: important incentives existed, especially for suboptimal producers, to increase participation in sponsored research. This factor has likely affected the balance of supply and demand in the market for academic research.

In light of the robust growth in the social consumption of academic research, one might on first impression conclude that social demand was the dominant factor in this market. In addition, as just seen, private universities have had good reason to resist or moderate any expansion of research capacity in their academic cores. But given the attractiveness of research for universities, it seems more likely that supply has on the whole exceeded demand.

Judging by effects, market forces appear to have worked to the advantage of consumers. In the case of industry, proactive policies by universities increased their share of industry-sponsored research beginning in the mid-1980s.[36] Liberal government subsidies also encouraged industrial consumption of academic research (see Chapter 5). In the case of federal grants, marginal decreases occurred during the 1990s in the price paid for research. Some agencies, particularly the National Science Foundation, asked universities to assume greater matching and cost-sharing obligations; and all paid lower indirect cost rates after 1991.[37] Most important, ample research capacity among universities stimulated greater competition.

One effect of increased competition should be to raise prices of key inputs. There is naturally a reciprocal relationship between spending power and the ability to bid up inputs, but most universities seem to have devoted greater resources (paid higher prices) to secure additional research funds. Most telling, the funds that universities themselves devote to separately budgeted research have been the most rapidly rising expenditure category in the current era. The proportion of these funds rose by about one-third, with most of the jump coming in the 1980s.[38]

Competition for faculty who bring in abundant grant support has been keen, but difficult to quantify. Some professorial "stars" are hired more for celebrity and brand-name enhancement than for prowess in research. Still, there can be little doubt that the price of hiring or keeping prolific researchers has risen disproportionately. Typically, private universities have led in the salary wars, while public universities have allocated far more of their own funds to sponsored research.

The competition for faculty spills over into a demand for facilities. Start-up costs for new faculty in the sciences have far outpaced salary costs and now routinely reach seven figures. Facilities may well be the most costly university input factor for maintaining competitiveness. The construction and renovation of research space is an ongoing process. Such spending peaked at the end of the 1980s, and that level was surpassed by another surge at the end of the 1990s.[39]

Research has become more expensive for universities in the current era, but more valuable too. Universities, on balance, have expanded the quantity of research they perform, its salience in their mix of activities, and its value to society. This could not have occurred if research were solely a joint product with teaching; more than ever it has become an autonomous role and a separate output. As such, research interacts at times in awkward ways with other university roles. Universities nevertheless face strong incentives to make substantial investments in their research role, above all because the payoffs are greatest to those who do it best.

Economic Development

No one can doubt that universities make substantial contributions to the economy. First and foremost, they create human capital through the transfer of knowledge and skills to students. Human capital makes graduates more productive in their occupations, and the returns to society are greater than the returns to individuals themselves. The second great contribution of universities is the creation of new knowledge through research. A third contribution, grown prominent in the current era, is technology development: specifically, the mobilization of university expertise to advance or create new technology. Fourth, one could cite the many services that universities offer, including direct technical assistance, agricultural extension, and continuing education.[40]

Each university produces a unique combination of these benefits. Although these benefits accrue to government, nonprofit organizations, and private industry, university assistance to industry has been most explicitly linked with economic growth. In the age of privatization, the litmus test for university involvement with the economy has been developing technology for the private sector.

Academic research and industrial R&D are two enormous subsystems of the national research economy with a fairly small area of overlap. For that reason the economic forces governing their interaction have been difficult to specify. Nuanced historical analysis rather than supply and demand curves led to the findings reported in Chapter 5. Industry largely draws on academic expertise to enhance the efficacy of its own internal R&D. Knowledge gained in this way constitutes an intermediate good, without intrinsic value, that the firm hopes will contribute to the development of marketable products. Consumption of such an uncertain commodity is naturally highly variable. It depends on the universities' eagerness to sell, industry's preference for vendors, and especially the nature of the industry. All these factors favored a growing volume of research after 1980.

The knowledge supplied in this enhancement role represents a positive spillover from the production of academic knowledge.[41] Firms pay for access to this knowledge through grants and contracts, but these transactions are priced at marginal cost. The direct costs calculated in university research agreements are literally marginal costs, and ICR represents only a small additional increment. Because the actual (or average) costs of creating and sustaining academic knowledge are far greater, industry benefits from this spillover.

Universities, for their part, have been eager to sell more research at these prices in order to enhance their knowledge-creating activity and cover a portion of their sunk costs. As universities sought greater collaboration, industry found it advantageous to purchase more research, particularly at favorable prices. Moreover, the appearance of new research technologies enlarged areas of interaction between the two subsystems.

This latter development, in particular, stimulated a second source of spillover. Academic research increasingly made discoveries of tangible value, sufficiently developed to foreshadow an ultimate product. Discoveries of this sort had always emerged from university research, but infrequently and unexpectedly. The new involvement with research technologies increased the odds. Biotechnology is the famous example. And the presence or likelihood of valuable inventions prompted universities to make accommodations that would continue to capture and enhance these spillovers.

Adopting this opportunistic strategy could have been expected. Spillovers, Lindblom notes, "represent gains that could be enlarged by parties to the transaction." Failure to do so constitutes "opportunities wasted."[42]

The technology transfer architecture erected (largely) in the 1980s was specifically intended to seize these opportunities. Several kinds of outcomes were foreseen. Universities hoped that the establishment of research parks, as well as other encouragement of research for industry, would enlarge research relations with industry, primarily for enhancement. Their explicit strategies were often vague, with propinquity perhaps being most prominent; and some expected that greater interaction with firms would somehow stimulate a second objective of technology development. To accomplish this on more than an occasional basis, however, required dedicated internal organizations—ORUs.

Universities were greatly assisted in this respect by the common interest of the states and federal government in technology development. The subsidies they provided created cooperative university-industry research centers focused on technology development in a targeted area. The outputs were somewhere in between enhancement of industrial R&D and the creation of new products, but the subsidized price made participation attractive for industry.

A third source of spillover to universities was the expectation of technology transfer itself. This process encompassed two related challenges: moving innovations from the academic laboratory to the marketplace and appropriating some portion of the value created. The organization of technology transfer offices (TTOs), business incubators, and in-house venture capital funds each addressed different pieces of this puzzle. These units aid the transformation of discoveries made in universities into intellectual property and eventual products. At most universities their operations begin with and rely heavily on the uncertain procedure of invention disclosures. The efficiency and efficacy of this triad of TTOs, incubators, and venture capitalists determine to a large extent how much of the potential value spillover can be captured by the institution. The role of the TTO in garnering disclosures and evaluating them for patenting and licensing is the key, but the proper capitalizing and nurturing of start-ups is also critical for inventions following that route.[43]

The rationalizing of university-industry research relationships has thus been a distinctive feature of the current era, and these formal arrangements have largely succeeded in capturing some degree of spillover. Universities have greatly enlarged the volume of the traditional research performed for industry to the benefit of both parties; and universities are now well prepared to take advantage of the decreasingly serendipitous occurrence of inventions in their laboratories. However, in the spirit of Lindblom's injunction, why should universities stop there? Why not seize more opportunities and realize greater gains? In effect, at least some universities have been doing precisely that, following this logic toward increasing commercialization. There are two paths toward this destination, one that emphasizes technology development, and another, in biotechnology, that focuses on patenting. Each would seem to have different implications for American universities.

The logic of commitment to economic development has drawn universities toward the role of technology innovation or development. Sustained technology development requires more than single grants or stand-alone centers. Rather, it presupposes the kind of dense networks that exist in agglomerations and that include participants at all levels of the creative process. Efficient mechanisms are also needed for moving innovations through the pipeline from discovery to patenting to commercialization. Such arrangements seem to demand a separate organization, or set of organizations, to accomplish these specialized tasks. These requirements pose a fundamental question for universities. When universities were induced to perform research above and beyond the scope of their teaching infrastructure, they responded by creating an autonomous research role. Is it possible for universities similarly to develop an autonomous role for technology development and transfer—a kind of enterprise zone within the university?

Georgia's Yamacraw Project, particularly at Georgia Tech, may represent the best model of such a development. An examination of its structure reveals the exacting requirements of such an undertaking. Financially, the project was launched by an enormous commitment of state funds specifically linked with job creation. Public subsidies would seem to be indispensable for supporting technology development, even though the ultimate objective may be a self-sustaining unit. Industry, which pays the full cost of its internal technology development, tends to contribute nominal amounts to participate in consortia. Organizationally, Yamacraw is embedded in a superstructure of state and Georgia Tech units. This complex structure is actually an asset, guaranteeing its autonomous status within the university. The structure also provides for the effective disposition of intellectual property through the channels already developed by Georgia Tech. Academically, by funding and appointing Yamacraw professors, the project created faculty who were committed from the outset to the role of technology development. Elsewhere, it might prove difficult to persuade professors already overburdened with teaching and research to dedicate time for technology as well. The essence of an autonomous technology role is the network interaction of university and industry scientists, which, however fruitful, still demands faculty time.

The Centennial Campus at NC State has approximated an autonomous technology role with a somewhat different formula. Although assisted by the state, the campus has not been financed by direct subsidies. Instead, it has pursued networking through design and organization. In this respect, the organizational superstructure has played a crucial role in facilitating collaboration and technology transfer. The faculty culture at NC State has apparently reinforced the commitment of significant time and effort to working with industry, at least among the faculty on the new campus.

Powerful trends are impelling universities toward commitments to autonomous technology development, but relatively few campuses are yet in a position to embrace this role. Superficially, it may appear that the potential revenues from commercialization are the foremost inducement, but that is not true. The big money from patent licenses, and probably start-ups too, is in biotechnology; and there a different dynamic is at work. Outside of the life sciences the principal incentive for universities comes from economic development rather than commercialization per se. Public funds to subsidize economic development, and to leverage private contributions, are far more valuable for building university resources than licensing revenues or equity in start-ups. Economic development represents a social contribution that is consistent with—in fact one facet of—the university's larger economic role. Commercialization is inherently connected with this role, but the cash nexus is more muted and more in line with normal patterns of small business entrepreneurship.

The path from academic research to technology development to commercialization follows a different route in biotechnology. First, universities are largely assured of aggregate research funding. The massive investment from the NIH and other supporters of biomedical research guarantees that the seedbeds of future technology will be assiduously cultivated. Second, patenting tends to precede rather than follow technology development. This is a subtle distinction, but one that fundamentally affects the life sciences.

In engineering and the physical sciences, patentable inventions tend to emerge from intensive research in laboratories that were created and designed for technology development. Inventions are in fact the expected outcomes, and the labs proceed from that point to licensing them and then developing practical applications. Patents in biotechnology are more likely to result from basic academic research. In the spirit of DNA pioneers Cohen and Boyer, biologists have a powerful incentive to patent the most basic processes, as soon as possible. This phenomenon amounts to *jackpot patenting*: the most lucrative biotech patents assert ownership over processes that have become essential to subsequent technologies (see Chapter 5). There is no relationship between the time and intellectual effort expended or the capital invested and the blockbuster earnings generated by a few lucky patents. As a consequence of jackpot patenting, the crucial stage of technology development follows the establishment of a patent, usually outside the university.

So the third major difference in biotechnology is that discoveries in academic laboratories tend to be developed in start-up firms or licensed to corporate laboratories. Thus the university has little role to play in technology development, and certainly no need to establish special university centers and an autonomous technology role. However, universities and their TTOs must act deftly to capture some of this value.

Again in contrast to other technologies, commercialization in biotechnology will occur whether or not the university claims its share or assists in the process. But the university is scarcely irrelevant. Life scientists depend on their universities to make continuing investments in the research technologies that propel these advancements. Genomics institutes and similar installations have received the highest priorities for facilities construction. But these scientific facilities are aimed at maintaining cutting-edge research and are not specifically dedicated to technology development.

The commercialization of university research at the dawn of the twenty-first century would seem to possess an inexorable momentum. Under the guise of economic development it carries the cachet of rendering public service. The form it has assumed in the life sciences is hitched to biocapitalism and beyond academic control. Those who fear the potential threat to disinterested inquiry must contend with the depressing spectacle of universities selling all manner of goods and services—their brand names, athletics, entertainment, real estate developments, executive MBAs—not to mention academic disdain for the very notion of disinterestedness. Clearly this is squishy ground on which to oppose the commercialization of research.[44] But are there more solid reasons for concern?

From the perspective of spillover benefits, as just presented, a case can be made for some degree of commercialization. If universities are producing knowledge with tangible value, who should reap the benefits? Surely universities should be entitled to some portion of that value. In a dynamic perspective, this argument becomes far more compelling. By making valuable knowledge more widely available, universities perform a public service, but one that consumes resources and requires compensation. A flow of commercial revenues then both enhances the amount of pubic service and enlarges the university's knowledge resources.[45] Moreover, the university's research role would seem to demand an extension into emerging research technologies that straddle the academic and commercial realms. University leadership in basic research depends on such growth, which can only be sustained through links with commercial users. Continued involvement with commercial markets, including the generation of revenue, will likely be a permanent facet of research universities, but caveats remain.

Critics have good reason to sense an incompatibility between the basic missions of instruction and research and the commercialization of knowledge. But these concerns for the reasons just stated, are unlikely to impede this phenomenon. More likely they represent normative standards that have constrained commercialization and will probably continue to do so.

The first caveat is the incongruity of nonprofit universities making profits. It is not a matter of profit per se—nonprofits are only barred from distributing profits. They must, and do, plow any surpluses back into the enterprise. Rather, a murky area surrounds the private individuals and companies that reap benefits from commercialization. What is economic development for a social scientist is profit for an entrepreneur. But private profits are derived in this case from publicly subsidized activities. Public universities in particular (because of the use of public funds) would prefer to obscure the fact that commercialization of technology brings wealth to a few. They risk the appearance of conflict of interest, and possibly the real thing.

The second caveat derives from the limitations of the academic core. As remarked throughout this study, nonacademic activities have grown out of all proportion to the academic core, and commercialization promises to increase this lopsidedness. The question has already been raised whether faculty would accept technology transfer as an additional mission. Striking an optimal balance between teaching and research has been an academic conundrum; adding technology transfer as another responsibility would compound these difficulties. As a case in point, one factor that plagued the ill-fated ventures to create on-line universities was the problem of defining the role of faculty and compensating them. The additional duties associated with such endeavors do not easily fit into the existing structure of faculty work.[46] Of course, pundits have prophesied the reinvention of the university to make it more compatible with these "inevitable" realities. Until that happens, the nature and coherence of the academic core will remain a constraint on unbridled commercialization.

And third, much the same could be said of the basic university mission of advancing and disseminating knowledge. The preeminence of the American university, as well as the synergistic activities that threaten to engulf it, all stem from the primacy of this commitment. This mission is lodged above all in the faculty, their expertise, behavior, and roles. In order for learning to be primary in the university, it must also be foremost in the motivation of the faculty. This mainspring requires a degree of insulation from commercialism. It also requires a continuous investment by universities in the learning of their faculty.

University patrons also play an important role in supporting and validating the commitment to disinterested knowledge, providing a very heavy counterweight, in effect, to the pull of commercial markets. Ultimately, the unique qualities of the American university as a center of learning generate the knowledge and expertise sought by the commercial realm. Commercial relations, should they become too dominant, would tend to corrode the very qualities responsible for producing those results. At the beginning of the twenty-first century an appropriate balance still held. But for universities that have shown themselves to be increasingly influenced by market forces, how long is this balance likely to endure?

The Paradox of the Marketplace

Time was when American universities were valued chiefly for the public good they engendered. Support from governments and philanthropy reflected an appreciation of those social benefits and was not intended to "coordinate" university behavior. Rather, institutions were accorded considerable freedom to determine how best to fulfill their role. Students were presumed to have earned the right to attend through merit and hard work. Universities tended to occupy well-understood niches in the system of higher education. Competition was relegated to the playing fields. Markets were an alien realm. But that was not the Golden Age of universities: the Golden Age is now.

Conditions have changed in higher education, and changed decisively in the current era. For universities in the twenty-first century none of those former traits prevail. The intangible social returns to higher education have been overshadowed by the private benefits attained by students and other consumers.

With private benefits predominating, the costs of universities have steadily shifted from public to private sources. Privatization has not merely been fiscal; it has also meant that revenue streams are now more closely linked with university functions, limiting the discretion of university leaders. Competition has also become keener, driven by the increased reliance on private revenues and, more fundamentally, by the national integration of the university system. The competition for students has bred consumerism—a reversal of attitude from students as clients, fortunate to attend, to students as customers who must be pleased. In all these areas, coordination of behavior has migrated from within universities to the markets governing these activities.

Prosperity has not come without a price. The intent of this study has been to gauge the dimensions of these developments, understand the forces at work, and fathom the consequences.

The current era has brought a revolution in the financing of universities. Private universities, capitalizing on federal and institutional financial aid, established a system of differential tuition that allowed them to escalate prices with minimal resistance. Public universities compensated for the slow growth in state funding by following their lead, nearly doubling the proportion of their costs derived from students. As these trends accelerated, competition intensified for the students who were best prepared for university study and best able to pay for it.

Growing market coordination in this case produced three social consequences. First, the total resources garnered by universities grew impressively. Per-student spending rose by 62 percent at public universities and more than double that at privates (see Figure 2). It is difficult to imagine another scenario that might have brought universities a similar augmentation of resources.

Second, market forces brought greater inequality among universities. Most notably, private universities dramatically outpaced their public counterparts. But within the private sector, disparities grew as well, as the top institutions enjoyed unparalleled prosperity. Inequality in the public sector actually declined in the 1980s, but the cause was greater state appropriations for laggard institutions, not the market. When privatization became more pronounced in the 1990s, inequality among public universities increased as well.

Third, the development of a more pronounced institutional hierarchy was accompanied by greater social stratification among students. This too is a market phenomenon. A policy of high-tuition/high-aid requires large numbers of students who can afford high tuition. However, this trend was exacerbated by the selectivity sweepstakes. The differential returns to selective schools were both a social fact and a self-fulfilling prophecy. That is, graduates of selective schools on average appear to achieve higher career earnings, but as this datum was publicized it increased both the attractiveness of these universities to students and their use as a screening device by employers. Highly competitive admissions placed a premium on preparation, favoring students from more privileged backgrounds and the cumulative advantage they possess. Merit in American higher education has a pronounced social gradient.

That said, American higher education in the current era has become more stratified by academic ability than ever before. The market forces that produced this result acted with particular power on both students and institutions. The emergence of a single national market for selective higher education has largely been responsible for the fine gradations of merit among students at selective institutions.

For institutions, each additional increment of selectivity has meant greater prestige and affluence. For that reason, the battle for high-ability students intensifies each year, not only with growing amounts of merit aid but also in conflicts over the rules of engagement.[47] Universities, ironically, have endeavored mightily to exempt some portion of entering classes from their own ruthless standards with special criteria based on race, ethnicity, or hardship. Social implications aside, the meritocratic stratification of American higher education has brought universities the most highly qualified students they have ever had. Moreover, matching the students best equipped to learn with institutions having the greatest learning resources is an efficient social outcome in itself.

Market coordination through the seeming irrationality of the selectivity sweepstakes has yielded a rational and efficient result. Another consequence is perhaps less welcome. Competition in the admissions market has contributed substantially to the ascendancy of student consumerism. Universities may have attracted the most capable students in their history, but in the process they have ceded some control over their learning.

An entirely different form of market coordination prevails in the research system. This administered market rigorously enforces standards of academic excellence through the predominance of peer-reviewed research grants. As a greater number of universities participated more actively in the research system in the current era, academic standards tended to rise. Universities faced strong inducements to participate because research contributed to enhancing prestige, enlarging resources, improving graduate education, and multiplying benefits to society.

But the resources needed to engage in research were by their nature in scarce supply. The competitive market for talented researchers and state-of-the-art research facilities determined which universities acquired how much research funding from the administered market. Most universities were able to expand their capacity for research during the current era.

The expansiveness of their actions in this market contrasted markedly with the strategy of increasing the selectivity rather than the size of undergraduate programs. This discrepancy meant that much of the growth in academic research occurred outside of core departments as part of an autonomous research role. Although the increasing ratio of researchers to faculty is a disconcerting trend, their separation from departmental structures may have been an important ingredient for success. Academic research proved quite effective at accommodating and incorporating the evolving demands for new knowledge. In doing so, academic research became more integrated with the economy and a more productive contributor to economic growth. That development brought a new set of market relationships.

The economic contributions of academic research have been a notable achievement of universities in the current era. Moreover, the coordinating effects of this portion of the research market, despite fears, have done little to destabilize the larger research enterprise. One reason is the predominance of the academic standards enforced by the administered research market. Another is the prominence of research technologies, which allow university scientists to pursue basic research that has a high probability of subsequent economic relevance.

A thicket of commercial activities has grown downstream from these research activities, as universities have responded to incentives to transfer technology to industry and to take their cut in the process. But on balance these activities have had a relatively minor impact on the research process itself. The weight of evidence about the nature of university-industry research relationships suggests that commercialization and its temptations continue to be largely compartmentalized. The risk here seems manageable, especially in relation to the benefits. Involvement with industry and with commercially relevant technologies has brought substantial additional resources to universities and has resulted in substantial returns to society in the form of new technologies.

Market relationships have the capacity to produce great wealth and to promote efficiency through the combination of incentives and free choice. The accentuation of market relationships among American universities since 1980 has done all of these things. Market relationships also generate negative outcomes or externalities, and this has been true in higher education as well.

Just as capitalist markets generate wealth inequality in the economy, the working of market forces in higher education has exaggerated wealth inequalities among universities. The wealth of some private universities is devoted both to wise, knowledge-enhancing investments and to wasteful competition. Other universities lack the resources to realize their potential. Consumer sovereignty exacerbates this situation, creating a kind of winner-take-all phenomenon typical of mass markets. Greater social stratification, furthermore, is the ineluctable result of colleges competing for preferred students and students competing for preferred colleges.

Markets, when unimpeded, have a tendency to exploit all the inherent possibilities—to drive good fortune to excess and thereby jeopardize the accomplishment itself. The differential pricing system for private higher education seems to have done just that. By exploiting federal and institutional aid to maximize net tuition income, private institutions pushed nominal prices to stratospheric levels. The greater the overpricing, the more precarious these arrangements become. Specifically, these artificial prices are vulnerable to the depredations of merit aid, increased competition from public institutions, fluctuations in the prosperity of the upper middle class, or changes in their taste in colleges. The same constellation of forces now motivates state universities to rectify their relative underpricing by raising tuition. Here a different set of externalities arises, as quality higher education for state residents becomes more expensive and exclusive. The worries about commercialization reflect a similar process. If universities were to exploit commercial possibilities to their fullest, the nature of the institution would indeed be altered and its contribution to society impaired.

The results of coordination through market systems are also affected by imperfections. Most of the markets in higher education discussed here may be decentralized and fairly competitive, but embedded in each is the heavy hand of government. The federal government chiefly administers the markets for research, and the states still provide three of every five dollars of general funds at state universities. Moreover, governments provide the bulk of the funds for student financial aid. And wherever economic development is invoked, public funds are sure to be found. In these latter cases, public funding has been supplied in ways that encouraged or incorporated market mechanisms. But forms of coordination shaped by artificial prices will always be sensitive to fluctuations in the levels and conditions of subsidization.

Hence the paradox of the marketplace for American universities: the marketplace has, on balance, brought universities greater resources, better students, a far larger capacity for advancing knowledge, and a more productive role in the U.S. economy. At the same time, it has diminished the sovereignty of universities over their own activities, weakened their mission of serving the public, and created through growing commercial entanglements at least the potential for undermining their privileged role as disinterested arbiters of knowledge.

The gains have been for the most part material, quantified, and valuable;

the losses intangible, unmeasured, and at some level invaluable. The consequences of the university's immersion in the marketplace are thus incommensurate. In the near term, no doubt, the tangible payoffs from these markets will prove greater than the intangible dangers. Nevertheless, increasing market coordination of universities should not be construed as a prescription for unceasing material gains. The markets that have shaped American universities were contrived by human rather than invisible hands. And what succeeded in one era, if left unchanged, has a strong likelihood of failing in the next.

The health of these national treasures will depend in the future, as it has in the past, on continual adjustment to changing conditions. Adaptation demands constant attention to the signals of the marketplace. But it also requires wise and deliberate coordination by the numerous actors who shape and lead these dynamic and enduring institutions.

APPENDIXES

Costs per FTE Student, 1980, 1990, 2000

The amount of money a university spends each year for the general purpose of educating students ought to be simple to calculate, but it is not. The figures conventionally used are usually based on the entire university budget or on "general and educational (G&E) expenditures," both of which are far too large. G&E expenditures include separately budgeted research, which is an independent form of revenue and spending. They also include expenditures for medical schools, which may have as many faculty as students. A better proxy would be the "general funds budget," excluding the medical school, but that figure is not readily available. The challenge for this study was to devise a measure of university costs that would be comparable across institutions and over time.

Since none of the reported data for expenditures could meet these criteria, the best approximation was the amount of money an institution had available to spend for general instructional purposes. Moreover, this approach was consistent with the revenue theory of costs, discussed in Chapter 2. Accordingly, the following formulas were used:

For private universities:

$$\frac{\text{Gross tuition revenue} - \text{institutional student aid} + \text{spending from endowment}}{\text{Full-time students} + \frac{1}{3}\text{ part-time students}}$$

For public universities:

$$\frac{\text{Gross tuition} - \text{institutional student aid} + \text{endowment spending} + \text{state appropriation}}{\text{Full-time students} + \frac{1}{3}\text{ part-time students}}$$

In Tables A1 and A2, these totals are converted to 1996$. Unless otherwise indicated, the financial comparisons in this study are based on these data, derived from the National Center for Education Statistics IPEDS database.

Private Universities: Net Revenue per FTE Student, 1980, 1990, 2000 (1996$)

Institution	1980	1990	2000
Boston University	7,500	13,690	17,350
Brandeis University	8,370	14,240	16,230
Brown University	8,900	16,020	21,710
California Institute of Technology	18,100	28,650	34,190
Carnegie Mellon University	10,100	17,110	21,300
Case Western Reserve University	9,400	15,150	19,510
Columbia University	11,740	18.560	24,070
Cornell University	12,060	16,720	26,370[a]
Dartmouth College	12,370	22,810	29,370
Duke University	7,070	14,850	21,520
Emory University	9,360	17,670	31,150
George Washington University	6,790	14,520	18,010
Harvard University	17,870	23,770	45,460
Johns Hopkins University	8,030	14,890	20,610
Massachusetts Institute of Technology	10,410	18.340	31,580
New York University	10,180	16,330	21,990
Northwestern University	10,290	14,980	24,390
Princeton University	15,780	27,260	50,620
Rensselaer Polytechnic Institute	8,060	13,070	15,100
Rice University	13,430	19,130	36,360
Stanford University	11,420	18,660	29,410
Syracuse University	7,880	11,660	14,110
Tufts University	9,620	15,680	19,410
Tulane University	6,950	12,020	15,450
University of Chicago	14,090	17,710	24,690
University of Miami	7,680	12,930	17,950
University of Pennsylvania	8,410	15,400	25,790
University of Rochester	10,710	13,730	17,610
University of Southern California	8,710	14,660	17,990
Vanderbilt University	8,410	13,600	21,110
Wake Forest University	7,840	13,630	20,230
Washington University	10,000	15,730	28,020
Yale University	11,400	18,120	37,850

[a]Endowed campus only

Public Universities: Net Revenue per FTE Student, 1980, 1990, 2000 (1996$)

Institution	1980	1990	2000
Arizona State University	5,760	9,650	10,540
Auburn University	7,930	10,260	13,980
Clemson University	11,930	13,550	14,820
Colorado State University	7,070	8,190	11,060
Florida State University	6,990	9,450	9,830
Georgia Institute of Technology	7,740	12,500	19,680
Indiana University, Bloomington	6,910	9,380	12,410
Iowa State University	8,580	11,840	14,630
Kansas State University	6,940	8,830	10,700
Louisiana State University	8,220	10,300	10,280
Michigan State University	8,610	11,540	14,770
New Mexico State University	6,310	7,170	10,700

Institution	1980	1990	2000
North Carolina State University, Raleigh	9,930	14,440	17,890
Ohio State University	8,060	11,900	15,550
Oregon State University	7,430	10,590	12,600
Pennsylvania State University, main campus	8,360	11,270	14,430
Purdue University, main campus	7,790	10,680	13,210
SUNY, Albany	9,270	9,740	10,410
SUNY, Buffalo	11,330	13,460	17,120
SUNY, Stony Brook	16,260	18,020	17,520
Texas A&M University, main campus	8,770	12,310	13,290
University of Alabama, Birmingham	16,620	16,500	18,930
University of Arizona	9,340	12,040	15,160
University of California, Berkeley	13,240	17,810	20,520
University of California, Davis	14,900	18,100	19,680
University of California, Los Angeles	14,720	17,820	19,360
University of California, Riverside	20,140	18,050	15,450
University of California, San Diego	15,990	16,340	17,380
University of California, Santa Barbara	8,870	11,980	11,820
University of California, Santa Cruz	12,170	12,990	14,520
University of Cincinnati	6,990	10,020	14,140
University of Colorado, Boulder	5,530	8,020	9,690
University of Connecticut	7,930	10,990	19,860
University of Delaware	7,910	11,790	14,570
University of Florida	11,030	16,510	15,180
University of Georgia	10,960	13,760	18,220
University of Hawaii, Manoa	10,010	16,010	16,090
University of Illinois, Chicago	13,120	14,890	17,420
University of Illinois, Urbana-Champaign	10,320	11,400	13,750
University of Iowa	11,660	11,340	15,340
University of Kansas	6,450	8,620	11,430
University of Kentucky	11,380	14,120	17,660
University of Maryland, College Park	6,620	12,740	14,950
University of Massachusetts, Amherst	7,090	9,900	14,220
University of Michigan, Ann Arbor	11,780	15,720	21,200
University of Minnesota, Twin Cities	9,060	15,820	20,290
University of Missouri, Columbia	9,840	10,500	14,010
University of Nebraska, Lincoln	7,230	9,420	12,450
University of New Mexico	5,890	8,990	13,670
University of North Carolina, Chapel Hill	11,460	16,570	22,210
University of Oklahoma, Norman campus	4,980	7,390	8,980
University of Pittsburgh	10,460	13,320	15,700
University of South Carolina, Columbia	7,530	11,460	14,070
University of South Florida	7,340	11,860	13,050
University of Tennessee, Knoxville	5,150	12,370	13,290
University of Texas, Austin	7,910	7,790	13,610
University of Utah	7,730	10,160	13,190
University of Virginia	11,440	13,800	15,940
University of Washington, Seattle	9,130	13,290	15,500
University of Wisconsin, Madison	10,220	13,470	16,350
Utah State University	7,910	8,560	9,760
Virginia Polytechnic Institute	9,040	13,120	13,310
Washington State University	9,460	11,660	13,780
Wayne State University	9,690	12,330	17,000

Research Share for Selected Universities, 1980, 1990, 2000

Comparing the expenditures of universities for separately budgeted research is far simpler than comparing education costs. These data have been carefully compiled by the National Science Foundation since the 1950s. But each institution's performance is obscured by the rising total volume of research and the effects of inflation. These factors are eliminated for companies over time by using "research share"— each university's research expenditures as a percentage of total national expenditures for academic research. For the calculations in Tables B1 and B2, the unique expenditures of the Applied Physics Laboratory at Johns Hopkins University have been eliminated from the total. Two-year average shares for 1979–80 and 1989–90 are taken from Roger Geiger and Irwin Feller, "The Dispersion of Academic Research in the 1980s," *Journal of Higher Education* 66 (1995): 336–60. All data are from the National Science Foundation.

TABLE B1

Research Share of Total Academic R&D, 66 Public Universities,
1979–80, 1989–90, 2000

Institution	1979–80	1989–90	2000
Arizona State University	0.14	0.35	0.36
Auburn University	0.39	0.41	0.31
Clemson University	0.33	0.42	0.39
Colorado State University	0.73	0.48	0.51
Florida State University	0.36	0.41	0.35
Georgia Institute of Technology	0.97	1.18	1.02
Indiana University, Bloomington	0.54	0.59	0.77
Iowa State University	0.90	0.75	0.59
Kansas State University	0.49	0.34	0.31
Louisiana State University and Agricultural and Mechanical College	0.92	0.89	0.85
Michigan State University	1.27	0.85	0.77
New Mexico State University	0.43	0.45	0.27
North Carolina State University, Raleigh	0.78	0.88	0.94
Ohio State University	1.26	1.21	1.22

Institution	1979–80	1989–90	2000
Oregon State University	0.79	0.63	0.48
Pennsylvania State University	1.28	1.64	1.45
Purdue University, main campus	1.10	0.88	0.79
Rutgers, the State University of New Jersey, New Brunswick	0.66	0.90	0.76
SUNY, Albany	0.12	0.16	0.28
SUNY, Buffalo	0.43	0.72	0.64
SUNY, Stony Brook	0.47	0.56	0.55
Texas A&M University	1.27	1.80	1.34
University of Alabama, Birmingham	0.55	0.73	0.79
University of Arizona	1.20	1.27	1.16
University of California, Berkeley	1.56	1.52	1.75
University of California, Davis	1.17	1.30	1.23
University of California, Irvine	0.39	0.50	0.53
University of California, Los Angeles	1.55	1.63	1.80
University of California, Riverside	0.44	0.37	0.28
University of California, San Diego	2.19	1.56	1.75
University of California, Santa Barbara	0.24	0.38	0.40
University of California, Santa Cruz	0.14	0.17	0.19
University of Cincinnati	0.51	0.50	0.58
University of Colorado, Boulder	1.03	1.03	1.20
University of Connecticut	0.78	0.77	0.54
University of Delaware	0.29	0.27	0.25
University of Florida	0.99	0.91	1.06
University of Georgia	1.00	1.04	0.87
University of Hawaii, Manoa	0.72	0.51	0.54
University of Illinois, Chicago	0.41	0.58	0.66
University of Illinois, Urbana-Champaign	1.50	1.51	1.26
University of Iowa	0.75	0.76	0.80
University of Kansas	0.35	0.41	0.50
University of Kentucky	0.56	0.50	0.68
University of Maryland, College Park	0.69	1.08	0.95
University of Massachusetts, Amherst	0.44	0.73	0.66
University of Michigan, Ann Arbor	2.06	2.03	1.87
University of Minnesota, Twin Cities	2.12	1.89	1.39
University of Missouri, Columbia	0.64	0.54	0.54
University of Nebraska, Lincoln	0.60	0.50	0.46
University of New Mexico	0.47	0.38	0.45
University of North Carolina, Chapel Hill	0.68	0.84	0.91
University of Oklahoma, Norman	0.35	0.39	0.51
University of Pittsburgh	0.58	0.79	1.00
University of South Carolina, Columbia	0.12	0.30	0.35
University of South Florida	0.09	0.47	0.49
University of Tennessee, Knoxville	1.19	0.86	0.55
University of Texas, Austin	1.40	1.45	0.92
University of Utah	0.69	0.59	0.64
University of Virginia	0.47	0.61	0.59
University of Washington, Seattle	1.99	1.61	1.79
University of Wisconsin, Madison	2.45	2.05	1.87
Utah State University	0.40	0.54	0.35
Virginia Polytechnic Institute and State University	0.59	0.78	0.65
Washington State University	0.54	0.42	0.35
Wayne State University	0.38	0.42	0.53
Total	52.75	53.64	51.23

TABLE B2

Research Share of Total Academic R&D, 33 Private Universities,
1979–80, 1989–90, 2000 (percent)

Academic Institution	1979–80	1989–90	2000
Boston University	0.43	0.48	0.
Brandeis University	0.18	0.21	0.16
Brown University	0.31	0.31	0.27
California Institute of Technology	0.76	0.70	0.75
Carnegie Mellon University	0.51	0.69	0.47
Case Western Reserve University	0.72	0.62	0.65
Columbia University	1.74	1.22	1.08
Cornell University	1.96	2.02	1.38
Dartmouth College	0.17	0.28	0.27
Duke University	0.72	0.93	1.21
Emory University	0.29	0.51	0.69
George Washington University	0.36	0.22	0.23
Harvard University	1.79	1.48	1.15
Johns Hopkins University	1.50	1.62	1.52
Massachusetts Institute of Technology	2.87	2.06	1.44
New York University	1.04	0.73	0.61
Northwestern University	0.75	0.86	0.83
Princeton University	0.51	0.60	0.46
Rensselaer Polytechnic Institute	0.24	0.30	0.14
Rice University	0.15	0.16	0.14
Stanford University	2.02	2.03	1.54
Syracuse University	0.28	0.24	0.13
Tufts University	0.20	0.33	0.35
Tulane University	0.23	0.35	0.30
University of Chicago	1.11	0.78	0.58
University of Miami	0.77	0.63	0.49
University of Pennsylvania	1.66	1.25	1.46
University of Rochester	1.19	0.87	0.66
University of Southern California	1.26	1.14	1.01
Vanderbilt University	0.38	0.48	0.58
Wake Forest University	0.11	0.26	0.29
Washington University	1.06	0.96	1.22
Yale University	1.28	1.21	1.00
Total	28.19	26.31	23.35

Notes

Introduction

1. The vast American system of higher education contains nearly 4,000 institutions and serves some 15 million students. Few meaningful statements can be made about it without specifying particular sectors. The subject of this study is *research universities*—those institutions most focused on advancing knowledge through research and scholarship, doctoral education, and undergraduate instruction. To monitor their evolution, I have collected information on ninety-nine of these institutions, identified in the appendices. Chosen for a combination of academic strength and research activity, these institutions form a crucial part of U.S. higher education. They perform nearly 75 percent of academic research, award 28 percent of bachelor's degrees, 34 percent of first professional degrees, and 68 percent of doctorates.

2. Daniel Bell, *The Coming of Post-Industrial Society: A Venture in Social Forecasting* (New York: Basic Books, 1973). This point has been noted by many social theorists, including Clark Kerr and Harold Perkin.

3. Charles E. Lindblom, *The Market System: What It Is, How It Works, and What to Make of It* (New Haven, Conn.: Yale University Press, 2001), quotations on pp. 23, 141, 142, 143.

Chapter 1

1. Burton R. Clark, *The Higher Education System* (Los Angeles: University of California Press, 1983), chapter 1.

2. Laurence Veysey, *The Emergence of the American University* (Chicago: University of Chicago Press, 1965), p. 338.

3. Howard R. Bowen, *The Costs of Higher Education* (San Francisco: Jossey-Bass, 1980), p. 20. The apparent simplicity of this law is deceiving: David Breneman calls it one of "only two basic theories [of college costs] that warrant consideration": "An Essay on College Costs," in National Center for Education Statistics, *Study of College Costs and Prices: 1988–89 to 1997–98*, vol. 2 (Washington, D.C.: NCES, 2001), pp. 13–20, quotation on p. 14. Bowen's law, and the second basic theory, are discussed further in Chapter 2.

4. See Chapters 2 and 6; also, Daniel Rodas, *Resource Allocation in Private Research Universities* (New York: Routledge Falmer, 2001).

5. Henry Hansmann, "Economic Theories of the Nonprofit Sector," in Walter W. Powell, ed., *The Nonprofit Sector: A Research Handbook* (New Haven, Conn.: Yale University Press, 1987), pp. 27–42.

6. Roger L. Geiger, "Finance and Function: Voluntary Support and Diversity in American Private Higher Education," in Daniel Levy, ed., *Private Choice and Public Policy in Private Education* (New York: Oxford University Press, 1986).

7. This situation has been changing as public and private universities have increased their borrowing for capital purposes. With low interest rates and high returns to endowments, this form of arbitrage has been attractive. However, as a result, students in effect now contribute to the facilities they utilize. And, in another example of universities in the marketplace, bond ratings are now an important concern of universities.

8. In fact, this description fits for-profit higher education.

9. Michael S. McPherson and Gordon C. Winston, "The Economics of Academic Tenure: a Relational Perspective," in David W. Breneman and T. I. K. Youn, eds., *Academic Labor Markets and Careers* (New York: Falmer Press, 1984), pp. 174–99.

10. Burton R. Clark, "The Modern Integration of Research Activities with Teaching and Learning," *Journal of Higher Education* 68 (1997): 241–55.

11. David A. Garvin, *The Economics of University Behavior* (New York: Academic Press, 1980), pp. 22–24.

12. For a distinction between reputation and prestige, see Dominic J. Brewer, Susan M. Gates, and Charles A. Goldman, *In Pursuit of Prestige: Strategy and Competition in U.S. Higher Education* (New Brunswick, N.J.: Transaction, 2002).

13. Roger L. Geiger, *To Advance Knowledge* (New York: Oxford University Press, 1986), pp. 38–39; David S. Webster, "Reputational Rankings of Colleges, Universities, and Individual Disciplines and Fields of Study, from Their Beginnings to the Present," in John Smart, ed., *Higher Education: Handbook of Theory and Research* 7 (1992): 234–304; discussed in Chapter 4.

14. Hugh Davis Graham and Nancy Diamond, *The Rise of American Research Universities* (Baltimore: Johns Hopkins University Press, 1997).

15. Derek Bok, *Universities in the Marketplace: The Commercialization of Higher Education* (Princeton, N.J.: Princeton University Press, 2003). Bok includes intercollegiate athletics as a paradigm for the baneful effects of commercialization.

16. National Center for Education Statistics, *Digest of Education Statistics, 2000* (Washington, D.C.: NCES), table 182.

17. Some colleges deliberately limited enrollments to enhance selectivity; see Elizabeth A. Duffy and Idana Goldberg, *Crafting a Class: College Admissions and Financial Aid* (Princeton, N.J.: Princeton University Press, 1998).

18. Richard Freeman, *The Over-Educated American* (New York: Academic Press, 1976).

19. Estimates of these phenomena vary depending on the units being monitored and the method of accounting for inflation: see NCES, *Digest of Education Statistics, 1999*, tables 342, 343; Kent Halstead, *Higher Education Revenues and Expenditures: A Study of Institutional Costs* (Washington, D.C.: Research Associates of Washington,

1991); and American Association of University Professors, "Annual Reports on the Economic Status of the Profession," published annually in the March–April issue of *Academe*.

20. Derek Bok, *Beyond the Ivory Tower: Social Responsibilities of the Modern University* (Cambridge, Mass.: Harvard University Press, 1982), p. 141. Bok nevertheless urged caution (p. 142), then and now (see note 15).

21. George Keller, *Academic Strategy: The Managerial Revolution in American Higher Education* (Baltimore: Johns Hopkins University Press, 1983), p. 57.

22. Ibid., p. 48.

23. Roger L. Geiger, *Research and Relevant Knowledge*, *American Research Universities since World War II* (New York: Oxford University Press, 1993), pp. 256–57; Roger L. Geiger, "Curriculum and the Marketplace," *Change* (Nov./Dec. 1980): 17–23; Duffy and Goldberg, *Crafting a Class*.

24. Duffy and Goldberg, *Crafting a Class*, pp. 64–67.

25. James C. Hearn, "The Paradox of Growth in Federal Aid for College Students, 1965–1990," in John C. Smart, ed., *Higher Education: Handbook of Theory and Research* 9 (1994): 94–153.

Chapter 2

1. National Commission on the Cost of Higher Education (NCCHE), *Straight Talk about College Costs and Prices* (Phoenix, Ariz.: Oryx Press, 1998).

2. The congressional mandate limiting the purview of this study is described in the second report: National Center for Education Statistics, *Study of College Costs and Prices, 1988–89 to 1997–98*, 2 vols. (Washington, D.C.: NCES, 2001).

3. National Commission on the Financing of Postsecondary Education, *Financing Postsecondary Education in the United States* (Washington, D.C.: GPO, 1973). This study was commissioned as part of the 1972 amendments to the Higher Education Act, which systematized federal programs for student financial aid. It consequently rationalized rather than shaped those programs.

4. Recent studies analyzing institutional behavior include Charles T. Clotfelter, *Buying the Best: Cost Escalation in Elite Higher Education* (Princeton, N.J.: Princeton University Press, 1996); Michael S. McPherson and Morton Owen Schapiro, *The Student Aid Game: Meeting Need and Rewarding Talent in American Higher Education* (Princeton, N.J.: Princeton University Press, 1998); Ronald G. Ehrenberg, *Tuition Rising: Why College Costs So Much* (Cambridge, Mass.: Harvard University Press, 2000); Jeffrey E. Olson, "The Cost-Effectiveness of American Higher Education: The United States Can Afford Its Colleges and Universities," in *Higher Education: Handbook of Theory and Research* 12 (1997): 195–242.

5. D. Bruce Johnstone, "Higher Education and Those 'Out of Control Costs,'" NCES, *Study of College Costs*, vol. 2, pp. 21–43, 22ff. The present study does not address cost functions in higher education; see Paul T. Brinckman, "Higher Education Cost Functions," in Stephen A. Hoenack and Eileen L. Collins, eds., *The Economics of American Universities* (Albany: State University of New York Press, 1990), pp. 107–28; Darrell R. Lewis and Halil Dundar, "Costs and Productivity in Higher Education: Theory, Evidence, and Policy Implications," in John C. Smart, ed., *Higher Education: Handbook of Theory and Research* 14 (1999): 39–102.

6. For this study data were gathered for ninety-nine universities (thirty-three pri-

vate and sixty-six public) that performed the largest amounts of research and had the largest number of rated doctoral programs (henceforth, RU database); see Appendix A. Some universities were omitted from certain analyses if the data for them were incomplete. Complete financial data were not available for Rutgers and UC Irvine, for example, so averages of public university costs are based on sixty-four institutions. Medical universities that do not teach undergraduates were omitted from this study. These ninety-nine universities were selected to represent research universities during the 1980s and 1990s. Inclusion or exclusion implies no judgment about any individual institution.

7. Howard R. Bowen, *The Costs of Higher Education* (San Francisco: Jossey-Bass, 1980), p. 20. Two decades after he wrote, exceptions to Bowen's spending rule are evident: the wealthiest universities no longer spend all their revenues, but in effect create savings; see later discussion in the text; and David W. Breneman, "An Essay on College Costs," in NCES, *Study of College Costs*, vol. 2, pp. 13–20. However, Breneman endorses Bowen's revenue theory of cost (pp. 14–15).

8. In October 1999, the National Association of College and University Business Officers (NACUBO) initiated a project to define the costs of undergraduate education at selected participating institutions. This project encountered severe difficulties defining instructional expenditures and finally recommended a methodology with more than twenty-five elements. The final report provided no comparable institutional data, but only aggregate figures; see NACUBO, *Explaining College Costs: NACUBO's Methodology for Identifying the Costs of Delivering Undergraduate Education* (Washington, D.C.: NACUBO, Feb. 2002).

9. Gordon C. Winston has argued that depreciation and opportunity costs, based on the value of land, buildings, and equipment, ought to be included in educational costs; see "Capital and Capital Service Costs in 2,700 U.S. Colleges and Universities," Discussion Paper 33, Williams Project on the Economics of Higher Education, Williams College, Dec. 1995. This approach was followed in NCCHE, *Straight Talk* (p. 32). These costs would seem to add about 15 percent to overall costs, perhaps more for wealthier institutions, but also introduce great uncertainty. See note 26 to this chapter.

10. These categories, elaborated by Gordon C. Winston, are widely employed for depicting university costs: "A Guide to Measuring College Costs," Discussion Paper 46, Williams Project on the Economics of Higher Education, Williams College, Jan. 1998.

11. For an overview of the transformation of federal student aid policy from grants to loans, see James C. Hearn, "The Paradox of Growth in Federal Aid for College Students, 1965–1990," *Higher Education: Handbook of Theory and Research* 9 (1994): 94–153.

12. NCES, *Digest of Education Statistics, 2000* (Washington, D.C.: NCES), tables 331, 359. Student expenses for room, board, and incidentals also rose during these years; however, Pell grants, state student aid, and institutional financial aid also increased the subsidy side. Hence, tuition and federal loans represent the largest change. This analysis is in substantial agreement with Arthur M. Hauptman and Cathy Krop, "Federal Student Aid and the Growth of College Costs and Tuitions: Examining the Relationship," in NCCHE, *Straight Talk*, pp. 70–83.

13. Ibid., p. 73. *Straight Talk* summarizes the case for denial and is unable to endorse either position (pp. 300–302).

14. McPherson and Schapiro, *Student Aid Game*, pp. 53–103.

15. Roger L. Geiger, "High Tuition—High Aid: A Road Paved with Good Intentions" (paper presented at meeting of the Association for the Study of Higher Education, Sacramento, Calif., Nov. 2002).

16. King, "Student Borrowing," pp. 6, 13; Thomas J. Kane, *The Price of Admission: Rethinking How Americans Pay for College* (Washington, D.C.: Brookings Institution Press, 1999).

17. Evidence of price sensitivity has been found for lower-income students, especially at nonelite institutions. However, McPherson and Schapiro found "no evidence that increases in net cost inhibited enrollment for more affluent students" (*Student Aid Game*, pp. 39–40).

18. The seminal study in this area is W. Lee Hansen and Burton A. Weisbrod, *Benefits, Costs, and Finance of Public Higher Education* (Chicago: Markham, 1969). See also W. Lee Hansen and Burton A. Weisbrod, "A New Approach to Higher Education Finance," in M. D. Orwig, ed., *Financing Higher Education: Alternatives for the Federal Government* (Iowa City: American College Testing Program, 1971), pp. 117–42; Carnegie Commission on Higher Education, *Priorities for Action: Final Report of the Carnegie Commission for Higher Education* (New York: McGraw-Hill, 1973), p. 66. One problem that the Carnegie Commission addressed was the perception, ironic in retrospect, that private colleges and universities were pricing themselves out of the market. The two-pronged solution was higher tuition in public institutions coupled with student aid for both sectors.

19. In 2000 the tuition ratios for sixty-five public universities in this study ranged from 22 percent to 71 percent, with a mean of 37 percent.

20. Mark Nerlove's 1972 analysis was particularly concerned with "the downward pressure on tuition at private institutions"; see "On Tuition and the Costs of Higher Education: Prolegomena to a Conceptual Framework," *Journal of Political Economy* 80 (May–June, 1972): S178–S218, quotation on p. S211.

21. Tuition data from Clotfelter, *Buying the Best*, pp. 71, 81.

22. Carolyn M. Hoxby, "How the Changing Market Structure of U.S. Higher Education Explains College Tuition," Working Paper 6326, National Bureau of Economic Research, Cambridge, Mass., Dec. 1997.

23. For the thirty-three private universities monitored in this study, net tuition remained remarkably constant: 69 percent of costs in 1980, 70 percent in 1990, 71 percent in 1996, but 66 percent in 2000. Institutional scholarships rose as a percentage of gross tuition revenues from 18 percent in 1980 to 20 percent in 1990, to 24 percent in 1996, and to 27 percent in 2000.

24. Indeed, without loans, institutional aid alone could not sustain actual tuition levels. For example, for guaranteed loans to be replaced by institutional aid in 1996, the tuition discount rate for the private universities in this sample would need to rise from 24 percent to an estimated 42 percent.

25. A student who pays full tuition, in other words, receives a negative subsidy, at least as far as direct costs are concerned. Whether institutional student aid is a real cost or a price discount has been a vexing question. Conceptually a distinction can

be made: at institutions with a surfeit of qualified applicants, aid is an investment in the quality of the student body; without such a surplus, it is a discount to optimize revenue; see William G. Bowen and David W. Breneman, "Student Aid: Price Discount or Educational Investment?" *Brookings Review* 11 (1993): 28–31. In reality, most institutions now combine both motives in a strategic manner; see McPherson and Schapiro, *Student Aid Game.*

26. Universities receive additional income from gifts and research grants, but these funds are largely earmarked for particular purposes. Students receive a significant subsidy in the use-value of the campus, buildings, and equipment, but this value is difficult to quantify because it depends upon interest rate assumptions for opportunity costs and uncertain assessments of real estate values; see note 9 in this chapter.

27. See the model in David W. Breneman, *Liberal Arts Colleges: Thriving, Surviving, or Endangered?* (Washington, D.C.: Brookings Institution Press, 1994); and the critique of tuition discounting in Madlynne Veil Griffiths, "The Financial Effects of Tuition Discounting: An Analysis of Private Colleges in Pennsylvania" (D.Ed. diss., Pennsylvania State University, 1996).

28. The implications are explored in Geiger, "High Tuition—High Aid."

29. This problem is less severe at private research universities than at other private institutions; see Lucie Lapovsky, "Institutional Financial Health: Tuition Discounting and Enrollment Management," in NCES, *Study of College Costs*, vol. 2, pp. 57–73.

30. The 10/90 tuition spread for 2001–2002 was $22,000 to $26,700, or 18 percent.

31. The practice of tuition discounting has been carried much further in many private colleges. A few, most notably Muskingum College, have repudiated this practice and drastically reduced tuition to more realistic levels; see Geiger, "Signposts on the Path to Privatization," p. 54; Ehrenberg, *Tuition Rising*, pp. 83–84.

32. Gordon C. Winston describes the degree of inequality for all U.S. higher education and foresees it increasing as a result of disparities in "savings" or endowment formation; see "Economic Stratification and Hierarchy among U.S. Colleges and Universities," Discussion Paper 58, Williams Project on the Economics of Higher Education, Williams College, Nov. 2000.

33. Patrick M. Callen and Joni E. Finney, eds., *Public and Private Financing of Higher Education* (Phoenix, Ariz.: Oryx Press, 1997), pp. 81–136.

34. Ibid., pp. 6–10.

35. Among public universities in the Big Ten, increases in tuition and fees ranged from 8 to 27 percent for 2002–2003. Comparisons are blurred by the addition of fees and differential charges. The tuition ratio for public universities has risen to roughly 40 percent.

36. *Chronicle of Higher Education Almanac* (Aug. 29, 1997): 12. This last fad was carried furthest in South Carolina, where a facilitator convinced a focus group of citizens that the process of funding state universities needed to be "reinvented." The system they invented, and which was enacted into law, tied all state appropriations to 37 performance indicators, some of which could not be measured; see William Trombley, "Performance-Based Budgeting: South Carolina's New Plan Mired in

Detail and Confusion," *National Crosstalk* 7, no. 1 (1998): 1, 14–16. This unworkable scheme has since been modified

37. See Donald E. Heller, "The Policy Shift in State Financial Aid Programs," in John C. Smart, ed., *Higher Education: Handbook of Theory and Research* 17 (2002): 221–62.

38. Donald E. Heller and Patricia Marin, eds., *Who Should We Help? The Negative Social Consequences of Merit Aid Scholarships* (Cambridge, Mass.: Harvard University, The Civil Rights Project, 2002).

39. William Trombley, "California's Improved Financial Aid Program," *National Crosstalk* 8, no. 4 (2000): 1, 8.

40. David W. Breneman, "The 'Privatization' of Public Universities: A Mistake or a Model for the Future?" *Chronicle of Higher Education* (July 3, 1997).

41. NCES, *Digest of Education Statistics, 1999*, table 343, adjusted to eliminate noninstructional components of education and general expenditures. See also Johnstone, "Higher Education," pp. 23–24.

42. Ibid., table 31. Spending for elementary and secondary education increased at a similar rate in the 1980s and 1990s.

43. Using a different measure, real expenditures per FTE student increased as follows from 1976 to 1995:

Universities: public: 20 percent; private: 59 percent
Four-year colleges: public: 13 percent; private: 34 percent
Two-year colleges: public: 12 percent (ibid., tables 349–53)

44. See Clotfelter, *Buying the Best*; Charles W. Smith, *Market Values in American Higher Education* (Lanham, Md.: Rowman and Littlefield, 2000), pp. 32–42.

45. See the discussion in Birnbaum, *Management Fads*, pp. 215–17; and William F. Massy, *Honoring the Trust: Quality and Cost Containment in Higher Education* (Bolton, Mass.: Anker, 2003), pp. 29–44.

46. Charles T. Goldman et al., *Paying for University Research Facilities and Administration* (Santa Monica, Calif.: Rand, 2000), chapter 3.

47. Smith, *Market Values*, pp. 8–9.

48. In addition, annual budget allocations are perceived by units as "property rights," which can be revoked only in the direst emergency; see William F. Massy, *Resource Allocation in Higher Education* (Ann Arbor: University of Michigan Press, 1996), p. 29.

49. RU database. Most of this increase occurred from 1980 to 1985, when regulatory burdens were rising. Data on administrative growth in general during the 1980s were reported by Karen Grassmuck, "Colleges Hired More Non-Teaching Staff Than Other Employees throughout the '80s," *Chronicle of Higher Education* (Aug. 14, 1991).

50. Johnstone, "Higher Education," p. 33.

51. From 1980 to 1996, physical plant expenditures declined from 13.2 percent to 10.6 percent at private universities; 13.4 percent to 11 percent at public universities (RU database).

52. See, e.g. (for Michigan and Stanford), William F. Massy and Joel W. Meyerson, eds., *Strategy and Finance in Higher Education* (Princeton, N.J.: Peterson's Guides, 1992), pp. 67–78, 87–100.

53. Caroline M. Hoxby, "Tax Incentives for Higher Education," in James M. Poterba, ed., *Tax Policy and the Economy*, vol. 12 (Cambridge, Mass.: MIT Press/National Bureau of Economic Research, 1998), pp. 49–81, esp. p. 60.

54. These data are compiled by the Delaware Study of Instructional Costs and Productivity; see Michael F. Middaugh, "Measuring Higher Education Costs: Considerations and Cautions," in NCES, *Study of College Costs*, vol. 2, pp. 87–116.

55. NCES, *Digest of Education Statistics, 1999*, tables 228, 229.

56. For Category I (doctoral level) universities, see "Annual Report on the Economic Status of the Profession, 2001–2002," *Academe* (Mar.–Apr. 2002): p. 32, table 4.

57. Roger L. Geiger, "The Competition for High-Ability Students: Universities in a Key Marketplace," in Steven Brint, ed., *The Future of the City of Intellect: The Changing American University* (Stanford, Calif.: Stanford University Press, 2002), pp. 82–106.

58. Leslie Christovich, "Top 100 R&D Performing Institutions Continue Increased Facilities Construction," *Data Brief* (Washington, D.C.: National Science Foundation, Division of Science Resources Studies, June 22, 2000); Goldman, *Paying for University Research*, p. xiii. Start-up costs for science faculty are considerable. A Cornell study found nearly half of these costs coming from general funds; see Ronald G. Ehrenberg, "Financing Higher Education Institutions in the 21st Century" (Cornell Higher Education Research Institute, Mar. 25, 2003, draft).

59. Clotfelter, *Buying the Best*. A seminal analysis of the complementarity of teaching and research argued that a socially optimal investment in basic research at universities "may well have the effect of making the provision of undergraduate educational services more expensive, but this increase in cost is desirable from society's point of view"; see Nerlove, "On Tuition and the Costs of Higher Education," p. S204.

60. William G. Bowen, *The Economics of Major Private Universities* (New York: Carnegie Commission on Higher Education, 1968). This effect is also credited to Bowen's collaborator, William J. Baumol, but Bowen first invoked it to explain the persistence of price increases in higher education.

61. Essentially the same dynamic operates for administrative and professional workers. Those working in business or technical services may be closer to the commercial economy, but notions of internal equity apply here too. Over time, increases in faculty and administrative salaries are quite similar.

62. For example, the divergence in salaries among newly appointed assistant professors is greater than that among full professors; see Ehrenberg, *Tuition Rising*, p. 119.

63. David A. Hollinger, "Money and Academic Freedom a Half-Century after McCarthyism: Universities and the Force Fields of Capitalism," in *Unfettered Expression* (Ann Arbor: University of Michigan Press, 2000), pp. 161–84.

64. The average faculty salary was 23 percent below other highly educated occupations in 1985 and 32 percent below in 1997; see Linda A. Bell, "More Good News, Why the Blues? The Annual Report on the Economic Status of the Profession," *Academe* (Mar.–Apr. 2000): 12–21.

65. F. King Alexander, "National Trends in the Relative Fiscal Capacity of Public Universities to Compete in the Academic Labor Market" (University of Illinois, typescript, n.d.).

66. Ibid., pp. 15–18; Ehrenberg, *Tuition Rising*, p. 119.

67. Professors in doctoral universities earned 29 percent more than those in the next category. Although the comparison is not exact, this premium would seem to cover a good part of the 32 percent "relative deprivation" (see note 65 to this chapter); also see Bell, "More Good News," pp. 15–16.

68. The University of Southern California outpaced all others by announcing in 2002 that it would invest $100 million in hiring 100 "world-class" senior faculty members, all in the College of Letters, Arts, and Sciences—an unprecedented enlargement of its knowledge resources.

69. From 1980 to 1996, salaries of regular faculty declined as a proportion of university spending and as a proportion of instructional budgets (RU database). This trend probably reflects greater use of part-time instructors and more departmental administration.

70. Patricia J. Gumport, "Universities and Knowledge: Restructuring the City of Intellect"; and Burton R. Clark, "University Transformation: Primary Pathway to University Autonomy and Achievement," in Brint, *TheFuture of the City of Intellect*, pp. 47–81, 322–43.

71. Roger L. Geiger, "Doctoral Education: The Short-Term Crisis vs. the Long-Term Challenge," *Review of Higher Education* 20 (1997): 239–51.

72. Harvard in particular has been criticized for conducting a campaign for funds it does not need. The release of endowment figures for 2000 incited further protest that these universities retain too much; see Kit Lively and Scott Street, "The Rich Get Richer," *Chronicle of Higher Education* (Oct. 13, 2000). Given a 4 percent spending rule, the value of 2000 endowments would produce the following per-student expenditures: Princeton, $52,000; Yale, $40,000; and Harvard, $38,000.

73. See discussion in Chapter 3.

74. Andrew Brownstein, "Upping the Ante for Student Aid," *Chronicle of Higher Education* (Feb. 16, 2001): A47–A49. The removal of loans was expected to cost Princeton $16 million in FY2002.

75. Princeton University, "Wythes Committee Report," Apr. 2000 (www.princeton.edu/pr/reports/wythes/).

76. Princeton had the largest endowment per student among universities, the lowest faculty:student ratio (7:1), and lavish campus facilities. Faculty size had grown steadily as new fields were covered, and increased revenues from the endowment were "applied almost exclusively to increased investments in physical facilities"; ibid., p. 26.

77. Princeton estimated that it could enroll a freshman class twice the current size of 1,150 with no loss of talent. The Wythes Committee argued that additional students would strengthen the class intellectually. Presumably, that would mean admitting more intellectually superior students and thereby diluting the legacies and athletes. Princeton has also been concerned that it enrolls *too many* full-paying (i.e., rich) students! Ibid.

78. Henry Hansmann, "Why Do Universities Have Endowments?" *Journal of Legal Studies* 19 (Jan. 1990): 3–42.

79. James J. Duderstadt, *A University for the 21st Century* (Ann Arbor: University of Michigan Press, 2000), p. 312. Tuition revenue increased from $78 million in 1980

to $513 million in 1998, a real increase of 244 percent. All figures for 1998–99 are from University of Michigan, *Financial Report for the Year Ended June 30, 1999*.

80. Larger endowments are held by the University of California System and by the Texas "Public Universities Fund," which largely benefits the University of Texas and Texas A&M but is not controlled by those institutions. For perspective: in 2000 the University of Michigan had roughly $100,000 in endowment for each student, while Princeton, Yale, and Harvard had $1 million or more. Spending from endowment at Michigan appears to be far less than 5 percent of $100,000 per student.

81. Duderstadt, *University for the 21st Century*, p. 312. Similar notions were floated in Wisconsin during the mid-1990s.

82. Departments were urged to locate highly desirable minority and women candidates and then given the funds to hire them; ibid., pp. 201–11. In 1997, Michigan's aggressive affirmative action policies became the target of two long-running lawsuits that were resolved by the Supreme Court in 2003.

83. Massy, *Resource Allocation*, pp. 26–31.

84. Robert Birnbaum, *Management Fads in Higher Education* (San Francisco: Jossey-Bass, 2000); Gary Rhoades, "Who's Doing It Right? Strategic Activity in Public Research Universities," *Review of Education* 24 (2000): 41–66.

85. Rhoades offers evidence that such approaches fail to resolve the "*managerial dilemma* [of] how to establish clear, fair, and rational criteria for allocating monies to prioritized activities in a highly variable and politicized environment" ("Who's Doing It Right?" p. 53).

86. Chancellor David Ward of the University of Wisconsin, Madison, interview by author, UC Berkeley Center for Studies in Higher Education, Oct. 5, 2000.

87. Other terms for decentralized budgeting include "Revenue Responsibility Budgeting." With quantitative performance measures factored in, it becomes "Performance Responsibility Budgeting" or "Value Responsibility Budgeting." See Massy, *Resource Allocation*, pp. 163–90, 293–324. Revenue Responsibility Budgeting was adopted at the Universities of Pennsylvania and Southern California in the 1980s; ibid., pp. 163–84.

88. Indiana University, RCM Review Committee, "Responsibility Centered Management at Indiana University, Bloomington" (Oct. 1996); Indiana University, RCM Review Committee, "Responsibility Centered Management at Indiana University Bloomington, 1990–2000" (May 2000).

89. For examples of strategic behavior by units under RCM, see Massy, *Resource Allocation*, pp. 171–72; and note 93 in this chapter.

90. President Miles Brand also implemented a $25 million plan called "Strategic Directions." It employed the foundationlike approach of soliciting and reviewing proposals for a broad range of goals. However, the awards went heavily to strengthen research, and the process was unpopular with faculty; Indiana University, "The Strategic Directions of Indiana University, 1994–1999" (n.d.).

91. The University of Illinois at Urbana-Champaign also implemented RCM but attempted to reserve considerable fiscal discretion for the provost.

92. David L. Kirp, *Shakespeare, Einstein, and the Bottom Line: The Marketing of Higher Education* (Cambridge, Mass.: Harvard University Press, 2003), pp. 122–29. Kirp also describes RCM budgeting as a failure at the University of Southern California (pp. 116–22).

93. Ehrenberg, *Tuition Rising*, pp. 157–70. Ehrenberg concludes, "internal transfer pricing systems [which RCM requires] set up economic incentives that do not always square with educational objectives. . . . Hence inefficiencies invariably result" (p. 165). The same basic problems with RCM were noted in a study of private universities: Daniel Rodas, *Resource Allocation in Private Research Universities* (New York: Routledge Falmer, 2001).

94. Burton R. Clark, *Creating Entrepreneurial Universities: Organizational Pathways of Transformation* (London: IAU Press, 1998), pp. 5–8.

95. Treatment of "soft-money" faculty varies widely among universities; see Marcia Barinaga, "Soft Money's Hard Realities," *Science* (Sept. 22, 2000): 2024–28.

96. *Annual Report of Sponsored Programs, University of Colorado at Boulder, Fiscal Year 1998–1999;* "The Plan: University of Colorado at Boulder, Master Plan"; interview with Carol Lynch (Sept. 7, 2000).

97. Donald Kennedy relates the "sudden torrent of private money" for science facilities to "the explosion of industry interest in basic research and the increased private support for research infrastructure in the universities"; see "Reshaping Basic Research," *Science* (Oct. 20, 2000): 451. The fiscal obligations such projects impose on universities are discussed by Ehrenberg, *Tuition Rising*, pp. 104–9.

98. Beckman Institute for Advanced Science and Technology, *Annual Report, 1999* (Urbana-Champaign, Ill., 1999).

99. This appropriation was motivated by considerations of economic development and made directly to the campus—bypassing the Illinois Board of Higher Education and the University of Illinois system office.

100. The Madison Initiative was supposed to be implemented over two budget cycles. For 1999–2001, the state appropriated $29 million to be matched by $20 million in private funds; for 2001–03, $28 million was promised with the same $20 million match. Private funding was largely guaranteed by the University of Wisconsin Foundation and the Wisconsin Alumni Research Foundation. In addition, UW Madison has been engaged in a large building program for (mostly) research facilities, based on a fifty-fifty split of state and private funds. The previous poor relations between the state and university (which returned with a vengeance in 2002) are discussed in David J. Weerts, *State Government and Research Universities: A Framework for a Renewed Partnership* (New York: Routledge Falmer, 2002), pp. 49–60.

101. Robin Wilson, "Stanford U. Freezes Faculty and Staff Salaries," *Chronicle of Higher Education* (Mar. 21, 2003): A14.

Chapter 3

1. The College Board was established in 1901 by the leading private universities to supplement their individual entrance examinations with a test to evaluate applicants who had not specifically prepared for those exams. The College Board did not become an inclusive organization until after World War II; see Harold S. Wechsler, "Eastern Standard Time: High-school–College Collaboration and Admission to College, 1880–1930," in Michael Johanek, ed., *A Faithful Mirror: Reflections on the College Board and Education in America* (New York: College Entrance Examination Board, 2001), pp. 43–80.

2. Harold S. Wechsler, *The Qualified Student: A History of Selective Admissions in*

America (New York: John Wiley and Sons, 1977); Marcia Graham Synnott, *The Half-Opened Door: Discrimination in Admissions to Harvard, Yale, and Princeton, 1900–1970* (Westport, Conn.: Greenwood Press, 1979); Roger L. Geiger, *To Advance Knowledge: The Growth of American Research Universities, 1900–1940* (New York: Oxford University Press, 1986), pp. 130–38, 215–19; Nicholas Lemann, *The Big Test: The Secret History of the American Meritocracy* (New York: Farrar, Straus and Giroux, 1999), pp. 38–40. On Harvard, see Morton Keller and Phyllis Keller, *Making Harvard Modern: The Rise of America's University* (New York: Oxford University Press, 2001), pp. 32–38. Other Ivy League schools followed Conant's lead with token employment of scholarship tests at the end of the 1930s. Swarthmore had recruited talented students for its honors program in the 1920s.

3. Wilbur J. Bender, "A Report on the Admission and Scholarship Committee for the Academic Year 1959–60," *Report of the President of Harvard College, 1959–1960* (Harvard University, 1960), pp. 52–62; David Karen, "Who Gets into Harvard? Selection and Exclusion at an Elite College" (Ph.D. diss., Harvard University, 1985), pp. 118–24; Synnott, *Half-Opened Door*, pp. 205–7; Keller and Keller, *Making Harvard Modern*, pp. 293–96; Roger L. Geiger, "Market History: Selective Admissions and American Higher Education since 1950," *History of Higher Education Annual* 20 (2000): 93–108.

4. The following discussion draws on Carolyn M. Hoxby, "The Changing Market Structure of U.S. Higher Education" (Harvard University, 1997, mimeo); and Elizabeth A. Duffy and Idana Goldberg, *College Admissions and Financial Aid, 1955–1994* (Princeton, N.J.: Princeton University Press, 1998).

5. The College Scholarship Service was established in 1954 by the elite institutions to provide uniform calculation of student financial need. Members pledged to award only need-based aid, not academic scholarships. Hoxby notes that they thus committed themselves to compete on the basis of quality (student preference for academic programs) and not on the basis of price; see "Changing Market Structure."

6. See Synnott, *Half-Opened Door*; Duffy and Goldberg, *College Admissions*, pp. 137–65; Karen, "Who Gets into Harvard," pp. 144–52.

7. Nicholas Thompson, "Playing with Numbers," *Washington Monthly* (Sept. 2000).

8. An analysis of the rankings found "severe and pervasive multicollinearity" (most variables measured the same things), and that average SAT scores were most significant; Thomas J. Webster, "A Principal Component Analysis of the *U.S. News & World Report* Tier Rankings of Colleges and Universities," *Economics of Education Review* 20 (2001): 235–44, quotation on p. 243.

9. For rankings and methodology see the *U.S. News* website (www.usnews.com/usnews/edu/college/rankings/).

10. James Monks and Ronald G. Ehrenberg, "The Impact of *U.S. News and World Report* College Rankings on Admissions Outcomes and Pricing Policies at Selective Private Institutions," Working Paper 7227, National Bureau of Economic Research, Cambridge, Mass., July 1999; also reported in *Change* (Nov./Dec. 1999): 43–51.

11. Caroline M. Hoxby, "How the Changing Market Structure of U.S. Higher Education Explains College Tuition," Working Paper 6323, National Bureau of Eco-

nomic Research, Cambridge, Mass., Dec. 1997. See also Hoxby, "Changing Market Structure."

12. These processes are also explained in Gordon Winston, "Subsidies, Hierarchy, and Peers: The Awkward Economics of Higher Education," *Journal of Economic Perspectives* 13 (Winter 1999): 13–36.

13. This is both an arcane economic finding (see notes 10 and 11 in this chapter) and conventional wisdom. *U.S. News* tells its readers, "the higher the caliber of the student body, the richer the educational experience in the classroom and on campus"; *U.S. News and World Report*, Oct. 16, 1989, p. 58.

14. Winston, "Subsidies, Hierarchies, and Peers," p. 28. Positional markets are explicated in Robert H. Frank and Philip J. Cook, *The Winner-Take-All Society* (New York: Free Press, 1995).

15. Gordon C. Winston has made wealth the criterion for analyzing status in American higher education in a series of papers in the Williams Project on the Economics of Higher Education; and Robert Zemsky has employed institutional wealth to define market segments in American higher education: Robert Zemsky, Susan Shaman, and Daniel B. Shapiro, "Higher Education as Competitive Enterprise: When Markets Matter," *New Directions for Institutional Research* 111 (Fall 2001).

16. Winston writes of this situation, "hierarchy based on donative resources becomes highly skewed"; however, any attempt to opt out of the arms race would be "fiduciary irresponsibility": "in a positional market, there's never too much of a good thing . . . and in the hierarchy, wealth is fundamentally a good thing" (ibid., pp. 27, 31).

17. National Center for Education Statistics, *Digest of Education Statistics, 1999* (Washington, D.C.: NCES).

18. Ibid. This list was compared with that in *Barron's Profiles of American Colleges, 1999 Edition*. There sixty-five institutions are classified as "Most Competitive" and another ninety as "Highly Competitive." These institutions annually enroll roughly 180,000 freshmen: 50,000 in ninety-six nondoctoral private colleges; 57,000 in thirty-six private doctoral universities; and 72,000 in twenty-three public doctoral universities. The *Barron's* scheme may be overly generous to liberal arts colleges.

19. In a large study of school choices by high-aptitude students that corresponded closely with group 3, two-thirds attended private colleges or universities; see Christopher Avery and Caroline M. Hoxby, "Do and Should Financial Aid Packages Affect Students' College Choices?" Working Paper 9482, National Bureau of Economic Research, Cambridge, Mass., Feb. 2003.

20. This population is well understood by admissions officers, but little studied. See Patricia M. McDonough et al., "College Rankings: Who Uses Them and with What Impact" (paper presented at the meeting of the American Educational Research Association, Mar. 1997).

21. Roger L. Geiger, "High Tuition—High Aid: A Road Paved with Good Intentions" (paper presented at the meeting of the Association for the Study of Higher Education, Sacramento, Calif., Nov. 2002).

22. The comparison is inexact. In 1981, 24.9 percent of wealthy students enrolled in selective institutions comprising 7.9 percent of enrollments; in 1998, 34.7 percent

of these students matriculated in selective institutions representing 9.8 percent of higher education. Thus the selective sector, as defined in this study, expanded; see Michael McPherson and Owen Morton Schapiro, "Reinforcing Stratification in American Higher Education: Some Disturbing Trends," Technical Report 3–02, Stanford University, National Center for Postsecondary Improvement, table 8.

23. Besides SAT or ACT scores, selective schools place considerable weight on high school academic records: grade-point average, class standing, and the rigor of courses taken, especially Advanced Placement courses. In addition, highly selective institutions place great emphasis on extra-academic factors in choosing among their largely high-ability applicants. See Jean H. Fetter, *Questions and Admissions: Reflections on 100,000 Admissions Decisions at Stanford* (Stanford, Calif.: Stanford University Press, 1995); Geiger, "Market History."

24. Data were compiled from *Barron's Profile of American Colleges* (1999) and *Peterson's Guide to Four-Year Colleges, 1999*. Standardized test scores are from 1997–98. Change in median SAT scores calculated by the author using data from the Lombardi Program on Measuring University Performance, University of Florida (www.TheCenter.edu).

25. Roger L. Geiger, "The Competition for High-Ability Students: Universities in a Key Marketplace," in Steven Brint, ed., *The Future of the City of Intellect: The Changing American University* (Stanford, Calif.: Stanford University Press, 2002), pp. 82–106, esp. p. 91.

26. George Goethals, Gordon Winston, and David Zimmerman, "Students Educating Students: The Emerging Role of Peer Effects in Higher Education," Discussion Paper 50, Williams Project on the Economics of Higher Education, Williams College, Mar. 1999; Gordon C. Winston and David J. Zimmerman, "Peer Effects in Higher Education," Discussion Paper 64, Williams Project on the Economics of Higher Education, Williams College, Jan. 2003. Ernest T. Pascarella and Patrick T. Terenzini found no convincing evidence that selective institutions, ipso facto, produced greater student learning, but they also offer reasons why such effects might be difficult to document or measure; see *How College Affects Students* (San Francisco: Jossey-Bass, 1991), pp. 73–83, 133–36.

27. Two studies of academic rigor based on analyses of course examinations came to different conclusions. The first found evidence of greater rigor at selective liberal arts colleges, but the second failed to find conclusive evidence of greater rigor at selective research universities; see John M. Braxton and R. C. Nordvall, "Selective Liberal Arts Colleges: Higher Quality as Well as Higher Prestige?" *Journal of Higher Education* 56 (1985): 538–54; John M. Braxton, "Selectivity and Rigor in Research Universities," *Journal of Higher Education* 64 (1993): 656–75.

28. David Zimmerman, "Peer Effects in Academic Outcomes: Evidence from a Natural Experiment," Discussion Paper 52, Williams Project on the Economics of Higher Education, Williams College, 1999; Bruce Sacerdote, "Peer Effects with Random Assignment: Results from Dartmouth Roommates," *Quarterly Journal of Economics* (2001).

29. Striking evidence of grade inflation is provided at www.gradeinflation.com. It is evident at nonselective institutions, starting from a much lower base. Most notable, grade inflation took off in the late 1980s after more than a decade of relative

stability. See also George D. Kuh and Shouping Hu, "Unraveling the Complexity of the Increase in College Grades from the Mid–1980s to the Mid–1990s," *Educational Evaluation and Policy Analysis* 21 (1999): 297–320; Henry Rosovsky and Matthew Hartley, *Evaluation and the Academy: Are We Doing the Right Thing?* (Cambridge, Mass.: American Academy of Arts and Sciences, 2002).

30. Pascarella and Terenzini, *How College Affects Students*, p. 82.

31. Institutional data from UC Berkeley reveal that graduates with the highest SAT scores majored in bioengineering, electrical engineering/computer science, physics, mechanical engineering, molecular and cellular biology, and mathematics. All averaged well over 700 on the math portion of the SAT. My thanks to Martin Trow for this information.

32. Educational costs per student at smaller regional state universities sometimes approximate those at flagship institutions, but the former lack this kind of resource base associated with extensive research.

33. "A high aptitude student surrounded by significantly worse peers may be able to use much more than his share of a college's resources. While some attributes of a college must be shared relatively equally by all students (faculty quality), others (such as faculty time) can be disproportionately allocated to certain students"; see Avery and Hoxby, "Financial Aid Packages." Internal differentiation and individual initiative would accentuate such "disproportionate allocation."

34. George Bradshaw, Suzanne Espinosa, and Charles Hausman, "The College Decision-Making of High Achieving Students" (paper presented at the annual meeting of the Association for the Study of Higher Education, Sacramento, Calif., Nov. 2000).

35. Avery and Hoxby, in "Financial Aid Packages," suggest that such students may be sacrificing human capital—the present value of lifetime earnings. However, there are many uncertainties in such calculations. Ann L. Mullin found that future earnings resulted from a complex interplay between field of study and selectivity of college attended; see "The Effects of Institutional Stratification on College Graduates' Career Trajectories" (paper presented at the meeting of the Association for the Study of Higher Education, Sacramento, Calif., Nov. 2002).

36. A quantitative analysis by Stephen D. Grunig found that "the amount of research performed by an institution contributes substantially to the reputation of the institution's undergraduate educational program"; see "Research, Reputation, and Resources: The Effect of Research Activity on Perceptions of Undergraduate Education and Institutional Resource Acquisition," *Journal of Higher Education* 68 (1997): 17–52, quotation on p. 42.

37. Numbers of students with SAT scores of 700+ were calculated for all Research I & II universities, but only the thirty-five with the highest totals are shown in Tables 1 and 2.

38. Hoxby writes, "market integration has a particularly intense competitive effect on initially selective public colleges, forcing them to compete against private colleges and other public colleges for their increasingly mobile, high ability, prospective students" ("How the Changing Market Structure Explains College Tuition," p. 40). Table 2 suggests that the strongest public universities are holding, some even increasing, their share in this market.

39. A full exposition of the critique was published in 1986 by Paul Von Blum, a disaffected academic in the University of California system: *Stillborn Education: A Critique of the American Research University* (Lanham, Md.: University Press of America, 1986). Lacking a condemnation of the university culture, it was largely ignored.

40. For one attempt to discern unity in these diverse writings, see Edward Jayne, "Academic Jeremiad: The Neoconservative View of American Higher Education," *Change* (May/June 1991): 30–41. Dinesh D'Souza (*Illiberal Education*) would relish the title of Neocon, but Page Smith, author of *Killing the Spirit* as well as *A People's History of the United States*, is decidedly of the Left.

41. The National Institute of Education published *Involvement in Learning* (1984); the American Association of Colleges, *Integrity in the College Curriculum* (1985); and the Southern Regional Education Board, *Access to Quality Undergraduate Education* (1985). See Joan S. Stark and Lisa R. Lattuca, *Shaping the College Curriculum: Academic Plans in Action* (Boston: Allyn and Bacon, 1997), pp. 80–104. The critique defined here seeks to isolate one strand of a wave of criticism that emphasized, among other things, the place of Western learning in the curriculum during the 1980s and political correctness on campus during the early 1990s.

42. Study Group on the Conditions of Excellence in American Higher Education, *Involvement in Learning: Realizing the Potential of American Higher Education* (Washington, D.C.: National Institute of Education, 1984). Full disclosure: the author wrote a background paper for the Study Group: Roger L. Geiger, "American Research Universities: Their Role in Undergraduate Education." This paper seems to have had no discernible influence on the final report.

43. It would be futile to seek the origins of so vague a concept, but *Change* apparently began a persistent advocacy with the issue of November/December 1985. It also convened its first annual assessment conference that year. The traditional view had long held that students were accountable individually for their learning and should be assessed in their classes.

44. For the different levels of evaluation or assessment, see Stark and Lattuca, *Shaping the College Curriculum*, pp. 282–309.

45. *Involvement in Learning* acknowledged the changing demographics. The only evidence of a decline in learning was a decrease in most graduate scores on the Graduate Record Exam (GRE). It interpreted this and other trends as "warning signals" (pp. 8–9). See also Clifford Adelman, *The New College Course Map and Transcript Files: Changes in Course-Taking and Achievement, 1972–1993* (Washington, D.C.: Department of Education, 1995).

46. The plausible case was built with implausible evidence. For example, results of the National Adult Literacy Survey were twisted by several critics to allege the incompetence of college graduates; see Wingspread Group on Higher Education, *An American Imperative: Higher Expectations for Higher Education* (Racine, Wisc.: Johnson Foundation, 1993), pp. 5–6. In fact, more than 40 percent of the sample surveyed were over 40 years of age, and no inferences could be drawn for current institutions of higher education: National Center for Education Statistics, *Adult Literacy in America* (Washington, D.C.: Office of Educational Research and Improvement, 1993).

47. Ernest L. Boyer, *College: The Undergraduate Experience in America* (New York: Harper and Row, 1987), pp. 126–27; Ernest L. Boyer, *Scholarship Reconsidered: Priorities for the Professoriate* (Princeton, N.J.:Carnegie Foundation for the Advancement of Teaching, 1991); Marvin Lazerson, Ursula Wagener, and Nichole Shumanis, "What Makes a Revolution? Teaching and Learning in Higher Education, 1980–2000," *Change* (May/June 2000): 12–19.

48. Russell Edgerton, "The Re-Examination of Faculty Priorities," *Change* (July/ Aug. 1993): 12–25. Symbolism: endorsements from Ernest Boyer and William Bennett grace the cover of Martin Anderson's rehash of the critique: *Impostors in the Temple: A Blueprint for Improving Higher Education in America* (Stanford, Calif.: Hoover Institution Press, 1996 [1994]).

49. Lynne V. Cheney, *Tyrannical Machines: A Report on Educational Practices Gone Wrong and Our Best Hopes for Setting Them Right* (Washington, D.C.: National Endowment for the Humanities, 1990), p. 27.

50. Carnegie Foundation for the Advancement of Teaching, *The Condition of the Professoriate* (Princeton, N.J.: Carnegie Foundation for the Advancement of Teaching, 1989); Gordon C. Winston, "The Decline in Undergraduate Teaching: Moral Failure or Market Pressure?" *Change* (Sept./Oct. 1994): 8–15; William F. Massy and Robert Zemsky, "Faculty Discretionary Time: Departments and the Academic Ratchet," Discussion Paper 4, Stanford Institute of Higher Education Research, Stanford University, May 1992.

51. According to a model suggested by Marc Nerlove and discussed in Chapter 6, introducing research into a purely teaching environment should *enhance* teaching; see "On Tuition and the Costs of Higher Education: Prolegomena to a Conceptual Framework," *Journal of Political Economy* 80 (May–June, 1972): S178–S218.

52. Martin J. Finkelstein, Robert K. Seal, and Jack H. Schuster, *The New Academic Generation: A Profession in Transformation* (Baltimore: Johns Hopkins University Press, 1998), pp. 1–5, 65–84. For changes in institutional research volume, see Roger L. Geiger and Irwin Feller, "The Dispersion of Academic Research in the 1980s," *Journal of Higher Education* 66 (1995): 336–60.

53. Peter Sacks, *Generation X Goes to College* (Chicago: Open Court, 1996).

54. David Riesman, *On Higher Education* (San Francisco: Jossey-Bass, 1980), quotation on p. xi; see also Sacks, *Generation X*.

55. National Association of Scholars, *The Dissolution of General Education, 1914–1993* (Princeton, N.J.: National Association of Scholars, 1996).

56. Stuart Roystaczer, *Gone for Good: Tales of University Life after the Golden Age* (New York: Oxford University Press, 1999), pp. 13–26. Or consider the views of Harvey Mansfield, who deplores grade inflation but believes it would be unfair to his students not to inflate his own grading: "Grade Inflation: It's Time to Face the Facts," *Chronicle of Higher Education* (Apr. 6, 2001): B24.

57. Peter Ewell, "Assessment: What's It All About," *Change* (Nov./Dec. 1985): 32–36, quotation on p. 33; see also Pat Hutchings and Ted Marchese, "Watching Assessment—Questions, Stories, Prospects," *Change* (July/Aug. 1990): 12–38; Lazerson, Wagener, and Shumanis, "What Makes a Revolution?" pp. 14–15.

58. John Robert Greene, *Syracuse University: The Eggers Years*, vol. 5 (Syracuse, N.Y.: Syracuse University Press, 1998).

59. Information drawn from Edward B. Fiske, *The New York Times Selective Guide to Colleges, 1982–83* (New York: Times Books, 1982); *Barron's Profiles of American Colleges* (Woodbury, N.Y.: Barron's, 1985); *The Insider's Guide to the Colleges*, by the staff of the *Yale Daily News* (New York: St. Martin's, 1985).

60. The research share of SU declined from 0.27 percent in 1980 to 0.22 percent in 1990 and 0.13 percent in 2000 (see Appendix B). Its rank for research expenditures fell from 106 to 147.

61. Greene, *Syracuse*, pp. 199–209.

62. The quotations and information in this discussion are from Syracuse University, "Self Study," 1996 (www.syr.edu/selfstudy/).

63. See Report of Task Force to Develop Guiding Principles for the Long-Range Budget Plan (www.syr.edu/acadaff/budgetguide.html/).

64. Gershon Vincow, "Annual Report to the Faculty," *Syracuse Record* (Jan. 31, 1994) (www.syr.edu/acadaff/1994faculty.html). Also summarized in Gershon Vincow, "The Student-Centered Research University," *Innovative Higher Education* 21 (Spring 1997): 165–78.

65. Ibid., p. 168. Vincow invoked Boyer's *Scholarship Reconsidered* for examples of more student-friendly "research" in his "Report to the Faculty."

66. Ibid. These efforts were part of the "Sears Project" at SU, which preceded and laid the groundwork for the student-centered concept. Surveys of faculty at research universities consistently showed the opposite, that is, a preference for spending more time on research. Such results are strongly influenced by the wording of questions and the group surveyed.

67. Ibid. SU evaluates all faculty annually according to the formula 40 percent for research, 40 percent for teaching and advising, and 20 percent for service. How to evaluate advising remained something of a mystery, and the 20 percent for service seemed an unreasonably high weighting.

68. SU Office of Budget and Planning, "Fiscal Restructuring at SU in the 1990's" (http://sumweb.syr.edu/ir/bud_retr.html); Syracuse University, "A Report to the Commission on Higher Education Middle States Association of Colleges and Schools," Jan. 15, 1998; and Syracuse University, "Visiting Team Report," Mar. 22–25, 1998 (www.syracuse.edu/selfstudy/). SU's characterization of itself changed in these years from *a* leading to *the* leading student-centered research university.

69. Edward B. Fiske, *Fiske Selective Guide to Colleges* (New York: New York Times Books, 2000), pp. 626–28.

70. In the AAUP's annual rating of faculty salaries given in the March issue of *Academe*, SU slipped from 2 (on a five-point scale) in 1980 to 4 in 1998. It recovered to 3 in 2003.

71. Syracuse University, "Visiting Team Report."

72. Deborah Freund, "The 2020 Vision of Syracuse University," Mar. 1, 2000; and Deborah Freund, "A 2020 Vision for Syracuse University: In Search of a New Standard of Excellence" (www.syr.edu/acadaff/vision.html).

73. Roger L. Geiger, *Research and Relevant Knowledge, American Research Universities since World War II* (New York: Oxford University Press, 1993), pp. 273–83.

74. Quoted in University of Arizona, "NCA Accreditation Self-Study Report," Nov. 16, 1999, chapter 2 (www.library.arizona.edu/nca/).

75. In the 1980s, undergraduate enrollments increased by 20 percent, full-time graduate students by 30 percent, and regular faculty by 7 percent.

76. Ibid., chapter 5. On Manuel Pacheco, see *Chronicle of Higher Education* (July 3, 1991); *St. Louis Post-Dispatch*, Mar. 9, 1997.

77. However, UA had an average freshman retention rate (78 percent) for selective, doctoral, public universities, despite being near the lower end of that range; see ACT Press Release: "National College Dropout and Graduation Rates, 1998" (www.act.org/news/04–01b99).

78. University of Arizona, "Proposed Measurable Goals for Linking Faculty Teaching Effort to the Improvement of the Quality of Undergraduate Education" (n.d., photocopy); University of Arizona, "NCA Accreditation Self-Study."

79. University of Arizona, "NCA Accreditation Self-Study," chapter 5.

80. Given the academic qualifications of its students, freshman retention at UA was equal to national norms, and its goals unrealistically high.

81. University of Arizona, "NCA Accreditation Self-Study," chapter 10.

82. According to *Barron's Profiles*, between 1984 and 1997, UA increased its freshman class by 1,200 (3,400 to 4,600); average SAT scores (recentered) remained the same; the ACT score increased from 22 to 23. And the *Barron's* rating increased from "competitive" to "very competitive," apparently on the basis of having received more applications.

83. University of Arizona, "NCA Accreditation Self-Study."

84. Peter Likens, "Testimony for Appropriations Committee," Feb. 12, 2002; University of Arizona, "Main Campus Strategic Plan: Transformation into the 21st Century—2000 Update" (www.arizona.edu/~ipass/maincampussstratplan).

85. Ibid. UA acquired bonding authority for capital projects in 1989. Debt service on these capital costs is paid from general revenues.

86. Peter Likens, "State of the University Address, November 1999," Nov. 5, 1999.

87. Michael S. McPherson and Morton Owen Schapiro, "The End of the Student Aid Era? Higher Education Finance in the United States," in Johanek, ed., *A Faithful Mirror*, pp. 335–76.

88. Michael S. McPherson and Morton Owen Schapiro, *The Student-Aid Game* (Princeton, N.J.: Princeton University Press, 1998).

89. Ben Gose, "Princeton Plans Major Increase in Aid for Middle- and Low-Income Students," *Chronicle of Higher Education* (Jan. 30, 1998): A35–A36; see also Chapter 2.

90. The economic issues are most fully explored by Caroline M. Hoxby, "Benevolent Colluders? The Effects of Antitrust Action on College Financial Aid and Tuition" (Department of Economics, Harvard University, n.d., photocopy). She found "evidence that [the] antitrust suit did affect financial aid in Overlap colleges, resulting in aid that was less progressive with respect to parents' income and slightly more sensitive to merit." She also observed that these changes "accelerated dramatically" after her data ended. McPherson and Schapiro observe: "the competitive maneuverings of Harvard, Yale, and others are exactly what an economist would predict when cooperative arrangements are suspended. Unfortunately, it is far from clear that . . . this is an arena where the pursuit of individual self-interest serves the collective good": "End of the Student Aid Era?" pp. 359–60.

91. An additional factor in the increasing competition over admissions is early admission practices, which in some cases allows lower-ranked institutions to steal students who might have been admitted to higher-ranked ones. Growing controversy over this practice reflects a disintegrating consensus; see James Fallows, "The Early-Decision Racket," *Atlantic Monthly* (Sept. 2001): 37–52; Eric Hoover, "Admissions of Uncertainty," *Chronicle of Higher Education* (June 21, 2002): A35.

92. David Karen, "'Achievement' and 'Ascription' in Admission to an Elite College: A Political-Organizational Analysis," *Sociological Forum* 6 (1991): 349–80.

93. James L. Shulman and William G. Bowen, *The Game of Life: College Sports and Educational Values* (Princeton, N.J.: Princeton University Press, 2001). Selective colleges have cut athletic programs, possibly in response to this concern.

94. Ronald G. Ehrenberg, *Tuition Rising: Why College Costs So Much* (Cambridge, Mass.: Harvard University Press, 2000), pp. 252, 255.

95. This trend has attracted notice from the national media; see Jonathan B. Weinbach, "Luxury Learning," *Wall Street Journal*, Nov. 10, 2000, pp. W1, W4.

96. Ehrenberg, *Tuition Rising*, 249; Time/Princeton Review, *The Best College for You, 1999*, p. 9. Ironically, Ehrenberg notes that "dining plays a very minor role in [student] decisions whether to enroll at the university"; however, the goal of Cornell Dining (and housing) "is to maximize student satisfaction" (*Tuition Rising*, p. 251).

97. Ehrenberg, *Tuition Rising*, pp. 256–61. He concludes, "although housing and dining are [auxiliary] enterprise units at Cornell, their behavior directly and indirectly affects the rest of the university" (p. 261).

98. Ibid., pp. 233–48; Shulman and Bowen, *Game of Life*, pp. 33, 211, and passim.

99. At Yale College, and undoubtedly elsewhere, the most popular elective courses obtained the largest enrollments. Hence the largest classes on balance were considered by students to be the best. However, today lecturing is out of favor and "active learning" is in, despite the different uses and strengths of these two approaches.

100. See www.northwestern.edu/provost/faculty/order/order4.

101. Winston, "Subsidies, Hierarchy, and Peers."

102. Frank and Cook, *The Winner-Take-All Society*, pp. 164–66; Ehrenberg, *Tuition Rising*.

103. For example, the Association of American Universities maintains a data exchange for its members; the National Association of College and University Business Officers gathers financial information in many areas; and most university conferences, like the Big Ten (for this purpose, the Consortium for Institutional Cooperation), maintain extensive data exchanges.

104. What follows is a collective portrait, drawn from interviews, publications, and websites from the public universities in this study. Hence the measures described may be inapplicable to some universities, and implementation may vary widely across institutions.

105. The seminal text on this subject is Lee M. Upcraft, John N. Gardner, and Associates, *The Freshman Year Experience: Helping Students Survive and Succeed in College* (San Francisco: Jossey-Bass, 1989).

106. Like many enhancements, the UCLA general education cluster courses

serve a minority of freshmen, disproportionately high achievers. A future goal is to reach half of the incoming freshmen (http://www.college.ucla.edu.ge/).

107. In March 2001 the University of Kentucky hosted 2,500 undergraduate students and their faculty mentors, most from smaller, regional public institutions, for a conference on undergraduate research. In November 2002 the Reinvention Center at SUNY Stony Brook hosted a conference on undergraduate research aimed chiefly at research universities.

108. In response to the volume of excellent applicants, as well as the controversy surrounding admissions, first UC Berkeley and then other UC campuses converted to a labor-intensive private university model, where each application is read multiple times and nonacademic criteria are carefully weighed.

109. Roger L. Williams, "Southern Research Universities and Their Ambitions for Pre-eminence" (University of Arkansas, 2000).

110. This distinction is my own, but information on honors programs may be gleaned from *Peterson's Honors Programs*, 2nd ed. (Princeton, N.J.: Peterson's, 1999), which is subtitled *The Official Guide of the National Collegiate Honors Council*. Most university web pages contain more complete information.

111. Williams, "Southern Research Universities," p. 2.

Chapter 4

1. Joseph Ben-David, *The Scientist's Role in Society: A Comparative Study* (Chicago: University of Chicago Press, 1971), pp. 139–68; Burton R. Clark, *Places of Inquiry: Research and Advanced Education in Modern Universities* (Los Angeles: University of California Press, 1995), pp. 116–58. Historical material illustrating both these processes is provided in Roger L. Geiger, *Research and Relevant Knowledge: American Research Universities since World War II* (New York: Oxford University Press, 1993).

2. On organizational fields, see Paul J. DiMaggio and Walter W. Powell. "The Iron Cage Revisited: Institutional Isomorphism and Collective Rationality in Organizational Fields," in DiMaggio and Powell, eds., *The New Institutionalism in Organizational Analysis* (Chicago: University of Chicago Press, 1991), pp. 63–82.

3. "The objective of basic research is to gain more comprehensive knowledge or understanding . . . without specific applications in mind"; "applied research is aimed at gaining the knowledge or understanding to meet a specific need"; and "development is the systematic use of the knowledge or understanding gained from research directed toward the production of useful materials, devices," etc.; National Science Foundation, *Science and Engineering Indicators, 1998* (Washington, D.C.: NSF, 1998), p. 4.9. In practice, such distinctions are not always obvious, so self-reporting is subjective and incomplete, and estimation is required. In the aggregate, however, these data are reasonably consistent. Thus year-to-year fluctuations can be capricious, but large trends are highly credible.

4. For background, see Roger L. Geiger, "Historical Patterns of Change in Academic Research," in Albert H. Teich et al., eds., *Science and Technology Policy Yearbook, 1994* (Washington, D.C.: American Association for the Advancement of Science (AAAS), 1994), pp. 403–18; Richard R. Nelson, "Historical Perspectives and Distinctions between Basic and Applied Research," in Albert H. Teich et al., eds., *Science*

and Technology Yearbook, 1996 (Washington, D.C.: AAAS, 1996), pp. 137–42; and Roger L. Geiger, "What Happened after Sputnik? The Shaping of the University Research System in the United States," *Minerva* 35 (1997): 349–67.

5. Much of the growth in industrial research for 2000 was reported without classification, and thus final totals had to be estimated. This created a larger element of uncertainty than usual. It seems quite possible that the extraordinary conditions of these years produced a "bubble" in research at young high-tech companies, although nothing like the bubble in their stock valuations. The major trend of increasing expenditures for basic research nevertheless appears intact. See *Data Brief* (Washington, D.C.: National Science Foundation, Division of Science Resources Studies, Nov. 29, 2000).

6. Geiger, *Research and Relevant Knowledge*, pp. 14–19. Ironically, most of Bush's career as an engineer and science administrator was associated with directing science toward practical ends.

7. Geiger, "Science, Universities, and National Defense," *Osiris* 7 (1992): 26–48; NSF, *Science and Engineering Indicators, 2000*, p. 2.32.

8. Frank Press, "Science and Technology for the Post–Vannevar Bush Era," address to the AAAS, Apr. 16, 1992.

9. Michael Gibbons et al., *The New Production of Knowledge: The Dynamics of Science and Research in Contemporary Societies* (London: Sage, 1994), pp. 2–16, quotation on p. 159.

10. In the early 1960s, historian of science Derek de Solla Price noted that since its inception in the seventeenth century scientific activity roughly doubled every fifteen years; see *Little Science, Big Science, and Beyond* (New York: Columbia University Press, 1963), pp. 1–29. This pattern not only continued from the 1960s, but as Table 4 shows, it held from 1980 to 1995, or from 1985 to 2000; see Geiger, "Historical Patterns of Change."

11. Michael S. McPherson and Gordon C. Winston, "The Economics of Academic Tenure: A Relational Perspective," in D. W. Breneman and T. I. K. Youn, eds., *Academic Labor Markets and Careers* (Philadelphia: Falmer Press, 1988), pp. 174–99.

12. Roger L. Geiger, "Organized Research Units in American Universities: Emergence, Evolution, Significance," *Journal of Higher Education* 61 (1990): 1–19.

13. Geiger, *Research and Relevant Knowledge*, pp. 47–61.

14. See Stuart W. Leslie, *The Cold War and American Science* (New York: Columbia University Press, 1993); Rebecca S. Lowen, *Creating the Cold War University: The Transformation of Stanford* (Berkeley: University of California Press, 1997); Geiger, "Science, Universities, and National Defense"; and Geiger, *Research and Relevant Knowledge*.

15. There are currently eighteen Federally Funded Research and Development Centers [FFRDCs] operated by universities, mostly in nuclear physics and astronomy. Another twenty-four are run by industry or nonprofit agencies. Funds for FFRDCs are not included in university budgets or reported as research expenditures. The Applied Physics Laboratory (APL) has confused this distinction by ceasing to be an FFRDC and reporting through Johns Hopkins. Academic research data reported here exclude APL.

16. Geiger, "Organized Research Units": The term "organized research unit" was first employed after World War II at the University of California and abbreviated as ORU. This has become a generic name for this phenomenon, although each university tends to have its own designation.

17. For the transformation of medical schools, see Kenneth M. Ludmerer, *Time to Heal: American Medical Education from the Turn of the Century to the Era of Managed Care* (New York: Oxford University Press, 1999), esp. pp. 139–61; for the early expansion of NIH, see Geiger, *Research and Relevant Knowledge*, pp. 179–85.

18. Ludmerer, *Time to Heal*, pp. xxii, 26–32.

19. For 1979–80, six medical universities were among the top 100 for R&D expenditures; for 1989–90, eight made the list; see Roger L. Geiger and Irwin Feller, "The Dispersion of Academic Research in the 1980s," *Journal of Higher Education* 65 (1995): 336–60. In 1999–2000, eleven medical universities were in the top 100.

20. NIH funding for academic research increased more rapidly than federal funding, but at times not fast enough for the burgeoning medical research community. From the late 1970s to the late 1990s it grew from 47 percent to 57 percent of federal support for academic research; see NSF, *Science and Engineering Indicators, 1998*, table 5.8.

21. Ludmerer, *Learning to Heal*, pp. 336. For elucidation of this development, see pp. 224, 283, 327–36.

22. Ibid., p. 355. This complex evolution is analyzed on pp. 349–99.

23. Alan I. Rapaport, "How Has the Field Mix of Academic R&D Changed?" *Issue Brief* (Washington, D.C.: National Science Foundation, Division of Science Resources Studies, Dec. 2, 1998); Ludmerer, *Time to Heal*, pp. 288–90.

24. Hugh Davis Graham and Nancy Diamond, *American Research Universities: Elites and Challengers in the Postwar Era* (Baltimore: Johns Hopkins University Press, 1997), pp. 74–83.

25. Robert M. Rosenzweig with Barbara Turlington, *The Research Universities and Their Patrons* (Berkeley: University of California Press, 1982), p. 1.

26. NSF, *Science and Engineering Indicators, 2000*, appendix table 6–19.

27. National Center for Education Statistics, *Digest of Education Statistics, 2000* (Washington, D.C.: NCES), table 234. The teaching and research roles are coextensive to a large degree; see Carol L. Colbeck, "Merging in a Seamless Blend: How Faculty Integrate Teaching and Research," *Journal of Higher Education* 69 (1998): 647–71.

28. The expansion of research in clinical medicine, discussed above, almost provided a counterexample. For a time, the economics favored expansion; and people in the field predicted a concentration of medical research in the largest health centers. Lately, this argument has been applied to biotechnology.

29. Lyle V. Jones, Gardner Lindzey, and Porter E. Coggeshall, eds., *An Assessment of Research-Doctorate Programs in the United States*, 5 vols. (Washington, D.C.: National Academy Press, 1982); and Marvin L. Goldberger, Brendan A. Maher, and Pamela Ebert Flatau, eds., *Research-Doctorate Programs in the United States: Continuity and Change* (Washington, D.C.: National Academy Press, 1995).

30. David S. Webster and Tad Skinner, "Rating Ph.D. Programs: What the NRC Report Says . . . and Doesn't Say," *Change* (May/June, 1996): 23–44; Nancy Dia-

mond and Hugh Davis Graham, "How Should We Rate Research Universities?" *Change* (July/Aug. 2000).

31. Diamond and Graham, "How Should We Rate Research Universities?"; Goldberger, Maher, and Flatau, *Research-Doctorate Programs*, p. 23.

32. Goldberger, Maher, and Flatau, *Research-Doctorate Programs*, appendix R.

33. Ibid., appendices J–N. The ceiling effect was exaggerated for universitywide average scores by the fact that more departments were rated for 1995 than for 1983: that is, the newly rated departments were likely to bring down the very high averages of the top universities.

34. Geiger and Feller, "Dispersion of Academic Research."

35. Goldberger, Maher, and Flatau, *Research-Doctorate Programs*, appendix R; Committee on Science, Engineering, and Public Policy, *Reshaping the Graduate Education of Scientists and Engineers* (Washington, D.C.: National Academy Press, 1995), pp. 65–68, 139–72.

36. For a fuller exposition, see Geiger and Feller, "Dispersion of Academic Research."

37. See ibid. for analysis of the twenty academic leaders. One of them, Rockefeller University, is not included in the present study.

38. The following draws upon interviews by the author with Arnold Levine and Hugo Sonnenshein, Princeton University, Mar. 3, 1993.

39. For the exceptions in nuclear physics, and Princeton's ambivalence toward them, see Amy Sue Bix, "'Backing into Sponsored Research': Physics and Engineering at Princeton University," *History of Higher Education Annual* 13 (1993): 9–52.

40. Molecular biology has continued to thrive at Princeton in its distinctive fashion. It has the resources to hire top scientists, but they are self-selected for a willingness to engage in undergraduate teaching, a commitment exemplified by President Shirley M. Tilghman. In 2000–2001 the Molecular Biology Department, with its new Institute for Integrative Genomics, brought in $23 million in research grants and fellowships; see Lynn W. Enquist, remarks at "A Symposium on the Princeton Model of Graduate Education," Princeton University, 2001.

41. Irwin Feller, "Social Contracts and the Impact of Matching Funds Requirements on American Research Universities," *Educational Evaluation and Policy Analysis* 22 (Spring 2000): 91–98.

42. David H. Guston and Kenneth Keniston, eds., *The Fragile Contract: University Science and the Federal Government* (Cambridge, Mass.: MIT Press, 1994).

43. These figures reflect a comparison between the twelve public and private universities with the highest average departmental ratings (1995); compiled from "The Annual Report on the Economic Status of the Profession, 2000–2001," *Academe* (Mar.–Apr. 2001).

44. Duke University, *Shaping Our Future: A Young University Faces a New Century* (Durham, N.C.: 1994), quotations on pp. 31, 16, 41–42.

45. Gains in shares of medical research masked loss of share in other fields at Johns Hopkins, Northwestern, Wake Forest, and Case Western Reserve.

46. Washington University, *A University Agenda for the 21st Century* (St. Louis: Apr. 1992), pp. 5, 31–32.

47. University of Pennsylvania, "Agenda for Excellence, 1995–2000," *Almanac*

Supplement (May 1, 2001); "Budget 2000–2001: President Rodin's Report to the University Council," *Almanac* (Apr. 3, 2001).

48. See Geiger and Feller, "Dispersion of Academic Research." Wisconsin, Washington, UC San Diego, Minnesota, and Purdue were the notable losers of research share in the 1980s.

49. University of Texas at Austin, *Agency Strategic Plan for the 2001–2005 Period* (June 1, 2000), p. 13.

50. Ibid.; University of Minnesota, "University Plan, Performance, and Accountability Report 2001" (http://www.irr.umn.edu/uplan/2001); Ben Gose, "The Fall of the Flagships: Do the Best State Universities Need to Privatize to Thrive?" *Chronicle of Higher Education* (July 5, 2002): A19–A21.

51. For budgetary history, see University of California, Office of the President, *Budget for Current Operations, 2000/2001* Oakland, Oct. 2000.

52. For the most part, this is the philosophy of the University of California and the Academic Senate, which plays an important role in upholding academic excellence. However, in addition to the academic core, research is shaped on four other campuses by schools of medicine, Davis has an agricultural extension station, and San Diego includes the Scripps Institute and a supercomputing center.

53. Joseph Cerny, vice-chancellor for Research, UC Berkeley, interview by author, Oct. 25, 2000. In addition, physicists and chemists at Berkeley work closely in some areas with the E. O. Lawrence Berkeley National Laboratory, which had a budget of almost $400 million for FY2000. Perhaps $30–35 million of research grants to Berkeley faculty are administered by this national lab.

54. At Berkeley, 400 senior faculty accepted retirement; however, 95 percent remained in the area, most of them still affiliated with the university (Cerny interview).

55. The University of Michigan's state appropriations have not been shabby: for 1998–99 they were $375 million, or more than $10,000 per student; see University of Michigan, *Financial Report* (year ended June 30, 1999).

56. University of Michigan, "Self-Study for Institutional Re-accreditation," Report of the Working Group on Faculty, 2000.

57. Lee Bollinger, "Letter on the Life Sciences Initiative," May 24, 2000 (http://www.lifesciences.umich.edu/). The initiative comprises several other elements, including new appointments of junior faculty, initiatives in bioinformatics and bioengineering, and a medical research laboratory. It also dovetails with the Michigan Life Sciences Corridor, a commitment by the state to spend $50 million per year for twenty years from its tobacco settlement on the life sciences. Although four recipients are named, the U of M has the resources to claim the lion's share of these funds.

58. James J. Duderstadt, *A University for the 21st Century* (Ann Arbor: University of Michigan Press, 2000), p. 266. Duderstadt called the Michigan version of opportunistic strategic planning "logical incrementalism" (p. 266).

59. University of Michigan, Office of the President, "A Strategy for Our Future," Spring 1996. This pamphlet advances a view of a far-reaching transformation of the University of Michigan in the next twenty years. His subsequent book, *A University for the 21st Century*, presented some of these ideas in a milder form. This is quite the

opposite of the usual pattern for presidential pronouncements: tepid in office and bold out of office!

60. Despite his accomplishments, it seems that style rather than substance was responsible for Duderstadt's ouster. He was an autocratic president, and his relations with some regents deteriorated, perhaps over petty matters (details unknown). His resignation announcement in September 1995 was due to lack of support from the regents; Maryanne George, "Letter Reveals U-M Tension: Duderstadt, Regents Were at Odds," *Detroit Free Press*, Nov. 14, 1995, p. 1A.

61. University of Washington, Office of Research, "Engine of the Knowledge-Based Economy," 2000 (http://depts.washington.edu/or/calcharts/).

62. University of Washington, "Funding Education at the University of Washington," 1999.

63. Among gainers of research share, 1990–2000: the University of Alabama at Birmingham (+0.06), Wayne State University (+0.11), and the University of Cincinnati (+0.08).

64. The University of Colorado at Boulder is part of a system that includes branches in Denver and Colorado Springs, and a separate Health Sciences Center. Management of the research university in Boulder is hamstrung by the system as well as close state regulation; see http://www.state.co.us/cche/hb1289/toc.html.

65. University of Colorado at Boulder, Office of the Chancellor, "NCA Evaluation Report: Chancellor's Executive Summary," Aug. 21, 2000; "2000 College Rankings," *U.S. News and World Report*, Aug. 1999.

66. The average departmental rating at the University of Colorado increased from 2.81 in 1982 to 3.15 in 1995. During this interval the university expanded its faculty by approximately 100 positions. Research share grew from 0.99 in 1989 to 1.18 in 1999, the sixth largest gain in the public sector.

67. University of Colorado, Boulder, Graduate School, "Self-Study for the North Central Association of Colleges and Schools," Dec. 15, 1999; University of Colorado, Boulder, "Sponsored Research at the University of Colorado at Boulder, 1998–1999," 1999. In addition, the National Center for Atmospheric Research ($60 million in FY1997), a federal laboratory, is located in Boulder.

68. Carol B. Lynch, associate vice-chancellor for research, University of Colorado, Boulder, interview by author, Sept. 7, 2000. The Colorado state legislature has only been willing to fund programs and capital costs related to undergraduate education.

69. University of Utah, *Discovery: Annual Report of the Office of the Vice President for Research* (1998 and 1999).

70. The University of Utah has approximately 5,000 graduate students who, unlike the undergraduates, are recruited nationally. The average departmental rating improved from 2.66 in 1982 to 3.04 in 1995.

71. Michael I. Luger and Harvey A. Goldstein, *Technology in the Garden: Research Parks and Regional Economic Development* (Chapel Hill: University of North Carolina Press, 1991), pp. 100–21.

72. Louis G. Tornatzky, Paul G. Waugaman, and Denis O. Gray, *Innovation U: New University Roles in a Knowledge Economy* (Research Triangle Park, N.C.: Southern Growth Policy Board, 2002), pp. 137–44; University of Utah, *Research and Enterprise: The University and New Industry* (n.d.).

73. Two careful analyses of the labor market for faculty predicted greater demand in the late 1990s: Howard R. Bowen and Jack H. Schuster, *American Professors: A National Resource Imperiled* (New York: Oxford University Press, 1986), pp. 188–200; William G. Bowen and Julie Ann Sosa, *Prospects for the Faculty in the Arts and Sciences* (Princeton, N.J.: Princeton University Press, 1989), p. 173. Faculty growth was muted throughout American higher education; see Douglas T. Shapiro, "Modeling Supply and Demand for Arts and Sciences Faculty: What We Can Say about the Projections of Bowen & Sosa after 10 Years?" (paper presented at conference of the Association for the Study of Higher Education, San Antonio, Tex., Nov. 1999).

74. Nancy Cantor, "Remarks" (paper presented at conference "The Boyer Commission Report: A Second Anniversary Retrospective," SUNY Stony Brook, Apr. 28, 2000). At the University of California, undergraduate admissions seems to have overshadowed most other issues.

75. Sloan Foundation, *Part-Time, Adjunct, and Temporary Faculty: The New Majority?* (New York: Alfred P. Sloan Foundation, 1998); elite universities often appoint a significant number of visiting or term faculty, who enrich the offerings for a year or two without obligating the institution—a phenomenon that could use further study.

76. This figure refers to regular faculty with appointments as full or associate professors; see AAUP faculty survey: *Academe*.

77. Geiger, "Organized Research Units"; and for additional background, see Geiger, *Research and Relevant Knowledge*, passim.

78. Chancellor David Ward of the University of Wisconsin, interview by author, Berkeley, Calif., Oct. 4, 2000.

79. The Beckman Institute for Advanced Science and Technology at the University of Illinois has since 1989 pursued a goal of becoming a preeminent center for multidisciplinary research (*Annual Report, 1999*). Interdisciplinary centers are widely used in the humanities to encourage greater focus and collaboration, but also to provide research assistance in fields where external funding is scarce.

80. Nathan Rosenberg, "Scientific Instrumentation and University Research," *Research Policy* 21 (1992): 381–90.

81. University of Illinois at Urbana-Champaign, Biotechnology Center, descriptive materials (2000); Harris Lewin, interview by author, University of Illinois, Urbana, Sept. 5, 2000; Fawwaz T. Ulaby, "Annual Report on Research, Scholarship, and Creative Activities at the University of Michigan, FY2000" (Dec. 14, 2000): Michigan's core technologies were: genomics, animal models, proteomics, structural biology, and bioinformatics.

82. National Science and Technology Council, "National Nanotechnology Initiative: The Initiative and Its Implementation Plan" (Washington D.C.: NSTC, 2002). Photonics is another research technology with vast potential and is the focus of new centers erected at Duke and Stanford; see "$50 Million Gift to Launch Centers for Advanced Photonics and Communications Systems at Stanford and Duke" (http://dknws2k.dukenews.duke.edu/arch/archoo/fitzpat5.htm). As a result of $25 million gifts to each school by Michael and Patty Fitzpatrick, Duke's engineering school launched a $100 million center, and Stanford's a $60 million one.

83. Walter W. Powell and Jason Owen-Smith, "The New World of Knowledge

Production in the Life Sciences," in Steven Brint, ed., *The Future of the City of Intellect* (Stanford, Calif.: Stanford University Press, 2002), pp. 107–32.

84. Universities, especially those with large endowments, are now welcome in capital markets. However, they are reluctant to borrow for other than self-supporting enterprises. Yale, for example, plans to cover as much as possible of its $1 billion commitment to science with donations and finance the rest. This would seem to recognize that research is at least partially self-supporting. However, it was precisely the practice of financing capital expenditures through ICR that brought Stanford to grief in the early 1990s.

85. Nannerl O. Keohane, quoted in "$50 Million Gift."

Chapter 5

1. For background, see Nathan Rosenberg and Richard R. Nelson, "American Universities and Technical Advance in Industry," *Research Policy* 23 (1994): 323–48; and Roger L. Geiger, "The Ambiguous Link: Private Industry and University Research," in William E. Becker and Darrell R. Lewis, eds., *The Economics of American Higher Education* (Boston: Kluwer, 1992), pp. 265–98. For the 1980s, see Roger L. Geiger, *Research and Relevant Knowledge: American Research Universities since World War II* (New York: Oxford University Press, 1993), pp. 296–309; and for more recent developments, see Irwin Feller, "Technology Transfer from Universities," in John Smart, ed., *Handbook of Theory and Research in Higher Education* 12 (1998): 1–42.

2. Geiger, "Ambiguous Link," pp. 272–74.

3. For a comprehensive view of the role of research in industry, see Richard R. Nelson, "Capitalism as an Engine of Progress," *Research Policy* 19 (1990): 193–214; and Nathan Rosenberg, "Why Do Firms Do Basic Research (with Their Own Money)?" *Research Policy* 19 (1990): 165–74. The implications of this depiction for universities are explored below.

4. National Science Foundation, *Science and Engineering Indicators, 2000* (Washington, D.C.: NSF, 2000), vol. 2, pp. 2-49–2-52, 2-58.

5. See Lucien Paul Randazzese, "Profit and Academic Ethos: the Activity and Performance of University-Industry Research Centers in the United States" (Ph.D. diss., Carnegie Mellon University, 1996), pp. 19–48.

6. Rosenberg and Nelson, "American Universities," p. 340. Rosenberg and Nelson also identify situations in which academic research is a substitute for industrial research: for example, in forestry and sometimes agriculture.

7. This distinction and the trade-offs depicted in Figure 13 are elaborated by Randazzese, "Profit and Academic Ethos." See also Business–Higher Education Forum, *Working Together, Creating Knowledge: The University-Industry Research Collaboration Initiative* (2001), pp. 27–43.

8. Wesley M. Cohen, Richard R. Nelson, and John P. Walsh, "Protecting Their Intellectual Assets: Appropriability Conditions and Why U.S. Manufacturing Firms Patent (or Not)," Working Paper 7552, National Bureau of Economic Research, Cambridge, Mass., 2000. The authors also note that "complementary marketing and manufacturing capabilities" protect a firm's innovations.

9. Randazzese, "Profit and Academic Ethos," p. 288; see also Edwin Mansfield

and Jeong-Yeon Lee, "The Modern University: Contributor to Industrial Innovation and Recipient of Industrial R&D Support," *Research Policy* 25 (1996): 1047–58.

10. Goldie Blumenstyk, "Vilified Corporate Partnership Produces Little Change (Except Better Facilities)," *Chronicle of Higher Education* (June 22, 2001): A24–A27. The Novartis agreement became effective in November 1998; the Novartis unit subsequently became the Torrey Mesa Research Institute of Syngenta Corporation. Syngenta, the world's largest agribusiness, was spun out of Novartis and Zeneca Corporations in November 2000.

11. Deborah Shapley and Rustum Roy, *Lost at the Frontier* (Philadelphia: ISI Press, 1985), p. 20. For GTRI, see http://www.gtri.gatech.edu/.

12. Pennsylvania's Ben Franklin program, although highly regarded nationally, apparently illustrates this tension. It was designed to provide access for small business to academic research, but Irwin Feller reports that faculty became "disenchanted" with their experiences. Participants had differing expectations and goals, leading to "mutual disappointment"; see Feller, "Technology Transfer," p. 25.

13. Mansfield and Lee, "Modern University," pp. 1054–55; Randazzese, "Profit and Academic Ethos," pp. 199–215.

14. Mansfield and Lee found that "distance is particularly important for universities with only adequate-to-good or marginal faculties; for such universities, the chances of support were quite low unless they are within 100 miles of the firm" ("Modern University," p. 1053).

15. Given the propensity of industry to support prestigious academic researchers, Randazzese suggests that firms may be misallocating research dollars — that more downstream benefits would accrue from adopting a local strategy; see "Profit and Academic Ethos," p. 288.

16. This is the argument of Rosenberg and Nelson, "American Universities," pp. 345–47; see also Mansfield and Lee, "Modern University."

17. See "50 Ways Penn State Has Shaped the World" (http://www.psu.edu/ur/archives/50ways/50ways.html). During most of this period MIT performed the most R&D for industry, but recently Duke has assumed this position, largely by conducting clinical trials. For an overview of all Penn State activities related to economic development, see Louis G. Tornatzky, Paul G. Waugaman, and Denis O. Gray, *Innovation U: New University Roles in a Knowledge Economy* (Research Triangle Park, N.C.: Southern Growth Policies Board, 2002), pp. 67–78.

18. I would like to thank Robert Killoren, vice president for research and head of Sponsored Programs, for providing these data. This sum was considerably less than the $66 million in industrially sponsored research that Penn State reported to NSF in fiscal 1999. Some of the university's reported total would have pertained to the Hershey Medical School, and many contracts undoubtedly are active for less than one year. Final reporting would also require some reclassification. The expenditure figures employed here are thus not comparable with reported annual totals.

19. Steve Sampsell, "Broad, Interdisciplinary Research Efforts Started Small, with Surface-Only Focus," *Science Journal* 18 (Summer 2001) (http://www.science.psu.edu/journal/Sum2001/Surface-Sum01.htm).

20. Rosenberg and Nelson, "American Universities," p. 347.

21. These ideal types are abstracted from some 300 individual grants. As such,

they represent clusters of grants of an identifiable character among an otherwise bewildering variety of activities.

22. Ammon J. Salter and Ben R. Martin, "The Economic Benefits of Publicly Funded Basic Research: A Critical Review," *Research Policy* 30 (2001): 509–32, esp. pp. 520–22, 527.

23. Ibid., pp. 520–24; Rosenberg, "Why Do Firms Do Basic Research?"; Rosenberg and Nelson, "American Universities," p. 340; Keith Pavitt, "What Makes Basic Research Economically Useful?" *Research Policy* 20 (1991): 109–19.

24. A true analysis of departmental research patterns would have to focus on the department members, not the unit that administered their research. Such an analysis would undoubtedly reveal the important role of ORUs, which is only suggested in these data.

25. For some perspective, in 1997 the firm ranked number 100 in R&D spent $180 million: NSF, *Science and Engineering Indicators, 2000*, vol. 2, p. 2-58.

26. Herbert Simon, *The Sciences of the Artificial* (Cambridge, Mass.: MIT Press, 1969). Rosenberg and Nelson emphasize this view in "American Universities," pp. 332–33.

27. Robert Killoren, interview by author, Pennsylvania State University, Sept. 4, 2001; Gary Weber, interview by author, Pennsylvania State University, Jan. 24, 2003.

28. Rosenberg and Nelson, "American Universities," pp. 332–33; Rosenberg, "Why Do Firms Do Basic Research?" pp. 169–70.

29. The following discussion draws on Rosenberg, "Why Do Firms Do Basic Research?"; Nelson, "Capitalism"; Pavitt, "What Makes Basic Research"; and Salter and Martin, "Economic Benefits."

30. Dennis K. Berman, "At Bell Labs, Hard Times Take Toll on Pure Science," *Wall Street Journal*, May 23, 2003, pp. A1, A8.

31. Industry differences in the conduct and use of research are addressed in Richard R. Nelson, "Capitalism," pp. 200–202; Rosenberg and Nelson, "American Universities," pp. 339–44; A. K. Klevorick et al., "On the Sources and Significance of Inter-University Differences in Technological Opportunities," *Research Policy* 24 (1995): 185–205.

32. Rosenberg, "Why Do Firms Do Basic Research?" p. 170.

33. Ibid., pp. 168–69. He further explains, "these connections are . . . extraordinarily difficult to trace. . . . But even if these difficulties could be overcome, the problems of evaluating the knowledge, and of providing the appropriate incentive system to reward the knowledge producers, would appear to be insuperable."

34. For example, Eli Lilly & Co. now maintains a website where it posts chemistry problems that its scientists need help with and for which Lilly will make grants for possible solutions; see *Wall Street Journal*, Dec. 24, 2001, p. B5.

35. Nathan Rosenberg, "Scientific Instrumentation and University Research," *Research Policy* 21 (1992): 381–90. Conversely, industry sometimes gives highly sophisticated instruments to universities because of the innovative uses devised by academic scientists.

36. Rosenberg points out that formal quantitative methodologies for evaluating research are quite prejudicial to basic (academic) research; see "Why Do Firms Do

Basic Research?" p. 168. Note that expenditures for enhancement would include many internal expenses, especially for personnel enhancement, and thus would not be recorded as university-industry interaction (e.g., industry scientists attending academic conferences).

37. For example, the charge to industry for $100 of research (direct costs) might be $140 at a public university; $160 at a private university; and $250 at an independent laboratory. Universities may have a somewhat lower cost base, but the chief difference probably can be ascribed to the disparity between average costs, which an independent lab must charge, and marginal costs, which university charges approximate.

38. In 1977, Congress authorized NSF to establish a program in State Science, Engineering, and Technology to encourage states to plan science and technology policies. Almost every state received a planning grant, but follow-on funding was never provided. This failed policy may nevertheless have encouraged states to consider initiatives; see Christopher Coburn, ed., *Partnerships: A Compendium of State and Federal Cooperative Technology Programs* (Columbus, Ohio: Battelle, 1995), p. 50.

39. Earlier developments include the Research Triangle in North Carolina (opened in 1959) and the University of Utah Park (1970). Both received government assistance, but it was given through ad hoc measures.

40. Ibid., 51; David Roessner, "Outcomes and Impacts of the State/Industry–University Cooperative Research Program" (NSF 01–110), National Science Foundation, 2001. NSF also launched a program for Science and Technology Centers in 1987. Although technology transfer was one explicit goal of these units, greater emphasis was placed on partnerships with other research performers and educational outcomes. These centers are consequently not included in the following discussion, although some merit inclusion.

41. Empirical studies of university-industry research centers usually include all academic centers that have some relations with industry, thus conflating basic science units with an occasional industrial grant and units designed to work with industry. Results are rarely analyzed according to the degree of industrial involvement. Cohen et al., for example, found that centers receiving the majority of their funding from industry "differ in their orientation, objectives and expectations" from others, but they devote less than one page to this phenomenon; see Wesley Cohen, Richard Florida, and W. Richard Goe, "University-Industry Research Centers in the United States" (Carnegie Mellon University, July 1994), p. 23.

42. Salter and Martin, "Economic Benefits," p. 520; Michael Gibbons et al., *The New Production of Knowledge* (London: Sage, 1994), passim; Frieder Meyer-Krahmer and Ulrich Schmoch, "Science-Based Technologies: University-Industry Interactions in Four Fields," *Research Policy* 27 (1998): 835–51, esp. pp. 840–41; Roessner, "Outcomes and Impacts," p. 11.

43. Linda Parker, "The Engineering Research Centers (ERC) Program: An Assessment of Benefits and Outcomes" (National Science Foundation, Dec. 1997), pp. 2, 7. According to one participant: "the benefits are considered large compared to the limited costs of participation" (ibid., p. 8).

44. Most Engineering Research Centers offer different classes of membership to encourage the greatest possible industrial participation. A relatively expensive cen-

ter offered "executive, research, and trial memberships for $25,000, $15,000, and $5,000; possibly the cheapest center offered full memberships for $5,000 and associate memberships for just $1,000. By any metric, participation is inexpensive, and the centers advertise the "leveraged" access to millions of dollars of NSF and university-supported research. For details see www.nsf.gov/pubs/2000/nsf00137/start. htm.

45. NSF, "Industry/University Cooperative Research Centers Program" (http://www.eng.nsf.gov/iucrc/Program/program.htm).

46. Roessner, "Outcomes and Impacts," p. 13.

47. The following summarizes benefits data given in Parker, "Engineering Research Centers"; and Roessner, "Outcomes and Impacts."

48. The NSF program for state IUCRCs started three new centers in 1996, but has since been closed to new applications.

49. Roessner, "Outcomes and Impacts," pp. 12–14.

50. Coburn, *Partnerships*, pp. 51–53.

51. This is also a conclusion of Cohen et al., "University-Industry Research Centers," although their sample included federal- and state-subsidized centers created in the 1980s.

52. That is, in the case of firms, private returns to research are inferior to social returns; in the case of states and localities, regional returns to research are inferior to national (or possibly international) returns. In economics the latter situation is known as geographic spillover; see Salter and Martin, "Economic Benefits," p. 318.

53. Martin Kenney, ed., *Understanding Silicon Valley: The Anatomy of an Entrepreneurial Region* (Stanford, Calif.: Stanford University Press, 2000); AnnaLee Saxenian, *Regional Advantage: Culture and Competition in Silicon Valley and Route 128* (Cambridge, Mass.: Harvard University Press, 1994). Silicon Valley and Route 128 outside of Boston are often paired in discussing this subject; however, Saxenian argues that universities played a much more prominent role in the former (pp. 66–68).

54. Martin Kenney and Urs Von Burg, "Institutions and Economies: Creating Silicon Valley," in Kenney, *Understanding Silicon Valley*, pp. 218–40, quotation on p. 224.

55. The literature on spillovers and localization is summarized by Salter and Martin, "Economic Benefits," pp. 517–20.

56. For studies supporting this point, see Salter and Martin, "Economic Benefits," p. 519.

57. Hans Weiler, "Proximity and Affinity: Regional and Cultural Linkages between Higher Education and ICT in Silicon Valley and Elsewhere," in Marijk van der Wende and Maartin van de Ven, eds., *The Use of ICT in Higher Education: A Mirror of Europe* (Utrecht: Lemma Publishers, 2003), pp. 277–97.

58. Michael S. Fogarty and Amit K. Sinha, "Why Older Regions Can't Generalize from Route 128 and Silicon Valley: University-Industry Relationships and Regional Innovation Systems," in Lewis M. Branscomb, Fumio Kodama, and Richard Florida, eds., *Industrializing Knowledge: University-Industry Linkages in Japan and the United States* (Cambridge, Mass.: MIT Press, 1999), pp. 473–509, quotation on p. 491.

59. Besides the postwar investment in defense research, these would include the creation of the Stanford Research Institute, the Stanford Industrial Park, and the commitment to making Stanford a top-ranked research university; see Kenney, *Understanding Silicon Valley*, passim.; Leslie, *Cold War*; and Geiger, *Research and Relevant Knowledge*, pp. 118–35.

60. The creation of university-linked venture capital funds is another strategy to promote or profit from economic development. Venture capital funds are not included in this discussion. Nor does this discussion consider the total economic impact of universities; see Michael I. Luger and Harvey A. Goldstein, "What Is the Role of Public Universities in Regional Economic Development?" in Richard Bingham and Robert Mier, eds., *Dilemmas of Urban Economic Development*, Urban Affairs Annual Reviews 47 (Thousand Oaks, Calif.: Sage, 1997), pp. 104–34.

61. Michael I. Lugar and Harvey A. Goldstein, *Technology in the Garden: Research Parks and Regional Economic Development* (Chapel Hill: University of North Carolina Press, 1991), pp. 76–99, 122–54, 187–91. Both of the defining characteristics of university-related research parks—the university nexus and research—are subject to interpretation. That is, university participation may be token, and research parks blend into office or industrial parks. Hence the population can only be approximate.

62. Jeffrey A. Bastuscheck, "Faculty Roles in University Related Research Parks" (Ph.D. diss., Pennsylvania State University, 1996).

63. Lugar and Goldstein analyzed employment growth in the regions of forty-five research parks; they found sixteen positive and fourteen comparatively negative outcomes; see *Technology in the Garden*, pp. 49–75, esp. p. 62.

64. This discussion assumes that research parks, where rents are relatively high, cater to more established businesses, while incubators, which can operate in relatively low-tech and therefore cheaper environments, are for true beginners. In fact, many parks serve start-ups as part of their mission, but it is more common for a university to have both, thus validating the distinction.

65. Lugar and Goldstein, *Technology in the Garden*. This detailed study found much to value in research parks, but in the climate of the early 1990s its findings were interpreted negatively. The authors themselves were cautionary about the creation of additional research parks (pp. 182–83).

66. Technically, internal economies are low, so firms have weak incentives to internalize transactions, and external economies are large, providing motivation for obtaining resources outside the firm; see Allan J. Scott, *Technopolis: High-Technology Industry and Regional Development in Southern California* (Berkeley: University of California Press, 1993), pp. 25–28. Saxenian refers to a similar phenomenon as "network systems" (*Regional Advantage*, pp. 150–56 and passim). Agglomerations are an ancient phenomenon, first analyzed by Alfred Marshall in *Principles of Economics* (1920).

67. North Carolina State University, "The New NC State: Becoming the Nation's Leading Land-Grant Institution," June 2000.

68. NCSU, "Centennial Campus Facts," 2002. The entire development is envisioned as a community, with residential housing, a school, a convention center, and a golf course.

69. "NC State's Next Big Bio Bet: Centennial Biomedical Campus," *Results: Research and Graduate Studies at North Carolina State University* (Spring 2002): 1–2.

70. Charles G. Moreland, "New NC State," p. 15; Louis G. Tornatzky, Paul G. Waugaman, and Denis O. Gray, *Innovation U: New University Roles in a Knowledge Economy* (Research Triangle Park, N.C.: Southern Growth Policy Board, 2002), pp. 43–53.

71. Interviews by author with Vice Chancellor for Research and Graduate Studies Charles G. Moreland and with Robert Geolas, Centennial Campus Coordinator, NC State, Apr. 12, 2002. The intent of the Centennial Campus in this respect is to recreate conditions of agglomerations, and particularly to foster conditions of affinity and reciprocity highlighted by Weiler in "Proximity and Affinity." Interestingly, much of the intermingling and interaction of the Centennial model have evolved spontaneously at the University of Utah Research Park; see Tornatzky, Waugaman, and Gray, *Innovation U,* pp. 138–39.

72. Another line of criticism has come from business: unfair competition. As a publicly subsidized real estate development it has not been popular with regional competitors. At the time of writing, hotels in the Raleigh area had prevented the construction of the projected convention center, which clearly would be financially viable.

73. For background, see Geiger, *Research and Relevant Knowledge*, pp. 283–95. The following draws on interviews by the author with Robert McMath, May 24, 2001, and Provost Michael Thomas, May 25, 2001.

74. Richard S. Combes and William J. Todd, "From Henry Grady to the Georgia Research Alliance: A Case Study of Science-Based Development in Georgia," Georgia Research Alliance, 1999. The universities were Georgia Tech, the University of Georgia, Emory University, Georgia State University, Georgia Medical College, and Clark Atlanta University.

75. Matt Kempner, "The Yamacraw Mission: State Secrets," *Atlanta Journal-Constitution*, Jan. 13, 1999.

76. *Yamacraw Forward* (Apr. 2002): 8; Georgia Tech also offers a large number of modular courses for Yamacraw through Continuing Education: *Yamacraw Forward* (Apr. 2001): 13.

77. Interview with Richard J. LeBlanc Jr., Yamacraw Director of Education, Apr. 16, 2002 (www.yamacraw.org).

78. A national study found the institute to be nationally preeminent in the range and comprehensiveness of its programs for this purpose. See Tornatzky, Waugaman, and Gray, *Innovation U*; Georgia Tech's extensive programs are described on pp. 27–41. The innovative universities in this study were nominated by a panel of forty experts: "by a comfortable margin, Georgia Tech received the highest number of nominations" (n. 26).

79. G. Wayne Clough, "Shaping Futures through Innovation: 2001 State of the Institute Address," Oct. 2001.

80. Geiger, "Ambiguous Link," pp. 289–91.

81. Gerald D. Laubach aptly terms this the "new biology," which far transcends recombinant DNA: "Perspectives on Industrial R&D Management," in Nathan Rosenberg, Annetine C. Gelijns, and Holly Dawkins, eds., *Sources of Medical Tech-*

nology: Universities and Industry (Washington, D.C.: National Academy Press, 1995), pp. 209–18, esp. pp. 213–14. For the purposes of this discussion, "biotechnology" represents the new biology, which is far too complex to summarize here.

82. Pharmaceutical Research and Manufacturers Association, "Pharmaceutical Industry Profile, 2001" (http://www.phrma.org/), chapter 2; Darren E. Zimmer, "Medical R&D at the Turn of the Millennium," *Health Affairs* (Sept.–Oct. 2001): 202–9.

83. For an overview circa 1995, see Enriqueta C. Bond and Simon Glynn, "Research Trends in Support for Biomedical Research and Development" in Rosenberg, Gelijns, and Dawkins, *Sources of Medical Technology*, pp. 15–40. The authors report 1,272 biotechnology companies (235 public) in 1993 (p. 26).

84. The portrayal of "Mode 2" science by Michael Gibbons and associates (*The New Production of Knowledge*) appears to be modeled largely upon biotechnology, although the importance of capital would seem to be missing from their analysis. As a characterization of contemporary science, ex biotechnology, Mode 2 is far more problematic. The analysis here seeks first to probe biotechnology on its own terms and then to relate its characteristics to academic science.

85. Wesley M. Cohen, Richard R. Nelson, and John P. Walsh, "Protecting Their Intellectual Assets: Appropriability Conditions and Why U.S. Manufacturing Firms Patent (Or Not)," Working Paper 7552, National Bureau of Economic Research, Cambridge, Mass., Feb. 2000), quotations on p. 18.

86. Richard Jensen and Marie Thursby, "Proofs and Prototypes for Sale: The Tale of University Licensing," Working Paper 6698, National Bureau of Economic Research, Cambridge, Mass., Aug. 1998. Faculty are less motivated by licensing revenues and more likely to seek patents as a means to increase sponsored research (ibid., p. 7), but this may be more characteristic of engineering and physical sciences (see below).

87. Charles Weiner, "Patenting and Academic Research: Historical Case Studies," *Science, Technology, and Human Values* 12 (1987): 50–62; Rebecca Henderson, Adam B. Jaffe, and Manuel Trajtenberg, "Universities as a Source of Commercial Technology: A Detailed Analysis of University Patenting, 1965–1988," Working Paper 5068, National Bureau of Economic Research, Cambridge, Mass., Mar. 1995; Association of University Technology Managers (AUTM), *AUTM Licensing Survey: FY 1999* (AUTM, 2000); Walter W. Powell and Jason Owen-Smith, "The New World of Knowledge Production in the Life Sciences," in Steven Brint, ed., *The City of Intellect* (Stanford, Calif.: Stanford University Press, 2002), life sciences royalties calculated from table 1. According to the *AUTM Licensing Survey: FY 1996* (AUTM, 1997), 80 percent of reported licensing revenue was biomedical.

88. David C. Mowery, Richard R. Nelson, Bhaven N. Sampat, and Arvids A. Ziedonis, "The Growth of Patenting and Licensing by U.S. Universities: An Assessment of the Effects of the Bayh-Dole Act of 1980," *Research Policy* 30 (2001): 99–119; Gary Matkin, *Technology Transfer and the American Research University* (New York: Macmillan, 1990).

89. The validity of this argument and the efficacy of ensuing policies are questioned by Mowery et al., "Growth of Patenting," pp. 116–18. Additional steps strengthening patents include: the creation of the Court of Appeals for the Federal

Circuit (1982), which hears appeals in patent cases and has largely favored patent holders; and "at least 14 Congressional bills passed during the 1980s focused on strengthening . . . protection of intellectual property rights" (ibid., 103). See also Risa L. Lieberwitz, "Science and the University" (paper presented at the conference "University Science Research Funding: Privatizing Policy and Practice," Cornell Higher Education Research Institute, May 2003), pp. 15–23.

90. Patent-related data from AUTM, *Licensing Survey: FY 1999*.

91. Jason Owen-Smith, "Public Science, Private Science: The Causes and Consequences of Patenting by Research One Universities" (Ph.D. diss., University of Arizona, 2000); U.S. General Accounting Office (GAO), *Technology Transfer: Administration of the Bayh-Dole Act by Research Universities* (May 1998).

92. Accounts emphasizing the difficulties of profiting from patenting include Geiger, "The Ambiguous Link"; and Irwin Feller, "Universities as Engines of R&D-based Economic Growth: They Think They Can," *Research Policy* 19 (1990): 335–48.

93. Provisional patents were apparently prompted by the GATT Uruguay Round Agreements (http://www.uspto.gov/web/offices/pac/provapp.htm).

94. AUTM, *Licensing Survey: FY1999*; GAO, *Technology Transfer*, pp. 46–75.

95. Henderson, et al., "Universities as a Source," pp. 14, 21–23.

96. *AUTM Licensing Survey: FY1999*. The comparable number of top research performers accounted for 37 percent of university R&D in 2000.

97. Preliminary results from a study of faculty in relevant departments at six patent-active universities found that roughly one-third of faculty members disclosed an invention to the university TTO over sixteen years. Two percent appeared to be active inventors, submitting disclosures in eight or more years. According to these data, disclosures of inventions by faculty are becoming less exceptional; see Jerry G. Thursby and Marie C. Thursby, "Patterns of Research and Licensing Activity of Science and Engineering Faculty," conference paper, "Science and the University," Cornell Higher Education Research Institute (May 2003).

98. William D. Gregory and Thomas P. Sheahen, "Technology Transfer by Spin-off Companies versus Licensing," in Alistair M. Breit et al., eds., *University Spin-off Companies: Economic Development, Faculty Entrepreneurs, and Technology Transfer* (Savage, Md.: Rowman and Littlefield, 1991), pp. 133–52.

99. GAO, *Technology Transfer*.

100. The study by Jason Owen-Smith, "Public Science, Private Science," provides valuable insight into these issues and the nature of the patenting process. However, the argument for an increasing cumulative advantage of the elite group is questionable. AUTM data, for example, show the five universities mentioned here accounting for about 30 percent of academic patents in the 1990s.

101. Ibid., chapter 4. The author writes that at an elite patenter, "a large, well-funded and experienced licensing office allows for flexible response to faculty schedules, fewer constraints on [staff] entrepreneurialism, relatively quick turn around, 'transparent' internal relationships, and a team based organizational structure [that] allows [licensing professionals] to specialize." In contrast, at a nonelite institution, he found that an "under-funded and understaffed office is often blamed for frustratingly long delays, inconvenient schedules, lax reporting, limited risk taking capacity, and a lack of understanding of the various demands of academic patenting"

(p. 178). In the latter case, the author reported that some inventions were "taken out the back door" and commercialized independently. It should be noted that TTOs are often expected to be self-supporting, The result can be a vicious circle of insufficient resources leading to a lack of patenting success and vice-versa.

102. Sixty-three percent in 1999; *AUTM Licensing Survey: FY1999*, p. 90.

103. Richard Jensen and Marie Thursby, "Proofs and Prototypes for Sale: The Tale of University Licensing," Working Paper 6698, National Bureau of Economic Research, Cambridge, Mass., Aug. 1998, p. 5. Twelve percent of academic inventions were "ready for practical or commercial use" (table 1).

104. "[S]mall businesses tend to be more entrepreneurial than large companies and are more interested in marketing new technologies" (University of Michigan); see GAO, *Technology Transfer*, p. 59.

105. Robert A. Lowe, "The Role and Experience of Inventors and Start-ups in Commercializing University Research: Case Studies at the University of California," Research and Occasional Paper Series (Berkeley, Calif.: Center for Studies in Higher Education, University of California, Dec. 2002).

106. GAO, *Technology Transfer*, pp. 53, 60; Owen-Smith, "Public Science, Private Science," pp. 213–24. Resistance to faculty start-ups nevertheless remains. Harvard warns that start-ups are not the first choice for licensing and that Harvard rules may work against them (GAO, *Technology Transfer*, p. 66); and the Howard Hughes Medical Institute considers the personal financial stake of faculty entrepreneurs to be incompatible with collaboration with the same company in university laboratories; see Thomas R. Cech, [discussion] in Hugo Sonnenschein, ed., *Research Universities and the Future of the Academic Disciplines* (Washington, D.C.: Association of American Universities, 2001), pp. 37–38.

107. The following discussion draws upon findings from case studies conducted by Owen-Smith, "Public Science, Private Science," pp. 165–86.

108. Ibid., pp. 213–16; Lynne G. Zucker, Michael R. Darby, and Jeff Armstrong, "Intellectual Capital and the Firm: The Technology of Geographically Localized Knowledge Spillovers," Working Paper 4946, National Bureau of Economic Research, Cambridge, Mass., Dec. 1994.

109. Walter W. Powell, Kenneth W. Koput, and Laurel Smith-Doerr, "Interorganizational Collaboration and the Locus of Innovation: Networks of Learning in Biotechnology," *Administrative Science Quarterly* 41 (1996): 116–45.

110. For example, Thomas R. Cech has described how his discovery of the human telomerase gene at the University of Colorado "involved a Swiss postdoc and a Japanese graduate student, a laboratory of collaborators in Texas, a mass-spectrometry facility in Heidelberg, [in addition to] a biotechnology company in Menlo Park." This was not unusual: "there are huge international consortia involved in making these projects work"; see "Biology's Revolution: Opportunities and Challenges for Universities," in Sonnenschein, *Research Universities*, pp. 5–14, quotation on p. 12.

111. Zucker, Darby, and Armstrong, "Intellectual Capital and the Firm"; Lynne G. Zucker and Michael R. Darby, "Star Scientists and Institutional Transformation: Patterns of Invention and Innovation in the Formation of the Biotechnology Industry," *Proceedings of the National Academy of Sciences of the United States of America*

93, no. 23 (1996): 12709–16; Lynne G. Zucker, Michael R. Darby, and Marilynn B. Brewer, "Intellectual Capital and the Birth of U.S. Biotechnology Enterprises," *American Economic Review* 88, no. 1 (1998): 290–306.

112. Zucker and Darby, "Star Scientists," p. 12714.

113. Powell, Koput, and Smith-Doerr, "Interorganizational Collaboration."

114. Jensen and Thursby, "Proofs and Prototypes."

115. Capital raised by biotech firms increased from $5.4 billion in 1998, to 11.8 billion in 1999, and to 37.6 billion in 2000. Biotech drug approvals, of which were a total of nineteen before 1995, topped thirty in 2000 alone; see Zimmer, "Medical R&D," pp. 206–7.

116. Bond and Glynn report: "the overwhelming majority of biotechnology companies are research organizations with essentially no revenues. Moreover . . . development efforts in the majority of these biotechnology companies are several years from approval" ("Recent Trends," p. 26).

117. "Their close ties to the academic system, their collegial atmosphere, and the possibility of using incentive-based compensation schemes . . . have given [new biotech firms] a comparative advantage in research." However, they are disadvantaged in bringing products to market. "As a result, many [new biotech firms] end up offering their skills or potential new products to larger firms for research collaboration and joint product developments." See Ashish Arora and Alfonso Gambardella, "The Division of Innovative Labor in Biotechnology" in Rosenberg, Gelijns, and Dawkins, *Sources of Medical Technology*, pp. 188–208, quotations on pp. 191, 192.

118. Ibid., pp. 193–99. However, Zimmer observes that pharmaceutical corporations must look increasingly to biotech firms for innovations, essentially outsourcing part of their R&D ("Medical R&D," p. 206).

119. For a recent example with all the clichés, see Eyal Press and Jennifer Washburn, "The Kept University," *Atlantic Monthly* (Mar. 2000): 39–54.

120. Martin Kenney, *Biotechnology: The University-Industrial Complex* (New Haven, Conn.: Yale University Press, 1986), p. 246; this is a valuable early study with a critical perspective.

121. Eric G. Campbell et al., "Data Withholding in Academic Genetics: Evidence from a National Survey," *Journal of the American Medical Association* (Jan.23/30, 2002): 473–80, quotations on p. 479. The reasons given for withholding data are both scientific (protecting future publishing) and mundane (problems associated with biomaterials), but are not easily linked to commercialization.

122. Scientists may well be reluctant to share important data with researchers *outside of* their own networks if they feel that the latter have little to offer in exchange. Thus the degree of withholding found by Campbell et al. (ibid.) may be consistent with the importance of networks.

123. Thomas J. Tighe, *Who's in Charge of America's Research Universities? A Blueprint for Reform* (Albany: SUNY Press, 2003), pp. 152–56; Derek Bok, *Universities in the Marketplace: The Commercialization of Higher Education* (Princeton, N.J.: Princeton University Press, 2003), pp. 144–51.

124. David Baltimore, "Response to Thomas Cech," in *Research Universities*, pp. 26–30, quotation on p. 28. Baltimore expressed concern that these conflicts have spread beyond biology, where they have caused "serious problems" (p. 29).

Chapter 6

1. Robert Kuttner, *Everything for Sale* (New York: Knopf, 1997).
2. Charles E. Lindblom, *The Market System* (New Haven, Conn.: Yale University Press, 2001).
3. Ibid., p. 175.
4. Ibid.
5. Michael S. McPherson and Morton Owen Schapiro, "The End of the Student Aid Era? Higher Education Finance in the United States," in Michael C. Johanek, ed., *A Faithful Mirror: Reflections on the College Board and Education in America* (New York: College Entrance Examination Board, 2001), pp. 335–78.
6. Caroline M. Hoxby, "Benevolent Colluders? The Effects of Antitrust Action on College Financial Aid and Tuition" (Harvard University, Department of Economics, n.d.).
7. The microeconomic consequences of this development are explained in Caroline M. Hoxby, "Tax Incentives for Higher Education," in James M. Poterba, ed., *Tax Policy and the Economy*, vol. 12 (Cambridge, Mass.: MIT Press/NBER, 1998), pp. 49–81. Much of the argument that follows is indebted to Hoxby's analysis summarized here (pp. 60–64) and documented in other papers.
8. As described in Michael S. McPherson and Morton Owen Schapiro, *The Student Aid Game* (Princeton, N.J.: Princeton University Press, 1998).
9. Roger L. Geiger, "High Tuition—High Aid: A Road Paved with Good Intentions" (paper presented at the meeting of the Association for the Study of Higher Education, Sacramento, Calif., Nov. 2002).
10. Two independent data sets show lower-income students increasing their presence at high-tuition/highly selective institutions, but wealthy students increasing far more; see Caroline M. Hoxby, "Testimony Prepared for United States Senate, Committee on Governmental Affairs, Hearing on "The Rising Cost of College Tuition and the Effectiveness of Government Financial Aid" (Feb. 9, 2000), pp. 7–8 (comparing 1972 with 1992); McPherson and Schapiro, "End of the Student Aid Era," pp. 374–76 (comparing 1981 with 1999).
11. Hoxby, "Tax Incentives," pp. 62–63. Lest the concept of a student "wage" be considered an abstraction, DePauw University (among many others) provides this information to prospective students on its website: an SAT score of 1,020 and a 3.25 GPA earned a tuition discount of $3,000; 1,200 SAT and 3.75 GPA earned $10,000: June Kronholz, "On Sale Now: College Tuition," *Wall Street Journal*, May 16, 2002, pp. D1, 6.
12. Note that Princeton has, in effect, preserved the old student aid philosophy while also paying very high wages to students. Recent changes created more generous financial aid packages for all qualifying students, while Princeton's subsidy to all students is the highest. The combination represents an enormous "wage" for all Princeton students without violating the student aid ethos. Only the wealthiest universities have been able to execute this strategy.
13. Price discrimination and rationing interact in complex ways. Some possibilities are modeled by Richard Steinberg and Burton A. Weisbrod, "Give It Away or Make Them Pay? Price Discrimination and Rationing by Nonprofit Organizations with Distributional Objectives," Indiana University, draft, June 17, 2002.

14. Described by Henry Hansmann as contract failure: "Economic Theories of the Nonprofit Sector," in Walter W. Powell, ed., *The Nonprofit Sector: A Research Handbook* (New Haven, Conn.: Yale University Press, 1987), pp. 27–42.

15. See McPherson and Schapiro, *Student Aid Game*. As in other things, the wealthier the institution, the less the incentive for sharp practices.

16. Gordon C. Winston, "The Positional Arms Race in Higher Education," Discussion Paper 54, Williams Project on the Economics of Higher Education, Williams College, Apr. 2000.

17. To opt out of the arms race, according to Gordon Winston, would border on "fiduciary irresponsibility": "In a positional market there's never too much of a good thing—or even much stomach for asking that question—and in the hierarchy, wealth is quite fundamentally a good thing": "Subsidies, Hierarchies, and Peers: the Awkward Economics of Higher Education," *Journal of Economic Perspectives* (Winter 1999): 13–36, quotation on p. 31.

18. These universities have sought to raise revenue through commercial channels, including selling logos and licensing inventions. To date, though, such sources have added little to general funds.

19. In a few states, elasticity of demand was a significant consideration. Local markets were such that increased prices at state universities would bring about enrollment losses. Quality must be factored into such situations: either the clientele is uninterested in paying for higher quality, or the quality differential does not match the price differential.

20. *Chronicle of Higher Education*, "Facts & Figures" for ninety-seven public universities offering the doctoral degree (http://chronicle.com/stats/tuition/2001/). The median tuition and fees were $4,000, and the lowest quartile charged $3,000 or less.

21. Hoxby, "Tax Incentives."

22. Endowment income per FTE student in sixty-six public universities rose from an average of $176 in 1980, to $195 in 1990, and to $448 in 2000; for thirty-three private universities the figures were: $2,536, $3837, $8124 (all in $1996).

23. Robert Birnbaum, *Management Fads in Higher Education: Where They Come from, What They Do, and Why They Fail* (San Francisco: Jossey-Bass, 2000).

24. Daniel Rodas, *Resource Allocation in Private Research Universities* (New York: Routledge Falmer, 2001), p. 15.

25. The argument is often made that tying resources to enrollments promotes quality teaching. But one need not be a cynic to concede that students may choose courses in order to maximize learning, entertainment, convenience, or leisure time—with corresponding incentives for course offerings.

26. The spread of enrollment management has been studied as a kind of organizational anomaly precisely because it is "so deeply problematic" for academic values; see Matthew S. Kraatz and Marc Ventresca, "Toward the Market Driven University: Pragmatic Institutionalism and the Spread of Enrollment Management" (paper presented at the conference "Universities and the Production of Knowledge," SCAN-COR, Stanford University, Apr. 2003), quotation on p. 37.

27. "Every tub on its own bottom" promotes autonomy among noncompeting units, and possibly quality; however, this system does not induce internal market coordination or promote efficiency.

28. Lindblom, *Market System*, p. 160. For college choice models, see Don Hossler, Jack Schmit, and Nick Vesper, *Going to College: How Social, Economic, and Educational Factors Influence the Decisions Students Make* (Baltimore: Johns Hopkins University Press, 1999), pp. 141–56.

29. Caroline M. Hoxby, "The Return to Attending a More Selective College: 1960 to the Present" (Department of Economics, Harvard University, n.d., photocopy).

30. David Brooks has dubbed such students "Organization Kids": "at the top of the meritocratic ladder we have a generation of students who are extraordinarily bright, morally earnest, and incredibly industrious. They like to study and socialize in groups. They create and join organizations with great enthusiasm." "The Organization Kid," *Atlantic Monthly* (Apr. 2001): 40–54, quotation on p. 42.

31. James D. Savage, *Funding Science in America: Congress, Universities, and the Politics of the Academic Pork Barrel* (New York: Cambridge University Press, 1999); Daryl E. Chubin and Edward J. Hackett, *Peerless Science: Peer Review and U.S. Science Policy* (Albany: SUNY Press, 1990).

32. Marc Nerlove, "On Tuition and the Costs of Higher Education: Prolegomena to a Conceptual Framework," *Journal of Political Economy*, pt. 2 (May 1972): S178–S218, quotation on p. S206.

33. A study by Carlo S. Salerno found that universities on the whole allocate faculty efficiently so that the marginal value of their research is equal to the marginal productivity of teaching; see Carlo S. Salerno, "On the Technical and Allocative Efficiency of Research-Intensive Higher Education Institutions" (Ph.D. diss., Pennsylvania State University, 2002).

34. Princeton is the exception that proves the rule. Recall that Princeton justified its decision to expand undergraduate enrollment by 500 by arguing that it expected to *increase* average student quality (see Chapter 2). Having in effect already expanded its academic core (including graduate education), it resolved to add undergraduate education to restore an optimal balance. For nearly all other universities, however, expanding undergraduate education would tend to dilute what Nerlove calls its "quality-adjusted" value.

35. Lawrence B. Mohr, "The Impact Profile Approach to Policy Merit: The Case of Research Grants and the University," *Evaluation Review* (Apr. 1999): 212–49.

36. Roger L. Geiger, "The Ambiguous Link: Private Industry and University Research," in William E. Becker and Darryl R. Lewis, eds., *The Economics of American Higher Education* (Boston: Kluwer, 1992), pp. 265–98.

37. Irwin Feller, "Social Contracts and the Impact of Matching Fund Requirements on American Research Universities," *Educational Evaluation and Policy Analysis* 22, no. 1 (2000): 91–98; Ronald G. Ehrenberg and Jaroslava K. Mykula, "Do Indirect Cost Rates Matter?" Working Paper 6976, National Bureau of Economic Research, Cambridge, Mass., Feb. 1999. Universities typically utilize indirect cost reimbursements to fund cost-sharing obligations.

38. In 2000, institutional support for research constituted 24 percent of research expenditures at public universities and 10 percent at privates. As an accounting category, this figure contains many different items, including matching funds, seed grants, and salary attributable to research. Earnings from research (licensing rev-

enues and part of ICR) are typically devoted to such purposes. Nevertheless, the trend has been in the direction of greater university contributions. Geiger and Feller found that universities devoting more of their own funds to research tended to gain in research share; see "Dispersion of Academic Research," pp. 344–45.

39. Leslie Christovich, "Top 100 R&D-Performing Academic Institutions Continue Increased Facilities Construction," *Data Brief* (Washington, D.C., National Science Foundation, Division of Science Resources Studies, June 22, 2000). The boom in construction of academic research space has no doubt accelerated into the new decade.

40. Universities are also large economic actors in themselves—major employers in their regions and important sources of capital investment, which is significant for economic impact rather than economic development. See Michael I. Luger and Harvey A. Goldstein, "What Is the Role of Public Universities in Regional Economic Development?" in Richard D. Bingham and Robert Mier, eds., *Dilemmas of Urban Economic Development*, Urban Affairs Annual Reviews 47 (London: Sage, 1997), pp. 104–34, esp. 106–15. For social returns see Larry L. Leslie and Paul T. Brinkman, *The Economic Value of Higher Education* (New York: Macmillan, 1988), pp. 70–80; for returns to research see Edwin Mansfield et al., "Academic Research and Industrial Innovation," *Research Policy* 20 (1991): 1–12.

41. Ammon J. Salter and Ben R. Martin, "The Economic Benefits of Publicly Funded Basic Research: A Critical Review," *Research Policy* 30 (2001): 509–32, esp. 517–20.

42. Lindblom, *Market System*, p. 153.

43. See the study by Jason Owen-Smith discussed in Chapter 5. Performance pressure in technology transfer has clearly intensified: Goldie Blumenstyk, "How Colleges Get More Bang (or Less) from Technology Transfer," *Chronicle of Higher Education* (July 17, 2002): A24–A26.

44. Derek Bok offers just such a case in *The University in the Marketplace: The Commercialization of Higher Education* (Princeton, N.J.: Princeton University Press, 2003).

45. Some universities have stretched this argument quite far; see Goldie Blumenstyk, "Knowledge Is 'a Form of Venture Capital' for a Top Columbia Administrator: Michael Crow Seeks Out Business Projects Designed to Exploit the University's Academic Prowess," *Chronicle of Higher Education* (Feb. 9, 2001): A29.

46. This is not to deny a role for the Internet in higher education, but rather to highlight one persistent obstacle. See Diane Harley et al., eds., *University Teaching as E-Business? Research and Policy Agendas* (University of California, Berkeley, Center for Studies in Higher Education, 2002).

47. The chief skirmish in the 2002 campaign occurred over early admissions, a practice that protects less-selective schools from more-selective rivals. Harvard threatened to ignore early-admission commitments, which would have made this market more efficient—and more relentlessly meritocratic.

Index

In this index an "f" after a number indicates a separate reference on the next page, and an "ff" indicates separate references on the next two pages. A continuous discussion over two or more pages is indicated by a span of page numbers, e.g., "57–59." *Passim* is used for a cluster of references in close but not consecutive sequence.